PHP and MySQL
Web Development:
A Beginner's Guide

Marty Matthews

New York   Chicago   San Francisco
Athens   London   Madrid   Mexico City
Milan   New Delhi   Singapore   Sydney   Toronto

Cataloging-in-Publication Data is on file with the Library of Congress

McGraw-Hill Education books are available at special quantity discounts to use as premiums and sales promotions, or for use in corporate training programs. To contact a representative, please visit the Contact Us pages at www.mhprofessional.com.

PHP and MySQL Web Development: A Beginner's Guide

1234567890   DOC DOC   10987654

ISBN   978-0-07-183730-9
MHID   0-07-183730-2

Sponsoring Editor   Brandi Shailer

Editorial Supervisor   Patty Mon

Project Manager   Namita Gahtori,
Cenveo® Publisher Services

Acquisitions Coordinator   Amanda Russell

Technical Editor   Christie Sorenson

Copy Editor   Lisa McCoy

Proofreader   Claire Splan

Indexer   Valerie Haynes Perry

Production Supervisor   George Anderson

Composition   Cenveo Publisher Services

Illustration   Cenveo Publisher Services

Art Director, Cover   Jeff Weeks

Cover Designer   Jeff Weeks

PHP and MySQL Web Development:

A Beginner's Guide

About the Author

Marty Matthews "played" with some of the first mainframe computers, and from those to the latest tablets and smart phones, he has never lost his fascination with computers. He has been everything from a programmer to a software company president. Throughout, he has worked to bring others along with him and help them make the best use of all that computers can do. Toward that end, Marty has written over 80 books on programming and computing subjects, with many becoming bestsellers and receiving many accolades.

His recent books include *Dynamic Web Programming: A Beginner's Guide*, *Windows 8.1 for Seniors QuickSteps*, *iPad for Seniors QuickSteps*, and *Windows 8 QuickSteps*.

Marty and his wife Carole, also a writer, are the co-creators of QuickSteps books and live on an island northwest of Seattle, Washington.

About the Technical Editor

Christie Sorenson is a senior software engineer at ZingChart. She has worked on PHP applications in analytics, content management, and business applications for over a decade. She has collaborated on and been the tech editor of several books, including *Ajax: The Complete Reference* and *JavaScript: The Complete Reference*. She lives in San Francisco with her husband, Luke, and daughters, Ali and Keira.

For Carole, always.

Contents at a Glance

Contents

Acknowledgments

This book, as with most, is a team effort of many truly talented people. Among them are the following:

Christie Sorenson, technical editor extraordinaire, who corrected many errors, added many tips and notes, and greatly improved the book. Throughout the process, Christie has been a joy to work with. Thanks, Christie!

Amanda Russell, editorial coordinator, queen of the McGraw-Hill Education labyrinth and Apple permissions, and a true Wonder Woman, who makes it all happen! She tries hard to keep us on schedule; accounts for all the chapters, pages, and illustrations; and gets everything to the right people. And she does all this with a light touch and a smile in her email voice. Thanks, Amanda!

Lisa McCoy, copy editor, who added to the readability and understandability of the book while not losing the author's voice. Thanks, Lisa!

Valerie Perry, indexer, who adds so much to the usability of the book, and does so quickly and with much thought. Thanks, Valerie!

Claire Splan, proofreader, who made sure that the words and illustrations actually work to tell a story that makes sense, as well as catching and correcting many last-minute errors. Thanks, Claire!

Namita Gahtori, project manager, who greased the wheels and straightened the track to make a smooth production process. Thanks, Namita!

Patty Mon, editorial supervisor, who is constantly involved with all aspects of the book and makes sure it is an outstanding product. Thanks, Patty!

Brandi Shailer, senior acquisitions editor, who is responsible for making this book a reality and had the faith and persistence to bring me on board. Thanks, Brandi!

Introduction

If you have done some website building with HTML, CSS, and possibly JavaScript and want to add more user interaction with better form handling, greater ease of moving information among pages, and a fully relational database to your sites with PHP and MySQL, then this is the book to help you do that.

PHP and MySQL Web Development: A Beginner's Guide takes the reader with a hands-on approach from building static web pages to creating comprehensive database-driven web applications. To do this, five of the most commonly used web programming languages (HTML, CSS, JavaScript, PHP, and MySQL) are introduced, explored, and demonstrated through the creation of common dynamic web elements.

The reader is assumed to have some experience with the creation of static web pages and wants to add database elements to their pages. To create a common foundation for all readers, the book starts out with a review of creating static web pages using HTML5 (Hypertext Markup Language) and then takes the reader through the use of CSS (Cascading Style Sheets) and templates to apply common features and formatting across a series of web pages. Next, the book provides an overview of JavaScript and how it is used to implement such client-side elements as changing an image when the mouse rolls over it, implementing a pop-up window, positioning the cursor in a form, and validating form entries.

PHP and MySQL Web Development: A Beginner's Guide then provides an in-depth discussion of PHP, including the parts of PHP, how it is used with HTML; its structure, control statements, arrays, and functions; and its use with forms. The discussion of PHP ends with a detailed demonstration of PHP's form and file handling capabilities to provide a secure user login and validation, along with controls to limit access to web pages and pass information among web pages.

Next, the book looks in detail at MySQL and the SQL language to discuss how it is used to store, select, and update information on a web page. The basic characteristics of the language, its command set, key words, operators, and functions, are all described and then demonstrated to let the reader explore the full power of MySQL.

Finally, the book discusses how PHP and MySQL are combined with HTML, CSS, and JavaScript to exercise the full power of a relational database system. In particular, the PHP MySQL functions are reviewed to show how information entered into website forms is used to create new records in database tables, and then how information in a database is read, formatted, and displayed on a web page. Finally, the book looks at how to detect and handle errors and security issues.

PHP and MySQL Web Development: A Beginner's Guide is a solutions-oriented book that concludes with the building of two detailed websites that demonstrate the full capability of PHP and MySQL. These are meant to be directly usable by the reader as templates with all the necessary code for building their own web pages with dynamic content fully exercising a MySQL/PHP database.

Conventions Used in This Book

PHP and MySQL Web Development: A Beginner's Guide uses several conventions designed to make the book easier for you to follow:

- **Bold type** is used for user input.
- *Italic type* is used for a word or phrase that is being defined or otherwise deserves special emphasis.
- A `monospaced typeface` is used for code snippets and listings.
- SMALL CAPITAL LETTERS are used for keys on the keyboard such as ENTER and SHIFT.

How This Book Is Organized

Although the focus of this book is dynamic web programming with PHP and MySQL, it is important that we have a common foundation with HTML, CSS, JavaScript, and the programming tools to create dynamic web pages.

Part I of the book is dedicated to establishing a common foundation with HTML, CSS, and JavaScript.

Chapter 1 discusses the tools needed to create, test, and support the coding of clean, error-free web pages. This includes an integrated development environment (IDE), with which to write the code that will provide support for not only HTML, but also JavaScript and PHP. You also want a test server running on your computer that supports all the languages, especially PHP and MySQL. Finally, you will need access to several popular browsers for testing HTML, CSS, and JavaScript (PHP runs in a server and so is browser neutral).

Chapter 2 reviews HTML and discusses how it is the foundation language of the Web and the structure providing the backbone of all web pages. To keep up with the latest browsers and web accessing devices, especially mobile devices, the chapter focuses on the most recent major revision of HTML, HTML5, and how it has changed from its recent predecessors. The chapter looks at both the commonly used legacy tags and their attributes, as well as many that are new to HTML5.

Chapter 3 covers CSS, which has the job of making all the pages in a website look consistently good in many browsers. The chapter explains how CSS is a collection of rules for specifying the colors, fonts, and layout of a web page, and how it is not only the primary way of formatting a web page, but it is also the most efficient. It allows you to separate the formatting of a web page from the content of a web page and be able to reuse the formatting on other pages.

Chapter 4 provides an overview of JavaScript that starts out by reviewing the JavaScript basics and then describing the elements and syntax of JavaScript. It next looks at various types of events that can occur on a web page, how JavaScript event handlers respond to them, and demonstrates several examples of their use. Finally, the chapter looks at forms, which are the web mechanism by which information flows from the user to the web page. The chapter discusses how forms are created and used, their methods and properties, how information in the form is validated, and how to carry out navigation in a website based on JavaScript navigation elements.

Part II shows how PHP, running in the server, provides another level of automation, including dynamically handling information and determining what a user sees next.

Chapter 5 introduces PHP, what it is, how it is used, how it is installed, the use of its many online resources, and what tools you should have running to work with PHP. The chapter discusses the parts of PHP, how it is tied into and used with HTML code, and the rules that need to be followed for good PHP code. Chapter 5 also discusses the structure of PHP, including strings, numbers, comments, constants, variables, arrays, and operators, with examples shown of their use.

Chapter 6 covers the PHP control statements and the conditions that control them, including `if-else`, `switch`, `for`, `foreach`, `while`, and `do-while` loops. The chapter also covers PHP's file handling capabilities, including opening, reading, writing, and closing files, as well as determining a file size and setting a pointer to a particular record. Finally, the chapter describes cookies and session and server variables and how to use them.

Chapter 7 describes and demonstrates PHP arrays in both single and multidimensions, how to work with them in loops, and with the many array functions. The chapter then looks at form creation and handling, including checking the existence of form data and accepting, validating, and transferring form data into an array.

Chapter 8 demonstrates how to use PHP form and file handling capabilities to set up a user login form, validate login information against a file, and establish controls that can restrict access to forms and information. Passing data among web pages is discussed and how the URL, session variables, and cookies are used to do that. Cookies are also discussed in terms of how they can be used to customize a page to a particular user.

Part III shows how MySQL, a full-fledged relational database management system (RDBMS), greatly enhances the process of reading, writing, maintaining, changing, searching, and rearranging information stored in computer files. It is the third major tool used to make websites dynamic, and while a website requires HTML and PHP in addition to MySQL, MySQL does the heavy lifting when it comes to the handling of data.

Chapter 9 introduces databases and describes what makes them relational; how tables, records, fields, keys, and relationships are used; and how to select the data types for different fields. In addition, the chapter shows how to create, initialize, and maintain a MySQL database using phpMyAdmin.

Chapter 10 explores SQL (Structured Query Language), the foundation of MySQL, discussing the basic characteristics of the language. MySQL is then introduced, showing how SQL has been implemented in MySQL. The basic command set for MySQL is described, as is making a database secure.

Chapter 11 describes MySQL's commands and keywords and the statements that marry them together, along with operators and functions to provide the full power of MySQL. The chapter reviews MySQL data types and makes extensive use of the MySQL Workbench and, to a lesser degree, phpMyAdmin and the MySQL command line to demonstrate how MySQL statements, their commands, and keywords operate.

Part IV shows how PHP and MySQL work together with HTML, CSS, and JavaScript to allow you to build extremely capable and powerful web applications to handle a wide range of needs.

Chapter 12 describes how PHP is used with MySQL to create, access, and query a database. It reviews the types of queries, how information entered into website forms is used to create new records in database tables, and then how information in a database is read, formatted, and displayed on a web page. Finally, the chapter looks at how to detect and handle errors and security issues.

Chapter 13 demonstrates the use of PHP and MySQL to create a web app to register students and the courses they sign up for, including constructing the forms and database tables, validating the data that is entered, querying the database, and presenting the information.

Chapter 14 demonstrates the use of PHP and MySQL to create a web app to handle online purchases. This will include presenting a catalog of items for sale, allowing the selection of items to be purchased, and handling the final checkout. In addition to the database aspects of this, the discussion will include authentication and access control, as well as protecting and encrypting vulnerable information.

Appendixes and Listings Online

Appendixes A and B and all of the listings in this book, including the complete User Authentication, Class Registration, and Online Purchasing systems, are available for download from McGraw-Hill Professional's Media Center at mhprofessional.com/mediacenter/. Enter this ISBN 0071837310 and click Find Product.

Part I

Getting Ready

Although the focus of this book is dynamic web programming with PHP and MySQL, it is important that we have a common foundation with HTML, CSS, JavaScript, and the programming tools to create dynamic web pages. Therefore, this part of the book is dedicated to establishing that foundation. In Chapter 1, we'll talk about the tools needed to create and test dynamic web pages. In Chapter 2, we'll review HTML; Chapter 3 will cover CSS; and Chapter 4 will provide a brief refresher of JavaScript. It is assumed that you already have some experience with all three of these tools and that what is presented here will reinforce what you already know.

Since you are reading this book, it is a pretty good bet that you already have a good idea what the acronyms in the previous paragraph stand for, but just so we all start out with the same understanding, here is the definition of each of them that I use:

- **HTML** stands for Hypertext Markup Language. It is the basic language used to build web pages, using tags to identify various elements of the page. HTML is used in a web browser to display a static web page. HTML5 is the latest version of HTML and, as of December 2012, is going through the official approval process by the World Wide Web Consortium (W3C). XHTML is a predecessor to HTML5 and was an attempt to use a number of the advances in HTML5 before HTML5 was officially recognized. This book will focus on HTML5. HTML files have the extension .htm or .html.

- **CSS** stands for Cascading Style Sheets. It is a language used to define styles that can then be repeatedly used on one or more web pages without having to repeat the style definitions. CSS files have the extension .css.

- **JavaScript** is a programming language used primarily to interact with the end user of a web page. JavaScript can be used on a static HTML page and have it respond to the end user selecting or entering something on the page. JavaScript is included and can operate in most browsers (called "client side"), but it can also work in a server that is delivering the web page (called "server side"). The most recent version of JavaScript is 1.8.5, which was released in March 2011 and is available for free. JavaScript has no relationship to Java. JavaScript files have the extension .js.

- **PHP** originally stood for Personal Home Page, but now stands for PHP: Hypertext Preprocessor. PHP is a general-purpose programming language used primarily with web applications to both automate a website and utilize a MySQL database. PHP runs in a server and so provides server-side processing. The most recent version of PHP is 5.5, which was released in June 2013 and is available for free. PHP files have the extension .php.

- ***MySQL*** stands for My Structured Query Language. It is pronounced either "My S-Q-L" or "My Sequel." MySQL is a relational database management system (RDMS) widely used in web applications, often with PHP. MySQL is an implementation of the standard SQL, as is Microsoft's SQL. MySQL is owned by Oracle Corporation, but is available for free. The latest version of MySQL is 5.6.15, released in December 2013. MySQL files have the extension .sql.

Chapter 1

Setting Up
Your Workstation

Key Skills & Concepts

- Picking a Development Tool
- Choosing a Testing Server
- Using Testing Browsers
- Considering Other Factors

As you get into dynamic web programming, you will be doing extensive coding and wanting all the support you can get to produce clean, error-free code. You will need to test not only how your code is structured, as you would with static web pages, but also how it runs, and not just on one browser, but on several. Therefore, you want a text editor, or its more advanced form—an integrated development environment (IDE)—with which to write the code that will provide support for not only HTML, but also JavaScript and PHP. You also want a test server environment running on your computer that supports all the languages, especially PHP and MySQL. Finally, you will need access to several popular browsers for testing HTML, CSS, and JavaScript (PHP runs in a server and so is browser neutral).

NOTE
This book is written for users of Microsoft Windows, from Windows XP to Windows 8.1. Although most of the discussion in the book is also applicable for Mac and Linux users, this particular section is dedicated to Windows. Mac and Linux have their own sets of editors, servers, and browsers, many of which are Mac versions of Windows apps.

Picking a Development Tool

The most important item that you need for dynamic web programming is a highly capable text editor or IDE that supports you in writing code without trying to do it for you. A number of such tools are available, ranging from Windows Notepad (see Figure 1-1), which comes free with Windows and allows you to type in and save code to a file, to Adobe Dreamweaver, which creates dynamic web code for you in a quasi-WYSIWYG (what you see is what you get) environment. Windows Notepad might do to enter a little code in a pinch, but when you see the level of features and support that is available with free downloadable IDEs, you'll relegate Windows Notepad to the software dustbin.

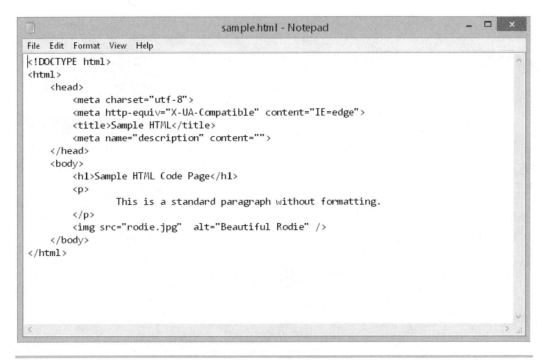

```
sample.html - Notepad
File   Edit   Format   View   Help
<!DOCTYPE html>
<html>
    <head>
        <meta charset="utf-8">
        <meta http-equiv="X-UA-Compatible" content="IE=edge">
        <title>Sample HTML</title>
        <meta name="description" content="">
    </head>
    <body>
        <h1>Sample HTML Code Page</h1>
        <p>
                This is a standard paragraph without formatting.
        </p>
        <img src="rodie.jpg"   alt="Beautiful Rodie" />
    </body>
</html>
```

Figure 1-1   Notepad provides the minimum ability to edit text.

NOTE

Someone may tell you that Microsoft Word will produce an HTML file from text and graphics that you lay out on a page in the word processor. Although this is true, the code that is produced is neither very efficient nor easy to change or customize. Also, Word does not offer any web programming support. Therefore, I strongly recommend against using Word for website development.

Full-Featured Development Packages

At the other end of the spectrum from Windows Notepad are Adobe Dreamweaver (see Figure 1-2) and Microsoft Visual Studio 2012. Both packages offer a great deal more than an editor and are meant to tie into the other tools offered by Adobe or Microsoft. Other than the cost, I have several major problems with these packages that prevent me from recommending their use:

- **Dedicated environment**   Both packages, but especially Visual Studio, assume, or even require, that you buy into the other programming tools provided by that company.

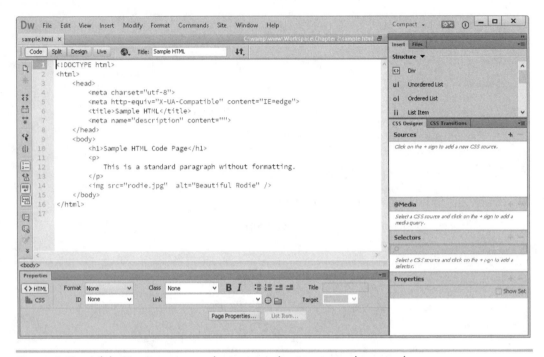

Figure 1-2   Adobe Dreamweaver, shown in code view, may do more than you want.

- **Marginal WYSIWYG**   The display of a web page depends on the browser that is used. Dreamweaver's attempts to allow you to edit in a page image that is close to the final displayed page is marginal at best and can significantly differ from the actual display. This can lead you to lay out a page differently than you would otherwise.

- **Complex and inefficient code**   The automatically generated code by Dreamweaver, especially using PHP, is complex, inefficient, and difficult to change and customize. If you want to do anything in PHP on your own with a page in which Dreamweaver has created PHP code, it is difficult.

Powerful Alternatives

In the products between Windows Notepad and Adobe Dreamweaver are a number of noteworthy web development tools that offer a lot more than Windows Notepad and are either free to download or have a relatively low cost. You can find comparisons of web development packages on a number of websites, including:

- **sixrevisions.com/tools/the-15-most-popular-text-editors-for-developers**   This site has many helpful articles on web development, but the software comparison is about five years old.

- **php-editor-review.toptenreviews.com**   This site (see Figure 1-3) provides a lot of detailed comparative information, but doesn't include price and seems to be missing several free packages, such as Aptana Studio, that I think should have been included. Note that TopTenReviews no longer updates this category and keeps it here for archiving purposes only.

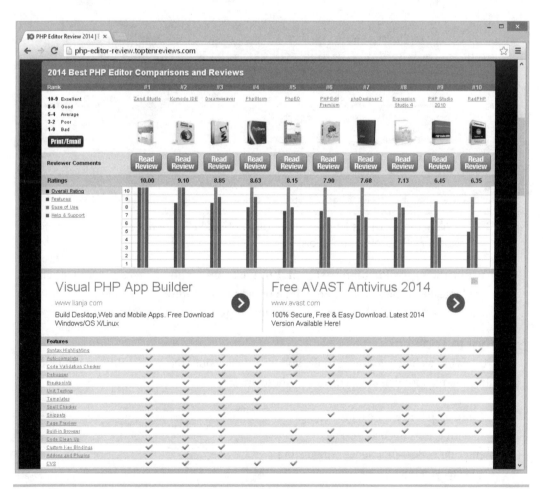

Figure 1-3   TopTenReviews provides a comprehensive and easy-to-use comparison.

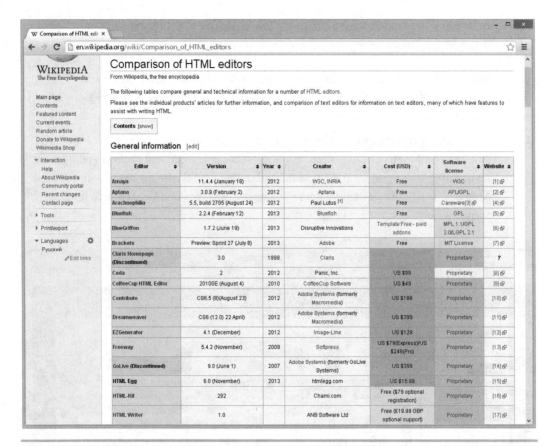

Figure 1-4   Wikipedia provides lengthy information about PHP, but not specific information about PHP development tools.

●   **wikipedia.org/wiki/comparison_of_html_editors**   This site (see Figure 1-4) covers the largest selection of software with a broad range of information and is probably the least biased. Not all HTML editors, though, provide good support for PHP.

What to Look For

In reviewing web development tools, you want to consider the availability of a number of features in the tool you choose. Among these are

●   **Code assistance**   Provides context-sensitive assistance as you are entering code—in essence, suggesting code as you type.

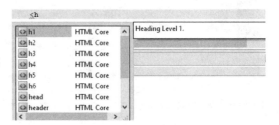

- **Code completion**   Automatically provides the ending tag for the opening 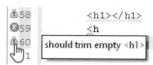 tag you typed.

- **Code highlighting**   Provides color-coding for various parts of the code so you can easily recognize it.

- **Code validation**   Reviews your code and tells you if it finds something that does not look correct—in essence, pointing out potential errors in your code.

- **Browser view**   Displays your code as it would appear in a browser within the development tool.

- **Outline view**   Provides an outline of your code, like this:

- **Line numbers**   Numbers each line of your code so that you can quickly find the line referred to in an error message.

- **Auto-indentation**   Provides automatic indentation for subordinate elements as you add new lines (see Figure 1-5).

- **Search and replace**   Allows you to change several instances of the same item in one operation.

- **Macro capability**   Allows you to record a set of steps so they can be repeated.

- **Multiple open files**   Allows you to have several code pages open at the same time to compare and copy code among them.

- **Multiple language support**   Provides support for multiple programming languages, such as HTML, CSS, JavaScript, PHP, and others. For this book, the first four are the most important.

- **File management**   Provides the capabilities of Windows Explorer from within the development tool.

```
<!DOCTYPE html>
<html>
    <head>
        <meta charset="utf-8">
        <meta http-equiv="X-UA-Compatible" content="IE=edge">
        <title>Sample HTML</title>
        <meta name="description" content="">
    </head>
    <body>
        <h1>Sample HTML Code Page</h1>
        <p>
            This is a standard paragraph without formatting.
        </p>
        <img src="rodie.jpg"  alt="Beautiful Rodie" />
    </body>
</html>
```

Figure 1-5 Indentation of your code allows you to more easily identify sections of it.

- **FTP transfer**   Allows you to upload and download your web pages and applications to a hosting server.

- **Version control**   Provides the ability to keep track of your site versions: which one is on the server, which is the most recent on the development computer, and which versions are archive copies.

- **Debugger/profiler**   Provides assistance in finding and correcting errors in your JavaScript and especially PHP.

Good Choices

As you saw by looking at comparisons on the Internet, there are many alternatives to choose from. Here are several text editors and IDEs that I know to be good products that will serve you well in building dynamic web applications:

- **Aptana Studio**, shown in Figure 1-6, is an IDE that combines text editing with a number of tools to help you produce clean code. Aptana has most of the features mentioned earlier (the illustrations were from Aptana), is free, and is supported by a large user community, as well as by its creators. Of particular importance to me is Aptana's ability to provide code assistance, code completion, and code colorization or syntax highlighting for all the languages discussed in this book. Aptana also can do code validation and file management within its window. You can download Aptana Studio for free from aptana.com.

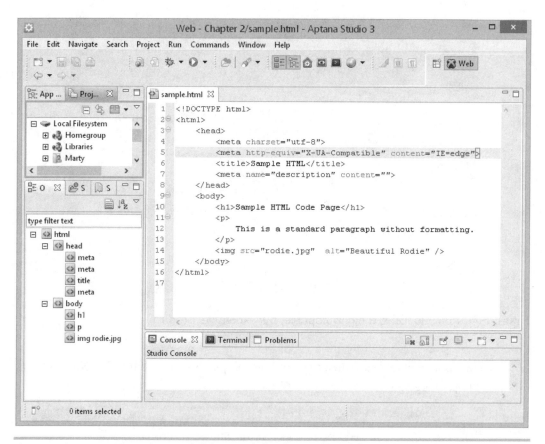

Figure 1-6 Aptana Studio is a full-featured development tool that is free and well supported.

- **Komodo IDE**, shown in Figure 1-7, is a highly rated IDE that includes all of the features mentioned earlier and adds a graphical debugger for PHP; the ability to reflect a change in multiple places at one time; built-in version control; and full smart editing, code intelligence, and debugging for HTML, CSS, JavaScript, and PHP. You can download the full version for a free 21-day trial and purchase Komodo IDE for $382. Komodo has a free smaller version without debugging/source control called Komodo Edit. See activestate.com/komodo-ide.

- **Notepad++** is a simple, but elegant, free text editor. It provides a customizable interface, as well as customizable syntax highlighting; allows for multidocuments with tabs;

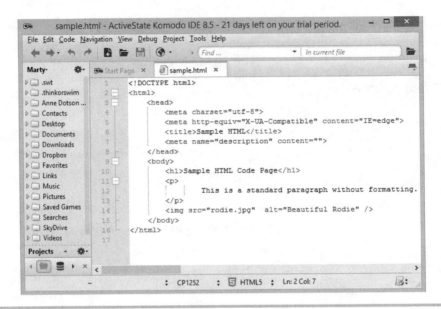

Figure 1-7 Komodo IDE is a highly capable, but expensive, product.

and has a comprehensive macro recording and playback capability. See NotePad-plus-plus.org.

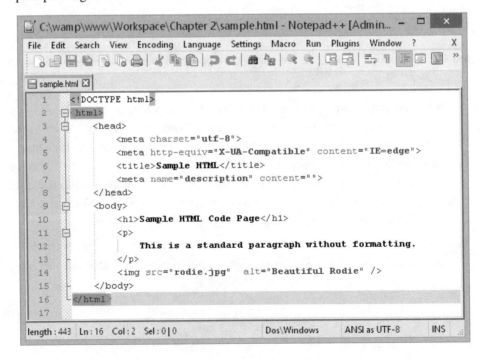

- **PHPStorm**, shown in Figure 1-8, is an IDE with many of the features mentioned earlier, plus a smart PHP editor that is current to the latest version of PHP, and a PHP code sniffer and mess detector. PHPStorm does not have a built-in browser, so you must go live to fully test a script. You can try out PHPStorm for free for 30 days and buy it for $199. See jetbrains.com/phpstorm.

- **UltraEdit**, shown in Figure 1-9, is a popular text editor for programmers that provides support for HTML, PHP, and JavaScript, among other languages. It provides color-coding of various elements of your script and allows you to toggle between code view and browser view. It allows you to define and repeatedly insert tags to save having to repeatedly type them, have multiple files open, use a built-in File Transfer Protocol (FTP) client, and it has a highly configurable interface. It provides HTML code validation, but does not do code completion. UltraEdit can be tested for 30 days for free and currently costs $79.95. See UltraEdit.com.

- **Zend Studio**, shown in Figure 1-10, was developed by two of the early developers of PHP and so is PHP-centric. Zend Studio is based on Aptana Studio and has much of the look and most of the features of Aptana described earlier in this section, including, most importantly, code assistance, code completion, code validation, and syntax highlighting for HTML, CSS, JavaScript, and PHP. Zend also has some powerful

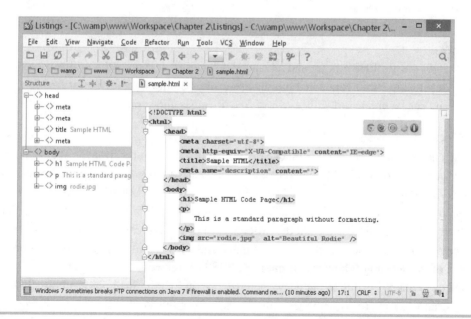

Figure 1-8   PHPStorm has a number of features to support PHP, but is missing others.

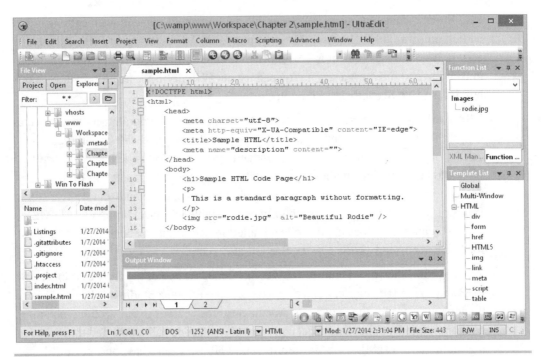

Figure 1-9 UltraEdit, currently in version 21, has many ardent followers in the programming community.

additions for PHP editing and advanced debugging. It even includes extensive tools for developing cloud-connected mobile apps. Zend Studio is available for free for 30 days and can be purchased with a year of free upgrades and support for $189. See Zend.com.

What to Choose

The choice is not easy. Since you can get all the listed programs for at least a trial period for free, I recommend that you do that and see what you like. Given the web programming PHP/MySQL focus of this book, I set aside Notepad++ and UltraEdit. PHPStorm is lacking several important features, and I don't think that Komodo is better enough than Zend—if it is at all—to warrant the difference in price. The choice to me is between the free Aptana and Zend, which includes Aptana and adds extensive PHP support for $189. Part of the decision is how important is the $189. If it is your food budget, then get Aptana and eat. Otherwise, due to the heavy dependence on PHP in this book, and possibly on what you want to do with the skills you gain from this book, I recommend Zend. Throughout the book, we will look at code in both Aptana and Zend, so you will not be

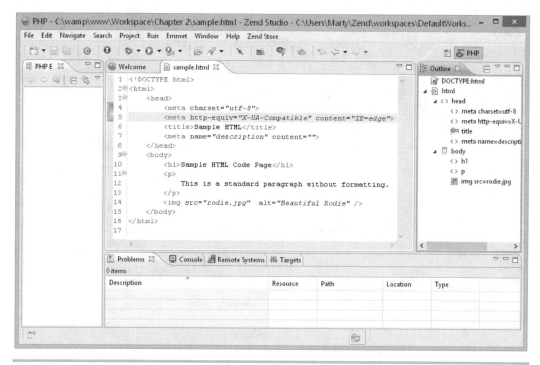

Figure 1-10   Zend Studio adds in-depth PHP support to Aptana Studio for a price.

left out if you only have Aptana; we will also look at the Zend PHP additions. Installation instructions for both Zend and Aptana follow.

Install Zend Studio

These steps are for Windows. Open the Zend Installation and Upgrade Guide for instructions for the Mac and Linux.

1. On the computer where you want to do your web development, open the zend.com website. Click Products in the menu bar, and click Zend Studio.

2. Click either Buy Now or Download Free Trial to use Zend for 30 days for free. This allows you to download Zend Studio, Studio Web Debugger, and Studio Browser Plug-ins (see Figure 1-11).

3. Click Windows MSI opposite Zend Studio. Register with Zend and click Download Zend Studio to begin the download process. The Thank You For Downloading Zend Studio screen will open. If downloading doesn't start, you should see a message to that effect; click Click Here To Download Zend Studio.

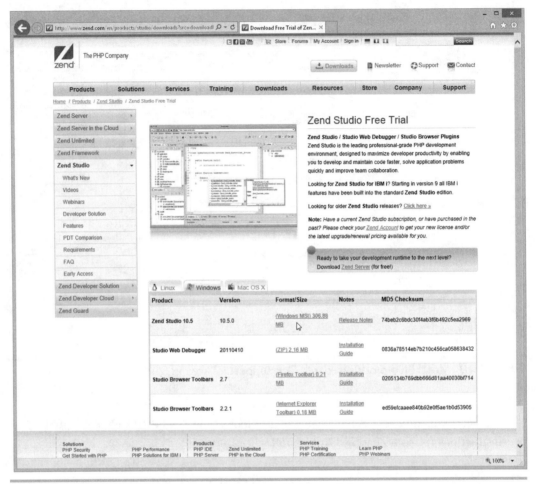

Figure 1-11 There is no reason not to take the initial free trial.

4. Click Run in answer to running or saving Zend Studio.

5. When the Zend Installer opens, click Next, keep the default install location and the default ways the features are installed by clicking Next twice, and then click Install.

6. Click Yes in the User Account Control dialog box to allow the installation, and click Finish when it completes.

7. As Zend Studio begins to load, you are asked to specify the default workspace. At this point, leave the default and click OK.

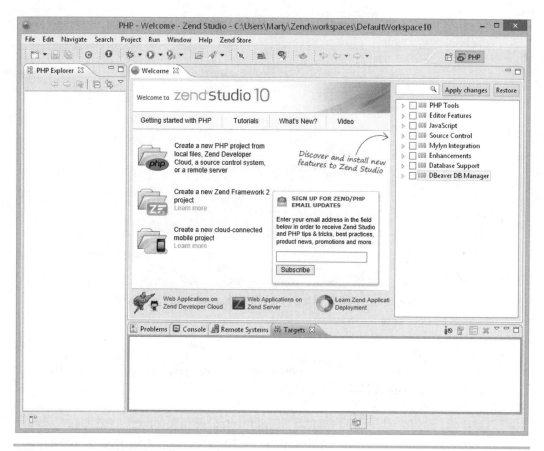

Figure 1-12   Zend Studio offers a number of add-on features and enhancements that you can choose to install.

8. Click Continue With Trial and then click Continue. Zend Studio will open as you see in Figure 1-12, if you have purchased Zend Studio

9. Open each of the new tools on the right and consider whether you want to add them. I think that the PHP Tools, Editor Features, JavaScript tools, Source Control tools, Enhancements, and DBeaver MySQL Driver can be useful as you expand your coding environment. Both JavaScript tools and Enhancements have conflicts that I have not been able to resolve. Database Support is for databases other than MySQL. Mylyn is a subsystem of Eclipse for task management that allows you to focus programming attention on a single task (Eclipse is a broad programming IDE developed by IBM in which Aptana can be plugged in). Both Mylyn and Eclipse are beyond the scope of this book.

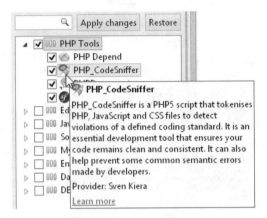

10. After you have selected the features you want to add to Zend Studio, click Apply Changes. You also might want to sign up for Zend/PHP email updates by entering your email address and clicking Subscribe.

Install Aptana

Even if you have Zend Studio, I recommend also installing Aptana, where you will see some advantages with HTML, CSS, and JavaScript.

1. On the computer where you want to do your web development, open the aptana.com website and click Download Aptana Studio 3. Keep the default Standalone Version, enter your name and email address, and once more click Download Aptana Studio 3.

2. Click Run in the Run vs. Save selection, and then click Yes to allow the installation. On the Welcome dialog, click Next, agree to the license agreement, click Next, keep the default destination folder, and again click Next.

3. Keep the suggested Start menu folder and the default file associations, clicking Next in both cases, and then click Install.

4. When the installation has completed, click Next and then click Close.

5. In the aptana.com/downloads/start web page note that Git is a required prerequisite and that a link to "PortableGit from msysgit" is provided (Git is a version-control and source-code management app that is used internally by Aptana). If Git is not already on your computer, click that link. Under Downloads, click the top entry, which at the time this was written was Git-1.8.4-preview20130916.exe, and then click that same name again at the top of the next page.

6. For a Git installation, click Run in the Run vs. Save selection, and then click Yes to allow the installation. The Welcome message will appear. Click Next seven times to accept all of the defaults. When the Git installation has completed, click Finish.

Choosing a Testing Server

Static web pages, and even some dynamic web pages that use JavaScript, are *client-side* scripts and run totally in a browser. All you need to test these pages is a browser. Dynamic web pages that use *server-side* features and run in the server instead of in the client's browser, such as those written in PHP and that use MySQL, require that you have a server on your development computer if you want to test your pages there. There are actually three server components that you need: a local web server, which is most often the Apache server; a PHP server; and a MySQL server. These three servers can be downloaded for free and individually installed. That process, though, is complex with a number of opportunities for error. As an alternative, there are several independent integrated packages that provide a much simpler installation of all three servers at the same time. These include *WAMP* (Windows servers for Apache, MySQL, and PHP), *XAMPP* (X for cross-platform servers for Apache, MySQL, PHP, and Perl), and Zend Server. All of these have versions for Windows, Macintosh, and Linux.

All three, WAMP, XAMPP, and Zend, include full versions of Apache, MySQL, and PHP (generally one version behind the latest), as well as *phpMyAdmin,* which is used for manual maintenance of a MySQL database. XAMPP, the oldest of the three, has become a bit dated and is the most difficult to use. WAMP is a more basic package, but has all the server and developmental tools you will probably need on your computer, and definitely all you'll need for this book. Zend Server also provides all you need and adds extra support for PHP, but I have found it difficult and time consuming to install. I assume that you will be using either WAMP or Zend Server, and I recommend that you download and install one of them now if you don't already have one (you can't use both at the same time). I'm going to be principally using WAMP.

Installing WAMP

If you do a web search on WAMP, you'll see you can get it from either wampserver.com or from sourceforge.net. In either case, what you will be downloading is WampServer. Wampserver.com skips the advertising and gives you several choices in the server to install. At this time (winter 2014), you want WampServer 2.4, either 32- or 64-bit, depending on your computer. WampServer uses standard Windows installer techniques to download and install Apache, PHP, and MySQL.

1. On the computer where you want to have your testing server, open the wampserver.com website. Click your language choice in the upper-right corner if it isn't already displayed, and then click Download at the top of the page, which will display the WampServer choices, as shown in Figure 1-13.

2. Click one of the top entries, which, as this is written, is either WAMPSERVER (32 BITS & PHP 5.4) 2.4 or WAMPSERVER (64 BITS & PHP 5.4) 2.4.

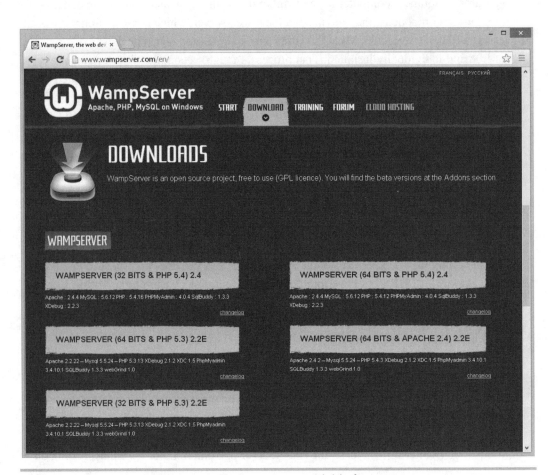

Figure 1-13 You generally want the latest version available for your computer.

3. You are given three warnings. The first, that you must have Microsoft Visual C++ 2010 SP1 Redistributable installed, is solved by clicking one of the two links that take you to the Microsoft site and installs the package. The other two warnings apply to installing over older versions of WAMP. If needed, follow the instructions given.

4. When you have handled the warnings, click the link at the top of the pop-up that says, "You can download it directly." Interestingly, this takes you to the SourceForge downloader, where the download will start and display a message at the bottom of the page.

5. Click either Run to do that directly or Save to save the file to your disk. Since this is a free package I can redownload, I don't see any need to save it, so I click Run.

6. When the download is complete, if you have User Account Control (UAC) turned on, click Yes to allow the program to run. The WampServer installer will open and display the version of each component to be installed. Click Next, accept the license agreement, and click Next again.

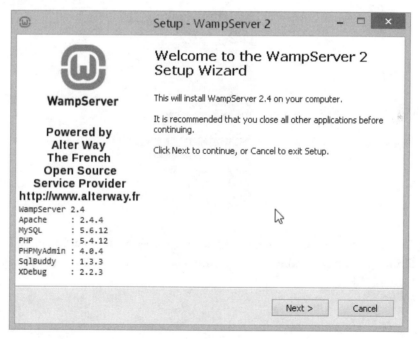

7. Select the destination (C:\WAMP is recommended) and click Next. Choose whether to add Quick Launch and/or desktop icons, and once more click Next. Finally, click Install. The installation will commence.

8. A dialog box will open and ask you to choose (really locate) your default browser. You will need to scroll the folders on the left to locate on your C: drive either the Windows folder and the Explorer.exe file, or the Program Files (x86) folder, and either Google\Chrome\Application\chrome or Mozilla Firefox\firefox. When you have located your default browser, click Open.

9. You will next be asked to specify your SMTP (Simple Mail Transfer Protocol) and email address. Under most situations, leave the default "localhost" for SMTP, and enter your email address.

10. When the installation is completed, make sure that Launch WampServer 2 Now is checked, click Finish, and click Yes to allow WampServer to load. You should see this icon in the system tray on the right of the taskbar.

11. Click the WampServer system tray icon to open the WampServer control panel. Click Start All Services. The control panel should automatically close.

12. To see if WampServer is running, open a web browser (Internet Explorer, Chrome, or Firefox), and type **localhost** in the address bar. WampServer should open as you see in Figure 1-14.

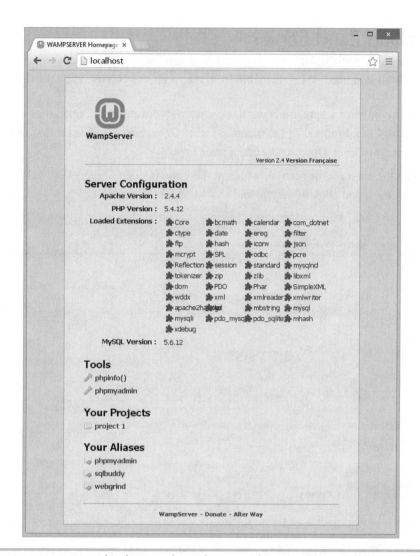

Figure 1-14   WAMP provides the Apache web server, the PHP programming environment, and the MySQL relational database program, among other programs.

Installing Zend Server

Zend Server is available in both a free and paid version. For your use in this book, the free version is all you need and is available from the same site you used to get the Zend IDE.

1. On the computer where you want to do your web development, open the zend.com website. Click Products in the menu bar, click Zend Server | Free Edition in the menu bar, and then click Download Zend Server Free.

2. Select the most recent version, which at this time is Zend Server (PHP 5.4) 6.2.0, as shown next, and click its format and size to begin the download.

3. Enter your email address and password and click Log In if you have used this site earlier, or register if you haven't. Click Run when asked if you want to run or save Zend Server. The Zend Server will be downloaded.

4. Click Yes in the User Account Control dialog box to allow the Zend Server to be installed. At the Welcome message, click Next.

5. Accept the license agreement and click Next. Click Custom for the Setup Type, and click Next.

6. Click MySQL Server to include it in the installation and click Next.

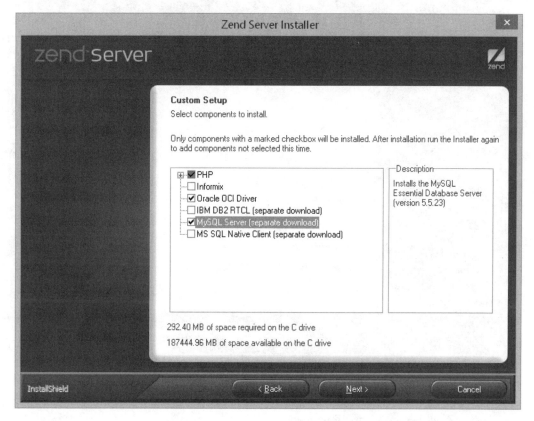

7. Accept the default installation of Apache, the default destination folder, and the default port assignments, clicking Next after each.

8. Review the installation settings and click Install. MySQL and the other elements will be downloaded and installed. If you are told that your firewall is blocking installation, click Allow Access.

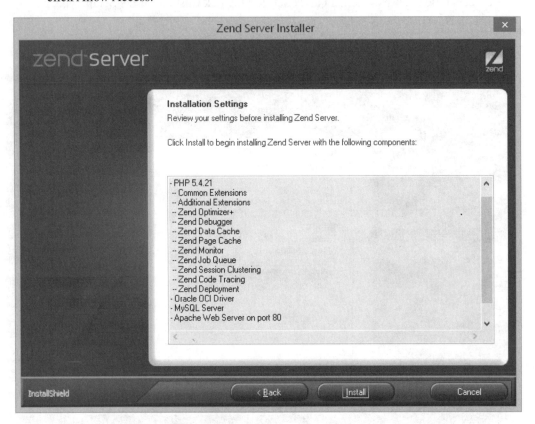

9. Click the check boxes to create a shortcut on your desktop and to start working with Zend Server, and then click Finish. Your browser will open, displaying localhost with the Zend Server license agreement.

10. Click the I Have Read check box, click Development as the working environment, enter and confirm an admin password, and acknowledge that all parts of the Zend libraries have been deployed, clicking Next as necessary.

11. Review the summary of the installation and click Launch. Zend Server will open in your browser.

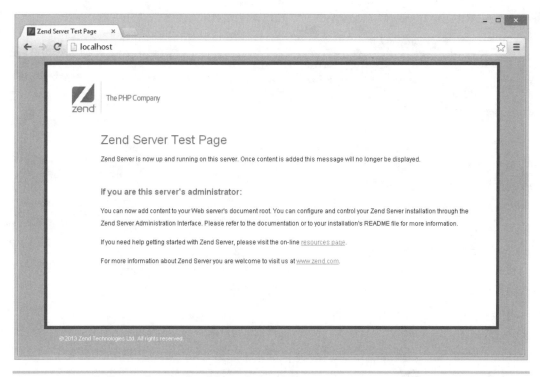

Figure 1-15   If all is well, you should see this Zend Server Test Page.

12. Click Administration | License | Use Free Edition. A list of features that are deactivated with the free edition is displayed. None of these will affect your using the Zend Server in development.

13. Click Continue; enter **admin** and the password you entered in step 10, and click Login. The Zend Test Page will open as you see in Figure 1-15.

Testing Environment

As you build websites, it is important that they are built and tested for the computers, operating systems, displays, and browsers used by your target audience. There is an important website, w3schools.com, that provides statistics on browser, operating system, and display usage (see Figure 1-16), as well as being an excellent resource for learning more about HTML, CSS, JavaScript, SQL, and PHP. You can use these statistics as a general guide, adjusted, of course, for your knowledge of the particular audience you are targeting.

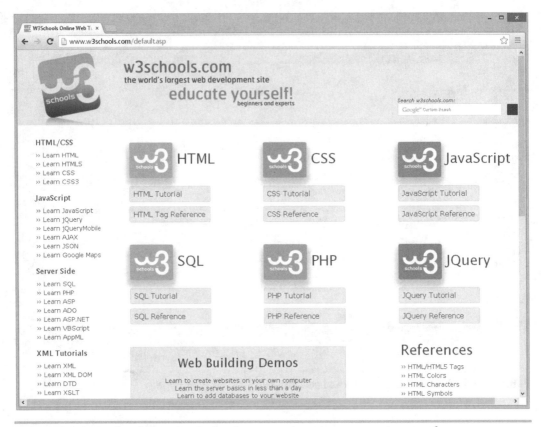

Figure 1-16 Get familiar with w3schools.com and use it as your primary reference.

Using Testing Browsers

Of the four components (computers, operating systems, displays, and browsers), the browser is the most important. The browser used by the person working with your website has a lot to do with how your site looks and behaves. As a result, it is very important that you test your site on the browsers used by your target audience. The majority of personal computer users access the Web using one of five browsers: Microsoft Internet Explorer, Mozilla Firefox, Google Chrome, Safari, and Opera).

As of May 2014, the usage of the various browsers is as follows (you can see the current lineup at w3schools.com/browsers/):

● Google Chrome: 59.2 percent

● Mozilla Firefox: 24.9 percent

- Microsoft Internet Explorer: 8.9 percent

- Apple Safari: 3.8 percent

- Opera: 1.8 percent

I recommend that you get at least the first three and test your sites on them all. You can download them at:

- Google Chrome: google.com/chrome and click Download Chrome.

- Mozilla Firefox: mozilla.org/firefox and click Firefox Free Download.

- Microsoft Internet Explorer: microsoft.com/download/internet_explorer.aspx. This provides the downloading of several versions of Internet Explorer (IE), including

  - IE 11, which came out in October 2013 with Windows 8.1.

  - IE 10, which came out in October 2012 with Windows 8.

  - IE 9, which came out in March 2011 and was a major upgrade.

  - IE 8, which came out in March 2009 and was used in the initial versions of Windows 7.

- Apple Safari: support.apple.com/kb/dl1531 and click Download.

- Opera: opera.com/computer/windows and click Free Download For Windows.

NOTE
You can have only one version of Internet Explorer on a computer at a time.

Considering Other Factors
The other components affecting how a user sees and experiences your website, while not quite as important as browsers, still can affect the perception of your site, and you need to give some thought to them and possibly do some testing on the alternatives.

Consider Display Size
When you lay out a web page, you need to consider the display real estate you have to work with. That is a combination of the display's physical size and its resolution. W3Schools.com has a display statistics table, shown next, that reveals the change in the screen resolution of their site's visitors over time. The summary message of the table is that the majority of screens are now high resolution, but it says nothing about screen size. It is my supposition, because I can't find any statistics, that the average screen size is getting smaller because of the new laptops with smaller screens and the proliferation

of tablets and smart phones. The resolution can stay the same and still display the same content on the smaller screen, but the size of the content is smaller to the point where it is uncomfortable to view. The point is that if you think your audience is going to view your site on smaller displays, you need to test it out and see if it works. This is especially true if you think your audience will be using smaller tablets and smart phones.

Web Statistics and Trends

Statistics are important information.

W3Schools.com is for people with an interest for web technologies. This fact indicates that the numbers below might not be 100% true for the average internet users. The average internet-user might have a lower screen resolution.

Anyway, our data, collected from W3Schools' log-files over many years, clearly shows the long term trends.

Screen Resolution Statistics

As of today, 99% of your visitors have a screen resolution of 1024x768 pixels or higher:

Date	Other high	1920x1080	1366x768	1280x1024	1280x800	1024x768	800x600	Lower
January 2014	34%	13%	31%	8%	7%	6%	0.5%	0.5%
January 2013	36%	11%	25%	10%	8%	9%	0.5%	0.5%
January 2012	35%	8%	19%	12%	11%	13%	1%	1%

Consider Operating Systems

W3Schools.com also has statistics on the operating system used by the people visiting their site. As of May 2014, 81 percent were Windows users, with 72 percent of those Windows 7 or 8. Ten percent were Mac OS X users, 5 percent were Linux users, and 4 percent were mobile users (iOS and Android). This tells me two major points. First, most effort needs to be on the Windows platform unless you are specifically targeting another, and second, I strongly question the mobile percentage and believe that the W3Schools website visitors are not representative of the universe of users. I think this last point needs to be considered with all the W3Schools statistics.

Consider Devices

I touched on tablets, smart phones, and smaller laptops in the discussion of displays, but if those devices are part of your target audience, you also need to consider how your website operates. The majority of those smaller devices do not use a mouse, and many use only touch. How do you handle that? It is a serious question that can affect whether your site is appreciated or not. Handling tablets and smart phones is beyond the beginner's guide focus of this book, but Zend Studio provides a lot of support for those devices, and there is considerable information on the Internet.

Chapter 1 Self-Test

The following questions are intended to help reinforce your comprehension of the concepts covered in this chapter. The answers can be found in the accompanying online Appendix A, "Answers to the Self-Tests."

1. What does "IDE" stand for?

2. Should you use Microsoft Word for website development?

3. What are at least 5 of the 15 features listed that should be in the web development tool you select?

4. What is the difference between code assistance and code validation?

5. Based on the discussion here, what are two good choices for IDEs?

6. What is Git?

7. What do "client side" and "server side" mean?

8. What is Apache besides a Native American tribe?

9. What does WAMP stand for?

10. What is the website used to test if you have your own web server running?

11. What is the website that is an excellent resource for learning about web programming and browser usage?

12. What are the four web environmental components of your audience to consider in building a website?

13. What is the most important environmental component?

14. What are the three browsers you should test your website with?

15. What is the summary message from the display statistics shown here?

Chapter 2

Building Web Pages with HTML

Key Skills & Concepts

- Using HTML5

- Setting Up Aptana

- Reviewing HTML

- Using Basic Tags

- Using Global Attributes

- Setting Paragraph Styles

- Applying Character Styles

- Displaying Special Characters

- Working with Images and Image Maps

- Adding Hyperlinks and Bookmarks

- Defining Forms

- Creating Tables

- Using New HTML5 Tags

- Understanding Deprecated HTML Tags

HTML (Hypertext Markup Language) is the foundation programming language of the Web and provides the backbone of all web pages. You may add JavaScript and PHP to your pages, but the structure around that code is HTML. Although HTML provides the critical infrastructure on a web page, it also has been around for a while, and browsers and devices, especially mobile devices, have put pressure on it for an update. As a result, there is a recent major revision of HTML and a significant supplement to it:

- **HTML5** is the first major standardized revision to HTML in 15 years. It replaces both HTML 4.01 and XHTML 1.1, as well as many ad hoc additions and revisions in common usage. A number of new tags and attributes were added, such as <audio>, <video>, <section>, and <header>. Other elements have been redefined, modified, or deprecated (no longer officially part of the language and whose use is discouraged). At the same time, HTML5 defines a number of processing situations so that they may be handled uniformly by browsers updated for HTML5. HTML5 is further discussed in this chapter and used throughout this book.

- **CSS (Cascading Style Sheets)** is a language used to describe the layout, formatting, and look of a web page. It is also used to carry a consistent set of styles across a number of pages in a website or even across several websites. CSS defines a prioritization scheme, or "cascade," to use when several style rules overlap. CSS is covered in Chapter 3.

This first part of the book provides an up-to-date foundation with HTML5 and CSS upon which you can build dynamic websites with JavaScript, PHP, and MySQL. Where applicable throughout the book, CSS and HTML5 replace the equivalent HTML.

HTML, HTML5, and CSS are controlled by recommended standards set by the World Wide Web Consortium (W3C—see w3.org). As of this writing, the latest CSS recommendation is CSS 2.1 dated June 2011. There are draft proposals for CSS 3 and CSS 4. HTML5, as of December 2012, is a candidate for recommendation and has taken 15 years to get to that status. It is awaiting the full approval of the many constituents of the W3C, which is expected to happen in 2014. Newer standards are in the works—CSS 3, CSS 4, HTML5.1, and HTML5.2—but the process is very slow, in part because the consortium is very large, including most organizations, academics, and individuals who are active on the Web.

CAUTION

To be sure that your websites are viewable in the maximum number of browsers, use only the recommended standards for HTML5 and CSS 2.1.

HTML5

HTML5 is a standard method of producing a web page. Being a standard means that many browsers can display the web page, so long as they are written to that standard. The standard defines what the tags do and how they are processed. The standard also presents a set of rules that determine how conflicts are handled—for example, how two tags with overlapping definitions work together—so that it's easier for a browser to interpret what it is you want to do.

This chapter will provide a good review of HTML and then talk primarily about HTML5. For simplicity, I'll often just say "HTML," unless I'm specifically talking about changes in HTML5. Much of what is said here also applies to HTML 4.01, but I strongly recommend that you pay attention to the changes in HTML5 and use them even though it may mean that you change what you have been doing in the past. Some elements of

HTML5 are easier to use, but I agree that is not universally true. Significant thought and effort by many people went into creating HTML5, and every new browser is reasonably compliant with it. Learn about the changes in HTML5, including the new rules, tags, and other modifications, and ignore the older tags that have been replaced with CSS or otherwise deprecated. This book assumes that is what you want to do, and the examples reflect it.

Using HTML5

Having just said that I strongly recommend using the changes in HTML5, I want to clarify that to mean I recommend using the HTML5 changes, additions, and deprecations to HTML tags and attributes, as described in this chapter. On the other hand, HTML5 loosened several of the rules of syntax in HTML (the way elements are formed, appear, and are arranged in a well-formed script) that I discourage you from following. In particular:

- HTML5 tags and attributes can be either upper- or lowercase, but for ease of identification and use, and to maintain an XHTML rule, I recommend using all lowercase for both tags and attributes.

- HTML5 doesn't require certain elements to have a closing tag or slash (/). I recommend strongly that you include all closing tags and slashes. For example, in HTML5, you can use `<p>` and `<img>` by themselves. I recommend you use `<p></p>` and `<img />`. Aptana, Zend Studio, and other integrated development environments (IDEs) provide ending tags and slashes automatically; they help you see where an element ends; and they assure that embedded CSS and JavaScript operate properly.

- HTML5 doesn't require the `<html>`, `<head>`, and `<body>` elements. I recommend that you keep these elements for the simple reason that they provide structure to your script, as does indentation, which also is not required.

- HTML5 doesn't require quotes around attribute values in *some cases*. I recommend that you use the quotes because of the last two words "some cases" and remove any ambiguity.

I will use all of these recommended syntax conventions in this book.

NOTE
A powerful reason for using a stricter syntax than that allowed by HTML5 is not that browsers need it to better display your page, although it can help in certain circumstances, but that humans, including the programmer, need it to better understand and follow a script. For the most part, browsers are good at rendering bad HTML, but that doesn't mean you should depend on that.

Setting Up Aptana

Throughout this book, I will demonstrate what is being discussed in the text and show the results both in an IDE and, where applicable, in a browser. For the early chapters, the code examples will be illustrated using Aptana. You can use other IDEs and achieve pretty much the same result, but what is described and shown here will be in Aptana. Here are the steps to set up Aptana starting with what was initially downloaded in Chapter 1, as shown in Figure 2-1, to what you see in Figures 2-2 and 2-3.

1. The first task after starting Aptana is to select a workspace. The default is in your Documents folder. That's fine until you want to use PHP, but you might as well prepare now for that event. You will need a workspace used by your web server. For WAMP, that is C:\wamp\www\. Use your Windows Explorer (File Explorer in Windows 8)

Figure 2-1   Aptana provides strong support for HTML5 and CSS.

to open that folder, and create and open a new folder named "Workspace." Copy that address into the Aptana Workspace Launcher and click OK.

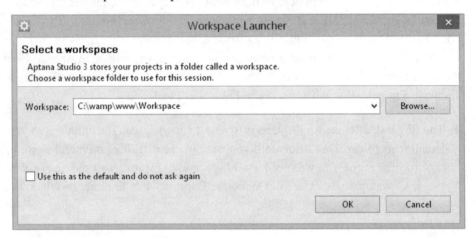

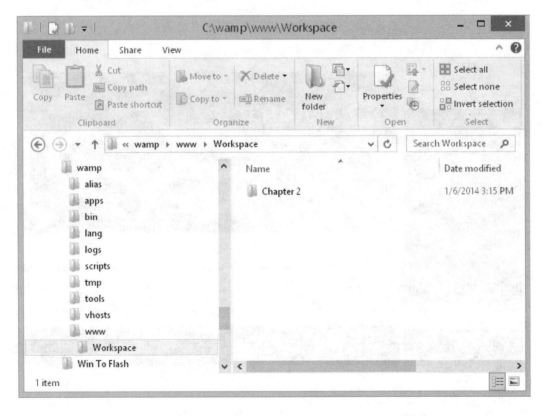

2. Next, create a new project by clicking the New icon down arrow on the left of the toolbar and clicking Web Project.

3. In the New Web Project dialog box that opens, click HTML5 Boilerplate, click Next, type **Chapter2** for the project name, and click Finish. This creates a lot of boilerplate we don't need right now, but it provides a place to start.

4. Click the close button on the Start Page tab to close that page. You can reopen it at any time by clicking the little red house icon in the middle of the toolbar.

5. Double-click index.html in the left column to open a web page. Here you can see all the extra boilerplate, as shown in Figure 2-2.

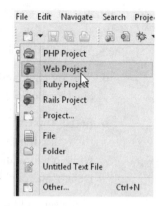

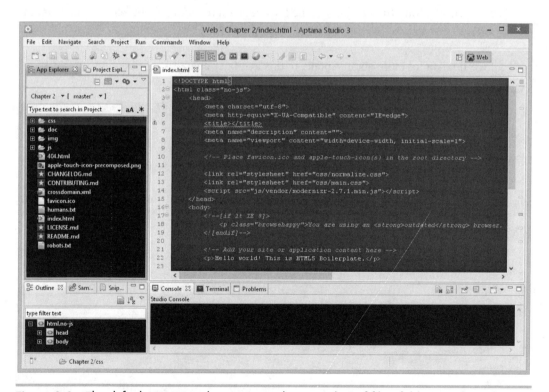

Figure 2-2 The default HTML5 web page provides a number of files, folders, and text that aren't initially needed.

6. Finally, let's clean up this page to leave only what we want to immediately discuss. We'll come back, both later in this chapter and in ensuing chapters, and look at other elements of this boilerplate. For now, we want to greatly simplify it.

    a. Start by changing the color from white and colored text on a black background to black and colored text on a white background as explained in the following Tip.

    b. In the App Explorer in the left column, delete everything except index.html by right-clicking the file or folder (select several files or folders by holding SHIFT while clicking the first and last ones and then right-clicking the selection), clicking Delete, and clicking OK.

    c. In the second line of index.html, delete "class="no-js"".

    d. Delete line 8 through line 14. After doing that, delete the newly renumbered lines 10 through 14. Then delete the again renumbered lines 11 through 25. The result is shown in Figure 2-3.

7. Save the resulting file by clicking the Save icon on the toolbar (the second one from the left).

We'll talk a lot more about Aptana in this and later chapters.

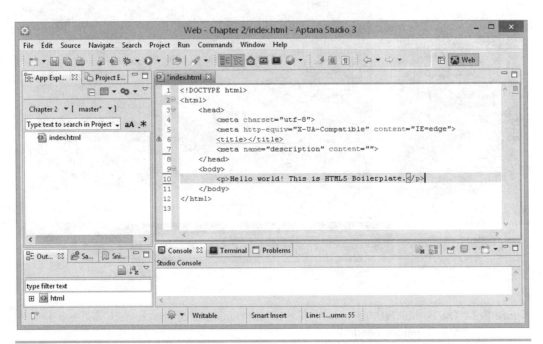

Figure 2-3 HTML5 !DOCTYPE and html tags are much simpler than those used previously.

TIP

If you don't like the white text on black background default look of Aptana 3, click the down arrow next to the color wheel icon in the toolbar (right of center), and click Aptana Studio 2.x theme, which gives you a black text on a white background that I like better (repeat this and click Aptana Studio to return to the white on black). Most of the screenshots in this book are taken with black text on a white background.

Reviewing HTML

HTML is a series of tags that identify the elements in a web page. *Tags,* or *markup tags,* consist of a tag name enclosed in angle brackets (`<>`) and normally come in pairs. Tags are placed at the beginning and end of an element, often text that you want to identify; the ending tag name is preceded by a slash. For example,

```
<title>This is a title</title>
```

uses the `<title>` tag to identify text that will be placed in the title bar of the browser window. Tags are placed around text to identify it and specify how it is handled.

NOTE

This chapter will not provide exhaustive coverage of HTML, nor will it cover every nuance of every HTML tag or attribute. Both areas are fully covered by sites on the Web, in particular, w3c.org and w3school.com, and in the excellent book *HTML: A Beginner's Guide, Fifth Edition* by Wendy Willard, published by McGraw-Hill Education.

In addition to a tag name, a tag may contain one or more *attributes* that modify what the tag does. For example, if you want to display an image on your web page, you could use this tag:

```
<img src="rodie.jpg" />
```

An *attribute* of the `<img />` tag is `src`, and the *value* of the `src` attribute is `rodie.jpg`. Attributes are related to their value with an equal sign, and the value is placed in full (double) quotation marks (single quotation marks are referred to as "apostrophes" and there is no difference between left and right double quotation marks).

NOTE

In the listings and HTML examples in this chapter, tags are shown in bold, whereas attributes and their values are not. Also, continuation lines are indented from their parents. These conventions are used solely for readability. Aptana, by default, color-codes and indents HTML for readability. Dark red is used for tags, bright red is used for attribute names, blue is used for attribute values, black is used for plain text, and green is used for comments.

Using Basic Tags

Every HTML script must contain a basic set of tags. These tags identify the document as being an HTML document and identify the major parts of the document. In HTML5, the tags must be included in a web page to conform to the standard. The basic tags are shown in Figure 2-3 and in Listing 2-1, and are described with their attributes in Table 2-1.

TIP

The listings here and in the rest of the book are available online at mhprofessional.com/mediacenter/. See the book's introduction on how best to use the online listings.

Listing 2-1   Basic Set of Tags

```html
<!DOCTYPE html >
<html>
    <head>
        <meta charset="utf-8">
        <meta http-equiv="X-UA-Compatible" content="IE=edge">
        <title></title>
        <meta name="description" content="">
    </head>
    <body>
        <p>Hello world! This is HTML5 Boilerplate.</p>
    </body>
</html>
```

NOTE

In the tables of tags and attributes in this chapter, tags are shown with their angle brackets, and attributes are indented from the left.

Using Global Attributes

Global attributes are attributes that can be used with virtually any HTML tag. Assume that these attributes, shown in Table 2-2, are added to the following lists of tag attributes in this chapter.

Setting Paragraph Styles

Paragraph styles include basic paragraph definition and headings; the line break; bulleted, numbered, and definition lists; preformatted paragraphs; comments; and horizontal lines or rules. Unless the preformatted style is used, normal line endings, more than one extra space, and tabs are ignored in HTML. Lines simply wrap to fit the space allotted for them

Tag or Attribute	Description
`<!DOCTYPE ...>`	Identifies the document as adhering to HTML standards.
`<html> </html>`	Identifies the intervening text as being HTML.
`<head> </head>`	Contains the title and document identifying information. The `<title>` tag is required in the `<head>` tag.
`<title> </title>`	Identifies the title that is placed in the browser's title bar.
`<meta ...>`	Assigns content to an element that can be used by a server or browser and that cannot otherwise be assigned in HTML. `<meta ...>` is an exception to the rule and does not have a closing tag.
charset	Identifies how to display characters on the page; `"utf-8"` is assigned to `charset` in Listing 2-1 and placed within the `<head>` tag.
content	Provides the text associated with `http-equiv` and/or `name`.
http-equiv	Identifies how the meta tag is used.
name	Provides information that can be used by search engines.
`<body> </body>`	Specifies the part of the page that is shown to the user and defines overall page properties.

Table 2-1 Basic Set of HTML Tags

unless you use the paragraph tag. Listing 2-2 shows examples of paragraph styles. This listing is combined with the tags in Listing 2-1 to produce the web page shown in Aptana in Figure 2-4 and in the Chrome browser in Figure 2-5. Paragraph styles are described in Table 2-3.

Tag or Attribute	Description
accesskey	Specifies a set of keystrokes (shortcut key) to go to (place the focus on) a particular element on a page
class	Identifies the class of an element for applying styles
dir	Sets the direction of text in an element
draggable	Specifies whether an element can be dragged
hidden	Specifies whether an element is hidden or not
id	Attaches a name for linking
style	Specifies the CSS style for an element
tabindex	Identifies the element's position in the tabbing order
title	Specifies a title for an element

Table 2-2 Global Attributes Applicable to All Elements

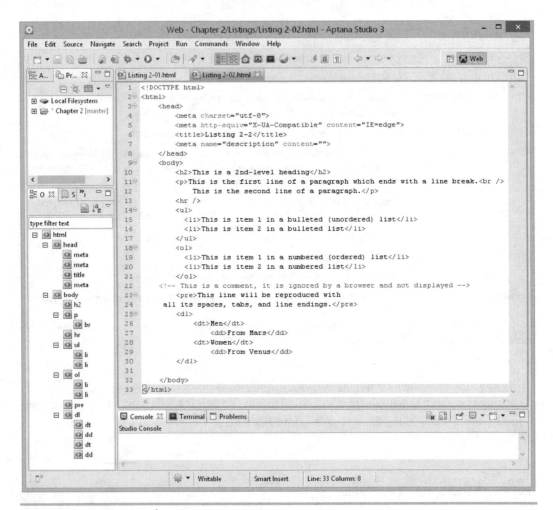

Figure 2-4 Listing 2-2 shown in Aptana

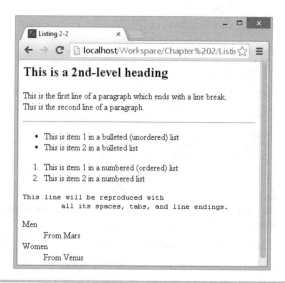

Figure 2-5   Listing 2-2 shown in Chrome

Listing 2-2   Paragraph-Style Tag Examples

```
<h2>This is a 2nd-level heading</h2>
<p>This is the first line of a paragraph which ends with a line
break.<br />
This is the second line of a paragraph.</p>
<hr />
<ul>
  <li>This is item 1 in a bulleted (unordered) list</li>
  <li>This is item 2 in a bulleted list</li>
</ul>
<ol>
  <li>This is item 1 in a numbered (ordered) list</li>
  <li>This is item 2 in a numbered list</li>
</ol>
<!-- This is a comment, it is ignored by a browser and not displayed
-->
<pre>This line will be reproduced with
 all its spaces, tabs, and line endings.</pre>
<dl>
  <dt>Men</dt>
    <dd>From Mars</dd>
  <dt>Women</dt>
    <dd>From Venus</dd>
</dl>
```

Tags or Attributes	Description
`<p> </p>`	Identifies the start and end of a paragraph
`<hn> </hn>`	Identifies a heading in one of six heading styles (n = 1 to 6)
` `	Forces a line break similar to pressing SHIFT-ENTER in Microsoft Word
`<hr />`	Creates a horizontal rule or line
`<ol> </ol>`	Contains an ordered (numbered) list
`reversed`	Specifies the list order will be reversed
`start`	Specifies the starting value of the list number
`type`	Specifies the type numbering of the list: 1 = numeric, A = uppercase alphabetic, a = lowercase alphabetic, I = uppercase Roman, I = lowercase Roman
`<ul> </ul>`	Contains an unordered (bulleted) list
`<li> </li>`	Identifies an item in a numbered or bulleted list
`value`	Specifies the numeric value of the list item from which the following list items will increment
`<dl> </dl>`	Contains a description list
`<dt> </dt>`	Identifies a term to be described, displayed on the left of a page
`<dd> </dd>`	Identifies the description of the term that immediately precedes it, indented from the left
`<address> </address>`	Identifies a paragraph of contact information, normally italicized
`<blockquote> </blockquote>`	Identifies a paragraph that is indented on both the left and right, as you might do with a quotation
`cite`	Identifies a URL for the `blockquote`
`<!-- -->`	Identifies a comment that the browser will ignore and not display
`<div> </div>`	Identifies a division of a page
`<pre> </pre>`	Identifies preformatted text in which all spaces, tabs, and line endings are preserved
`<style> </style>`	Defines style information for a page
`scoped`	Limits the use of the style information to a parent element and its descendants

Table 2-3   Paragraph-Style HTML Tags

NOTE
You can nest lists within lists and get automatic indenting.

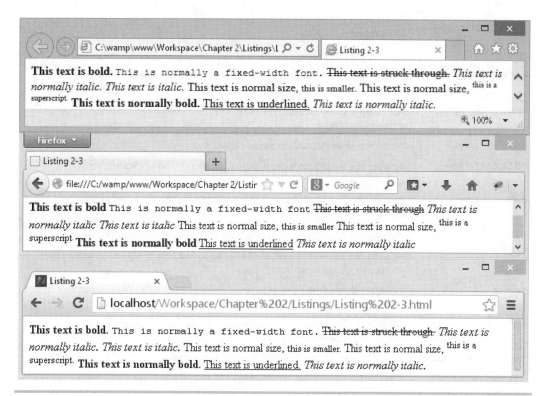

Figure 2-6   Character-style tags displayed in Internet Explorer, Firefox, and Chrome

Applying Character Styles

Character styles, which determine how one or more characters will look or behave, come in two forms. *Logical* character styles are defined by the browser and may be displayed in any way that the browser has established. *Physical* character styles have a strict definition that will be the same in all browsers. Examples of character-style tags are shown in Listing 2-3, and Figure 2-6 shows how Microsoft Internet Explorer 11, Mozilla Firefox 26, and Google Chrome 36 display them. Note the lack of differences. Table 2-4 describes most character styles.

NOTE

Figure 2-6 demonstrates that browsers ignore line endings unless they are marked with `<p>`, `<br />`, or other paragraph styles.

Tag	Description
`<b> </b>`	Applies the Bold physical character style to the enclosed characters.
`<cite> </cite>`	Applies the Citation logical character style to the enclosed characters; normally italic.
`<code> </code>`	Applies the Code logical character style to the enclosed characters; normally a fixed-width font.
`<del> </del>`	Applies a strikethrough to the enclosed text.
`<dfn> </dfn>`	Applies the Definition logical character style to the enclosed characters; normally italic.
`<em> </em>`	Applies the Emphasis logical character style to the enclosed characters; normally italic.
`<i> </i>`	Applies the Italic physical character style to the enclosed characters.
`<kbd> </kbd>`	Applies the Keyboard logical character style to the enclosed characters; normally a fixed-width font.
`<s> </s>`	Identifies deleted text and applies a strikethrough to it. W3C recommends not using this for just a strikethrough; use `<del>`.
`<samp> </samp>`	Applies the Sample logical character style to the enclosed characters; normally a fixed-width font.
`<small> </small>`	Makes the enclosed characters one size smaller.
`<strong> </strong>`	Applies the Strong logical character style to the enclosed characters; normally bold.
`<sub> </sub>`	Applies the Subscript physical character style to the enclosed characters.
`<sup> </sup>`	Applies the Superscript physical character style to the enclosed characters.
`<u> </u>`	Applies an underline to the enclosed text.
`<var> </var>`	Applies the Sample logical character style to the enclosed characters; normally italic.

Table 2-4 Character-Style HTML Tags

Listing 2-3 Character-Style Tag Examples

```
<b>This text is bold.</b>
<code>This is normally a fixed-width font.</code>
<del>This text is normally struck through.</del>
<em>This text is normally italic.</em>
<i>This text is italic.</i>
This text is normal size, <small>this is smaller.</small>
This text is normal size, <sup>this is a superscript.</sup>
<strong>This text is normally bold.</strong>
<u>This text is underlined.</U>
<var>This text is normally italic.</var>
```

NOTE

Character styles and formatting have a number of deprecated tags in HTML5, such as
`<big>`, `<center>`, `<font>`, `<strike>`, and `<tt>` (see a list of deprecated tags toward
the end of the chapter). Some of these make sense, like `<strike>`, which is replaced
with `<del>` and does the same thing. Others are hard to understand, like `<big>`,
when they have kept `<small>`. Yes, CSS can handle both of these, but then why not
deprecate them both? Two other character-style tags, `<u>` and `<s>`, were considered
deprecated in XHTML, but are not in HTML5. As a rule, you should not use deprecated
tags, but most browsers still handle them to display legacy web pages.

Displaying Special Characters

HTML defines the less-than, greater-than, and ampersand characters as having special
meanings, and therefore they cannot be used as normal text. Also, the quote mark and
apostrophe can be problematic. To use these characters normally, replace them as follows:

To Display	Type
Quote mark (")	`&quot;` or `&#34;`
Ampersand (&)	`&amp;` or `&#38;`
Apostrophe (')	`&apos;` or `&#39;`
Less than (<)	`&lt;` or `&#60;`
Greater than (>)	`&gt;` or `&#62;`

NOTE

Unlike the rest of HTML, escape sequences are case-sensitive—for example, you cannot
use < for the less-than symbol.

All other characters that you can type on your keyboard will be displayed as they are
typed. In addition, HTML has defined a number of other characters that can be displayed
based on entering an *escape sequence* where you want the character displayed. The escape
sequence can take either a numeric or a textual format, as was shown with the special
characters just mentioned. In either case, the escape sequence begins with an ampersand
(&) and ends with a semicolon (;). In the numeric format, the ampersand is followed by
a number symbol (#) and a number that represents the character. All characters, whether
they are on the keyboard or not, can be represented with a numeric escape sequence.
The textual format has been defined only for some characters and excludes most characters
on the keyboard. Additional examples of the two formats are shown in Table 2-5.

Character	Name	Numeric Sequence	Text Sequence
€	Euro	€ or €	&euro;
…	Horizontal ellipsis	… or …	&hellip;
•	Bullet	• or •	&bull;
™	Trademark	™ or ™	&trade;
©	Copyright	&#169;	&copy;
Æ	AE ligature	&#198;	&aelig;
Ä	A umlaut	&#228;	&auml;
É	E acute accent	&#233;	&eacute;
Õ	O tilde	&#245;	&otilde;

Table 2-5 Samples of Character Escape Sequences

TIP

For lists of the character escape sequences, go to w3.org/markup/html-spec/html-spec_13.html or e3schools.com/tags/ref_ascii.asp. Neither of these lists is totally complete. The most complete list I've found with all the 8000 series numbers is ascii .cl/htmlcodes.htm. The W3C list shows that &#127; through Ÿ are unused, although they work, as you see next for the Euro, ellipsis, bullet, and trademark. The standard has replaced those numbers with the 8000 series numbers as shown in Table 2-5.

```
<body>
    <p>Quote Mark   &quot;  &#34;</p>
    <p>Ampersand   &amp;  &#38;</p>
    <p>Apostrophe   &apos;  &#39;</p>
    <p>Less-than   &lt;  &#60;</p>
    <p>Greater-than   &gt;  &#62;</p>
    <p>Euro   &euro;  &#128;</p>
    <p>Horizontal Ellipsis   &hellip;  &#133;</p>
    <p>Bullet   &bull;  &#149;</p>
    <p>Trademark   &trade;  &#153;</p>
    <p>Copyright   &copy;  &#169;</p>
</body>
```

NOTE

The   (which can also be) in the previous illustration is a nonbreaking space and is used either to add space or with just the Paragraph tags to create a blank line (paragraph) that HTML will retain.

Working with Images and Image Maps

Images are added to a web page by use of the Image (`<img />`) tag, which specifies the path and filename of the image, as well as a number of attributes, such as size, positioning, margins, and border. One of the attributes, `ismap`, identifies the image as having an image map attached to it. The image map is a separate MAP file used by the server to relate areas of the image to URLs. To use `ismap`, you must include the Image tag in an Anchor tag (see the next section, "Adding Hyperlinks and Bookmarks"). A couple of examples are given in Listing 2-4 and shown in Figure 2-7. Many of the Image attributes are described in Table 2-6.

Listing 2-4   Image Tag Examples

```
<p><img src="hibiscus.jpg" alt="A picture of a hibiscus"
  width="166" height="190" /> This is a picture of a hibiscus...</p>
<p> </p>
<p><img src="undercon.gif" alt="Under
  Construction" width="40" height="38" />
  This is the Under Construction symbol...</p>
```

Figure 2-7   Example using the Image tag in Listing 2-4

Tag or Attribute	Description
`<img />`	Defines an image that will be linked to a page
`alt`	Identifies alternative text that is displayed if the image cannot be displayed
`height`	Specifies the height, in pixels, of the image
`ismap`	Specifies a server-side image map
`src`	Identifies the path and filename or URL of the image
`usemap`	Specifies a client-side image map
`width`	Specifies the width, in pixels, of the image

Table 2-6   Image Tag Attributes

TIP

Specifying the `height` and the `width` speeds up loading because a quick placeholder will be drawn for the image, allowing the text to continue to be loaded while the image is drawn. Without these dimensions, the loading of the text must wait for the image to be drawn and thereby determine where the remaining text will go. Current browsers will automatically scale the other dimension based on the current aspect ratio of the image if just one of the dimensions (`height` or `width`) is given.

Adding Hyperlinks and Bookmarks

Hyperlinks provide the ability to click an object and transfer what is displayed by the browser (the *focus*) to an address associated with the object. HTML implements hyperlinks with the Anchor tag (`<a> </a>`), which specifies that the text or graphic that it contains is a hyperlink or a bookmark or both. If the tag is a *hyperlink* and the contents are selected, then the focus is moved either to another location in the current page or website, or to another website. If the tag is a *bookmark,* then another Anchor tag may reference it and potentially transfer the focus to it.

An image used as just described assumes that the entire image is the hyperlink. An image may also be broken into sections, where each section is a link or a *hotspot*. To break an image into multiple links requires an *image map* that is implemented with the Map tag. The Map tag contains Area tags that define the shape of a specific area of the image and the link that it is pointing to.

Listing 2-5 provides some examples of the Anchor, Map, and Area tags, which are shown in Figure 2-8. Table 2-7 describes these tags and their attributes.

NOTE

The finger in Figure 2-8 is pointing to the hotspot labeled "screen," as shown at the bottom of the window (".../Listing 2-5.html#screen").

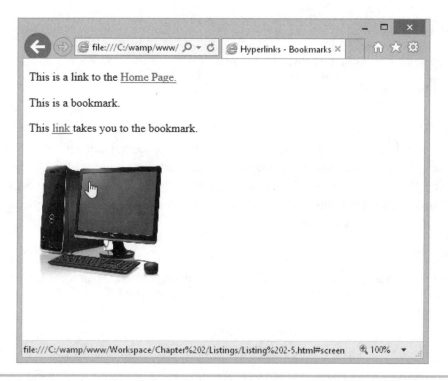

Figure 2-8   Hyperlinks and bookmarks defined in Listing 2-5, including a hotspot link (Dell XPS 8700 desktop computer; photo courtesy of Dell)

Listing 2-5   Hyperlinks and Bookmarks Examples

```
<p>This is a link to the <a href="default.html">Home
  Page.</a></p>
<p><a name="This ">This </a>is a bookmark.</p>
<p>This <a href="#This ">link </a>takes you to the bookmark.</p>
<p><map name="ComputerMap">
  <area shape="poly" coords="163, 121, 197, 145, 91, 183, 55,
    157" href="#keyboard">
  <area shape="poly" coords="6, 90, 147, 87, 148, 115, 46, 145,
    2, 124" href="#processor">
  <area shape="rect" coords="30, 6, 124, 70" href="#screen"></map>
  <a href="computer.map">
    <img align="bottom" src="Dell desktop.png" width="200" ismap
      usemap="#computermap" height="186" /></a></p>
```

NOTE

The shape attribute of the **area** tag may be left out, and a rectangular shape will be assumed. Also, with most browsers, you can use the shape attribute's values "polygon" and "rectangle" in place of "poly" and "rect" although they are not officially recognized.

Defining Forms

A form in HTML is defined by the input fields that it contains. Each input field is defined by its type, name, and potentially a default value. There are a number of field types around which you can wrap text and formatting to get virtually any form you want to define. One example is shown in Listing 2-6 and displayed in Figure 2-9. Table 2-8 describes the tags and attributes related to forms.

TIP

You can fix the sloppy drop-down list in Chrome by removing the multiple attribute from the <select> tag, but then you cannot have multiple selections. Currently, this is a bug in Chrome.

Tags or Attributes	Description
`<a> </a>`	Specifies the definition of a hyperlink
`href`	Identifies the destination URL, which can be a bookmark, page, or website
`name`	Identifies the bookmark at this location
`<map> </map>`	Specifies the definition of an image map
`name`	Identifies the name of the image map
`<area> </area>`	Specifies the definition of one image area
`coords`	Identifies the coordinates of the shape being defined using x and y positions in terms of image pixels for each point
`href`	Identifies the bookmark or URL to which the focus is transferred
`nohref`	Indicates that a given area causes no action to take place
`shape`	Specifies the type of shape being defined to be `circ`, `circle`, `poly` (polygon), or `rect`, (rectangle)

Table 2-7 Anchor, Map, and Area Tags and Their Attributes

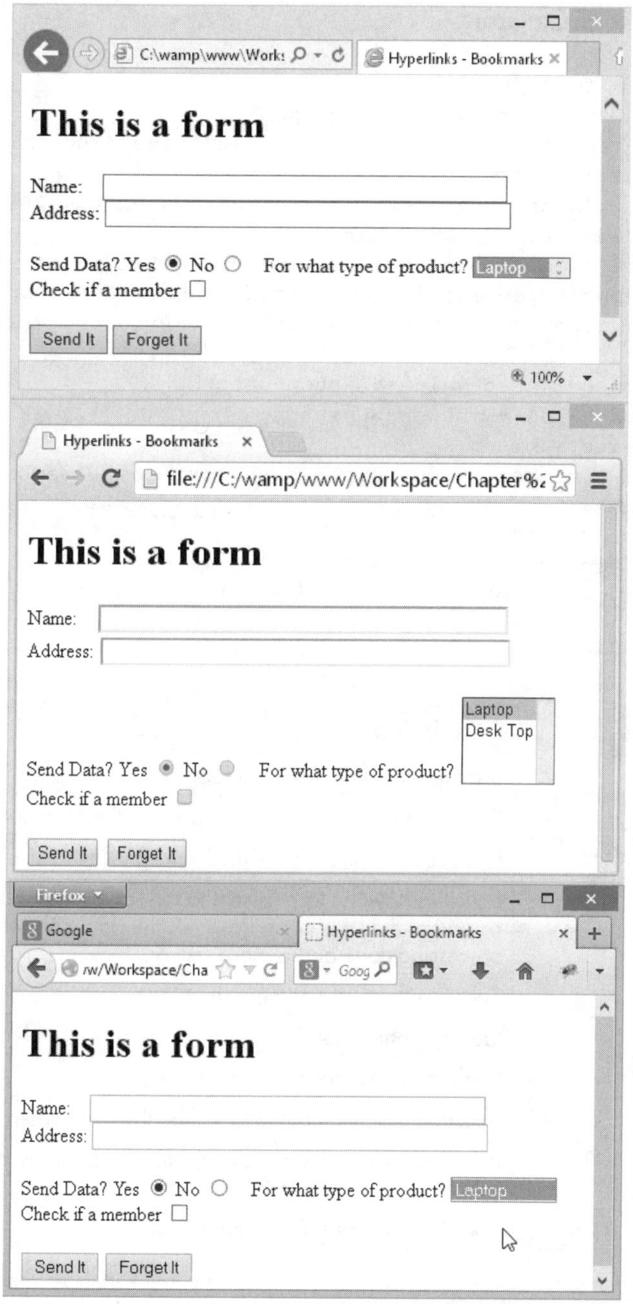

Figure 2-9 Form created with Listing 2-6. Note the differences between Internet Explorer at the top, Chrome in the middle, and Firefox at the bottom.

Listing 2-6   Form Example

```
<h1>This is a form</h1>
<form action="saveresults" method="post">
    Name:     <input type="text" size="50" maxlength="256"
    name="name"><br />
    Address: <input type="text" size="50" maxlength="256"
    name="address" /><br /><br />
    Send Data? Yes <input type="radio" name="Send" value="Yes" />
    No <input type="radio" name="Send" value="No" />   
    For what type of product? <select name="Product" multiple
    size="1">
    <option selected value="Laptop">Laptop
    <option value="Desktop">Desktop
        </select><br />
    Check if a member <input type="checkbox" name="Member"
    ="true">
    <br /><br />
    <input type="submit" value="Send It" />
    <input type="reset" value="Forget It" />
</form>
```

Tags or Attributes	Description
`<form> </form>`	Specifies the definition of a form.
`action`	Specifies the URL with code to process the form upon submittal.
`autocomplete`	Enables autocomplete for the form.
`method`	Specifies how the form is sent to the server: `get` transmits the data as part of the URL; `post` transmits the data only when queried by the processing code and is more secure.
`name`	Specifies the name of the form.
`<input />`	Identifies one input field.
`autocomplete`	Enables autocomplete for the input field.
`autofocus`	Specifies that the input field will be the focus when the page opens.
`checked`	If `type=checkbox` or `radio`, determines if, by default, they are selected (`true`) or not (`false`).
`disabled`	Specifies that the field cannot be used.

Table 2-8   Form Tags and Attributes *(continued)*

Tags or Attributes	Description
form	Specifies the form the drop-down list belongs to.
list	Identifies the default element for the input field.
max	Specifies the maximum value for the input field.
maxlength	Specifies the maximum number of characters that can be entered in an input field.
name	Specifies the name of the field.
readonly	Specifies that the field contents cannot be changed.
size	Specifies the width of a text field in characters, or the width and height in characters and lines of a text area.
src	Specifies the URL of an image if `type=image`.
step	Specifies the granularity of `value` for a given `type`.
type	Specifies the field type as `button`, `checkbox`, `date`, `datetime`, `email`, `file`, `hidden`, `image`, `month`, `number`, `password`, `radio`, `reset`, `search`, `submit`, `tel`, `text`, `time`, or `week`. See "Handling Date and Time Input" later in this chapter.
value	Specifies the default value of the field.
\<select\> \</select\>	Specifies the definition of a drop-down list.
autofocus	Specifies that the drop-down list will be the focus when the page opens.
disabled	Specifies that the definition cannot be used.
form	Specifies the form the drop-down list belongs to.
multiple	Specifies that multiple items can be selected in a menu (the user must be told to hold CTRL or COMMAND to select multiple items).
name	Specifies the name of a menu.
required	Specifies that the user must select a value.
size	Specifies the height of the menu.
\<option\>	Identifies one option in a menu.
disabled	Specifies that the option cannot be used.
label	Specifies the label of the option.
selected	Specifies that this option is the default.
value	Specifies the value if the option is selected.

Table 2-8 Form Tags and Attributes

Creating Tables

HTML provides a very rich set of tags to define a table, its cells, borders, and other properties. Table tags went unchanged in HTML5, but a number of attributes have been removed from table elements with the understanding that table formatting will be done with CSS. Listing 2-7 provides an example of the HTML for creating the simple table shown in Figure 2-10. Table 2-9 shows the principal table tags and their attributes.

Listing 2-7   Table Example

```html
<h2>A New Table</h2>
<table border="1">
  <caption>This Is The Table Caption</caption>
  <tr>
    <th>Cell 1, a header</th>
    <td colspan="2">Cell 2, This cell spans two
      columns</td>
    <td>Cell 3</td>
    <td>Cell 4</td>
  </tr>
  <tr>
    <td>Cell 5</td>
    <td>Cell 6</td>
    <td>Cell 7</td>
    <td></td>
  </tr>
  <tr>
    <td rowspan="2">Cells 9/13, These cells are
    merged</td>
    <td>Cell 10</td>
    <td>Cell 11</td>
    <td>Cell 12</td>
  </tr>
  <tr>
    <td>Cell 14</td>
    <td>Cell 15</td>
    <td>Cell 16</td>
  </tr>
</table>
```

TIP

There is no rule that the `<tr>` and`</tr>` tags must be on separate lines, as shown in Listing 2-7, but doing so makes it much easier to distinguish rows (`<tr>` `</tr>`) and cells (`<td>` `</td>`).

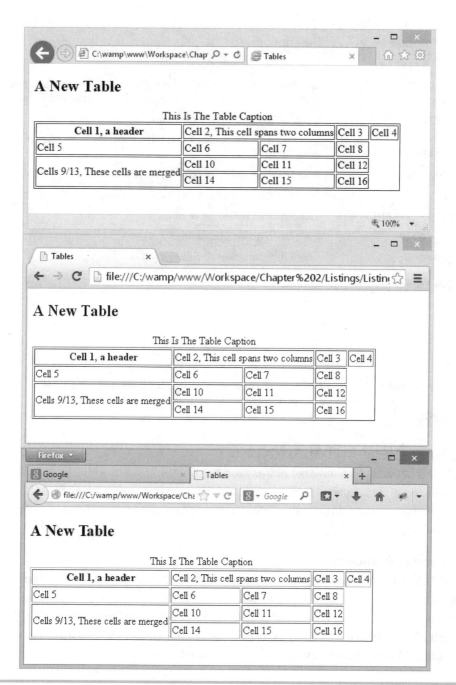

Figure 2-10   Table created with Listing 2-7. Notice almost no difference across IE, Chrome, and Firefox.

Tags or Attributes	Description
`<table> </table>`	Specifies the definition of a table.
`border`	Specifies the size, in pixels, of a border to be drawn around all cells in a table. HTML5 limits this to values of 0 ("") and 1. 1 is the default.
`<tr> </tr>`	Identifies the cells in a single row of a table.
`<td> </td>` `<th> </th>`	Identifies a single data cell in a table (`<td>`) or a header cell in the table (`<th>`).
`colspan`	Specifies the number of columns a cell should span.
`rowspan`	Specifies the number of rows a cell should span.
`<caption> </caption>`	Identifies the caption for a table.
`<col> </col>`	Identifies a group of columns.
`span`	Specifies the number of columns in the column group.

Table 2-9 Table Tags and Attributes

TIP

A table without the `border` attribute will not have a border, but will take up the same space as if it had a border of 1. Therefore, specifying a border of zero (0) will take up less space.

Using New HTML5 Tags

HTML5 has added a number of new tags and attributes, some of which have been mentioned in earlier parts of this chapter, but there are three areas where HTML5 has made significant additions: audio-video handling, date and time form input, and page sectioning.

Including Audio and Video

HTML5 added four new tags and related attributes to handle the inclusion and playing of audio and video files, as shown in Table 2-10. As this is written, there is not universal coverage by all browsers of all audio and video formats, but MP3 audio files and MP4 video files are both handled in Firefox, Internet Explorer, and Chrome. Listing 2-8 and Figure 2-11 demonstrate how `<video>` can be used.

Figure 2-11 Audio and video can add some real pizzazz to your website.

Listing 2-8 Video Example

```
<h1>Play This Video</h1>
<video src="win 8 intro.mpg" width="360" height="240" controls
    poster="win 8 QS Cover.jpg">
    Your browser does not support videos.
</video>
```

NOTE

Floating text between the starting and ending `<audio>` or `<video>` tags is displayed if the browser can't play the audio or video files.

NOTE

HTML5 also added the `<canvas>` tag that is used to contain and support graphics drawn by a scripting language, generally JavaScript. Only the latest browsers support `<canvas>`, and even there the support is spotty. The full use of `<canvas>` with JavaScript is beyond the scope of this book.

Tags or Attributes	Description
`<audio> </audio>`	Identifies a sound file that may be played
autoplay	Specifies that the audio will automatically start playing when the page is loaded (ignored if `preload` is present)
controls	Specifies that audio controls such as play, pause, and stop will be displayed
loop	Specifies that the audio will continue to replay
muted	Specifies that the audio will be muted
preload	Identifies how the audio should be loaded when the page loads: `auto` to load the entire file, `metadata` to load the metadata, or `none` to not load any of the audio file
src	Identifies the path and filename or URL of the audio file
`<video> </video>`	Identifies a video file that may be played (all the `<audio>` attributes are available with the `<video>` tag)
height	Specifies the height, in pixels, of the image
width	Specifies the width, in pixels, of the image
poster	Specifies a still image to display until the video starts
`<source> </source>`	Specifies the definition of an image map
src	Identifies multiple alternative audio files
`<track> </track>`	Specifies the text tracks, such as captions or subtitles, that are to be displayed while an audio or video file is being played
kind	Identifies the kind of text, including `captions`, `descriptions`, and `subtitles`
src	Identifies the source of the text track

Table 2-10   Audio and Video Tags and Attributes

Handling Date and Time Input

Prior to HTML5, the standard HTML only provided for the entry of dates and times into blank text boxes (later in this book, you'll see how to use JavaScript and PHP to do this). HTML5 provides a set of six form input types that include date and time "pickers" that pass on formatted dates and times, as shown in Table 2-11. Figure 2-12 shows that neither Internet Explorer 11 nor Firefox 26 (both the current release as of January 2014) has implemented the date and time input types in Listing 2-9. Chrome provides input

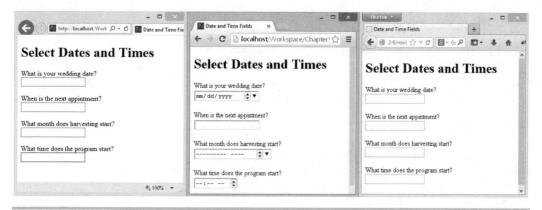

Figure 2-12   Not all browsers have kept up with HTML5.

formatting on all but `datetime`, and if the user clicks the down arrow on the right of the input box, they will see a full date picker.

Listing 2-9   Date and Time Examples

```
<h1>Form with Date and Time Entries</h1>
<form>
    What is your wedding date?<br/>
    <input type="date"/><br/><br/>
    When is the next appointment?<br/>
    <input type="datetime"/><br/><br/>
    What month does harvesting start?<br/>
    <input type="month"/><br/><br/>
    What time does the program begin?<br/>
    <input type="time"/><br/><br/>
</form>
```

NOTE

There are several additional new input types besides those for dates and times that provide specifically formatted types of fields. These include `email`, for e-mail addresses, `number` for numeric values, `tel` for telephone numbers, and `url` for web addresses. Although most form validation is done with JavaScript (see Chapter 4), HTML5 has added several validation attributes, including `list` for a list of predefined options for a form field, `min` and `max` for the minimum and maximum values for a form field, `multiple` to allow multiple values in a form field, `pattern` to specify a pattern that must be followed, and `required` to force an input field to be filled out.

Input Types	Description
date	Provides a date picker that outputs a year, month, and day.
datetime	Provides a date and time picker that outputs a year, month, day, hour, minute, second, and fraction of a second.
datetime-local	Provides a date and time picker that outputs a year, month, day, hour, minute, second, and fraction of a second.
month	Provides a picker that outputs year and month.
time	Provides a time picker that outputs hour, minute, second, and fraction of a second.
week	Provides a picker that outputs year and week.

Table 2-11   Date and Time Input Types

Tag	Description
`<article> </article>`	Identifies a self-contained area of a page or site
`<aside> </aside>`	Identifies an area of a page that is related to but not contained in the main body of the page
`<footer> </footer>`	Identifies an area of a page or subelement with such information as author, date of creation, and copyright
`<header> </header>`	Identifies an area of a page or subelement with introductory or navigational content
`<nav> </nav>`	Identifies an area of a page used to contain links to other parts of a site
`<section> </section>`	Identifies a generic section of a page or site

Table 2-12 Sectioning or Container Tags and Attributes

Using Page Sectioning

Prior to HTML5, you could divide a web page or site into various areas using the `<div>` tag. The `<div>` tag was often used to set off an area of a page or site for a header, footer, or a left or right column to provide a container for specific information in that area. HTML5 provides six additional tags, listed in Table 2-12, to section or identify containers on a page. In and of themselves, these tags do not provide placement or alignment on a page; you must do that separately with CSS styling (see Chapter 3). They simply provide identification of an area of a page for the script creator or reader. You can use these tags multiple times on a page or site, and they can be nested inside one another. For example, a page with a header and/or footer can have several article containers with their own header and/or footer, as shown in Figure 2-13. The new sectioning tags do not have their own attributes, but they make heavy use of the global attributes `class`, `id`, `style`, and `title`. Listing 2-10 shows a possible way the script might be laid out to provide the start of what you see in Figure 2-13, but remember that you will need to use styles discussed in the next chapter to get the actual layout in Figure 2-13; otherwise, it will look like the illustration on the right.

This represents the header content
Nav content
This represents the section content
Article 1 content
Footer 1 content
Article 2 content
Footer 2 content
This represents the aside content
This represents footer 3 content

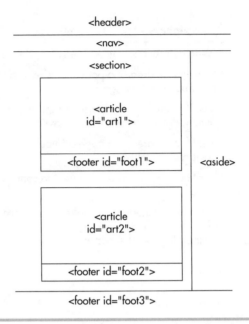

Figure 2-13 Sectioning tags allow you to identify containers for elements on a page.

Listing 2-10 Sectioning Example

```
<body>
    <header>
        This represents the header content
        <nav> Nav content </nav>
    </header>
    <section>
        This represents the section content
        <article id="art1">
            Article 1 content
            <footer id="foot1"> Footer 1 content </footer
        </article>
        <article id="art2">
            Article 2 content
            <footer id="foot2"> Footer 2 content </footer
        </article>
    </section>
    <aside>
        This represents the aside content
    </aside>
    <footer id="foot3">
        This represents footer 3 content
    </footer>
    </body>
```

Understanding Deprecated HTML Tags

With the increased use and desirability of CSS, a number of formatting and layout tags have been identified to be removed from the recommended HTML standard. These tags are called *deprecated tags,* meaning they have fallen out of favor. Currently, W3C deprecated tags are

- `<acronym>` (define an acronym; use `<abbr>`)
- `<applet>` (a Java applet; use `<object>`)
- `<basefont>` (font characteristics; use CSS)
- `<big>` (larger text; use CSS)
- `<center>` (a center-aligned element; use CSS)
- `<dir>` (directory list; use CSS)
- `<font>` (font change; use CSS)
- `<frame>` (create a frame)
- `<frameset>` (define a frameset)
- `<noframe>` (alternative to a frame)
- `<strike>` (strikethrough text; use `<del>`)
- `<tt>` (define Teletype text; use CSS)

NOTE

Frame-related tags are deprecated by the W3C because frame pages can foul up search engines.

In addition to the tags, several attributes of acceptable tags have been deprecated. Some of these are replaced with CSS. They include

- `align` (align left, right, center)
- `alink`, `link`, `vlink` (link color)
- `background` (background image)
- `bgcolor` (background color)
- `compact` (reduce interim spacing)

- `target` (specify a frame)

- `text` (text color)

- `type` (type style) deprecated in `<li>`, `<ul>`, and `<ol>` list tags, but is often used with other tags

NOTE

Even though there is a standards body for the Web (W3C), compliance with its standards is voluntary. As a result, you cannot count on all web browsers to interpret your HTML code identically. Some differences are relatively minor, whereas others are not. It's always best to test your work in the major browsers (IE 9, IE 11, Chrome, and Firefox) before publishing it.

HTML Authoring Resources

A number of excellent resources on HTML authoring are available on the Web. The following is a list of the ones that are most important. Some of these documents are ancient by Internet standards (several years old), but the basic information is still valid. It is important to understand that HTML has become a mature web language. Nonetheless, a solid understanding of HTML, which these documents will provide, will give you a firm foundation for dynamic web programming.

NOTE

URLs change quickly. While every effort was made to get the following URLs correct when this book went to print, some probably will have changed by the time this book reaches the bookstores. If you are having trouble with a URL, drop off right-hand segments, delineated by slashes, until it works. Microsoft's site changes faster than anybody's, so if one of their URLs isn't working, don't be surprised. The best work-around is to go to microsoft.com/ and work forward.

The following is a list of resources available online:

- **W3C** provides an excellent and detailed *HTML5 Reference* that provides information on each element, as well as lists of conforming and obsolete elements, and a comparison of HTML 4.01 and HTML5, at **dev.w3.org/html5/html-author/**. W3C also has a dated, but good, "Getting Started with HTML," "More Advanced Features," and "Adding a Touch of Style" by Dave Raggett of W3C that provide a foundation for understanding HTML and CSS from the organization that sets the standards. This was last updated May 24, 2005. The "Getting Started" document has links to the other two, and is available at **w3.org/MarkUp/Guide/**.

- **W3 Schools** is a major resource for HTML, HTML5, CSS, JavaScript, and PHP. It has tutorials, references, examples, and forums on all subjects for free. You can access it at **w3schools.com/**.

- **HTML Goodies** provides a good HTML/HTML5 primer and a number of advanced resources for HTML, HTML5, CSS, JavaScript, and PHP at **htmlgoodies.com/**.

- "Composing Good HTML" by James "Eric" Tilton (last updated July 13, 1998). Available at **ology.org/tilt/cgh/**.

- "HTML Tags," a free online cheat-sheet by VisiBone at **html-tags.info**. Well done, but not updated for HTML5.

- "Style Guide for Online Hypertext" by Tim Berners-Lee (the originator of the World Wide Web). Last updated May 1995. Available at **w3.org/Provider/Style/**.

Among a number of other good books on the Web and HTML authoring are

- *HTML: A Beginner's Guide, Fifth Edition* by Wendy Willard (McGraw-Hill Education, 2013)

- *HTML and CSS: The Complete Reference, Fifth Edition* by Thomas A. Powell (McGraw-Hill Education, 2010)

- *HTML, XHTML, and CSS QuickSteps, Second Edition* by Guy Hart-Davis (McGraw-Hill Education, 2009).

Try This 2-1   An HTML Web Page

Build a simple web page using only HTML5 (don't worry about formatting; we'll add that in Chapter 3). In this website, include

- At least two sectioning containers
- Several levels of headings
- A horizontal rule or line
- Several paragraphs including line breaks
- At least two different character formats
- A picture or two
- At least one list (either bulleted or numbered)

- A table with two or more rows with at least three cells each

- A form asking for a name and e-mail address (don't worry where the data goes; that's in later chapters)

When you are done, and only then (!), compare your page with my example in Appendix B.

Chapter 2 Self-Test

The following questions are intended to help reinforce your comprehension of the concepts covered in this chapter. The answers can be found in the accompanying online Appendix A, "Answers to the Self-Tests."

1. What does HTML mean, and what is the latest version to be recommended for approval?

2. What is the name of the standards committee recommending the latest version of HTML?

3. What does "HTML syntax" mean?

4. Is HTML5 case sensitive and should you follow that standard?

5. What is the primary component of an HTML element, and how are they identified?

6. How are the primary components of an HTML element modified, and what is the nomenclature for showing this modification?

7. What must every HTML script begin with, and what are three of the four primary elements in that?

8. Where can you use global attributes?

9. What are at least four paragraph-defining tags?

10. Is it correct that if you put line endings and spaces in most paragraph tags, they will be displayed on a web page?

11. What are the two forms of character styles, and how do they differ?

12. Can you use < > and & in a normal text line you want to display on a web page?

13. Why should you include height and width attributes with your image tags?

14. How is a hyperlink used?

15. What are four field types used with form input?

16. What are three of the tags used to define a table?

17. What are the three areas where HTML5 has made significant additions to HTML?

18. Is it correct to say that the new sectioning tags, such as `<header>`, `<footer>`, and `<aside>`, provide placement or alignment on a page?

19. Can you use tags such as `<big>`, `<center>`, and `<font>` and, if so, what are the ramifications?

20. What is the one website you should keep in mind as the primary HTML reference?

Chapter 3

Styling with CSS

Key Skills & Concepts

- Attaching CSS

- Understanding CSS Rules

- Selecting What to Format

- Applying CSS Concepts

- Using Text Properties

- Implementing Page Properties

- Laying Out with CSS

With HTML5, you can build the structure of a web page, but if you follow the strict definition of HTML5 and don't use any of the deprecated HTML tags, you can't make the page look very good, and it may look different in different browsers. Making a page consistently look good in many browsers is the job of *CSS* (Cascading Style Sheets). CSS is a collection of rules for specifying the colors, fonts, and layout of a web page. Today, it is not only the primary way of formatting a web page, but it is also the most efficient. It allows you to separate the formatting of a web page from the content of a web page and be able to reuse the formatting on other pages.

In this chapter, we'll look at the structure of CSS rules, how style sheets are added to a web page, how rules are applied, what the more common rules are, and examples of their use. We will be talking here about CSS 2.1, which became a formal World Wide Web Consortium (W3C) recommendation in June 2011. While CSS 2.1 was working its way to a formal recommendation (it was first proposed in February 2004), proposals for both CSS 3 and CSS 4 have been put forth with many additions to CSS. For the most part, I have ignored the CSS 3 and 4 additions for two reasons: they are still reasonably fluid, and many of them are not implemented in the latest browsers. Also, as I mentioned in Chapter 2, you should not consider this chapter an exhaustive review of CSS 2.1; rather, I have tried to briefly cover the most important aspects of CSS that are in common usage.

NOTE

In hopes of simplifying the discussion in this chapter, several terms are meant in their generic sense. These include the following:

Page or "web page" is the original area or "canvas" on which the web designer lays out the elements to be displayed.

Browser is any software that can render the page so it can be read.

Screen is any device that can display the page, including handheld devices and printers.

Creating CSS

CSS is simply lines of text (the rules) embedded in an HTML5 (from here on referred to as *HTML*) page, or, more commonly, in a separate CSS file, where it can be applied to a number of HTML pages. CSS is designed to be very compact, with many features that keep it from being verbose, as shown in Listing 3-1.

Listing 3-1   CSS Example

```
body {
      background:yellow;
      color:red;
      font: 12pt Arial;
     }
h1, h2 {
       color:blue;
       font: 24pt "Comic Sans MS";
      }
```

In the CSS listing shown in Listing 3-1, the HTML `<body>` tag on the web page to which this CSS is attached is assigned a background color of yellow, a text color of red, and a font of 12-point Arial. In addition, both the `<h1>` and `<h2>` heading tags are assigned a text color of blue and a font of 24-point Comic Sans. This also shows how CSS cascades: the `body` attributes are assigned to the elements on the page, except the `h1` and `h2` elements, which have their own attribute assignments.

Attaching CSS

A CSS is attached to HTML pages or files in one, two, or both ways:

- **Embedded** in the HTML file using the `<style>` tag.
- **Linked** as an external CSS file using the `<link>` tag.

Listing 3-2 shows how the `<style>` tag is used. Note that the CSS is embedded in the `<style>` tag. Listing 3-3 shows the `<link>` tag. Both of these tags only appear in the `<head>` section of an HTML document, but you can have multiple `<link>` tags if needed. Figure 3-1 shows that the two methods of attaching a CSS produce exactly the same result (you have to use your imagination for the color, but it is as stated), while Table 3-1 shows the tags and their attributes.

NOTE

CSS style elements can also be applied directly to HTML tags using the `style` attribute, but that negates the primary benefit of CSS of being able to apply consistent styles to multiple tags. The `style` attribute is and should be infrequently used.

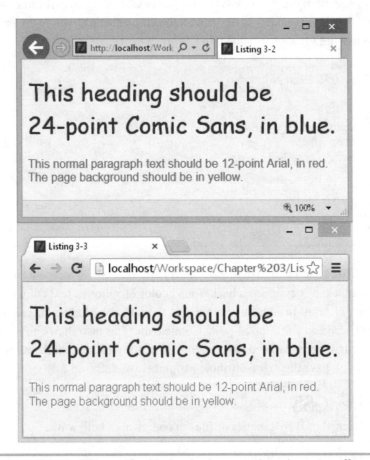

Figure 3-1 Both a linked and an embedded style sheet produce the same effect, but a linked one can be used on multiple pages.

Tags or Attributes	Description
`<style> </style>`	Allows the embedding of CSS rules in an HTML document.
`type`	Specifies the style sheet content type, normally `text/css`. This attribute must be supplied.
`media`	Specifies the intended medium for the styles. The default is `screen`.
`<link />`	Attaches an external CSS to an HTML document.
`rel`	Specifies the relationship between the HTML document and the style sheet. It is most commonly `stylesheet`, but it can also be `alternate` to specify an alternative style sheet with a name.
`href`	Specifies the URL or filename of the style sheet.
`type`	Specifies the style sheet content type, normally `text/css`. This must be supplied.
`media`	Specifies the intended medium for the styles. The default is `screen`; an alternative is `print`.
`title`	Specifies the name of an alternative style sheet.

Table 3-1 Style and Link Tags

Listing 3-2 HTML Page with `<style>` Tag

```
<!DOCTYPE html>
<html>
    <head>
        <meta charset="utf-8">
        <meta http-equiv="X-UA-Compatible" content="IE=edge">
        <title>Listing 3-2</title>
        <meta name="description" content="">
        <style type="text/css">
            body {
                    background:yellow;
                    color:red;
                    font: 12pt Arial;
                    }
            h1, h2 {
                    color:blue;
                    font: 24pt "Comic Sans MS";
                    }
        </style>
    </head>
    <body>
        <h1>This heading should be<br />24-point Comic Sans, in blue.</h1>
        <p>
            This normal paragraph text should be 12-point Arial, in red.<br />
            The page background should be in yellow.
```

```
      </p>
    </body>
</html>
```

Listing 3-3   HTML Page with `<link>` Tag

```html
<!DOCTYPE html>
<html>
    <head>
        <meta charset="utf-8">
        <meta http-equiv="X-UA-Compatible" content="IE=edge">
        <title>Listing 3-3</title>
        <meta name="description" content="">
        <link rel="stylesheet" type="text/css" href="Listing 3-1.css" />
    </head>
    <body>
        <h1>This heading should be<br />24-point Comic Sans, in blue.</h1>
        <p>
            This normal paragraph text should be 12-point Arial, in red.<br />
            The page background should be in yellow.
        </p>
    </body>
</html>
```

Understanding CSS Rules

A CSS rule in its simplest form is a line of text with three components: a selector, a property, and a value. For example:

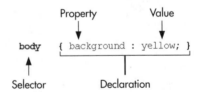

where the *selector* is generally a tag, such as **<body>**; the *property* is a feature of the tag, such as background; and the *value* is an aspect of the feature, such as yellow. The property and value are separated by a colon, and together they form the *declaration,* which is enclosed in curly braces ({}). A single selector can have multiple property/value pairs, as shown in Listing 3-1, which are separated by a semicolon. With only a single property/value pair, or for the last property/value pair, a semicolon is not necessary, but it is suggested simply for consistency and to promote good habits.

Within CSS rules, you can add as many spaces, tabs, and newlines as you want to make CSS easy to read. It is recommended that you spread out the rules so that you can easily see what is affecting the various parts of your web pages.

You can both help your own memory of what you did in a style sheet and tell others about it by adding comments, either after completing a rule on the same line, or on a separate line. To do this, enclose the text comment within a /* */ pair, as shown here:

```
body { background : yellow; }   /* Makes the background yellow */
```

Selecting What to Format

The selector part of a CSS rule identifies the element of a web page that will be affected by the rule. You can have selectors that cover the entire page, such as **body**, or a single type of tag, such as **h1**, as you have seen in Listings 3-1 and 3-2. You can also have selectors that identify parts of a page, or just some of a particular tag, some **h1**s, for example. So a selector can be a tag name; a tag name modified by a class, an ID, an attribute, an event, or its context; or parts of an element identified by a tag.

Class and ID Selectors

You can add class names and/or IDs to most tags to identify just the ones that you want affected by a style, by adding the class or ID to the selector. A class is added to a selector by following the tag name with a period (**.**) and the class name. An ID is added to a selector by following the tag name with a pound sign (**#**) and the ID. For example, Listing 3-4 and Figure 3-2 show the selectors needed to specifically format a class of paragraphs and a particular heading with an ID when headings and paragraphs not so identified are formatted differently.

Figure 3-2   ID and class attributes let you style particular elements.

NOTE

In Listing 3-4, and in the remaining listings in this chapter, the `<!DOCTYPE>` and `<meta>` tags, as well as the `<html>` attributes, have been left out for compactness.

Listing 3-4   Class and ID Selectors

```html
<html>
   <head>
      <title>Listing 3-4</title>
      <style type="text/css">
         h1 {font : 24pt "Arial Black";  }
         p { font : 14pt "Times New Roman"; }
         h1.big { font : 36pt "Eras Bold ITC"; }
         p#special { font : 16pt "Gill Sans MT Condensed"; }
      </style>
   </head>
   <body>
      <h1>This is a normal heading.</h1>
      <p>This is a normal paragraph.</p><br />
      <h1 class="big">This is the "big" heading.</h1>
      <p id="special">This is the "special" paragraph.</p>
   </body>
</html>
```

TIP

A CSS selector can be just a class or an ID, with its identifier (`.` or `#`) and without a tag name. For example, `.legal { font : 16pt "Franklin Gothic Book"; }` would apply to all tags with the `legal` class. While you can do the same thing with an ID (`#note { font : 16pt "Franklin Gothic Book"; }`), only one element in an HTML document can have a particular ID.

Other Selectors

The most often used selectors are tag names followed by a class or ID. However, five other types of selectors use events, attributes, context, location, or groups to identify what is to be styled:

- **Events** consider the interactive events affecting a tag and are generally used with a hyperlink in the `<a>` (Anchor) tag. For example:

  `a:link   { color : green; }`

  colors the link green if it has not been visited. Five possible events can be styled; all are preceded by a colon (`:`) immediately following a tag:

  - `link`, for hyperlinks that have not been clicked.

  - `visited`, for hyperlinks that have been clicked.

- **active**, for elements that are in the process of being clicked.

- **hover**, for elements on which the mouse is pointing.

- **focus**, for elements selected but not activated, like with the TAB key.

- **Attributes** of a tag, where the attribute is enclosed in square brackets (`[]`). For example:

  `input[readonly]   { background : gray; }`

  applies a gray background to form fields that have a `readonly` attribute. You can also style just those tags with an attribute that has a particular value. For example:

  `table[border="1"]   { border-color : blue; }`

  sets only the table borders of tables with an attribute of `border="1"` to blue. In addition, a tag with an attribute value that is one of a list of values can be styled with

  `area[coords~="147"]   { background-color : yellow; }`

  which places a yellow background behind the area(s), one of whose coordinates is 147. Finally, a tag with an attribute value that is the first value in a list of values can be styled with

  `area[coords|="60"]   { background-color : fuchsia; }`

  which places a fuchsia background behind the area(s), whose first coordinate is 60.

- **Context** of a tag considers where a tag is in relationship to another tag and has four possibilities (see Listing 3-5):

  - **Descendant** selectors, where the tag to be styled, called a *descendant* tag, is contained any place in another tag, called the *ancestor*, including inside a third tag. As a selector, the descendant follows the ancestor, with a space separating them. For example:

    `div em { font-family : "Comic Sans MS" }`

    makes the contents of any **<em>** within a **<div>** Comic Sans, like this:

    - This line is *FUNNY!*
    - This line is *FUNNIER!!*

Listing 3-5   Example of Context Modified Selector

```
<html>
   <head>
      <title>Listing 3-5</title>
      <style type="text/css">
         div em { font-family : "Comic Sans MS"; }
      </style>
   </head>
   <body>
```

```
<div>
   <ul>
      <li>This line is <em>FUNNY!</em></li>
      <li>This line is <em>FUNNIER!!</em></li>
   </ul>
</div>
</body>
</html>
```

- Child selectors, where the tag to be styled (called a child tag) is contained immediately within its parent tag. It cannot be within a third tag. As a selector, the child follows the parent, with a > (greater-than) separating them. For example:

  `ul > li { font-family : "Comic Sans MS"; }`
  makes the contents of both `<li>` Comic Sans, like this:

  - This line is *FUNNY!*
  - This line is *FUNNIER!!*

- First child selectors, where the tag to be styled is a child tag and immediately follows its *parent* tag. As a selector, `:first-child` follows the parent. For example:

  `ul:first-child { font-family : "Comic Sans MS"; }`
  makes the contents of the first `<li>` Comic Sans, like this:

  - This line is *FUNNY!*
  - This line is *FUNNIER!!*

- **Adjacent** selectors, where the tag to be styled is immediately preceded by its *sibling* tag at the same level. As a selector, the tag to be styled follows the sibling, with a plus (+) separating them. For example:

  `li+li { font-family : "Comic Sans MS"; }`
  makes the contents of the second `<li>` Comic Sans, like this:

  - This line is *FUNNY!*
  - This line is *FUNNIER!!*

- **Location** within an element, where either the *first letter* or *first line* of an element is to be styled. For example:

  `p:first-letter { font : 18pt "Copperplate Gothic Bold"; }`
  will make the first letter enclosed in a `<p>` tag 18pt Copperplate Gothic Bold, as you can see next, where each paragraph is in separate `<p> </p>` tags.

F our score and seven years ago our fathers brought forth on this
continent, a new nation, conceived in Liberty, and dedicated to
the proposition that all men are created equal.

N ow we are engaged in a great civil war, testing whether that nation,
or any nation so conceived and so dedicated, can long endure. We are
met on a great battle-field of that war. We have come to dedicate a
portion of that field, as a final resting place for those who here
gave their lives that that nation might live.

- **Groups** of tags that have the same declaration can be listed as a common selector,
  separated by commas. For example:
  ```
  h1, h2, h3 { font-family : "Copperplate Gothic Bold"; }
  ```
  will set the first three heading levels to use the Copperplate Gothic Bold font.

TIP
You can combine many of the methods of specifying a selector to refine what is to be
styled. For example:
```
p#first span { font : 18pt "Copperplate Gothic Bold" ; }
```
will make the text in the <span> tag(s) that are a descendant of the <p> tag with an ID
first 18pt Copperplate Gothic Bold.

CSS Properties and Values

The properties and values that you can use in a CSS rule are many and varied, but roughly
fall into three groups: text properties, page properties, and layout properties, which are
each discussed in their own section later in this chapter. To understand and appropriately
use these properties and values require an initial understanding of the fundamental
concepts upon which CSS is built.

Applying CSS Concepts

Seven fundamental concepts underlie CSS:

- Cascading and inheritance
- Box and visual models of page layout
- Element positioning
- Units of measure

- Use of color
- Text and fonts
- Tables and lists

Text and fonts are discussed with the text properties. The box and visual models of page layout, as well as positioning and tables and lists, are discussed with layout properties. The rest are discussed here.

Cascading and Inheritance

In CSS, every property must have a value. That value can be specific, computed, or inherited. To arrive at the actual or final value that will be used with a property, a browser must go through three sets of processes. The first of these is the *cascade,* which determines the order of precedence of various factors that can influence the final property value. The second is *inheritance,* which considers the influence of values determined for elements that are parents to the current element. The third process is the *calculation* of the final value.

Cascading Order In cascading order, a value is determined by the influence that is found to be most important in a given hierarchy. For CSS, the cascading order of precedence, in ascending order where 1 is least important and 6 is most important, is

1. Conventions and settings in the browser or viewing software.
2. Default settings made by the user or viewer of the web page.
3. Imported or linked style sheet property values.
4. If a selector, for example `<p>`, appears more than once in a style sheet and refers to the same property, the last one in the sheet takes precedence over earlier ones.
5. Embedded style sheet property values.
6. Inline style attribute property values.
7. Settings made by the user or viewer as the page is being viewed.

In other words, the browser begins with its own settings, which may be changed by the user, replaced by first an external style sheet and then by an embedded style sheet, followed by an inline style attribute, and finally is adjusted in the viewed program by the user.

If you want a particular style to override what would otherwise occur with the cascade, you can give that style an `!important` declaration and it will do so. An example of such a declaration is

```
h1 { font : 24pt "Arial Black" !important ; }
```

Inheritance   Through inheritance, an element's value can be determined by the values of elements that are earlier in the document tree. For example, Listing 3-6 shows a simple web page with the document tree as displayed by Aptana's outline view, shown next:

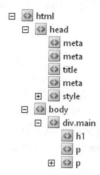

Listing 3-6: Document Tree Example

```html
<html>
   <head>
      <title>Listing 3-6</title>
      <style type="text/css">
         div.main { font : 12pt "Bodoni MT"; }
         em { font : 14pt "Script MT Bold"; }
      </style>
   </head>
   <body>
      <div class="main">
         <h1>The main heading.</h1>
         <p>The first paragraph.</p>
         <p>The second, <em>yes, second</em> paragraph.</p>
      </div>
   </body>
</html>
```

In this document tree, as in most, `<body>` is the root of the tree and the first child is `<div class="main">`, which in turn has three children: `<h1>`, `<p>`, and `<p>`. The second `<p>` has one child, `<em>`. Without a style sheet or the users making changes in their browser, the default style settings in the browser would flow through the entire tree based on the cascade. When a style sheet is introduced with a font style for `<div class="main">`, this style will flow to its children and its children's children unless interrupted by another style. This is the fundamental principle of inheritance. As you can see next, the font set for `<div class="main">` appears in the `<h1>` and two `<p>`s, except for the text enclosed in `<em>`, which has its own style.

The main heading.

The first paragraph.

The second, *yes, second,* paragraph.

Inheritance works for those properties, such as `font`, that allow it. In the lists in later sections of this chapter, you'll see a column labeled "Inherited?," which shows the properties that can be inherited. If you want a property that isn't normally inherited to be inherited, you can create a style for the element and use `inherit` for its value.

Units of Measure

Horizontal and vertical measurement values in CSS are used with a number of properties, including `border-width`, `font`, `line-height`, `margin`, and `text-indent`. Units of horizontal and vertical measurement can be in two forms: relative to some other measure and absolute.

Relative units scale the current element to the element's font size, to the element's font "x-height" (the size of the lowercase x), or relative to the output device's resolution. The relative units of measure are

- `em`, which scales the element to its font size. `1em` is the same size as the font or equal to 100 percent. So `1.4em` is 140 percent of the font, and `.6em` is 60 percent of the font size.

- `ex`, which scales the element to its "x-height," is similar to `em`. `1ex` is the same size as the "x-height" or 100 percent of it. As a default, `1ex` is considered equivalent to `.5em`.

- `px` or pixel, which scales the element to the viewed resolution. On a computer screen at 96 dpi (dots per inch) viewed at arm's length, or about 28 inches, `1px` is approximately 0.01 inch or 0.26 mm, and is slightly smaller (72 percent) than a point (`pt`, see next list), which is 0.01389 inch.

NOTE
When **em** is used with a font, it is relative to or a percent of the parent element's font.

Absolute units of measurement are specific measurements in any of the following units:

- `cm`, centimeters, 0.3937 inch
- `in`, inches, 2.54 centimeters

- **mm**, millimeters, 0.1 centimeter, 0.03937 inch

- **pc**, picas, 1/6 of an inch, 12 points

- **pt**, points, 1/72 of an inch, 1/12 pica

TIP

When you use absolute units, you should be pretty certain of the dimensions of the displaying device. As handheld devices become more common, using relative units become more important.

Listing 3-7 and Figure 3-3 show examples of the application of various units of measure.

Listing 3-7   Units of Measure

```
<html>
   <head>
      <title>Listing 3-7</title>
      <style type="text/css">
         body {
               margin : .5in ;
               font : 14px "Arial";
               }
         h1    {
               font : 2em "Arial Black"; /* twice the body font */
               line-height : 1.5em ; /* 150% of font or 36 points */
               margin : -.32cm ; /* outdented about a third of the margin */
               }
```

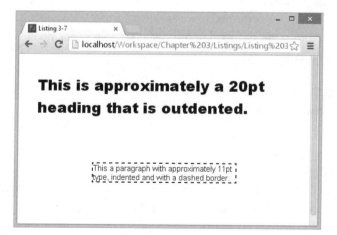

Figure 3-3 Web-based documents will scale much better with relative units of measure.

```
p  {
        margin : 25mm ; /* about twice the body margin */
        font : 1.1em; /* 110% of the body font*/
        border : .25ex dashed; /* 25% of the font's x-height */
     }
   </style>
 </head>
 <body>
    <h1>This is approximately a 20pt heading that is outdented.</h1>
    <p>
        This a paragraph with approximately 11pt type, indented and
           with a dashed border.
    </p>
 </body>
</html>
```

Use of Color

In CSS, you can add color to the background of a page with the `background-color` property or to one of three foreground elements: text, with the `color` property; borders, with the `border-color` property; and outlines, with the `outline-color` property. The value for each of these properties is a specific color identifier, plus, in the case of `border-` and `outline-color`, you have the option of `transparent`, which lets you see what is beneath the object.

The color identifier can be a color name or a numerical representation of a color using the RGB (red, green, blue) color specification. The color name can be one of the classic color names: `aqua`, `black`, `blue`, `fuchsia`, `gray`, `green`, `lime`, `maroon`, `navy`, `olive`, `orange`, `purple`, `red`, `silver`, `teal`, `white`, or `yellow`, or it can be one of the over 140 extended color names implemented in most browsers and shown at w3.org/TR/css3-color/.

The RGB color can be specified in four ways (shown in examples for making paragraph text the color cyan):

- As a six-digit hexadecimal (hex) number preceded by #, for example:
  `p`.cyan { color: #00ffff }.

- As a three-digit hex number preceded by #, for example:
  `p`.cyan { color: #0ff }.
  The three-digit hex number only works when each of the three colors, normally represented by two digits, has two digits of the same character. The three digits are expanded to six digits by doubling each of the original digits.

- As a set of three percentages, separated by commas, enclosed in parentheses, and preceded by `rgb`, where hex 00 is 0% and hex FF is 100%, for example: **p**.cyan { color: rgb(0%,100%,100%) }.

- As a set of three decimal numbers, separated by commas, enclosed in parentheses, and preceded by `rgb`, where hex 00 is 0 and hex FF is 255, for example: **p**.cyan { color: rgb(0,255,255) }.

The two-digit hexadecimal number used to represent the RGB color component can have 256 values (ranging from 0 to 255 decimal or 00 to FF hexadecimal). The combination of the three colors or six hex digits allows for over 16 million colors, compared with the 140 named colors. The colors range from black at decimal 0,0,0 or hex #000000 (the absence of any color) to white at decimal 255,255,255 or hex #ffffff (the sum of all color). Red is 255,0,0 or #ff0000, lime (not green) is 0,255,0 or #00ff00, and blue is 0,0,255 or #0000ff.

TIP

An easy way to convert between decimal and hexadecimal notation is to use the Windows 7 Calculator in Programmer mode. Open the calculator from Start | All Programs | Accessories | Calculator, and then select View | Programmer (in Windows 8 desktop, you can do a File Explorer search on "Calculator" to get the same one as you see in Windows 7). Click either the Hex or Dec option, enter a hexadecimal or decimal number, and click the opposite option (Hex or Dec).

In the past, any discussion of color on the Web focused on the Web Safe palette—216 colors that would display correctly on virtually any monitor. One reason the earliest browsers had only 16 named colors was that many systems wouldn't support more than 16 colors. Today, this situation, like everything else connected with the Web, is vastly different. At this point, it makes little sense to adhere to a standard that has been made obsolete by advanced technology. This doesn't mean that named colors should not be used when they fit the application, only that the importance of adhering to this standard has greatly diminished.

A number of color charts are available on the Internet in addition to the one at W3C mentioned earlier. Do a search on "Internet Color Chart." One of the best, and my favorite, is at html-color-codes.com, and is produced by Bob Stein of VisiBone (visibone.com, which has many other charts and guides, a number of which are mentioned in this book).

Using Text Properties

CSS provides a wide variety of properties and values to facilitate the styling of text, as set out in Table 3-2, and as shown in many of the listings, figures, and illustrations in this chapter. Text styling has two major components: the application of fonts and font characteristics, and the alignment and spacing of text. You can combine several properties, such as size, weight, and font in a single style declaration, as you'll see in "Application of Fonts" later in this chapter.

Property	Allowed Values	Inherited?
color	The color of text. See "Use of Color" earlier in this chapter.	Yes
direction	Determines the direction in which text flows with `ltr`, left to right, the default and `rtl`, right to left, and `inherit` the alternatives.	Yes
font	A combination of font size and font family, but can include `font-variant`, `-weight`, `-style`, and `line-height`, which must be preceded by a slash (/).	Yes
font-family	One or more font names in quotation marks and separated by commas, and optionally a generic font type (`serif`, `sans-serif`, `cursive`, `fantasy`, and `monospace`) as a fallback if the specified font is unavailable.	Yes
font-size	A font size as an absolute value (`xx-small`, `x-small`, `small`, `medium`, `large`, `x-large`, `xx-large`); a specific numeric value in one of the units of measure; a relative size (`larger`, `smaller`); or a percentage (120%).	Yes
font-style	`normal`, `italic`, `oblique`.	Yes
font-variant	`normal`, `small-caps`.	Yes
font-weight	`normal`, `bold`, `bolder`, `lighter`, `100-900`.	Yes
letter-spacing	`normal` or a specified added space between letters in one of the units of measure.	Yes
line-height	`normal` or a specified height in one of the units of measure, a number to multiply by the font size, or a percentage multiplied by the font size.	Yes
text-align	`left`, `right`, `center`, `justify`.	Yes
text-decoration	`none`, `underline`, `overline`, `line-through`, `blink`.	No
text-indent	A specified amount in one of the units of measure for indenting the first line of text.	Yes
text- transform	`capitalize`, `uppercase`, `lowercase`, `none`.	Yes

Table 3-2 Text Properties *(continued)*

Property	Allowed Values	Inherited?
vertical-align	Aligns text relative to the line containing it: baseline, sub (subscript), super (superscript), top, text-top, middle, bottom, text-bottom, a positive or negative percentage, or a specific amount relative to the baseline. The default is baseline.	No
white-space	normal (collapse any white space and allow all line breaks), pre (prevent collapsing white space and allow some line breaks), nowrap (collapse white space and ignore line breaks), pre-wrap (prevent collapsing white space and allow all line breaks), pre-line (collapse white space and allow some line breaks).	Yes
word-spacing	normal or a specified added space between words in one of the units of measure.	Yes

Table 3-2 Text Properties

Application of Fonts

The key ingredient in the application of fonts is for the browser to present to the user the font that the web designer specified in the correct size, weight, variant, and style. Most browsers have an algorithm for choosing a substitute font if the specified one with its attributes is not available. The W3C provides a model for such substitution at http://w3.org/TR/CSS21/fonts.html. As a designer, you can do several things to assist this process: choose common fonts, add alternative fonts, and add a generic font.

For example, if you wanted to specify Garamond as the font family for the main division of your page, you might use the following rule:

```
div.main { font-family : "Garamond", "Palatino Linotype", "Times", "serif"; }
```

The fonts are listed in priority order from left to right, so Garamond is used first if it is available, and the generic serif font is only used if all three of the named fonts cannot be found.

NOTE
Font names do not need to be in quotes if they do not contain a space or a special character. Nevertheless, it's a good practice to put all font names in quotes.

Considerations to keep in mind with the various font properties include the following:

- A value of italic for the font-style will select both italic and oblique font names, while a value of oblique will only select oblique font names.

- The numeric values for `font-weight`, such as `200` and `600`, are names, and you *cannot* interpolate between them, for example, by using `250`. The value `400` is the same as `normal`, and `700` is the same as `bold`. Fonts with "light" in their name are `300`; "book," "regular," and "roman" are all normal or `400`; "medium" or "demi" is `500`; "heavy" is `800`; and "black" is `900`.

- The `font` property allows you to combine in one property the values for the other five font properties, plus `line-height`, as you can see in Listing 3-8 where the individual properties listed in the first rule are combined into one at the end. In the `font` property, you must have a font size and a font family, and the size must precede the family. You can have zero to three of the other font properties. Among themselves, they can be in any order, but they all must precede the font size. The line height must be between the size and the family and, when combined, it must be preceded by a slash.

Listing 3-8   The Same Rule

```
p  {
   font-style : italic;
   font-variant : small-caps;
   font-weight : 800;     /* 25% bolder than "bold" */
   font-size : 16px;
   line-height : 1.5em;
   font-family : "Garamond", "Palatino Linotype", "Times", "serif";
   }
p  { font : italic small-caps 800 16px /1.5em "Garamond"; }
```

Alignment of Text

The properties for the alignment of text are reasonably self-explanatory, but several of the less obvious features include the following:

- The `text-indent` property applies only to the first line of a block of text and can be negative to move the line of text to the left, as shown next and in Listing 3-9, but if you don't have a margin to contain the outdented text, it will be cut off.

FOUR SCORE AND SEVEN YEARS AGO our
fathers brought forth on this continent, a new nation, conceived in Liberty,
and dedicated to the proposition that all men are created equal.

Listing 3-9   Using `text-indent`

```
<html>
   <head>
      <title>Listing 3-9</title>
      <style>
         p#first {
            margin : .5in ;
            text-indent : -.25in ;
            }
         p#first span { font : 18pt "Copperplate Gothic Bold" ; }
      </style>
   </head>
   <body>
      <p id="first">
         <span>Four score and seven years ago</span> our fathers brought
forth on this continent, a new nation, conceived in Liberty, and dedicated
to the proposition that all men are created equal.
      </p>
   </body>
</html>
```

- The algorithm used with `text-align : justify` is unique to each browser, and therefore may produce different results, and may conflict with rules incorporating word and letter spacing.

- The `text-decoration` property is applied to text within an element, including the white space between characters, words, and sentences, using the same text color as that specified for the element.

- The `blink` value for the `text-decoration` property is an optional value and does not work in the current versions of Internet Explorer, Chrome, or Firefox browsers.

- The `letter-spacing` and `word-spacing` property values are in addition to the normal spacing between characters, words, and sentences. When the spacing is changed with these properties, the `text-align : justify` value cannot further adjust the spacing to justify lines of text.

- The `vertical-align` property aligns text relative to the line of text (called a *line-box*) it is in. It does *not* do vertical alignment with a paragraph or other containing block.

- The `white-space` property determines how a browser treats the space at the beginning and end of lines of text. Spaces, tabs, and carriage returns are all considered "white space," which is eliminated by use of the `normal`, `nowrap`, and `pre-line` values, but not with the `pre` and `pre-wrap` values.

NOTE
Where applicable, most properties default to values of `auto`, `normal`, `medium`, or none, as appropriate, unless otherwise specified.

Implementing Page Properties

Page properties, shown in Table 3-3, when used with the `<body>` tag, are applied to the entire page, but you can also apply them to segments of a page using `<div>`, `<article>`, `<aside>`, `<footer>`, `<header>`, `<nav>`, `<section>`, `<h1...>`, `<p>`, `<table>`, and other elements that define space on a page.

Property	Allowed Values	Inherited?
`background`	Any combination of `background-attachment`, `background-color`, `background-image`, `background-position`, or `background-repeat`.	No
`background-attachment`	`scroll` or `fixed` with regard to the viewer, with `scroll` the default.	No
`background-color`	A color (see "Use of Color" earlier in this chapter) or `transparent`, with `transparent` the default.	No
`background-image`	The filename or URL of the image, or none.	No
`background-position`	A horizontal percentage or absolute distance, `left`, `center`, or `right`; and/or a vertical percentage or absolute distance, `top`, `center`, or `bottom`. The default is 0%, 0%, the top-left corner.	No
`background-repeat`	`repeat` (both horizontally and vertically), `no-repeat`, `repeat-x` (horizontally), or `repeat-y` (vertically), with `repeat` the default.	No
`border;` `border-top,` `-right, -left,` `-bottom`	Any combination of `border-width`, `border-style`, and `border-top-color`. (See the point later about how one or more properties can apply to two or more borders.)	No
`border-color;` `border-top-color` `-right-, -left-,` `-bottom-`	A specific color (see "Use of Color" earlier in this chapter) or `transparent`, with `transparent` the default.	No
`border-style;` `border-top-style` `-right-, -left-,` `-bottom-`	Up to four (one per side) of `dashed`, `dotted`, `double`, `groove`, `hidden`, `inset`, `outset`, `ridge`, and none. The default is none.	No

Table 3-3 Page Properties *(continued)*

Property	Allowed Values	Inherited?
border-width; border-top-width, -right-, -left-, -bottom-	Up to four (one per side) of thin, medium, thick, or a specific value in one of the units of measure. The default is medium.	No
cursor	A type of cursor: auto, crosshair, default, pointer, move (four-headed arrow), text (I-beam), wait (hourglass), progress (spinning beach ball); or moving one of the sides of the cursor, where a side is specified by n-resize (north side), ne-resize (northeast side), e-resize, se-resize, s-resize, sw-resize, w-resize, and nw-resize; or the filename of an image to use for the cursor.	Yes
orphans	The minimum number of lines that must be left at the bottom of the page. The default is 2.	Yes
outline	Any combination of outline-color, outline-style, and outline-width.	No
outline-color	A specific color (see "Use of Color" earlier in this chapter) or invert (an inversion of the element color), with invert the default.	No
outline-style	Up to four (one per side) of dashed, dotted, double, groove, inset, outset, ridge, and none.	No
outline-width	Up to four (one per side) of thin, medium, thick, or a specific value in one of the units of measure.	No
overflow	visible (content flows out of the box), hidden (content clipped at the edge of the box), scroll (scroll bar added to see content), auto (normally the same as scroll).	No
page-break-after page-break-before	auto (neither force nor forbid a page break), always (force a page break before/after a box), avoid (forbid a page break before/after a box), left (force one or two page breaks so the page is a left-hand, even-numbered page), right (force one or two page breaks so the page is a right-hand, odd-numbered page).	No
page-break-inside	auto (neither force nor forbid a page break), avoid (forbid a page break before/after a box).	Yes
widows	The minimum number of lines that must be left at the top of the page. The default is 2.	Yes

Table 3-3   Page Properties

NOTE

While you can apply many of the page properties to the <html> tag, the effect is almost always the same as applying them to the <body> tag.

Considerations to keep in mind with the page properties include the following (see Listing 3-10 and Figure 3-4 for examples of applying the background and border properties):

- The background property can be a color, an image, or both. If you have both, the color will be displayed until the image is generated. The color will also show though any transparent areas of the image. The background covers the content, padding, and border of the element to which it is assigned.

- Backgrounds, colors, or images are at the "bottom" (furthest away from the viewer) of the stack of elements on the screen and can be covered up by other elements. This can be controlled by the z-index property, discussed in "Laying Out with CSS" later in this chapter.

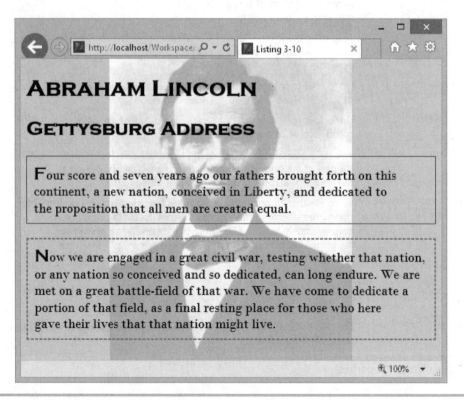

Figure 3-4 If you use a background image, be sure that the text can be read against it.

- If you use the `background` property with, for example, the `<p>` tag, you will want to add some padding around the `<p>` to allow the background to extend slightly beyond the text.

- If you use an image as the background, you normally want to use a small image so that it will download quickly. To have the image cover the element, it will probably have to be repeated, which is the default of the `background-repeat` property, so it does not need to be stated.

- If you want a single image centered both horizontally and vertically on a page, you need to use the `no-repeat` value, but only one `center` value.

- With `border-style` and `border-width` properties, if there is one value, it applies to all sides; if two values, the first refers to the top and bottom, and the second refers to the left and right; if three values, the first is the top, the second is the left and right sides, and the third is the bottom; if four values, the order is top, right, bottom, and left.

- Borders produced with the `border` property are placed on the outside of the element's content plus any padding that has been added, but on the inside of the margin. See "The Box and Visual Models of Page Layout" in the "Laying Out with CSS" section later in this chapter.

- Similar to the `background` property, if you add a border, you will want to add some padding around the `<p>` and other content areas to place the border slightly outside the text.

- The `outline` property draws lines on top of objects, not outside, like borders, and therefore the lines do not take space. They take the shape of the object, which may be nonrectangular, such as a button. The outline is the same on all sides.

- The `orphan` and `widow` properties are only considered if there is not enough room on the first page for a block of text. Also, if there is not enough text to satisfy both an `orphan` and `widow` property, and there is not enough room on the first page for the full block of text, then the full block of text is moved to the second page.

- The three `page-break` properties control whether page breaks can occur before, after, or within an element block, such as a paragraph, an image, or a table. The default is that all three are allowed but not forced. If page breaks are allowed, then the widow and orphan properties control how that is done.

Listing 3-10   Page Properties

```html
<html>
  <head>
    <title>Listing 3-10</title>
    <style type="text/css">
      body {
           background : #dcdcdc url('alincoln-transparent.jpg')
           no-repeat center;
           }
      h1, h2 {font-family : "Copperplate Gothic Bold"; }
      h1 { font-size : 24pt; }
      h2 { font-size : 20pt; }
      p {
         font : 14pt "Bodoni MT";
         padding : .5em;
         }
      p:first-letter  { font : 18pt "Copperplate Gothic Bold" ; }
      p#one { border : thin double blue}
      p#two { border : .1em dashed red}
    </style>
  </head>
  <body>
    <h1>Abraham Lincoln</h1>
    <h2>Gettysburg Address</h2>
    <p id="one">
       Four score and seven years ago our fathers brought forth on ...
    </p>
    <p id="two">
       Now we are engaged in a great civil war, testing whether that ...
    </p>
  </body>
</html>
```

Laying Out with CSS

While CSS is often thought of for formatting and styling a web page, it is at least equally useful for laying out a web page. With CSS' layout properties, shown in Table 3-4, you can position an element on a page in a number of different ways: you can determine how elements interact with each other and the amount of separation between them, how lists and tables are formed, and the characteristics and behavior of a page. As mentioned earlier in this chapter, several basic concepts are important to the layout properties, including the box and visual models, positioning, and tables and lists.

Property	Allowed Values	Inherited?
border-collapse	collapse or separate for tables, with separate the default.	Yes
border-spacing	One or two absolute distances between table and cell borders. One value specifies both the horizontal and vertical distances. With two values, the first is the horizontal distance, and the second is the vertical distance. 0 is the default.	Yes
bottom, left, top, right	A specific distance in one of the units of measure that an element side is separated from its containing block, a percentage of the containing block's height (bottom or top) or width (left or right) or auto.	No
caption-side	top (position the caption above the table), bottom, with top being the default.	
clear	The top border of the current box is placed beneath both, left, or right, border of another floating box, or none.	No
clip	auto (the element is not clipped), or rect (*top, right, bottom, left*), where *top, right, bottom,* and *left* are specific distances in one of the units of measure, separated by commas, that the side of an absolutely positioned element is clipped or offset from its upper-left corner (may be negative).	No
display	block (displays the element as an independent block), inline (displays the element within the block of another element), inline-block (displays the element as an independent block within the block of another element), list-item (displays a set of elements as a parent block with a set of inline children), run-in (displays an element as an independent block that adjoins another independent block), table, inline-table, table-*element* (displays elements as tables or table elements, independently or inline), none (causes the element and its descendants to have no effect on the layout).	No
float	Positions a block box to the left or right of other elements, closest to the left or right of the containing box, or none.	No
height, width	A specific distance in one of the units of measure of an element's height or width, a percentage of the containing block's height or width or auto. Excludes padding, borders, and margins.	No
list-style	Sets any of the properties for list-style-type, list-style-position, and/or list-style-image, in that order.	Yes
list-style-image	Filename of the image to be used for the list item marker, or none. Replaces list-style-type marker.	Yes
list-style-position	Positions the list-item marker inside or outside (as in a hanging indent) the list-item box, with outside the default.	Yes

Table 3-4 Layout Properties *(continued)*

Property	Allowed Values	Inherited?
list-style-type	Specifies the list-item marker as disc, circle, square, decimal, decimal-leading-zero, lower-roman, upper-roman, lower-alpha, upper-alpha, lower-greek, or none.	Yes
margin; margin-top, -right, -left, -bottom	A specific distance in one of the units of measure that an element side is separated from its containing block, a percentage of the containing block's height (bottom or top) or width (left or right), or auto. The default is 0. If one value, it applies to all sides. If two values, the first refers to the top and bottom, and the second refers to the left and right. If three values, the first is the top, the second is the left and right sides, and the third is the bottom. If four values, the order is top, right, bottom, and left.	No
max-height max-width min-height min-width	A specific minimum or maximum length in one of the units of measure of an element's height or width, a percentage of the containing block's height or width, or none.	No
padding; padding-top, -right, -left, -bottom	A specific distance in one of the units of measure that an element's side is separated from its containing block, a percentage of the containing block's height (bottom or top) or width (left or right) or auto. Default is 0. If one value, it applies to all sides. If two values, the first refers to the top and bottom, and the second refers to the left and right. If three values, the first is the top, the second is the left and right sides, and the third is the bottom. If four values, the order is top, right, bottom, and left.	No
position	absolute (a box is removed from the normal flow and positioned and sized relative to the containing block's upper-left corner by the top, right, bottom, left properties), fixed (a box is positioned as in the absolute value, but then fixed in that position when the page is scrolled), relative (a box's position is offset relative to its normal position, determined by the normal flow, using the top, right, bottom, and left properties), and static (a normal box that behaves in the normal flow of elements; it is the default).	No
table-layout	fixed (uses the specified table, column, cell, and border widths) or auto (reflects the data in the table and doesn't require specific widths).	No
visibility	visible (box is visible), hidden (box is invisible, but affects layout), collapse (in tables, collapses rows and/or columns; otherwise, the same as hidden).	Yes
z-index	An integer, representing the stacking level from the viewpoint of the screen with what the viewer sees being "on top," or the highest stacking level; or auto.	No

Table 3-4 Layout Properties

The Box and Visual Models of Page Layout

In the simplest sense, a web page is a series of boxes within boxes, next to other boxes, and above and below still other boxes. The process of laying out a web page can be thought of as sizing and arranging the boxes so they all fit in the order you want, like this:

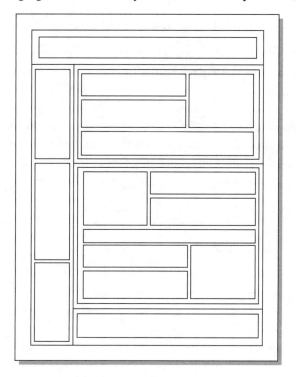

Elements on a web page are in one of two classes:

- **Block-level elements** take a specific, unique area of the screen and generate a block that is a containing block for its descendants. This called a *block-level box,* or just a "block box." Block-level elements include `<body>`, `<div>`, `<article>`, `<aside>`, `<footer>`, `<header>`, `<nav>`, `<section>`, `<h1...>`, and `<p>`.

- **Inline-level elements** do not take a unique area of the screen, nor do they, by default, form a unique block. Inline-level elements are inside (in line with) the blocks created by block-level elements. Inline-level elements include `<em>`, `<cite>`, `<dfn>`, and `<kbd>`. For the sake of layout, inline-level elements can be thought of as being contained in an "inline box."

The `display` property can make block-level elements inline-level and make inline-level elements block-level.

Block-level elements not only have an invisible box that contains them, but also that box can be contained in up to three additional boxes associated with the element:

- **Padding**, the area separating the content from the border.

- **Border**, the normally visible line or decoration that surrounds the padding.

- **Margin**, the area separating the border from its containing block, such as a page or a parent block.

The total size of a block-level element is the sum of the content, padding, border, and margin, as shown next. If the padding, border, and margin are all 0, which is the default, the content immediately abuts its containing block.

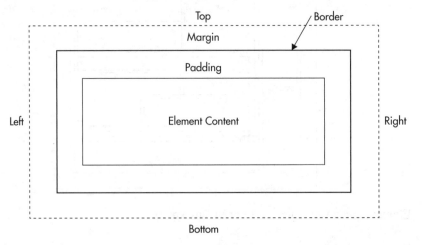

As a web page is rendered on a screen or other device, it flows on in a specific order, and later elements can both affect and be affected by earlier elements. As each element comes in, it generates none, one, or more boxes. How these boxes appear on the screen and affect other boxes is called the *visual formatting model,* or just "visual model." Components of the visual model affect how the final page appears on the screen and include

- **Viewpoint**, the area that the user sees; I have called this the *screen.* This may be larger or smaller than the designer's page or canvas, and has to be considered by both the browser and the designer.

- **Containing block** is a block created by an element higher in the hierarchy, either a parent or an ancestor, which contains the current element, which itself may be a

containing block for its children and descendants. For example, as shown next, the
`<body>` element contains a `<div>` element, which contains `<h1>` and `<p>` elements.
The `<body>` element containing block holds the other three elements as either a child
or descendants. The `<h1>` and `<p>` elements are in the containing blocks of both the
`<div>` and `<body>` elements, which are parent and ancestor, respectively.

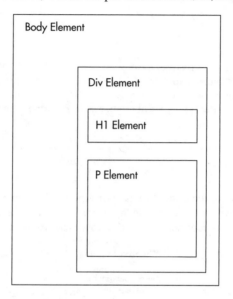

- **Box generation** occurs as elements are flowed onto a page. Depending on the type
  of element and the `display` property, the element generates a *block box,* which is
  displayed in a separate area of the page, or an *inline box,* which is displayed within
  another element's block box. In the example shown next, the `<p>` tag generates a block
  box that contains the `<span>` inline box.

```
<p> <span>Four score and seven years ago</span> our fathers brought...</p>
```

- **Run-in box**, created with the `display` property `run-in` value, allows a block-level
  element to share the same block with a sibling (at the same level) block-level element.
  For example, a heading that runs into a following paragraph, as shown in Listing 3-11,
  with the result shown next:

The first heading. The first paragraph into
which the first heading is run-in.

The second heading. The second paragraph
into which the second heading is run-in.

Listing 3-11   Run-in Example

```
<html>
   <head>
      <title>Listing 3-11</title>
      <style type="text/css">
         h4 { display : run-in; }
      </style>
   </head>
   <body>
      <h4>The first heading.</h4>
      <p>The first paragraph into which the first heading is run-in.</p>
      <h4>The second heading.</h4>
      <p>The second paragraph into which the second heading is run-in.</p>
   </body>
</html>
```

NOTE

Listing 3-11 only produces the desired results just shown in Internet Explorer beginning with IE 8, which came with Windows 7. In the current versions of both Chrome and Firefox, the run-in value does not work and produces the results shown here:

The first heading.

The first paragraph into which the first heading is run-in.

The second heading.

The second paragraph into which the second heading is run-in.

Positioning

Positioning determines how element boxes are sized and aligned relative to each other as the elements flow onto a page. The positioning is done using one of five methods that are determined by the position, top, right, bottom, left, float, clear, and z-index properties. The five positioning methods are

- **Normal flow** is the default flow of elements and their boxes onto a page, with all of the positioning properties set to their default or initial values; in particular, position is set to static, which negates the other positioning properties.

- **Relative positioning** starts with the normal flow and then offsets the element's box relative to its "normal" position by the values of the `top`, `right`, `bottom`, and `left` properties. Boxes that follow a relative-positioned box are positioned as though the box were normally positioned.

- **Float positioning** also starts with the normal flow and then offsets the element's box to the left or right as far as the containing box allows.

- **Absolute positioning** determines an element's position and possibly its size relative to the sides of the containing block by using the values of the `top`, `right`, `bottom`, and `left` properties. An absolute-positioned element has no impact on the layout of other elements, and its margins do not collapse with other margins.

- **Fixed positioning** is the same as absolute positioning, and additionally, the element remains at a fixed position (its original position) on the screen as a page is scrolled.

Normal Flow   In the normal flow, block boxes flow onto the page, starting at the top, and are positioned vertically one after the other, separated by their margins. The left edge of a block box is positioned against the left edge of the containing block. Inline boxes flow onto the page starting at the top left and are positioned horizontally across the containing block to the right edge, where they then move down and start another horizontal set of boxes. Such a set of inline boxes that stretches across the width of a containing block is called a *line box*. A set of inline boxes may be aligned within the line box horizontally with the `vertical-align` property and aligned vertically with the `text-align` property.

Float Positioning   Float positioning allows you to pull a block box out of its normal flow's vertical position and attach it to the left or right side of the containing block. Once attached, the floated block will allow other blocks on its unattached side. This is the primary and recommended way of producing multiple columns. That said, it is not always the easiest way to do that. Tables, discussed later in this chapter, can produce sure placement of information on a page if your only audience is a 1920 ×1080–pixel computer screen. The beauty of a floated block is that it is flexible and can look good on many different viewing devices, *if* you can get all the pieces to "float" where you want them.

In Listing 3-12, you'll see a CSS and the related HTML5 used to create a common three-column page with header and footer blocks, as shown in Figure 3-5.

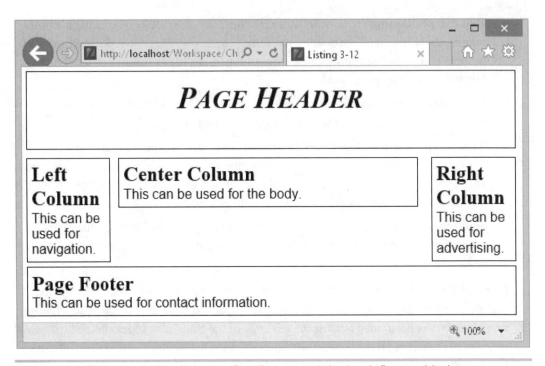

Figure 3-5 Multicolumn layout is most flexibly accomplished with floating blocks.

Listing 3-12 Floating Columns—CSS

```
body            {
                width : 600px;
                margin : 0;
                padding : 0;
                }
div, h1, h2, p  {
                margin : 0;
                padding : 0;
                }
h2              {font : 600 24px "Futura" ; }
p               {font : 16px "Arial", "Helvetica", "sans-serif" ; }
header          {
                top : 0px;
                left : 0px;
                height : 80px;
                margin : 5px;
                border : thin solid;
```

```
                    padding : 5px;
                    }
h1#title            {
                    font : italic small-caps 600 36px /1.5em "Futura" ;
                    text-align : center;
                    }
aside#left           {
                    float : left;
                    width : 15%;
                    margin : 5px;
                    border : thin solid;
                    padding : 5px;
                    }
section#main           {
                    position : relative ;
                    float : left;
                    width : 58%;
                    margin : 5px;
                    border : thin solid;
                    padding : 5px;
                    }
aside#right           {
                    position : relative ;
                    float : right;
                    width : 15%;
                    margin : 5px;
                    border : thin solid;
                    padding : 5px;
                    }
footer      {
                    clear: both ;
                    margin : 5px;
                    border : thin solid;
                    padding : 5px;
                    }
```

Floating Columns—HTML

```
<html>
   <head>               <title>Listing 3-12</title>
       <link rel="stylesheet" type="text/css" href="Listing 3-12.css" />
   </head>
   <body>
     <header>
       <h1 id="title">Page Header</h1>
     </header>
     <aside id="left">
```

```
        <h2> Left Column </h2>
        <p> This can be used for navigation.</p>
    </aside>
    <section id="main">
        <h2> Center Column </h2>
        <p> This can be used for the body.</p>
    </section>
    <aside id="right">
        <h2> Right Column </h2>
        <p> This can be used for advertising.</p>
    </aside>
    <footer>
        <h2> Page Footer </h2>
        <p> This can be used for contact information.</p>
    </footer>
</body>
</html>
```

In the CSS portion of Listing 3-12, much is obvious, but several areas are not:

● It makes sense to float left the left column and float right the right column, but you might not guess that *you also need to float left the middle column.* If you don't do this, the right column does not know that it can scoot up beside the middle column, and the middle column shifts to the left, like this:

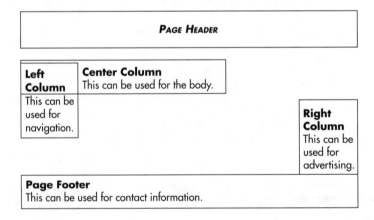

● If you give each of the two outer columns 15 percent of the space, you should be able to give the middle column 70 percent and have it all fit. But if you do that, you will find it doesn't fit, as shown next. As you can see in the listing, I had to reduce the middle column to 58 percent to get it to fit. The reason for this is that the height and width properties set the *content height or width and exclude the padding, border, and margin,* which must be added to the height or width values. You can see this best by looking at the absolute number instead of percentages (although using percentages is preferred for their flexibility).

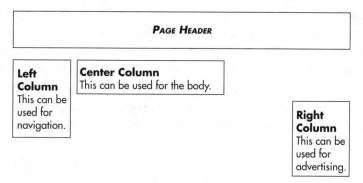

- The body width = 600 pixels.
- Left and right columns, both: `margin` = 5 pixels × 2, `border` = 1 pixels × 2, `padding` = 5 pixels × 2, a total of 22 additional pixels in each column, plus the 90-pixel content width, for a total of 112 pixels.
- The middle column also has 22 pixels in the margins, border, and padding.
- If the two columns and the 22 added pixels in the middle are subtracted from the 600-pixel body width, it leaves 354 pixels for the content of the middle column, or 59 percent.

You'll notice that at the top of the CSS part of Listing 3-12, I zero-out the `padding` and the `margin` for all basic elements. The reason for this is that all browsers set a default value for these elements (and apply the default differently from browser to browser). When you set your own values, it becomes additive to the browser set values and makes the elements look different from what you want. The next illustration shows how the three-column-float example looks without zeroing-out the basic elements. Compare this illustration with Figure 3-5, which includes the zeroing-out of the elements:

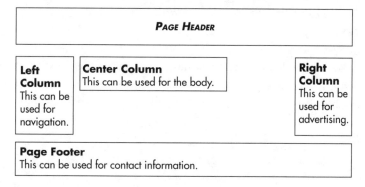

Tables and Lists

Tables and lists are a powerful set of HTML elements for handling tabular information. Tables can also be used for laying out a web page, but that is discouraged because of the limited flexibility it provides, as well as the difficulty of maintenance. Tables divide an area of a web page, or the whole page, into rows and columns, creating *cells* where the two intersect. *Lists* are an indented set of items, which can be automatically numbered or have a small image at the beginning of each line, called a *bullet*. As shown in Chapter 2, there is an extensive set of HTML tags for making tables and lists, but there is an equally extensive set of CSS properties and values that can be applied for formatting and laying out tables and lists.

NOTE

The table values in the `display` property (`table`, `table-row`, `table-row-group`, `table-column`, `table-column-group`, `table-cell`, `table-caption`, `table-header-group`, `table-footer-group`), which are meant for creating table elements, are for languages other than HTML, like XML, that do not define table elements. In HTML, this function is performed with the table tags, and the display properties are ignored when applied to HTML table elements.

Table Layout and Formatting   A table's formatting is the sum of the formatting applied to the various table elements based on a hierarchy that can be thought of as a set of layers. For formatting—for example, a border or a background—to appear to the viewer, it either must be applied on the top layer, or the layers above it must be transparent, which is the default. The layers, from top (closest to the viewer) to bottom, are

1. Cells (`<td>` or `<th>`)
2. Rows (`<tr>`)
3. Row groups (`<tbody>`)
4. Columns (`<col>`)
5. Column groups (`<colgroup>`)
6. Table (`<table>`)

If you want a simple table with a number of styles applied to it, start with the basic HTML as you see in Listing 3-13a, and look at how the sequential application of styles affects the table.

Listing 3-13a   Table HTML–Only Example

```html
<html>
   <head>
      <title>Listing 3-13</title>
   </head>
   <body>
      <table cellspacing="0">
         <caption>UR 771 Part Cost</caption>
         <colgroup id="part" />
         <colgroup span="2" id="costs" />
         <thead>
            <tr>
               <th>
                  Name
               </th>
               <th>
                  Annual
               </th>
               <th>
                  Hours
               </th>
            </tr>
            <tr>
               <th class="line">
                  of Part
               </th>
               <th class="line">
                  Cost
               </th>
               <th class="line">
                  to Repair
               </th>
            </tr>
         </thead>
         <tbody>
            <tr>
               <td class="name">
                  Gauge
               </td>
               <td class="data">
                  $425
               </td>
               <td class="data">
                  12
               </td>
            </tr>
```

```
            <tr>
                <td class="name">
                   Switch
                </td>
                <td class="data">
                    $158
                </td>
                <td class="data">
                    8
                </td>
            </tr>
            <tr>
                <td class="name">
                   Control
                </td>
                <td class="data">
                    $218
                </td>
                <td class="data">
                    10
                </td>
            </tr>
        </tbody>
    </table>
  </body>
</html>
```

1. With just the table and no styling or formatting except the default for the various elements, as shown in Listing 3-13a, you get the table shown next. Notice how the header rows are bold and centered, while the body rows are normal weight and left aligned. Also, there are no borders.

UR 771 Part Cost		
Name of Part	**Annual Cost**	**Hours to Repair**
Gauge	$425	12
Switch	$158	8
Control	$218	10

2. Give the `<table>` tag background, width, and border properties, and get the table shown next.

UR 771 Part Cost		
Name of Part	**Annual Cost**	**Hours to Repair**
Gauge	$425	12
Switch	$158	8
Control	$218	10

3. Add a background to the `<thead>` tag. This background overlays the table background except for where cell borders would be.

UR 771 Part Cost

Name of Part	Annual Cost	Hours to Repair
Gauge	$425	12
Switch	$158	8
Control	$218	10

4. Add the `<table>` tag attribute `cellspacing="0"` to eliminate the space between the cells. Also, give the `<colgroup id="part">` the same background as the heading, and give the cell class `<td class="name">` the `font-weight : bold`.

UR 771 Part Cost

Name of Part	Annual Cost	Hours to Repair
Gauge	$425	12
Switch	$158	8
Control	$218	10

5. Finally, spruce up the formatting of the caption, add some padding beneath it, add a bottom border under the heading, right-align the numbers with some padding on the right so they are not hard against the right edge of the cells, and right-align the part names, again with some padding on the right. The result is shown here—quite a change from the unformatted table. Listing 3-13b shows the styles that were added to the HTML shown earlier in Listing 3-13a.

UR 771 Part Cost

Name of Part	Annual Cost	Hours to Repair
Gauge	$425	12
Switch	$158	8
Control	$218	10

Listing 3-13b   Added CSS Example

```
<style type="text/css">
  table {
       background : #dcdcdc;
       border : thin solid;
       width : 240px;
       }
  thead, #part { background : #fffacd; }
  .name {
```

```
                    font-weight : bold;
                    text-align : right;
                    padding-right : 12px;
                   }
            caption {
                    font : bold 14px "arial";
                    padding-bottom : 5px;
                   }
            .line { border-bottom : medium solid #00008b }
            .data {
                    text-align : right;
                    padding-right : 12px;
                   }
         </style>
```

NOTE

Table grouping elements such as `<thead>` and `<colgroup>` have limitations on the style properties that can be used with them. For example, the bottom border does not show up if it is added to `<thead>`, and the font bolding does not work with `<colgroup>`.

Styling Lists   HTML contains several ways of displaying lists, including ordered (numbered) lists, unordered (bulleted) lists, and definition (indented) lists. CSS adds to this several properties for styling, positioning, and replacing the marker (the number, letter, or bullet on the left end of each list item). Listing 3-14 produces a list of lists—a definition list that contains first an unordered and then an ordered list. The notes after the listing provide some added definition of the CSS list properties. Figure 3-6 shows these lists without either CSS or HTML styling.

Listing 3-14   List of Lists

```html
<html>
   <head>
      <title>Listing 3-14</title>
      <style type="text/css">
         body { background : #dcdcdc; }
         dl {
             background : #fafad2;
             padding : 5px;
            }
         dt { font : bold 12pt arial; }
         ul { list-style-type : square; }
         ol { list-style-type : lower-alpha; }
      </style>
```

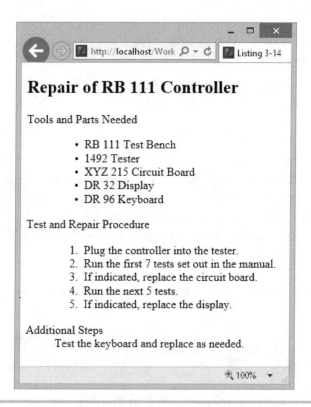

Figure 3-6 Initial list of lists without any styling or a CSS

```
</head>
<body>
    <h2>Repair of RB 111 Controller </h2>
    <dl>
        <dt> Tools and Parts Needed </dt>
        <dd>
            <ul>
                <li>RB 111 Test Bench </li>
                <li>1492 Tester </li>
                <li>XYZ 215 Circuit Board </li>
                <li>DR 32 Display</li>
                <li>DR 96 Keyboard </li>
            </ul>
        </dd>
        <dt> Test and Repair Procedure </dt>
        <dd>
            <ol>
                <li>Plug the controller into the tester. </li>
                <li>Run the first 7 tests set out in the manual. </li>
                <li>If indicated, replace the circuit board. </li>
```

```
            <li>Run the next 5 tests. </li>
            <li>If indicated, replace the display. </li>
        </ol>
    </dd>
    <dt> Additional Steps  </dt>
    <dd> Test the keyboard and replace as needed.  </dd>
    </dl>
  </body>
</html>
```

To the basic HTML code, add CSS styles to `<body>` and `<dl>` elements for contrasting backgrounds; add padding to `<dl>` so the text is not on the edge of the background; format the `<dt>` elements so they are more like headings; and then change the `<ul>` marker to a square, and the `<ol>` marker to lowercase letters. The result is shown in Figure 3-7.

TIP

Not all properties and values work in all browsers, and you need to test your code in the browsers that you think will be viewing your pages.

Figure 3-7 List of lists with simple CSS styling

Here are some notes on using the CSS list properties:

- If you apply a background to a list item, the marker will not share that background (it is transparent) if the marker is positioned "outside."

- If you have both `list-style-image` and `list-style-type` properties, the `list-style-image` will be used.

- The types of numbering and alphabetic systems that are available are

  - `decimal`: 1, 2,...9

  - `decimal-leading-zero`: 01, 02,...99

  - `lower-roman`: i, ii, iii, iv...

  - `upper-roman`: I, II, III, IV...

  - `lower-latin` or `lower-alpha`: a, b, c,...z

  - `upper-latin` or `upper-alpha`: A, B, C,...Z

  - `lower-greek`: α, β, γ,...ω

- The HTML and CSS specifications do not state what happens when a list has run through an alphabet, so you should use numbering for long lists.

TIP

Go to W3C (w3.org/tr/css2/) for the latest and most detailed explanation of CSS, and test your CSS code with the W3C CSS Validator (jigsaw.w3.org/css-validator). Also, Wendy Willard's book *HTML: A Beginner's Guide, Fifth Edition* (McGraw-Hill Education, 2013) has a large amount of information on CSS.

Try This 3-1 Add a CSS to Your Personal Web Site

Add a CSS to the personal website you built in Chapter 2. Make this style sheet a separate document and attach it using the `<link>` tag. Create styles for:

- The page background

- Several levels of headings specifying the font, its size, and its color

- At least two different paragraphs

- The table specifying how to handle the table heading, cell spacing (considering padding), borders and margins, and positioning cell content

- The bulleted or numbered list, specifying the marker or number, the font, and its color

- The layout of your page's box model and how you will accomplish the positioning

After you have tried this, see Listing B-2 and Figure B-2 in Appendix B for my example solution.

Chapter 3 Self-Test

The following questions are intended to help reinforce your comprehension of the concepts covered in this chapter. The answers can be found in the accompanying online Appendix A, "Answers to the Self-Tests."

1. What does "CSS" mean, and what is its purpose?

2. What are the two primary and one secondary way CSS styles are attached to an HTML page?

3. What is a CSS rule, and what are its four primary components?

4. How are at least three of a CSS rule's components used?

5. How are the CSS rule's components expressed or combined in a rule?

6. How do you differentiate among multiple instances of selectors, such as several `<p>` tags, and how do you identify these in a CSS rule?

7. What are four of the seven fundamental concepts behind CSS?

8. How is inheritance used?

9. What are the two primary components of text styling?

10. What can you do to assist the application of fonts?

11. What are four of the at least ten tags you can apply page properties to?

12. What can you do with layout properties?

13. What is the box and visual model?

14. Besides the size of an element on a web page, what three other features will affect the amount of space the element will take?

15. What is positioning, and what are three of the five positioning methods?

16. What is float positioning, and what is its benefit?

17. Why is it *not* a good idea to use tables to lay out a web page?

18. What are three of the seven ways an ordered list can be numbered?

Chapter 4

Adding Dynamic Elements with JavaScript

Key Skills & Concepts

- Characteristics of JavaScript
- Using JavaScript with HTML Pages
- Writing and Testing JavaScript
- Variables, Constants, and Operators
- Statements, Expressions, and Functions
- Conditional Statements
- Using Event Handlers
- Displaying Messages When a Page Opens/Closes
- Placing and Removing Focus
- Resizing a Window
- Using Mouse and Keyboard Event Handlers
- Working with onclick, ondblclick, and Arrays
- Creating and Automating Forms
- Form Properties and Methods
- Understanding Validation
- Using Validation with Passwords

JavaScript allows you to interact with the user of your website. It allows you to give them choices they can select and ask them for information they can enter. JavaScript can then respond to what the user selects or enters by displaying related information or opening a specific web page. JavaScript can also validate what the user enters to make sure that the response to the user is appropriate.

NOTE

There are some similarities between JavaScript and PHP. To provide the necessary coverage of both topics, some duplication occurs between the two discussions.

Chapter 4 provides an introduction and review of JavaScript and assumes that the user already has some knowledge of the subject or will use other means to supplement what is presented here. The chapter starts out by reviewing the JavaScript basics and then describing the elements and syntax of JavaScript. It next looks at various types of events that can occur on a web page, how JavaScript event handlers respond to them, and demonstrates several examples of their use. Finally, the chapter looks at forms, which are the web mechanism by which information flows from the user to the web page. They collect information that is then used by the site. JavaScript can add automation to a form to respond to what the user enters. The chapter discusses how forms are created and used, their methods and properties, how information in the form is validated, and how to carry out navigation in a website based on JavaScript navigation elements.

NOTE

JavaScript has no direct connection with Java, except that they both come from Sun Microsystems, now part of Oracle, and share some common syntax and keywords.

Introducing JavaScript

JavaScript is a programming language designed for web computing. A programming language is simply a set of rules, called *syntax,* that govern how you communicate with a computer using various elements of the language. JavaScript uses a model called *OOP* (object-oriented programming). You have *objects* (such as a window) that have *properties* (say, length) and *methods,* or actions, that the object can perform (such as open), while responding to *events,* or actions performed upon the objects (for example, a click). Once you are familiar with the basic terminology and syntax, JavaScript programming is only a matter of writing a sequential set of *statements* for the computer and its software to understand and act upon.

Characteristics of JavaScript

How and where this interaction takes place between the computer and the user is what differentiates JavaScript (and other scripting languages) from conventional languages, such as C or Java. Programming languages that create applications (for example, the Word.exe file for Microsoft Word) require special software to create the code and then must be run through a *compiler* in order to become computer readable. A compiler is software that checks the code for errors and then translates the written code into the computer's machine code. Although this method allows for very serious computing, it takes time and resources to accomplish.

JavaScript Is Interpreted

In contrast, JavaScript is referred to as an *interpreted* language, which means its code is run on the fly, without the need to compile it. All that is needed is a text editor to create the files that contain the code, and a web browser that provides the underlying interpretation of the code, as is true with HTML and CSS. While interpreted code like JavaScript tends to not perform as efficiently or as quickly as compiled code, its performance for the sorts of tasks used in creating dynamic web pages is good enough, and its advantages of being easy to edit and embed on a page more than make up for its shortcomings. Also, compiled code tends to be platform specific (Windows versus Mac), while interpreted JavaScript is not.

JavaScript Is Client-Side Computing

As the names imply, client-side and server-side computing refer to where the programming code is being executed. With server-side programming such as PHP, a request from a user's web page is sent to the hosting web server, is executed, and then the results are sent back to a web page in the user's browser. While having a server and its available networked resources and databases provides almost unlimited access to information and computing power, it requires a round-trip of information to pass from client to the server and back. In addition, a server's resources are shared among other users, thus opportunities exist for delays. Client-side computing performs the code execution on the client's computer, freeing the server to perform more intensive tasks and providing the user with a faster experience. (Many web applications use both server-side and client-side computing to split the workload and take advantage of the benefits offered by each.) JavaScript is a client-side program, which allows for faster execution of code and more responsive feedback to the user. JavaScript can be turned off in the client, so you may want to do any checks on the server side too even if they are duplicated from the client side.

JavaScript Programming Tools

To effectively work with JavaScript, you need to have a development environment that supports both the writing and the testing of JavaScript. You'll need tools for

- **JavaScript script writing**, with code assistance and validation as you write the script
- **JavaScript script testing** on your development computer
- **Developmental support** in a browser, to help debug

The tools described and recommended in Chapter 1 work well with JavaScript, including

- **Aptana Studio** integrated development environment
- **WAMP**, a combination of the Apache web server, the MySQL database server, and the PHP server
- **Internet Explorer, Chrome**, and **Firefox** browsers, needed to test and debug your scripts

If you do not already have Aptana Studio, WAMP, Internet Explorer, Chrome, and Firefox, return to Chapter 1, and follow the instructions to download and install them. They are recommended for the discussion in the remaining chapters of this book.

JavaScript Introduction

The elements of any language only work together in an understandable form if they all operate in concert, according to a set of rules and a given format. This section describes the basic techniques and conventions used in JavaScript to get you started, and offers you shortcuts and suggestions to make working with scripts easier and more efficient.

Using JavaScript with HTML Pages

You can use JavaScript code on HTML pages in one of two ways: directly on the HTML page where it's being used, or in a separate file. Scripts that you write for singular uses are most easily written directly on the affected page. As you become better acquainted with JavaScript and develop more advanced uses, you will find saving your longer scripts to separate .js files provides for cleaner web pages and the ability to use the same code on several pages within your website.

NOTE
The terms "code" and "script" are used interchangeably for describing the various elements of the JavaScript language placed within the `<script>` tag found on HTML pages and in separate .js files.

Entering JavaScript Directly on an HTML Page
An easy way to start coding JavaScript is to enter the script directly on an HTML page within the tag set `<script></script>`. The `<script>` tag can be placed either in the `<head>` or `<body>` section of the page. Typically, code that writes output directly to the page is placed within the HTML in the `<body>` section. Scripts placed in the `<head>` section are generally used for linking to external JavaScript pages, with functions called

by code placed in the `<body>` section. Both Firefox and Chrome, for the most part, ignore *active* JavaScript that tries to change elements on the page in the `<head>` section, but this works well with Internet Explorer. Listing 4-1 shows how the `<script>` tag can be inserted in both the `<head>` and `<body>` sections. Listing 4-4 later in this chapter shows how both of these are used.

Listing 4-1   Example Script Placement

```
<!DOCTYPE html>
<html>
    <head>
        <meta charset="utf-8">
        <title>Listing 4-1</title>
        <script type= "text/javascript">

        </script>
    </head>
    <body>
        <script type= "text/javascript">

        </script>
    </body>
</html>
```

Using JavaScript Files

As your scripting becomes more complex and you find repetitive uses within your website for your code, you can minimize the size of your HTML pages and reuse the same code by placing the JavaScript code in a separate text file with the .js file extension. Whenever you want to employ the code in the .js file (for example, myjavascript.js), you can request its action by adding an attribute to the `<script>` tag, such as:

```
<script type = "text/javascript" src = "myjavascript.js"></script>.
```

JavaScript Basics

Before you start trying to create scripts, review several general aspects of JavaScript syntax.

Commenting Your Script

JavaScript allows you to add comments to your script in two ways:

- On a single line starting with //

    ```
    //This is a comment
    ```

- On multiple lines enclosed with `/* */`

  ```
  /* This is a comment that can
  be on several lines. */
  ```

TIP
It is strongly recommended that you comment your scripts to help you in deciphering and debugging your work.

Coding Conventions

JavaScript is fairly easygoing as far as conventions are concerned, but there are some conventions you need to be aware of:

- Some JavaScript elements are case sensitive—in particular, function and variable names. For example, if you define **person** as a variable name and later use the word **Person**, JavaScript will not recognize the second instance as the original variable. The best rule of thumb is to use all lowercase. When employing other JavaScript elements such as objects, properties, methods, and event handlers from other sources, use the case referenced in the source you are using to assist you.

- Each *statement,* which is a piece of code that is complete and correct in its syntax to perform a task, typically ends with a semicolon. Although it is not always required, it will prevent errors, make debugging easier, allow you to put several statements on a single line, and it gets you in the habit of doing it for use in other languages that do insist upon it (for example, PHP, described later in the book).

- You can encapsulate your scripts within HTML tags to identify them as character data and not have them misinterpreted by either older browsers or validators. To protect your code from possible problems (at least problems of this nature), enclose your scripts within an HTML comment `<!-- -->`. Another concern is that some HTML validators will consider something in JavaScript to be in its purview and will produce an error. To avoid this, you can precede your scripts with `//<! [CDATA [` and terminate them with `//]]>`. This book does not include this added code because it is now rare for someone to use a browser that will display an error or a validator that is old enough to give you an error. If you find you are having a problem, you can add this containing HTML.

- Text, any combination of letters and numbers, called a *string,* needs to be enclosed in quotation marks, either single (`' '`) or double (`" "`)—differences in their use are explained in a Note later in the chapter. Quotation marks must be in like pairs.

- Legitimate numbers, which can have a decimal point, should not be in quotation marks. Numbers being read as strings cause many bugs in JavaScript.

- Multiple arguments are separated by commas (**,**).

- Most functions require that their arguments be enclosed in parentheses.

Special Characters and Escape Sequences

You may have wondered since quotation marks are used to identify a string, how you display a quotation mark that is part of the string to be displayed on an HTML page. For this purpose, JavaScript uses the backslash (\) in what is called an *escape sequence,* which tells JavaScript to treat the following character not as part of the scripting syntax, but as a *literal,* or part of the text string. For example:

```
document.write("My name is \"Marty\"");
```

The double quotes on either side of *Marty* within the outer pair would produce an error if they weren't "escaped" by preceding each with the backslash.

Another way of looking at this is that you want to add a literal character, in this case, double quotes. In this usage, we typically say we are adding a JavaScript *special character*. Actually, both escape sequences and special characters share the same codes and accomplish the same result. The only difference between the two is whether you're calling the glass half full or half empty.

Most of the characters that JavaScript assigns a special use for or as an escape sequence are preceded with a backslash. Here are some of the more common escape sequences or special characters:

- \" produces a double quotation mark.

- \' produces a single quotation mark.

- \\ produces a backslash.

- \b produces a backspace.

- \r produces a carriage return.

- \n produces a linefeed.

- \t produces a tab.

NOTE

While either single or double quotation marks can be used to enclose a string, in some circumstances, one or the other is preferable. With single quotation marks enclosing the string, you can use literal double quotation marks without the backslash in the string, as shown next. With single quotation marks, though, escape sequences other than \' or \\ will display the backslash and not perform their function. With double quotation marks, all escape sequences work.

```
document.write('My name is "Marty"');
```

Avoiding Reserved Words

Several words, called *reserved* words or *keywords* (see Table 4-1), should not be used to name elements in JavaScript because they are a part of the language and have special meaning to the JavaScript interpreter.

NOTE

If you do an Internet search on "JavaScript reserved words," you'll find a number of different lists. Table 4-1 is, for the most part, a superset of these lists that includes words reserved for future use and words that are used in the proposed next version of JavaScript.

Writing and Testing JavaScript

As an interpreted language, JavaScript can be written, checked for errors, and tested without anything more than a text editor. You can start writing JavaScript using any text editor you would otherwise use to write HTML; Aptana Studio, described in earlier chapters, is fine for this purpose.

As was mentioned, due to differences in how browsers interpret some aspects of HTML and scripting, it is important to test your work with popular browsers to determine if the differences affect your intent. A sample of JavaScript code shown in Listing 4-2 is used to display a message box slightly differently in three popular browsers (see Figure 4-1). In this case, the differences are slight and cosmetic, not a cause for concern. However, that will not always be the case. Don't be concerned about the appearance or your lack of understanding of the code in Listing 4-2 at this point. All will make sense in the rest of this chapter.

abstract	boolean	break	byte	case
catch	char	class	const	continue
debugger	default	delete	do	double
else	enum	export	extends	false
final	finally	float	for	function
goto	if	implements	import	in
instanceof	int	interface	label	let
long	native	new	null	package
private	static	static	static	static
static	super	switch	synchronized	this
throw	throws	transient	true	try
typeof	var	void	volatile	while
with	yield			

Table 4-1 Reserved Words in JavaScript

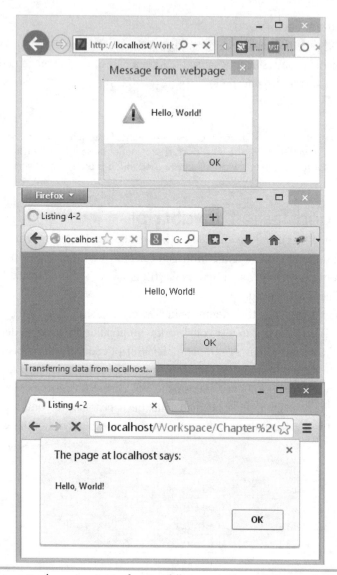

Figure 4-1 Internet Explorer (top), Firefox (middle), and Chrome (bottom) use similar but slightly different interpretations to display message boxes.

NOTE

The listings shown in the rest of the chapter have omitted some default HTML code found in web pages, such as the DOCTYPE declaration, to provide a more concise example.

Listing 4-2   Browser Differences Example

```html
<html>
    <head>
        <title>Listing 4-2</title>
    </head>
    <body>
        <script type= "text/javascript">
            // This code produces the classic Hello World! message
            window.alert("Hello, World!");
        </script>
    </body>
</html>
```

Parts of JavaScript

Much as a spoken language comprises elements of speech such as nouns, verbs, adverbs, adjectives, and other parts of speech, programming languages have their own set of components. In this part, we'll cover the more common elements of JavaScript, providing the groundwork for constructing working scripts in later parts of the chapter. In this section, we explore JavaScript information types, variables, operators, statements, and functions. In the following part, we explore statements that act as control structures.

NOTE

As with any language, JavaScript contains many elements in each part of the language, far more than can be covered here. To look at a comprehensive list, go to javascriptkit .com/jsref/, w3schools.com/js/, or webreference.com/javascript/reference/core_ref/ contents.html.

Variables and Constants

Information (or data) used in JavaScript falls into one of two categories. In either case, it is defined by a name you assign to it and its category of data, or *data type*.

- **Variables**, which are items that can contain different values at different times during script execution, start with the keyword **var** and are followed by a name that you give them.

- **Constants** contain the same value throughout the execution of your script.

Types of Data

JavaScript will generally recognize the data type you are using by its context within your scripts, shielding you from assigning a specific type. However, in instances where JavaScript misinterpreted your intent, it's helpful to have an understanding of the available data types and some of their characteristics. The more common data types are shown in Table 4-2. Here are some points to keep in mind:

- The Boolean `false` is equivalent to the integer 0, the floating point number 0.0, an empty string or a string of `"0"`, an array of zero elements, or `null`. Everything else is `true`.

- Integers are, by default, decimal (base 10) numbers. To make a number octal (base 8), precede it with `0` (zero). To make a number hexadecimal (base 16), precede it with `0x`.

- Very large integers (larger than 2,147,483,647) are considered floating point numbers.

- If you divide two integers, you get a floating point number, unless the numbers are evenly divisible.

- Floating point numbers are not accurate to the last digit because of the infinite progression of fractions like one-third. Therefore, you should not compare two floating point numbers for equality.

- A string containing a number (either integer or floating point) immediately following the left quote can be used as a number. For example, `"18.2"` and `"4 cars"` can both be used as numbers, while `"his 4 cars"` cannot.

Data Type/Subtype	Name	Description	Examples
Boolean	bool	Either `true` or `false` and is case sensitive	`true, false`
Numeric/Floating point numbers	float	A fractional number with a decimal; may be negative, and may use scientific notation	7.34, −21.89, 2.31e3
Numeric/Integers	int	A whole number without a decimal; may be negative	43, 928, −4
Numeric/Null	null	The absence of any value	`null`
String	string	A series of characters (one of 256 letters, numbers, and special characters) enclosed in either single or double quotation marks	`"Mike"`, `'Seattle'`, `"14 W. 18th St"`
Undefined		A named variable that has not been assigned a value	

Table 4-2 JavaScript Data Types

NOTE

In this book, two additional pseudo-types are used for discussion purposes only: "mixed" is used for any combination of other types, and "numbers" is used for a combination of integers and floating point numbers.

Naming Conventions

The name that you give to either variables or constants (or any other label in JavaScript) is case sensitive (see "JavaScript Basics" earlier in the chapter); can begin with either the letters *a–z* (or *A–Z*, though not recommended) or an underscore (_); can be of any length; and can contain letters, numbers, underscores, and the characters in Western European alphabets. While you may find that some special characters will be allowed, the best practice is to not use them. Blank spaces are not allowed.

A good practice is to make variable and constant names more self-descriptive, and in the process, stay away from any possibility of conflict with a predefined name. For example, if you are collecting a buyer's name and address, you might be tempted to use name, street, and city. While there is nothing wrong with those names, it is better to get in the habit of using compound names that are both more descriptive and that stay away from common names—for example, buyer_name, buyer_street, and buyer_city. It may take a couple of seconds more to type these names, but they won't be confused with other names. Also, most programmers get really good at cutting and pasting to reduce typing.

It is a good practice to *declare* a variable as such with the keyword var. JavaScript may often figure this out without var, but humans may not be so smart. Begin the statement with var and end it with a semicolon. You may declare several variables with a single var by putting a comma between them. Once you declare a variable, you don't have to repeat the var. For example:

```
var a = 7 ;
var car = "Ford" ;
var city = "Seattle" , state = "WA" ;
```

TIP

If you are having trouble finding a problem, or bug, in a program, look at the names you have assigned to variables and constants; try changing any that could possibly have a conflict with predefined or reserved names, such as changing name to buyer_name, or private to my_own.

Operators

Having created a variable or a constant, you are going to want to give it a value through assignment, calculation, or comparison. JavaScript has defined a number of operators of various types, as shown in Table 4-3, to do this.

Operator Type	Name	Example	Explanation
Arithmetic			Performs arithmetic calculations on two operands, which can be variables, numbers, or a number and a variable.
+	Add	a + b	Sums two operands.
-	Subtract	a - b	Returns the difference between two operands.
*	Multiply	a * b	Multiplies two operands.
/	Divide	a / b	Divides two operands.
- -	Decrement	--a a--	Subtracts 1 from a and returns a. Returns a, then subtracts 1 from it.
++	Increment	++a a++	Adds 1 to a and returns a. Returns a, then adds 1 to it.
%	Modulus	a % b	Returns the remainder from a divide operation.
=	Unary negation	=a	Converts a negative to a positive, or a positive to a negative.
Assignment			Replaces a value with another.
=	Assign	a = 7	a is set to 7.
+=	Add and assign	a += 2	a is incremented by 2 and assigned the new value.
-=	Subtract and assign	a -= 2	a is decremented by 2 and assigned the new value.
*=	Multiply and assign	a *= 2	a is multiplied by 2 and assigned the new value.
/=	Divide and assign	a /= 2	a is divided by 2 and assigned the new value.
%=	Modulus and assign	a %= 2	a is divided by 2 and assigned the remainder.
Bitwise			Logical consequences turn specific bits in an integer on or off.
&	And	a & b	Bits in both a and b are set.
|	Or	a | b	Bits in either a or b are set.

Table 4-3 JavaScript Operators *(continued)*

Operator Type	Name	Example	Explanation
^	Xor	`a ^ b`	Bits in a or b but not both are set.
~	Not	`~a`	Bits in a are not set.
<<	Shift left	`a << b`	Shift bits in a by b steps to the left (each step is multiplying by 2).
>>	Shift right	`a >> b`	Shift bits in a by b steps to the right (each step is dividing by 2).
Comparison			Compares two values and returns `true` or `false`.
==	Equal	`a == b`	`true` if a equals b.
===	Identical	`a === b`	`true` if a is identical to b.
!=	Not equal	`a != b`	`true` if a is not equal to b.
!==	Not identical	`a !== b`	`true` if a is not identical to b.
<	Less than	`a < b`	`true` if a is less than b.
>	Greater than	`a > b`	`true` if a is greater than b.
<=	Less than or equal to	`a <= b`	`true` if a is less than or equal to b.
>=	Greater than or equal to	`a >= b`	`true` if a is greater than or equal to b.
Logical			Logical consequence.
&&	And	`a && b`	`true` if both a and b are true.
||	Or	`a || b`	`true` if either a or b is true.
!	Not	`!a`	`true` if a is not true.
Other			
?:	Conditional	`Condition ? value : value`	An if-then-else statement where a condition is set to the left of the ? and values are placed on either side of the :.
`delete`	Delete	`delete window2`	Deletes an object, a property, or an array element.

Table 4-3 JavaScript Operators

NOTE

The conditional operator, also called a "ternary operator," will be discussed in the section "Control Structures" later in this chapter.

If you combine several operators in a single expression, the order of precedence is as follows, beginning with the highest or first executed: ++, --, !, delete, *, /, %, +, -, ., <<, >>, <, <=, >, >=, ==, !=, ===, !==, &, ^, |, &&, ||, ? :, =, +=, -=, *=, /=, &=, and, xor, or.

You can use parentheses to get around the order of precedence. Other notes about the JavaScript operators include the following:

- When the arithmetic (+) operator is used to combine text (for example, `window.alert ("Marty" + "Matthews")` to display "Marty Matthews" in a dialog box) or text with numbers (for example, `window.alert (1234 + "Broadway, " + "Anytown")` to display "1234 Broadway, Anytown"), the operation is referred to as *concatenation.*

- The modulus (%) does not yield a percentage; rather, it gives the remainder, the part that is left after whole division.

- The equal sign (=) does not mean "equal"; it means "assign" or "replace."

- To compare two variables, you can use equality (==) or identical (===). The difference is that == tests if two values are equal, independent of the type of value, while === tests if two values are not only equal in value, but also of the same type.

- If a = "2" and b = 2.0, they are not identical because one is a string and the other is a floating point number, but they are equal in value.

Listing 4-3 shows examples of the use of JavaScript variables and operators. The results that this script returns are shown here:

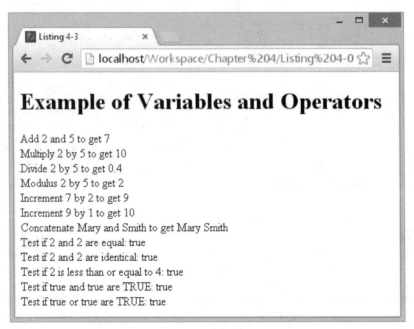

Example of Variables and Operators

Add 2 and 5 to get 7
Multiply 2 by 5 to get 10
Divide 2 by 5 to get 0.4
Modulus 2 by 5 to get 2
Increment 7 by 2 to get 9
Increment 9 by 1 to get 10
Concatenate Mary and Smith to get Mary Smith
Test if 2 and 2 are equal: true
Test if 2 and 2 are identical: true
Test if 2 is less than or equal to 4: true
Test if true and true are TRUE: true
Test if true or true are TRUE: true

Listing 4-3   Examples of Variables and Operators

```html
<html>
    <head>
        <title>Listing 4-3</title>
    </head>
    <body>
        <h1>Example of Variables and Operators</h1>
        <script type= "text/javascript">                //Math
            var a = 2;
            var b = 5;
            document.write("Add ", a, " and ", b, " to get  ",
                a+b, "<br />");
            document.write("Multiply ", a, " by ", b, " to get  ",
                a*b, "<br />");
            document.write("Divide ", a, " by ", b, " to get  ",
                a/b, "<br />");
            document.write("Modulus ", a, " by ", b, " to get  ",
                a%b, "<br />");
        //Assign, Increment and Concatenate
            a = 7;
            document.write("Increment ", a, " by 2 to get ", a+=2,
                "<br />");
            document.write("Increment ", a, " by 1 to get ", ++a,
                "<br />");
            var first_name = "Mary ", last_name = "Smith";
            document.write("Concatenate ", first_name, " and ",
                last_name, " to get  ", first_name + last_name,
                    "<br />");
        //Comparison
            a = "2"; b = 2.0; c = 4;
            var d = a == b;
            var e = a === b;
            document.write("Test if ", a, " and ", b,
                " are equal:  ", a==b, "<br />");
            document.write("Test if ", a, " and ", b,
                " are identical:  ", a===b, "<br />");
            document.write("Test if ", a, " is less than or equal
                to ", c, ":  ",     a<=c, "<br />");
        //Logical
            document.write("Test if ", d, " and ", e, " are true:  ",
                d&&e, "<br />");
            document.write("Test if ", d, " or ", e, " are true:  ",
                d||e, "<br />");
        </script>
    </body>
</html>
```

Statements and Expressions

JavaScript scripts contain either comments or statements. A *statement* is a line of code that is complete and correct in its syntax to perform a task, typically anything that is in between semicolons and the opening and closing `<script>` tags. Often, a statement is a single line of code ending in a semicolon, but you can have several statements on a single line, and you can have statements that take several lines. Statements contain one or more expressions.

Expressions are anything that has a value. *Values* are anything that can be assigned to a variable, so values can be any of the data types: integer, floating point, string, or Boolean. While the `null` data type is the absence of a value, it is still considered a value for this discussion.

Expressions can contain expressions, or said another way, expressions are building blocks that can be used to build other expressions. For example, `a = 2` is three expressions: 2, a, and a = 2.

Functions

A function is a piece of script (a *snippet*) that does something and can be repeatedly called within a larger script. Global functions already exist, and you write user-defined functions. Some functions require that you pass them values or *arguments,* which the function uses to return a value to you. Other functions simply return a value when they are called.

Global Functions

Unlike other languages and programs such as PHP or Microsoft Excel, JavaScript does not have a large library of internal, global functions to perform day-to-day tasks that are not *object*-specific. On the other hand, JavaScript contains a full complement of *methods,* which are function calls that are related to objects. (Methods and objects are described later in the chapter.) In this manner, you can achieve essentially the same results using JavaScript methods as you can by using internal functions found in other languages and programs. The more commonly used JavaScript global functions are listed in Table 4-4.

Function	Description
`eval( )`	Evaluates a string of JavaScript code without reference to a specific object
`isFinite( )`	Evaluates an argument to determine if it's a finite number
`isNaN( )`	Evaluates an argument to determine if it's not a number (NaN)
`parseFloat( )`	Parses a string argument and returns a floating point number
`parseInt( )`	Parses a string argument and returns an integer

Table 4-4 Global Functions

User-Defined Functions

As you write JavaScript code, you'll often find that you want to repeatedly use the same code. You could simply copy the code to all the places you want to use it, but if you want to change that code, you would have to change it everywhere it was copied. The solution for this is to create a function containing the code you want to repeat and simply call that function everywhere you want to use it. Functions also let you segment or compartmentalize your code, making it easier to debug and maintain.

There is even a bigger reason for using functions. Up to now, all the JavaScript code in this chapter is meant to run when the page is loaded. But if you don't want that, you can create a function, place it in the HTML `<head>` section, and it won't be run until it is called.

Like predefined or global functions, user-defined (just "user" from here on) functions may have arguments that are passed to them and return a value after they are executed. Once a user function has been defined, it is *called,* that is, a statement in the script requests the function perform the action it is designed to do. The function itself can do anything you can do with JavaScript using all of the features of JavaScript, including calling other functions, or even calling itself to create a recursive function (this should not be done over 100 times, however, or errors may occur).

User functions are defined with the `function` keyword using this form:

```
function name(argument1, argument2,...)
{
    [any JavaScript statements];
    return returnValue;
}
```

Functions are called to perform their actions in a script in this form:

```
name(argument1, argument2,...)
```

NOTE

Functions without arguments are defined by providing a *name* and an empty set of parentheses, for example: `function calrate()`.

The name that you give to a function uses the same naming rules as variables, constants, and other labels. It is case sensitive; can begin with either the letters *a–z* or *A–Z* or an underscore (_); can be of any length; and can contain numbers, underscores, and the characters in Western European alphabets.

Listing 4-4 shows an example of a user function with the result shown next.

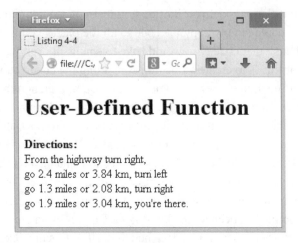

Listing 4-4   User-Defined Function

```html
<html>
    <head>
        <title>Listing 4-4</title>
        <script type= "text/javascript">
            function tokm(miles)
            {
                var km = miles * 1.6;
                return km;
            }
        </script>
    </head>
    <body>
        <h1>User-Defined Function</h1>
        <script type= "text/javascript">
            document.write("<b>Directions:</b><br />");
            document.write("From the highway turn right,<br />");
            document.write ("go 2.4 miles or " + tokm(2.4) +
                " km, turn left<br />");
            document.write("go 1.3 miles or " + tokm(1.3) +
                " km, turn right<br />");
            document.write("go 1.9 miles or " + tokm(1.9) +
                " km, you're there.<br />");         </script>
    </body>
</html>
```

Objects

As I mentioned earlier in this chapter, JavaScript is an object-based programming language. Objects can be the visual elements of a web page such as windows, buttons, check boxes, and dates, and they can be more abstract elements such as math calculations and arrays. You will probably find that the predefined objects in JavaScript are all you will need for your basic programming work, but you can also create your own objects. And to make things even more interesting, objects can have child-objects, which can begin to resemble a family-tree hierarchy of the elements that constitute a web page.

TIP

There are dozens of predefined JavaScript objects, many associated with several properties and methods—far too many to list in this book. I suggest you obtain both online and hardcopy reference charts that list objects with their constituents. References I've found useful are javascriptkit.com and *JavaScript: The Complete Reference, Third Edition* by Thomas Powell and Fritz Schneider (McGraw-Hill Education, 2012).

Predefined objects are identified by a keyword name, and custom objects are given a unique name, using the same naming rules as described earlier in the chapter for naming variables. You can have several instances of an object in a web page. Take, for example, the **window** object. Each window or frame in a web page is uniquely identified by name; is further defined by its characteristics, or *properties*; by the things it can do, called *methods*; and by which user *events* (for example, a mouse click) affect it. The relationship of an object to its constituents is shown through the use of the *dot syntax,* whereby the object name is separated from its constituent by a period. At the beginning of this chapter (see Listing 4-2), you saw the use of the **alert** method being applied to the window object to produce an alert dialog box (Hello World!):

```
window.alert("Hello, World!");
```

where **window** is the predefined object, **alert** is a method that displays an alert message box, and "Hello, World!" is the method value that displays text in the message box.

TIP

The object **window** is implicit in the method **alert** and you don't need it, which is why **alert** works by itself, as well as **window.alert**.

Another example of the dot syntax you've seen so far in this chapter is the commonly used statement that displays scripting results to the browser:

```
document.write("From the highway turn right,<br />");
```

Custom Objects

You can create your own objects, such as furniture items for sale on a store's website. You can use either of two ways to create the objects:

NOTE

A *constructor* function is used to create objects. The function is not a global function, but rather, it's a way to use the standard syntax of a user function to structure an object by naming it, declaring its parameters, and assigning the parameter values to the properties of the object. Also, you don't have to return anything from a constructor function even though something is assigned with the **new** keyword.

- **Use a constructor function** to first create the structure of the object, and then use the new keyword to create an instance of the object.
- **Use an object initializer** to name the object and to assign property values in one statement.

Using the constructor function, you first name an object, and then its parameter values are assigned to the properties of the object. For example:

```
function furniture(era, wood)
{
    this.era=era;
    this.wood=wood;
}
```

NOTE

The JavaScript keyword **this** is used in the sense **this** *object*, that is, the parameter, is assigned to *this object* being defined.

Next, you have to create an instance of the object as a variable, using the keyword **new**, and assign it values. For example:

```
var buffet = new furniture("Eastlake", "Oak");
```

The object initializer method accomplishes the same result, but in a more shorthand fashion, directly creating an object instance:

```
var buffet = {era: "Eastlake", wood: "Oak"};
```

Using objects in scripting will be covered in greater depth later in this chapter.

Properties

Objects have properties that allow you to describe an object, distinguishing different variations of the same object from one another, as well as to customize an object to fit your needs. For example, you can modify a window by its outer height and width dimensions (`outerHeight`/`outerWidth`), as well as its inner, or display area, dimensions (`innerHeight`/`innerWidth`). Some objects have several properties (such as a `window`), while others have few (the string object has only one property, `length`). Also, different types of objects can have the same property (but they would be unlikely to share the same values of those properties).

Properties are applied to an object by using the dot syntax in the form `objectname .propertyname="value";`. You'll see many examples of this in this chapter.

Methods

The actions that objects can perform are called *methods.* In many cases, you can think of methods as being predefined functions for an object. For example, to return the square root of three, you would use the math object's square root method. Using the dot syntax, this would be in the form: `math.sqrt(3)`. Another example of using methods to elicit actions from an object was shown in the earlier section on objects where the `alert()` method was used to display a message box. As with properties, different object and object types share many of the same methods.

TIP

Since both an object's properties and methods are written in the form `object.method` or `object.property`, how can you determine which is which? The values associated with a property are set by use of the equal sign and often by enclosing the value in quotes (`document.bgColor="dodgerblue"`). Values used in methods are enclosed in parentheses alone (`Math.sqrt(3)`).

Event Handlers

JavaScript allows you to easily take advantage of events, or *triggers,* such as mouse clicks and page openings performed by a user on your web page, through the use of predefined *event handlers.* The event handlers recognize the event taking place and then perform one or more tasks, adding interactivity between the web page and the user. For example, when a user hovers the mouse pointer over a button, an alert dialog box opens, warning of the consequences of clicking the button (the clicking action being directed to another action by a second event handler). You'll see examples of event handlers later in this chapter.

Table 4-5 lists the most common JavaScript event handlers and the triggers needed to perform their assigned tasks.

Event Handler	Event Trigger
onabort	An image's loading is interrupted.
onblur	Focus is removed from an element.
onchange	Contents of a form are changed.
onclick	An element is single-clicked.
ondblclick	An element is double-clicked.
ondragdrop	An object is dragged and dropped into a window.
onerror	An error occurs when loading a web page or picture.
onfocus	The user places the focus on an element.
onkeydown	The user presses a defined key.
onkeypress	The user presses and holds down a defined key.
onkeyup	The user releases a defined pressed key.
onload	A web page completes loading in a browser.
onmousedown	The user presses a mouse button.
onmousemove	The user moves the mouse pointer.
onmouseout	The user moves the mouse pointer from a link.
onmouseover	The user moves the mouse pointer to a link.
onmouseup	The user releases a mouse button.
onmove	A window or frame is moved.
onopen	A web page opens in a browser.
onreset	A form is reset.
onresize	A window or frame is resized.
onselect	A field in a form is selected.
onsubmit	A user submits a form.
onunload	A user opens another web page.

Table 4-5   JavaScript Event Handlers

Control Structures

Simple scripts are executed from the first statement to the last statement without interruption or change of direction. Often, you will want to ask if the script should go one way or another, or go back and re-execute a particular piece of code. That is the purpose of control structures, which include **if/else** statements and **while**, **do-while**, **for**, and **switch** statements, among others.

If/Else Statements

The **if/else** statement is the primary decision-making construct in JavaScript. It allows you to specify that **if** some expression is true, then a group of statements will be executed, **else** a different group of statements will be executed. It takes this form:

```
if (conditional expression) {
   statements executed if true;
   }
else   {
   statements executed if false;
   }
   if (outer conditional expression) {
       statements executed if first conditional is true;
       if (inner/nested conditional expression){
           statements executed if second conditional is true;
       }
       else {
           statements executed if second conditional is false;
       }
   }
  else {
    statements executed if first conditional is false;
}
```

In all cases, the conditional expression must result in a Boolean true or false (1 or 0). If a variable simply exists, that is, it has been defined as containing something other than null, false, or 0, then it is true.

CAUTION

If you define a variable as containing a constant like null, true, *or* false, *you must remember* not *to put the constant in quotation marks.*

Many conditional expressions are comparisons that test if two elements are equal, greater than, or less than. Remember that when you test for equality in JavaScript, you must use a double equal sign (==), not a single one, which means assignment.

Listing 4-5 shows several examples of if/else statements, the results of which are shown next. A number of examples will be shown in the following chapters.

Listing 4-5   If/Else Statements

```html
<html>
    <head>
        <title>Listing 4-5</title>
    </head>
    <body>
        <h1>If/Else Examples</h1>
        <script type= "text/javascript">
            //if the variable "a" is declared, return True/write
            //   True; else return False/write False. Since no variable
            //   "a" declared, expect False;
            if (a){
                document.write("True <br />");
            }
            else {
                document.write("False <br />");
            }
            //If the variable "a" is declared, return True/write
            //   True; else return False/write False. Since variable
            //   "a" is declared, expect True;
            var a = "Something";
            if (a){
                document.write("True <br />");
            }
            else {
                document.write("False <br />");
            }
            //If variable "state" equals "WA", return True/write
            //   "Pacific Northwest;" else return False/write "Somewhere
            //   Else." Since variable "a" equals "CA", expect False;
            var state="CA";
            if (state=="WA"){
                document.write("Pacific Northwest <br />");
            }
            else {
                document.write("Somewhere Else <br />");
            }
        </script>
    </body>
</html>
```

Ternary Operator

A shorthand method of doing **if/else** decision making in JavaScript scripts uses the ternary operator (**? :**), where **?** replaces the **if** test and follows the conditional expression, and the **:** replaces **else**. For example, `(a==3)` **?** True **:** False;

While and Do-While Statements

The `while` and `do-while` statements are looping constructs that allow you to repeatedly execute a piece of code until a conditional expression is no longer `true`. The `while` statement is the foundation of this set of statements and takes the following form:

```
while (conditional expression) {
      statements executed while true;
      }
```

The `do-while` statement is similar to the `while` statement, except that the conditional expression is at the end of the statement instead of at the beginning, allowing the `do` portion to execute even if the `while` statement is `false`. The `do-while` statement takes this form:

```
do {
    statements executed while true;
    }
while (conditional expression);
```

The most common conditional expression is to compare a counter with some end value—in other words, to initialize a counter and then to loop though some statements, incrementing the counter with each loop, until the counter exceeds the end value. Listing 4-6 shows examples of this for both `while` and `do-while`, with the results shown next. You can see that the `while` statement runs until the counter ends. In the case of the `do-while` statements, the `do` statement is `true` and executes once, but the `while` statement is `false`, doesn't loop, and doesn't execute the `write` statement.

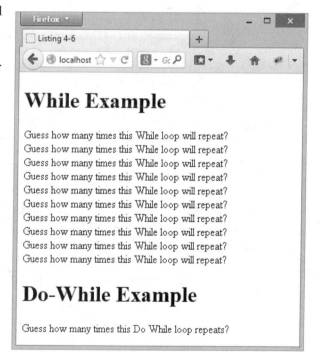

Listing 4-6   While and Do-While Examples

```html
<html>
    <head>
        <title>Listing 4-6</title>
    </head>
    <body>
        <h1>While Example</h1>
        <script type= "text/javascript">
            var i = 1;
            while (i <= 10) {
                document.write("Guess how many times this
                    While loop will repeat?<br />");
                i += 1;
            }
        </script>
        <h1>Do-While Example</h1>
        <script type= "text/javascript">
            var i = 10;
            do {
            document.write("Guess how many times this Do While loop
                repeats?<br />")
            i += 1;
            } while (i < 11);
        </script>
    </body>
</html>
```

For Statement

The `for` statement is another looping construct. The `for` statement, which is similar to its counterpart in other languages, places the initialization of the counter, its conditional limit, and its incrementing all in a series of expressions immediately following the `for`. The `for` statement takes the following form:

```
for (initializing expression; conditional expression; incrementing
expression)
        {
        statements executed while true;
        }
```

In its basic form, the `for` expression might be for (i = 1; i <= 5; i++), where i++ increments i after it is used. If any of these expressions is handled elsewhere in the script, they can be left blank in the for expression, which at its minimum is **for** (; ;).

Listing 4-7 shows examples of the `for` statement, with the results shown next. The `for` statement can be used in a manner very similar to `while`.

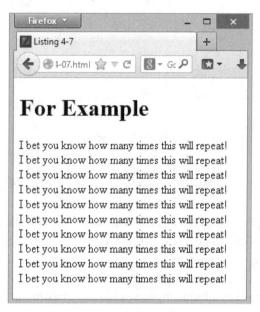

Listing 4-7   For Example

```
<html>
    <head>
        <title>Listing 4-7</title>
    </head>
    <body>
        <h1>For Example</h1>
        <script language="javascript" type= "text/javascript">
            for (i=1; i <= 10; i++) {
            document.write("I bet you know how many times this will repeat!<br
/>");
            }
        </script>
    </body>
</html>
```

Switch Statements

The `switch` statement is similar to a series of `if/else` statements. The `switch` statement is used where you want to compare a single variable with a number of different values and to do something different depending on the value. Three additional keywords are used with **switch**: **case**, **break**, and **default**, taking this form:

```
switch (a variable) {
    case "1" :
        statements executed while true;
        break;
    case "2" :
        statements executed while true;
        break;
    case "3" :
        statements executed while true;
        break;
    default :
        statements executed when all cases are false;
    }
```

Each **case** expression in the **switch** statement compares the **switch** variable with the **case** value, which can be a string. If it is equal, the statements following the **case** expression are executed, and then the **break** expression sends the script's flow to the first statement after the **switch**'s closing curly brace. If none of the **case** expressions is successful, the statements following the **default** expression are executed, and the script's flow exits the **switch** statement. Listing 4-8 demonstrates how this works, which provides these results:

NOTE

In Listing 4-8, Math.random is used to generate a random number between 0 and 1, which is then multiplied by 6 (to exercise the last option); then Math.ceil is used to take the resulting number and round it to the next higher integer.

Listing 4-8   Switch Statement Example

```html
<html>
    <head>
        <title>Listing 4-8</title>
    </head>
    <body>
        <h1>Switch Statement Example</h1>
        <p><b>The Computer Wizard!</b></p>
        <p>Ask a Yes/No question and click Refresh.</p>
        <script language="javascript" type= "text/javascript">
            var randNum = Math.ceil(6*Math.random());
            switch (randNum) {
            case 1 :
                document.write("Definitely Yes!");
                break;
            case 2 :
                document.write("Probably Yes!");
                break;
            case 3 :
                document.write("Definitely Maybe!");
                break;
            case 4 :
                document.write("Probably No!");
                break;
            case 5 :
                document.write("Definitely No!");
                break;
            default :
                document.write(randNum,"<br />");
                document.write("Computer Malfunction, Try Again");
            }
        </script>
    </body>
</html>
```

In the balance of this chapter, you'll see how to take the many pieces of JavaScript and weave them into a script that actually does something useful, like passing data between web pages or between sessions, or reading and writing files on the server to create a guest book, or authenticating a user.

Introducing Event Handlers

The discussion of event handling is organized around four basic categories of event handler use:

- **Window** event handlers deal with events such as opening, closing, resizing, and moving that a user does to the window that contains the web page.

- **Mouse** event handlers work with the actions of the mouse pointer, such as clicking or double-clicking an element, or moving the mouse pointer on to or off of an element.

- **Keyboard** event handlers respond to key presses on the keyboard.

- **Form** event handlers react to the user's actions within a data collection form, such as selecting form elements, resetting the values in a form, or submitting the form to a recipient or database (covered later in this chapter).

When a browser interprets an event as happening, it invokes, or triggers, a JavaScript object, called an *event handler,* to perform a certain action (see the list of the JavaScript event handlers earlier in this chapter). For example, when you move your mouse pointer over a link or image, often you will see a pop-up message informing you about the nature of the link or image. In this case, the *event* of placing the mouse pointer over the link *triggers* the onmouseover *event handler* to display the message. When you move the mouse pointer away from the link or image, typically, the onmouseout event handler closes the message.

NOTE
Not every event handler listed in this chapter is fully described or demonstrated. Many are so closely related that to detail their use would be redundant.

Placing Event Handlers in Your Code

Event handlers are a unique feature of JavaScript in that they can be used outside of the <script> tags normally used to encapsulate scripts.

You can add JavaScript event handlers to a number of HTML tags as an attribute. Which tags are available depends on the particular event handler. For example, the window-type event handler onload can be used with the <body>, <frame>, <frameset>, <iframe>, <img>, <link>, and <script> tags, while a click-type event handler such as onclick is compatible with dozens of tags. However, the majority of common uses occur within the <body>, <form>, and <link> tags. An example of this usage is

```
<body onload="window.alert('Welcome to Past Times Antiques');">
```

which adds the JavaScript onload event handler to the HTML <body> tag as an attribute.

Understanding Event Handler Syntax and Usage

When using JavaScript as an attribute in an HTML statement, you need to surround the JavaScript in double quotes. Text strings within the double quotes, such as message text for alert message boxes, are identified by using single quotes. Event handlers are added to HTML tags in the form:

```
<HTML tagname eventhandlername="JavaScript Statement; JavaScript
    Statement; …;">
```

where:

- < identifies the start of an HTML tag

- **HTML tagname** is one of the available tags associated with the event handler

- **eventhandlername** is the event handler you are using

- = assigns the JavaScript statement(s) to trigger when the event occurs

- **"** the opening double quote starts the JavaScript code

- **;** ends each JavaScript statement, separating multiple statements

- **"** the ending double quote completes JavaScript code

- > identifies the end of the HTML tag

As you can see, you can string together several JavaScript statements within one argument, separated by semicolons. While this is acceptable for short statements and statements that will be used only once, a much more efficient (and elegant) way to accomplish this is to create a function that contains the statements and then to call the function as needed in the body of your web page.

Working with the Window Event Handlers

In this section, we'll work with a number of the event handlers associated with the web page itself, referred to as "window events." Table 4-6 lists the related event handlers.

Displaying Messages When a Page Opens/Closes

Very common uses for event handlers are to display messages when users first open a web page or when they leave the page. An example of using an `onload` event handler would be to pop up a *modal* message box when the page finishes loading that requires the user to click OK to close the message box (presumably after reading the message). A modal

Event Handler	Event Trigger
onabort	An image's loading is interrupted.
onblur	Focus is removed from an element.
onerror	An error occurs when loading a web page or picture.
onfocus	The user places the focus on an element.
onload	A web page completes loading in the browser.
onmove	A window or frame is moved.
onresize	A window or frame is resized.
onunload	A user opens another web page.

Table 4-6   Window Event Handlers

window (in this case, an alert message box) is a window that requires user input to close it before the focus can change to another window or web page. The event handler that triggers the message box is onload.

Some other ways to use the onload event handler with more scripting include checking to see the type and version of the user's browser and then loading pages customized to that browser, or requesting a user's name and storing that information in a cookie so that subsequent visits can greet the user by name.

Using the syntax described in the previous section, Listing 4-9 shows the code to create an alert message box using the onload event handler, shown next.

NOTE
The alert() method that is called by the onload event handler can be contained in a JavaScript statement within the <**head**> section of a web page or in the <**body**> section. The difference is in the timing of the appearance of the message box. In the <**head**> section, the message box is displayed immediately, often before any page elements finish displaying. When it is in the <**body**> section, you can be assured that all page elements, including pictures and other media, will display before the message box appears, perhaps giving the user a better sense of the nature of the message box.

Listing 4-9   `onload` Example

```html
<html>
    <head>
        <title>Listing 4-9</title>
    </head>
    <body onload="window.alert('Please let us know if you
        have problems with our site.');">
    </body>
</html>
```

The `onunload` event handler would simply replace the `onload` event handler in the previous script with a different message to provide a message to a user when they leave the page by any number of methods: clicking a link, using File I Open, closing the browser window, and so forth.

Placing and Removing Focus

Focus is used to describe which window, or which element in a window, has the user's attention. For example, in the case of windows, the active window has the focus and inactive windows don't (in the last two listing examples, the message box has the focus). Another example is in data input forms, where the form element that will next accept user input has the focus and the other elements are called "blurred," although they aren't visually. Focus can be transferred by the user by clicking or tabbing to a different window or web page element, or programmatically by programmers by using scripts.

To see how you can use the `onfocus` event handler in your scripting, Listing 4-10 first creates a function in the `<head>` section to produce the result we want. Then in the `<body>` section, the code to call the function is added to the `onfocus` event handler so a change in focus will trigger the result we want—a change in the background color of a text box within a form (forms are covered in more detail later in this chapter) when a user moves the focus to it, as shown next.

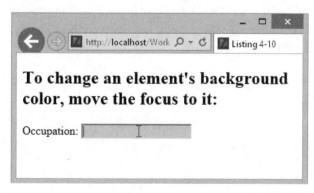

Listing 4-10   `onfocus` Example

```html
<html>
    <head>
        <title>Listing 4-10</title>
        <script type= "text/javascript">
            function chgTextColor(i){
            document.getElementById(i).style.background="lightblue";
            }
        </script>
    </head>
    <body>
        <h2>To change an element's background color, move the focus
            to it:</h2>
        <form>
        Occupation: <input type="text" onfocus="chgTextColor(this.id);"
            id="Occupation">
        </form>
    </body>
</html>
```

The `onblur` event handler, which works when the focus is removed from an element, comes in handy when you want to remind users of something they should have done to the element that had the focus or want to question them about some aspect of that element. You could take the `onfocus` example, add a second text box where the focus can be changed from the original text box (by clicking the text box or pressing TAB), and then create a message box that users have to attend to before they can continue.

Resizing a Window

The `onresize` event handler triggers and executes JavaScript code when a web page window is resized. There are times (and those times can happen more often with certain browsers than with others) when content on a web page doesn't resize when the web page window itself is resized. To slap the browser into recognizing the change, you can force a refresh, or reload, of the page using the `onresize` event handler. Listing 4-11 shows how to do this, as displayed in Figure 4-2.

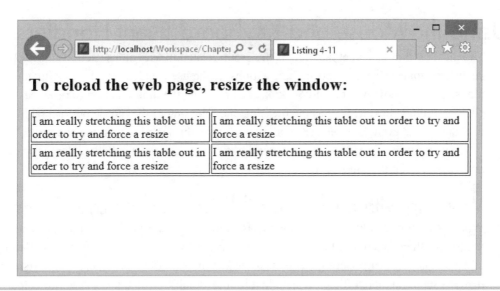

Figure 4-2   Internet Explorer 11 seems to do a constant reload with this code. Chrome and Firefox behave as expected.

Listing 4-11   `onresize` Example

```
<html>
    <head>
        <title>Listing 4-11</title>
    </head>
    <body onresize="window.location.href=window.location.href;">
        <h2>To reload the web page, resize the window:</h2>
        <table border="1" width="100%">
            <tr>
                <td width="41%" height="21">I am really stretching
                this table out in order to try and force a resize</td>
                <td width="59%" height="21">I am really stretching
                this table out in order to try and force a resize</td>
            </tr>
            <tr>
                <td width="41%" height="21">I am really stretching
                this table out in order to try and force a resize</td>
                <td width="59%" height="21">I am really stretching
                this table out in order to try and force a resize</td>
            </tr>
        </table>
    </body>
</html>
```

Using the Mouse and Keyboard Event Handlers

The most used of the event handlers is the group related to user mouse actions and keyboard inputs. Mouse events include actions by the user, such as simply moving the mouse pointer, moving it on and off links, and pressing the mouse button to produce a click or double-click, as well as the pressing and releasing of the mouse button. Table 4-7 lists the related event handlers. (Keyboard events are discussed later in the chapter.)

In the next few sections, I'll use several of the mouse event handlers to demonstrate how these can be used in your code.

Working with onclick, ondblclick, and Arrays

While any number of elements on a web page can react to a user's click, none is more ubiquitous than the button. In this first example, along with the `onclick` event handler, I add a couple of other scripting elements to make things a little more interesting. First, an *array* is set up to more efficiently handle multiple variables. Next, a *function* is created to display messages when called. Finally, the `onclick` event handler is attached to screen elements to trigger the action.

Introducing Arrays

An *array* is a JavaScript object that allows you to store similar variables, indexed by number, so they can be used later in your script. By assigning values a number, not only do you reduce typing when you want to use them (write once, use many), but then you also can employ other scripting features such as loops to further your efficiency. An array is created from a morphing of how we create variables and functions, in the form:

```
var arrayname=new Array()
```

Event Handler	Event Trigger
onclick	An element is clicked.
ondblclick	An element is double-clicked.
ondragdrop	An object is dragged and dropped into a window.
onmousedown	The user presses a mouse button.
onmouseup	The user releases a mouse button.
onmousemove	The user moves the mouse pointer.
onmouseout	The user moves the mouse pointer from a link.
onmouseover	The user moves the mouse pointer to a link.

Table 4-7 Click Event Handlers

where *arrayname* is a unique name you provide using the standard JavaScript syntax for naming variables and objects, and **var**, new, and Array() are scripting keywords that assign the soon-to-be-added variables to a new array.

You can assign variables (or parameters) to an array at the time you create the array (typically in the **<head>** section) or anywhere in your script thereafter. To assign variables after creating an array, you list them in the form:

```
var arrayname=new Array(3)
arrayname[0]="variablename0";
arrayname[1]="variablename1";
arrayname[2]="variablename2";
```

In this case, we know there will be three parameters in this array, so we set up the array as containing only three parameters, that is, new Array(3). Later in our script, we can add parameters in sequence, either by continuing the original list, or simply by adding a line of code with the assignment. Alternatively, we could create the array with no parameters, that is, new Array(), and add variables as we need them. As objects, arrays have properties and methods that make them very useful tools in your scripting toolbox.

CAUTION

Arrays are efficient data-storage mechanisms that can easily lose their efficiency if used incorrectly. When you run a script with, say, a 100-parameter array, 100 bytes of data is placed in the memory stack. If you create a 100-parameter array but inadvertently assign the last parameter an index of 500—for example, DogsInKennel[500]="lassie";—you've just created a 500-parameter array, taking up 400 unused bytes in the stack. So check to be sure your index numbers are sequentially assigned.

Putting the Script Together

In the **<head>** section of Listing 4-12, the logic_list array is defined and populated with three variables. The callalert function is defined with a statement to display a message box when called. In the body, three buttons are created (shown next) that use the onclick event handler to call the callalert function with each of the three variables in the logic_list array.

Listing 4-12   onclick and **array** Example

```html
<html>
    <head>
        <title>Listing 4-12</title>
        <script type= "text/javascript">
            var logic_list= new Array(3);
            logic_list[0]="Boy, do I need a European vacation";
            logic_list[1]="If only I had the money";
            logic_list[2]="Therefore, I need to keep working to earn
                enough money for my European vacation";
            function callalert(logic_list){
                window.alert(logic_list);
            }
        </script>
    </head>
    <body>
        <h2>Circular logic</h2>
        Click here for a solution...
        <input type="button" onclick="callalert(logic_list[0]);">
        that has a small problem...
        <input type="button" onclick="callalert(logic_list[1]);">
        that seems to have a solution \
        <input type="button" onclick="callalert(logic_list[2]);">
    </body>
</html>
```

Other Mouse Click Event Handlers

The ondblclick event handler functions identically to the onclick event handler, except it requires a little extra effort on behalf of the user (a second click!). Two other event handlers react to mouse clicks: onmousedown and onmouseup. Depending on the action you are expecting the user to perform, these event handlers can often provide less error-prone results than onclick and ondblclick. Take, for example, the situation where a user clicks a link or button, but moves the mouse pointer off the target before releasing the mouse button. (Remember the definition of a click; that is, a click involves both the pressing and releasing of the mouse button.) If you use the onclick event handler, the trigger will not fire. If you use the onmousedown event handler, the trigger will fire on the initial press, irrespective of where the mouse pointer is when the button is released.

Moving the Mouse Pointer to Trigger Events

Like the click-type event handlers, a few handlers work when the mouse pointer is moved over an element or off an element. The most common is the `onmouseover` and `onmouseout` pairing, which can be used for a variety purposes, but most notably in rollovers, where near-identical images are switched as the mouse pointer enters and leaves an image to give a sense of animation, as shown next. Listing 4-13 shows the code to include these two event handlers within the Anchor tag (**`<a href`**) to create a link to an image. To create this script, you need two images that have the same dimension, as one is replaced by the other when the mouse pointer is moved on and off the image. The code includes the following details:

- **`<a href="http://someLinkToPictures.com"`** includes the opening tag, which creates a link to the image if the user clicks it instead of simply moving the mouse pointer on/off it.

- `onmouseover="document.swan.src='../Art/swan-onmouseover.jpg';"` displays the image in the `src` path when the image named "swan" is triggered by a mouse-over event.

- `onmouseout="document.swan.src='../Art/swan-onmouseout.jpg';">` displays the image in the `src` path when the image named "swan" is triggered by a mouse-out event (the mouse must move off the picture).

- **`<img`** `name="swan" border="0" width="307" height="230" alt="Dutch Swan" src="../Art/swan-onmouseout.jpg">`**`</img>`** defines the image that initially appears on the page.

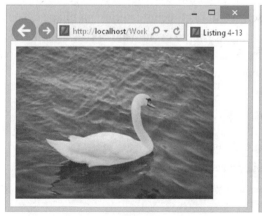 

NOTE

For the code examples in Listing 4-13 to be meaningful, I have used a public domain graphic file. If you want to replicate these examples, substitute a URL or path in the applicable `src` attribute to files of your choosing.

Listing 4-13   `onmouseover` and `onmouseout` Example

```html
<html>
    <head>
        <title>Listing 4-13</title>
    </head>
    <body>
        <a href="http://someLinkToPictures.com"
            onmouseover="document.swan.src='../Art/swan-onmouseover.jpg';"
            onmouseout="document.swan.src='../Art/swan-onmouseout.jpg';">
        <img name="swan" border="0" width="307" height="230" alt="Dutch Swan"
            src="../Art/swan-onmouseout.jpg"></a>
    </body>
</html>
```

NOTE

There are a number of variations on using the rollover to add interactivity to your scripts. The example shown in Listing 4-13 is really just the starting point for what you can do. The Web is full of examples you can mimic legally to find the one that performs the actions you are specifically trying to achieve.

Using the Keyboard Event Handlers

In addition to receiving user input from the mouse, you can trigger events based on key actions from the keyboard, listed in Table 4-8. A majority of these events are related to online data entry forms, which are described in more detail later in this chapter. The `onkeyup` event handler is used to demonstrate keyboard event handlers. In conjunction with a coding sample and an event handler from earlier in this chapter, and two functions, a key release event is used to trigger a random message to the user.

Event Handler	Event Trigger
onkeydown	The user presses a defined key.
onkeypress	The user presses and holds down a defined key.
onkeyup	The user releases a pressed defined key.

Table 4-8   Keyboard Event Handlers

The `<body>` section in Listing 4-14 performs three actions besides including some narrative HTML:

- `<body` `onload="setfocus();">` fires the `setfocus` function when the `onload` event handler is triggered.

- `<input` `input id="text1" type="text" onkeyup="presskey();">` creates a text box named `text1` and fires the `presskey` function when the user releases a pressed key.

The `<head>` section defines these two functions:

- **function** `setfocus()` encapsulates a statement that sets the focus to the text box (places the blinking insertion point at the left end of the box so it is ready to be entered) when the page is loaded.

- **function** `presskey()` encapsulates the `switch` statement demonstrated earlier in this chapter to randomly display comments in alert message boxes.

Listing 4-14 *onkeyup* Example

```html
<html>
    <head>
        <title>Listing 4-14</title>
        <script type= "text/javascript">
            function setfocus(){
                document.getElementById("text1").focus();
            }
            var randNum = Math.ceil(6*Math.random())
            function presskey(){
                switch (randNum) {
                    case 1:
                        window.alert("Hey dude, can you press a little
                        softer, please?");
                        break;
                    case 2:
                        window.alert("Ouch, take it easy, bub");
                        break;
                    case 3:
                        window.alert("C'mon, type like you mean it!");
                        break;
                    case 4:
                        window.alert("Is that all you got?");
                        break;
                    case 5:
                        window.alert("Try pressing in the middle of
                            the key");
                        break;
                    default:
                        window.alert("Where did you learn to spell?");
                }
            }
        </script>
    </head>
    <body onload="setfocus();">
        <h2>A little joke to play on your friends the next time they ask
            you to create a form:</h2>
        <ol>
            <li>Start typing a word in the text box below</li>
            <li>After closing the alert, refresh your screen.</li>
            <li>Continue until you've had enough.</li>
        </ol>
        <input id="text1" type="text" onkeyup="presskey();">
    </body>
</html>
```

Event Handler	Event Trigger
onsubmit	A user submits a form.
onselect	A field in a form is selected.
onreset	A form is reset.
onchange	Contents of a form are changed.

Table 4-9   Form Event Handlers

Reviewing Forms

This section provides a short primer on forms and how to create them using HTML. Several of the event handlers that focus on actions in a form are listed in Table 4-9. Many of these are demonstrated in the following discussion.

Understanding Forms

A form, much like its paper incarnation, is an area on a page that contains subelements to allow a user to input information, an example of which is shown in Figure 4-3. The user is given boxes to fill in, options to select, and choices to make. Online forms have several advantages over paper forms:

- Online forms are easily and cheaply produced.
- Input elements can be constructed to enforce user discipline, that is, data can be verified to exist (no blank fields), to be of a certain length, or to otherwise fit certain criteria.
- Data is provided in digital form and is immediately able to be entered into a database.

There are three cardinal rules in creating a form: keep it simple, keep it short, and make it clear what the user is supposed to do (remember the KISS principle).

When designing a form, ask yourself what type of information you want from the user, for example, contact information, account information, or ordering information. The answer to that question will dictate the questions you need to ask. For example, when soliciting contact information, ask for a name (and the format, such as *Full* or *Last, First*), title, address, e-mail address, and phone numbers. Make sure your text labels clearly convey to the user what you want from the user, as shown in Figure 4-3.

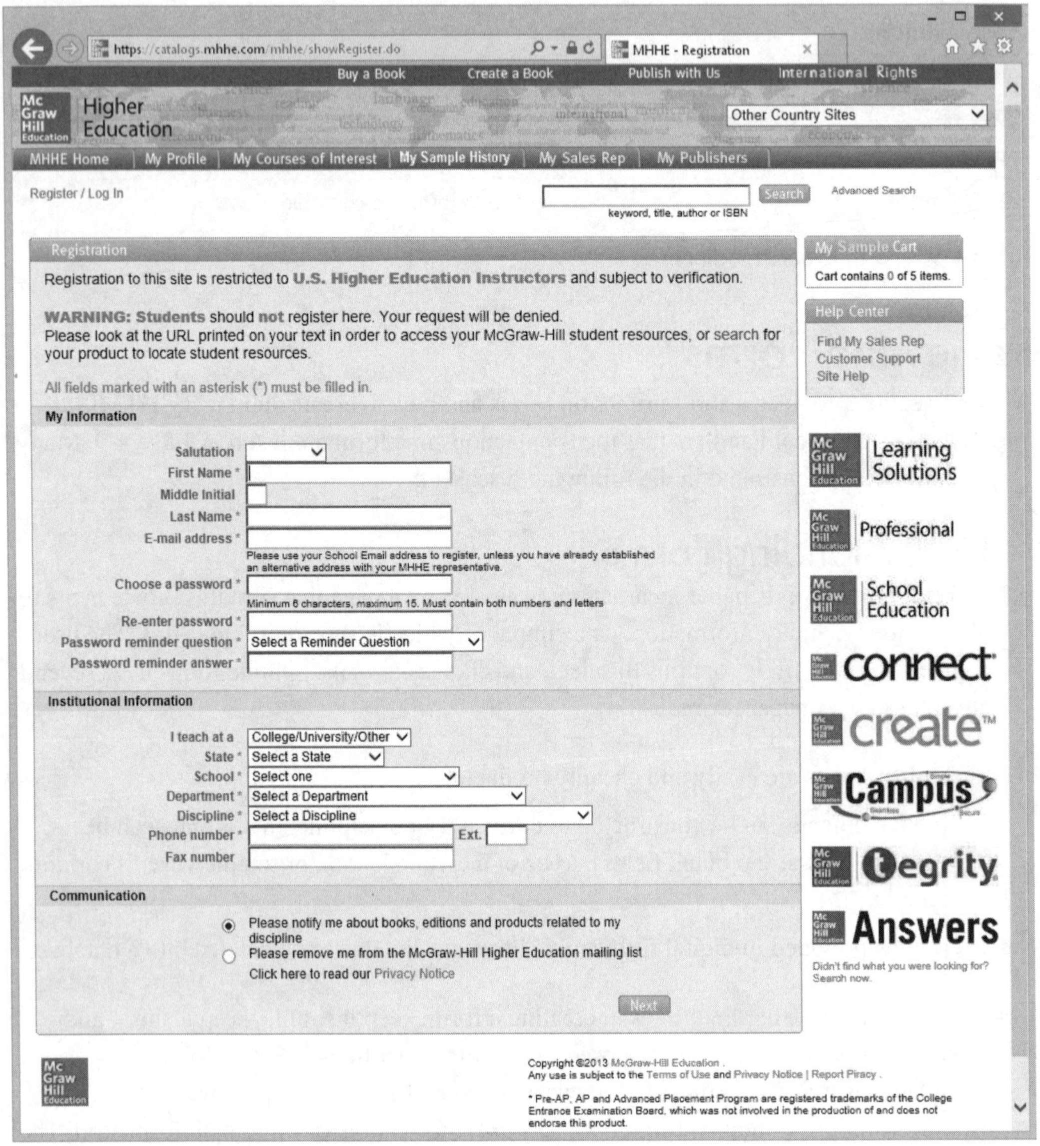

Figure 4-3 A web-based form has a similar appearance to its paper brethren.

Form Element	JavaScript Object Name	Usage
Button	`button`	Directs the user to another URL
Check box	`checkbox`	Obtains a yes/no-type response; can be used in a nonmutually exclusive grouping
Fieldset	NA	Allows you to display other form elements in a visible framed box, optionally with a legend (a nonscripting element)
Hidden field	`hidden`	Creates a field invisible to the user; commonly used to index submissions to the server
Password field	`password`	Creates a text box that displays asterisks (*) to mask entered characters
Radio (option) button	`radio`	Obtains a yes/no-type response within a mutually exclusive grouping
Reset button	`reset`	Returns a form to its default settings
Select box	`select`	Creates the infrastructure for a drop-down list box
Submit button	`submit`	Sends the data entered into a form to a destination such as a database or e-mail address
Text area	`textarea`	Allows large amounts of text to be entered, typically constrained only by the browser; useful for paragraphs, blogs, and essays
Text box	`text`	Allows for shorter, one-line text entries; typically 20 characters by default

Table 4-10   Form Elements

Next, consider which form elements best serve the type of information you are gathering. Each form element, described in Table 4-10, caters to a specific purpose, and with the exception of `fieldset`, also has associated JavaScript objects, which allow you to validate and set values from a script. Many of these JavaScript objects are demonstrated later in this chapter.

Creating Forms Using HTML

Forms are constructed in two steps. First, use HTML to create and place the form and its elements on the web page. Second, use JavaScript to activate your form to do something using functions and other scripting.

A form is created by enclosing its elements within the `<form></form>` tags, effectively creating a form object. Optionally, you can divide a form into visible discrete sections using the `<fieldset></fieldset>` tag set. Listing 4-15 shows an example of a basic form with several form elements, as shown next. The following sections will show you how to add scripting to activate a form.

Listing 4-15   Form Example

```
<html>
    <head>
        <title>Listing 4-15 Sample Form</title>
    </head>
```

```
<body>
    <h2>Acme Securities</h2>
    <form name="menu" action="mailto:teacher64@isp.com">
        <fieldset>
            <legend>Request for Investment Information</legend>
            Name: <input type="text" size="24" />
            Address: <input type="text" /><br />
            Telephone: <input type="text" />
            Email:      <input type="text" /><br />
            Married: Yes <input type="checkbox" /> No <input
                type="checkbox" /><p></p>
            Describe your anticipated retirement lifestyle:<br />
            <textarea name="report" rows="15" cols="50"></textarea>
            <br />Choose the investment products in which you are
            interested<br />
            <select name="investments" onchange="window.location=
                document.menu.investments.options
                [document.menu.investments.selectedIndex].value;">
            <option selected value="">Investments</option>
            <option value="stocks.html">Equities</option>
            <option value="bonds.html">Bonds</option>
            <option value="cds.html">CDs</option>
            </select>
            <select name="insurance" onchange="window.location=
                document.menu.insurance.options
                [document.menu.insurance.selectedIndex].value;">
            <option selected value="">Insurance</option>
            <option value="term.html">Term </option>
            <option value="whole.html">Whole Life</option>
            <option value="annuities.html">Annuities</option>
            </select>
        </fieldset>
    </form>
    <input type="submit" value="Submit Information" />
    <input type="reset" value="Reset Form" />
</body>
</html>
```

Using JavaScript in Forms

To apply JavaScript properties and methods to forms and their elements, a naming convention must be set up to identify to which form and element scripting statements are being applied. In this section, you will first see how to identify forms and then be introduced to their properties, as well as to properties and methods associated with form elements.

Naming Forms on a Web Page

Forms are identified in one of two ways. The most straightforward of the two conventions, and the one described here, is to simply name the form (the other method, detailed in the following section, utilizes the `length` property of the form object). By naming the form, you create an instance of the form object.

NOTE

A downside of naming forms instead of using the `document.forms.length` property to identify forms is that you cannot use a form array to loop through each of the elements in your forms. This limitation is normally outweighed by the convenience of quickly knowing which form is which without having to figure out the index number of a particular form. Of course, if you're working with only a couple of forms, either method is fine.

Naming forms allows you to access forms on a web page by a unique, meaningful name. To name a form, add the name attribute to the `<form>` tag, as in the following syntax:

```
<form name="formname">
```

To call the form from a statement in your scripts, use this method:

```
document.formname
```

Listing 4-16 employs the `length` property of the form object to count the number of elements in a form (the `length` property is described later in the chapter and is used in other examples and listings). Note the naming of the form at the beginning of the `<body>` section and how it's called in the `alert` statement to provide information for the text in the message box. Several form elements are added using the HTML `<input>` tag set, shown next. These, and others like them, will be the basis on which we add scripting statements later in the chapter.

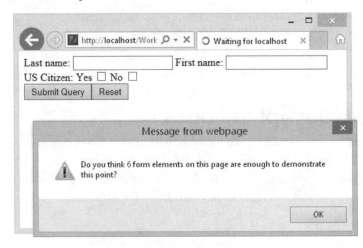

Listing 4-16 Naming and Calling Forms example

```html
<html>
    <head>
        <title>Listing 4-16</title>
    </head>
    <body>
        <form name="count_elements">
            Last name: <input type="text" />
            First name: <input type="text" /><br />
            US Citizen: Yes <input type="checkbox" />
                No <input type="checkbox" /><br />
            <input type="submit" /><input type="reset" />
        </form>
        <script type= "text/javascript">
            window.alert("Do you think "+document.count_elements.length+"
                form elements on this page are enough to demonstrate this
                point?");
        </script>
    </body>
</html>
```

Form Properties and Methods

Table 4-11 lists and describes the properties and methods associated with the form object. While most of the form properties only contain values that relate to the attributes in the <**form**> tag (similar to the name attribute described in the previous section), a few provide more meaningful actions. These, and some of the form methods, are discussed in this section.

action Property

The action attribute of <**form**> directs the browser to send submitted form data to a destination, typically a URL where a server-side CGI or PHP processing script appends the data to a database. Alternatively, the form data could be directed to a JavaScript function that would handle the processing, or to an e-mail address. The action property allows you to recall these values, an example of which is shown here and coded in Listing 4-17. In the listing, the script has a write statement containing one argument with a concatenated literal text value and the dot syntax:

```
"+document.mailto.action);
```

JavaScript Element	Type	Description
action	Property	Specifies the destination of the CGI (Common Gateway Interface) or PHP script; value corresponds to the `<form>` action attribute
elements[]	Property	Specifies an array used to access elements in the form
encoding	Property	Specifies the type of encoding used in the form; value corresponds to the `<form>` `enctype` attribute
length	Property	Specifies the number of elements in the form; value corresponds to the length of the elements array associated with the form
method	Property	Specifies the type of method used when a form is submitted; value corresponds to the `<form>` method attribute
name	Property	Specifies the name of a form; value corresponds to the `<form>` name attribute
target	Property	Specifies the window where CGI or PHP output is directed; value corresponds to the `<form>` target attribute
reset()	Method	Resets the input in form elements to default values without the user clicking a button
submit()	Method	Sends the form values to a specific script without the user clicking a button

Table 4-11 Form Properties and Methods

where `document` denotes the document object, `mailto` is the form object name, and `action` is the form property that returns the value in the `<form>` action attribute.

CAUTION

When using `mailto:` in the `action` attribute, the user's e-mail client opens a new message form, which is populated with the form data. The user must then click Send to send the mail data. The data isn't saved or processed for inclusion in a database or spreadsheet.

Listing 4-17   `action` Property Example

```html
<html>
    <head>
        <title>Listing 4-17</title>
    </head>
    <body>
        <form name="mailto" method="post" enctype="text/plain"
            action="mailto:teacher64@isp.com">
            <fieldset>
                <legend>Vacaciones de la Primavera</legend>
                Name: <input type="text" />
                Email: <input type="text" name="email_address" /><br />
                Describe what you did during your spring break, in Spanish,
                    por favor!:<br />
                <textarea name="report" rows="15" cols="50"></textarea><br />
            </fieldset>
                <input type="submit" />
                <input type="reset" />
        </form>
        <script type= "text/javascript">
            document.write("Note: Upon clicking Submit Query you are
                sending your report to me at: "+document.mailto.action);
        </script>
    </body>
</html>
```

`reset()` and `submit()` Methods

The `reset()` and `submit()` methods allow you to programmatically perform the actions of the Reset and Submit form element buttons, that is, to clear a form to its default values and to submit form values to a specified destination. Listing 4-18 and Figure 4-4 show how you can submit a form without a user manually performing that action, by using the `onblur` event handler to submit the form when focus is removed from a form element. (The `reset()` method works in a similar fashion.) Stealing a little thunder from the next section, this example uses the form property of the `textarea` element in conjunction with the **this** keyword to identify which form the element belongs to. This construction (`onblur="this.form.submit();"`) is an alternative to naming the form and then referring to it by name in the scripting attribute (`onblur="document.myformname.submit();"`).

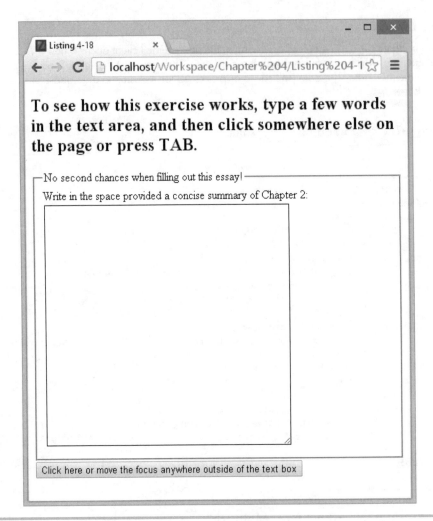

Figure 4-4 A form can be submitted by an event handler action such as a click.

NOTE
Using either the reset() method or the Reset form element button will reset a form to its default values. If you want to completely clear a form, including default values, you need to add scripting that individually identifies each element and returns it to a cleared state.

Listing 4-18   `submit()` Example

```html
<html>
    <head>
        <title>Listing 4-18</title>
    </head>
    <body>
        <h2>To see how this exercise works, type a few words in the
            text area, and then click somewhere else on the page
            or press TAB.</h2>
        <form action="http://matthewstechnology.com/essay.php">
            <fieldset>
                <legend>No second chances when filling out this
                essay!</legend>
                Write in the space provided a concise summary of Chapter 2:
                    <textarea rows=20 cols=40 onblur="this.form.submit()">
                    </textarea><br />
            </fieldset>
            <input type="submit" value="Click here or move the focus
            anywhere outside of the text box">
        </form>
    </body>
</html>
```

Working with Form Element Properties and Methods

Earlier in the chapter, Table 4-10 listed the form elements that a form comprises. Here, Table 4-12 lists several properties and methods that are applicable to each. As you can see, many of these properties/methods are shared by several elements.

This next section provides an example of how these properties and methods can be used with form elements to achieve certain results. Many of the properties/methods that are not shown behave in a very similar manner to the one being demonstrated.

defaultValue Property

In text boxes and text areas, you can display a default value for your users. If they change that value and then decide to return to the default value, they might be tempted to reset the entire form, which works but obliterates any other entries they may have made. A slicker way to handle this is to create a way that simply returns an element to its default value. Listing 4-19 shows the code for creating a function that returns the value of a text box to its default value when called by clicking the Return to Default Citizenship button. An `onclick` event handler does the calling in the `<body>` section. Try it for yourself, as shown in Figure 4-5.

Property/ Method	Used by These Elements	Description
`checked`	Check box, radio button	Indicates if a check box is checked (true) or not (false)
`defaultChecked`	Check box, radio button	Indicates whether a check box is checked by default (true)
`defaultValue`	Text area, text box	Indicates the default value in a text area or text box
`form`	All	Returns the name of the parent form
`name`	All	Sets or returns the name of the element
`options[]`	Select box	Provides an array for options within an option list
`selectedIndex`	Select box	Indicates the index value of the selected option within the option list
`type`	All	Returns the type value of the element; for example, the type value for a check box is checkbox
`value`	All except select box	Sets the value of a specified element
`blur()`	All except hidden field	Removes the focus from an element
`click()`	All except hidden field, select box, text area, and text box	Acts as a click event on an element
`focus()`	All except hidden field	Places focus on an element
`select()`	Text area, text box	Selects the text area box or text box

Table 4-12 Form Element Properties and Methods

Listing 4-19 `defaultValue` Property Example

```html
<html>
    <head>
        <title>Listing 4-19</title>
        <script type= "text/javascript">
            function default_cit(){
            document.contact.citizen.value=document.contact.citizen
                .defaultValue;
            }
        </script>
    </head>
    <body>
        <form name="contact">
            <fieldset>
                <legend>Personal Information</legend>
                Name: <input type="text" name="fullname" />
                Email: <input type="text" name="email" /><br />
                Citizenship: <input type="text" name="citizen"
                value="United States" />
```

```
            <input type="button" value="Return to Default Citizenship"
                onclick="default_cit();" />
        </fieldset>
        <input type="submit" value="Submit Personal Info" />
        <input type="reset" />
    </form>
  </body>
</html>
```

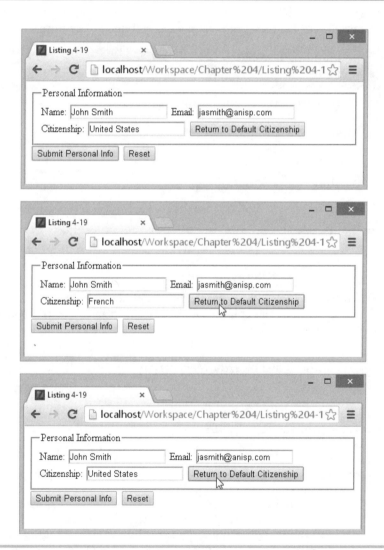

Figure 4-5 You can reset a field without resetting the entire form by using the `defaultValue` property.

Focus and `Blur` Methods

The `focus()` and `blur()` methods perform the same actions as the event handlers of the same names described earlier in this chapter. `focus()` places the focus in a field through a user mouse click or tabbing action, and `blur()` removes the focus from an element. The main difference between the two is how each is activated in the script. You simply include methods, similarly to the properties described earlier in the chapter, in the hierarchical dot syntax in a scripting statement. The example shown in Listing 4-20 uses these two methods as attributes of the `onclick` event handler, producing the form shown next.

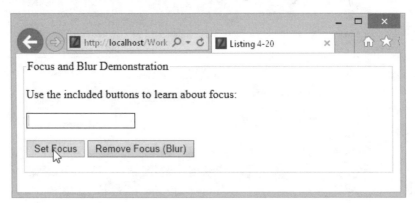

TIP
A handy way to use the `focus()` method in a form is to place the focus in a form element (that is, place the cursor in the element) after a validation script has returned the user to the element to correct his or her input. Validating JavaScript is described in more detail in the following section.

Listing 4-20   `focus()` and `blur()` Methods

```
<html>
    <head>
        <title>Listing 4-20</title>
    </head>
    <body>
        <form name="focusandblur">
            <fieldset>
                <legend>Focus and Blur Demonstration</legend>
                <p>Use the included buttons to learn about focus:</p>
                <input type="text" name="demo" size="20" /><p>
                <input type="button" name="focus" value="Set Focus"
```

```
                     onclick="document.focusandblur.demo.focus();" />
           <input type="button" name="blur" value="Remove Focus
               (Blur)"
                     onclick="document.focusandblur.demo.blur();" />
           <p>
        </fieldset>
     </form>
  </body>
</html>
```

Validating a Form

Earlier in the chapter, the basic functioning and layout of a form were reviewed, and the sections that followed illustrated ways you could use JavaScript to get your forms to perform certain actions. The one aspect missing so far is one of the most common ways JavaScript is used in forms. This section discusses form validation and demonstrates ways you can use it in your forms.

Understanding Validation

Validation is a way of checking for correctness of user input in a form. Since most input typically is added to a database for further processing and future use, it's imperative that the data coming in is accurate and is in the correct format. Submitted data is generally sent to a CGI or PHP script running on a server that certainly has the wherewithal to handle validation tasks. However, that requires a return trip to the browser, which can slow down the response to the user. A faster way to handle the validation is to perform it locally on the user's computer in conjunction with the web browser—client-side validation.

For the most part, client-side validation can be as simple as verifying that a form element has not been left blank, checking for the presence of required characters, or accessing external databases for security confirmation.

Using Validation with Passwords

One of the best demonstrations of client-side validation is ensuring basic information is provided correctly by the users. You can check that users enter characters they believe to be their password by having them enter it twice. (The actual verification to determine if the password is stored in a database is handled on the server side.) Listing 4-21 at first glance appears to be an overly complex script, especially for the minimal output shown here, but taken in pieces related to the ways a validation script works and the different ways validation can be performed, it becomes quite tame.

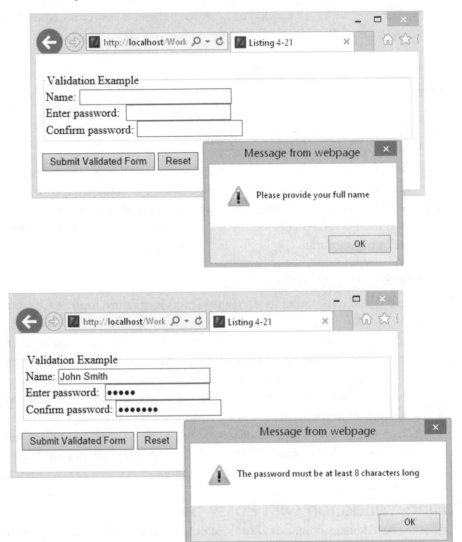

Listing 4-21   Validation Example

```html
<html>
    <head>
        <title>Listing 4-21 Validation</title>
        <script type= "text/javascript">
```

```
        var minlength=8;
        function validateform(){
            if (document.passwordform.fullname.value==""){
                window.alert("Please provide your full name");
                document.passwordform.fullname.focus();
                return false;
            }
            if (document.passwordform.pwd1.value==""){
                window.alert("Please enter a password");
                document.passwordform.pwd1.focus();
                return false;
            }
            if (document.passwordform.pwd1.value.length < minlength){
                window.alert("The password must be at least
                "+minlength+" characters long");
                document.passwordform.pwd1.focus();
                return false;
            }
            if (document.passwordform.pwd1.value !=
              document.passwordform.pwd2.value){
                window.alert("Your two password entries are not
                the same");
                document.passwordform.pwd1.focus();
                document.passwordform.pwd1.select();
                return false;
            }
            else {
                window.alert("Thank you for submitting correct
                data");
                return true;
            }
        }
    </script>
  </head>
  <body>
    <form name="passwordform" onsubmit="return validateform();"
        action="http://myserver.com/cgi-bin/formresults.com">
        <fieldset>
            <legend>Validation Example</legend>
            Name: <input type="text" name="fullname" size="30"
            /><br />
            Enter password:  <input type="password"
            name="pwd1" /><br />
            Confirm password: <input type="password"
            name="pwd2" /><br />
        </fieldset>
        <p></p>
        <input type="submit" value="Submit Validated Form" />
        <input type="reset" />
    </form>
  </body>
</html>
```

Using the `onsubmit` Event Handler

The `<body>` section in Listing 4-21 appears much the same as you've seen in other examples in this chapter, producing the basic short form. The one interesting aspect in this construction is the argument in the `onsubmit` attribute, that is, `onsubmit="return validateform();"`. This construction is a key element in how the validation process works.

When the user clicks the Submit Validated Form button, instead of sending the form values directly to the server specified in the `action` attribute, as has been the case in previous examples, the `onsubmit` event handler in the `<form>` tag set intercepts the request, calls the `validateform()` function (which is described in the next section), and using the **return** keyword, sees if the function returns a **true** or **false**. If **true**, the values are sent to the server; if **false**, no data is sent.

Dissecting the Function

The `validateform()` function comprises several **if** statements that perform the validation checks within the text box and two password boxes. If the condition of an **if** statement is true, the code continues running uninterrupted. If the condition is false, an alert message box appears to the user apprising them of a problem.

The first two **if** statements in Listing 4-21 are nearly identical and simply check to make sure the Name text box and first password box are not blank. If either is blank, an alert is displayed, a **false** is returned to the `onsubmit` event handler in the `<body>` section, and no form data is sent.

```
if (document.passwordform.fullname.value=="") {
    window.alert("Please provide your full name");
    document.passwordform.fullname.focus();
    return false;
}
```

NOTE

It is important to use fully qualified form field names—`document.passwordform`
`.fullname` and not just `passwordform.fullname`—if you want scripts to work in older browsers, where "document" refers to the current page being displayed in the browser.

If an alert is displayed, note that the focus is brought back to the affected element when the user closes the message box.

In the third `if` statement, the length of the password entered by the user is compared with the length specified in the `minlength` variable. If it's less than the value, an alert is displayed, a **false** is returned to the `onsubmit` event handler in the `<body>` section, and no form data is sent.

In the fourth and final `if` statement, the values of the two password boxes are compared to ensure the entered password is identical to the password entered in the confirmation box. As in the other `if` statements, a **false** generates an alert, and a **true** continues the script.

TIP

If you were to just compare the two passwords (`passwordform.pwd1 !=`
`passwordform.pwd2`) and not their values, it is possible that you would not get
equality when the two passwords are the same because the other attributes of the
variable, such as length, may differ.

The final actions in the function are handled by the **else** and final **return** statements. When all the `if` statements return **true**, the code processing reaches the **else** statement, which displays a confirmation alert to acknowledge to the user that all is well. When the alert is acknowledged, the function returns a **true**, which is received by the `onsubmit` event handler, which finally gives the green light for the form data to be sent to the URL specified in the `action` attribute.

While this is a rather long example, it really is the tip of the iceberg in terms of what validation checks you can perform. For example, in addition to what was checked here, you could check to see that the password was a "strong" password by verifying that some capital letters, numbers, and special characters were included. Or, in the case of an e-mail text box, you could check to see if the user included both the @ character and a period (you'll see an example of this later in the book). Using variations on the examples in Listing 4-21, you can construct your own validators to check the parameters important to your forms.

Try This 4-1   Create a Registration Form

Create a form to collect registration information for an individual using JavaScript to automate and validate the form. The form should have at least four different types of form elements. In the JavaScript, include at least one variable, one function, one conditional, and several objects with methods and properties. Place and return the focus so the user is positioned correctly in the form, or use mouse and/or keyboard event handlers. Place the JavaScript on a separate .js page, and use CSS to make the form look a bit better.

Chapter 4 Self-Test

The following questions are intended to help reinforce your comprehension of the concepts covered in this chapter. The answers can be found in the accompanying online Appendix A, "Answers to the Self-Tests."

1. What is JavaScript?

2. JavaScript is a complied language, true or false?

3. JavaScript is primarily client-side computing, true or false?

4. Client-side computing is done in a browser, true or false?

5. All JavaScript is contained within HTML, true or false?

6. In HTML, into what two sections can JavaScript be placed?

7. What HTML tags surround JavaScript?

8. What is one of the two ways you can add comments to JavaScript?

9. Should you use upper- and lowercase in JavaScript?

10. What should JavaScript statements end with?

11. What is a string, and how is it identified in JavaScript?

12. What are several types of JavaScript operators, and what are several examples of each?

13. What are statements, expressions, and values?

14. What is a function?

15. What is an object?

16. What are properties?

17. What are methods?

18. What are event handlers?

19. What are three of the four types of control structures?

20. What is focus and blur?

21. What is an array?

22. What are five of the eleven types of form elements?

23. Forms are created with JavaScript, true or false?

24. What is one of the two ways a form is identified in JavaScript?

25. What is validation, and what are three examples?

Part II

Exercising the Server with PHP

In Part I of this book, you saw how JavaScript activated dynamic web elements with scripts running in the client browser. In Part II, you'll see how PHP, running in the server, provides another level of automation, including dynamically handling information and determining what a user views next.

Chapter 5 introduces PHP, what it is, how it is used, how it is installed, the use of its many online resources, and what tools you should have running to work with PHP. The chapter discusses the parts of PHP, how it is tied into and used with HTML code, and the rules that need to be followed for good PHP code. Chapter 5 also discusses the structure of PHP, including strings, numbers, comments, constants, variables, arrays, and operators, with examples shown of their use.

Chapter 6 covers `if-else` and `switch` statements and the conditions that control them, along with `for`, `foreach`, `while`, and `do-while` loops. The chapter also covers PHP's file-handling capabilities, including opening, reading, writing, and closing files, as well as determining a file size and setting a pointer to a particular record. Finally, the chapter describes cookies and session and server variables and how to use them.

Chapter 7 describes and demonstrates PHP arrays, in both single and multidimensions, how to work with them in loops, and with the many array functions. The chapter then looks at form creation and handling, including checking the existence of form data and accepting, validating, and transferring form data into an array.

Chapter 8 demonstrates how to use PHP form- and file-handling capabilities to set up a user login form, validate login information against a file, and establish controls that can restrict access to forms and information. Passing data among web pages is discussed and how the URL, session variables, and cookies are used to do that. Cookies are also discussed in terms of how they can be used to customize a page to a particular user.

Chapter 5

Fundamentals of PHP

Key Skills & Concepts

- Preparing a PHP Workstation

- Integrating PHP with HTML

- Writing and Testing PHP

- PHP Basics

- Types of Information

- Variables and Constants

- Operators

- Statements and Expressions

- Functions

PHP provides server-side programming, giving the web developer access to the web server that is hosting the website, and to everything that is stored and/or runs there. Among these are other web pages, stored on that server or another server; web applications such as shopping carts and billing programs; and databases to both collect and display information. PHP also has access to the server's file system so it can read and write information independent of the database. Most importantly, PHP can be used to build the web pages that are sent to the client so the pages are customized to the person at the client, for example, to display an invoice of purchases or selected information in a class.

This chapter will introduce PHP, how it is integrated with HTML, and how it is written and tested on your computer. The chapter will then discuss the parts of PHP and the rules that need to be followed for good PHP code.

About PHP

PHP is a scripting language for developing dynamic web pages. PHP, which runs in a web server, is *interpreted,* meaning that the original human-readable script written by the developer is converted to computer instructions each time it is used. This contrasts with languages such as C and Java (not JavaScript), which are *compiled* instead of interpreted, meaning the original code is converted to computer instructions as a one-time process and stored in the converted form, so when it is used, it can immediately be executed and does not have to wait for interpretation. While interpreted languages like PHP may be slightly slower, they can be changed immediately before they are used, giving them a lot of flexibility and making development much easier—something you'll appreciate as you go through the remainder of the book.

PHP began life in 1994 when Rasmus Lerdorf developed it to help him add some dynamic elements to his *personal home page,* hence PHP. Since then, it has spread like wildfire because it is powerful and easy to use, it integrates well with HTML, and it supports a number of databases, most importantly, MySQL. Rasmus also put it in the public domain, which means that not only is it free to use, but anybody with the skill can enhance it. As a result, a number of people have worked on it. Today, it is in its fifth major revision (PHP 5), with a number of minor revisions along the way (as this is written, the latest stable version is PHP 5.5.9, with PHP 5.6 in developmental testing). PHP is now a fully mature professional scripting language, as you can see from its website, php.net. It has a large number of user groups all over the world (valuable for getting help—see the PHP site for one in your area), sizable steering and documentation committees, and many developers working on it, for the most part, on a volunteer basis. It also now has a more official sounding, if recursive, name—"PHP: Hypertext Preprocessor." While it is impossible to get an accurate count, many millions of web pages have been developed using it, and many professional web developers believe that PHP and MySQL are the best way to add a database to a website of any size.

Tools Needed for PHP

To effectively work with PHP, you need to have a development environment that supports both the writing and the testing of PHP scripts. You'll need tools for:

- **PHP script writing**, with code assistance and validation as you write the script
- **PHP script testing** on your development computer
- **Developmental support** in a browser, to help debug

Chapter 1 describes and recommends packages that you can download for these tools. For the first part of this book, I recommended that you use Aptana Studio integrated development environment (IDE) and the WAMP (Windows servers for Apache, MySQL, and PHP) server group. While you can continue to use these if you wish, I recommend that you switch to Zend Studio IDE and Zend Server because they both provide powerful support for PHP (they were developed by a couple of the early PHP developers). Zend Studio, which uses the same foundation as Aptana, provides better PHP debugging help.

Preparing a PHP Workstation

If you do not already have Zend Studio and Zend Server, return to Chapter 1 and follow the instructions to download and install them. They are used in the discussion in the remaining chapters of this book and will prove very beneficial to your PHP work.

Setting Up Zend Server

When you have completed downloading Zend Server, use these steps to set it up and prepare it for use.

1. After completing the installation of Zend Server, you are left with a Thank You page in your browser, as you see in Figure 5-1.

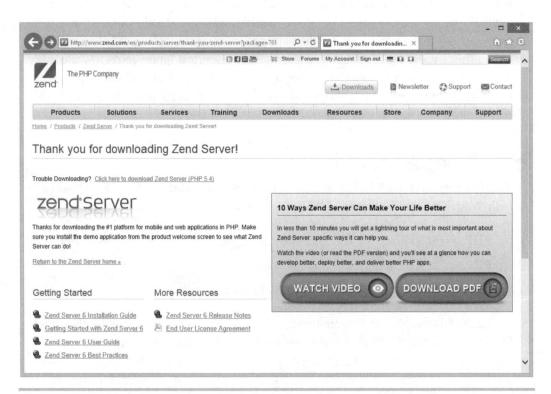

Figure 5-1 Zend Studio provides a number of pages to review to prepare for its use.

2. Open the Getting Started link | Zend Server User Guide | Getting Started. You did step 1 as a part of the installation, so begin with step 2 and work down each of the steps. Here are some tips:

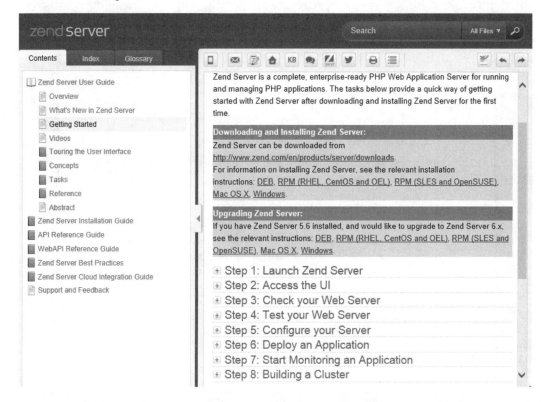

a. The Apache server component of Zend Server that provides the localhost in your browser is automatically started whenever you boot your computer. You can tell the Apache server is running by hovering over this symbol in the notification area of the taskbar or in the hidden icons.

b. Test the localhost in a browser by opening a browser and typing **localhost** in the address bar. The Zend Server Test Page should appear.

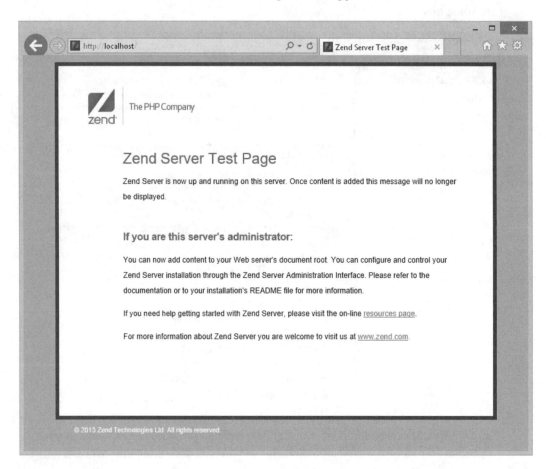

c. Open the Zend Server user interface (UI) in your browser by typing **localhost:10081/zendserver**. You are asked to log in. For the username, type **admin**, and then enter the password you entered in step 10 near the end of the installation. This should open the page shown in Figure 5-2.

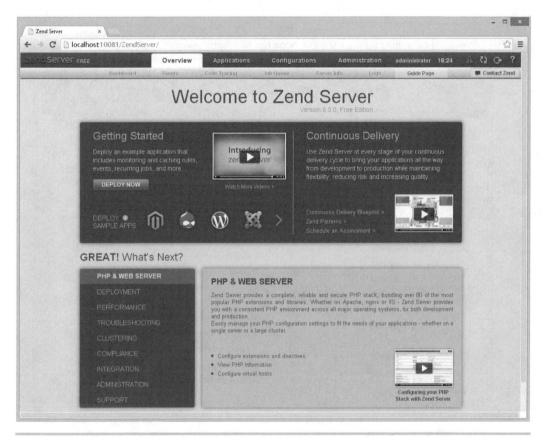

Figure 5-2   The initial view of the Zend Server UI should be the Overview Guide Page.

d. For files to appear in your browser at localhost, place them in the folder at
c:\program files (x86)\zend\apache2\htdocs, assuming that Zend Server is installed
in the default folder c:\program files (x86).

TIP

If you download the listing scripts from this book (go to mhprofessional.com/ mediacenter/), unzip (extract) the .zip file into the htdocs folder so it looks like this:

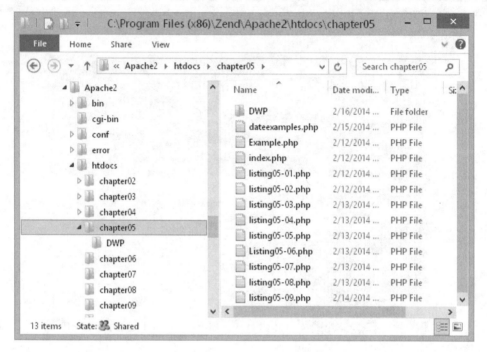

Setting Up Zend Studio

When you finished installing Zend Studio, it should have left a shortcut on your desktop. Use that shortcut to start Zend Studio, and with the following steps, set up Zend Studio for use.

1. When Zend Studio first opens, the Workspace Launcher is displayed with the default workspace. Based upon what we just did in the steps for Zend Server, enter or browse to the c:\program files (x86)\zend\apache2\htdocs folder, click Use This As The Default, and click OK. Zend Studio should open, as you see in Figure 5-3.

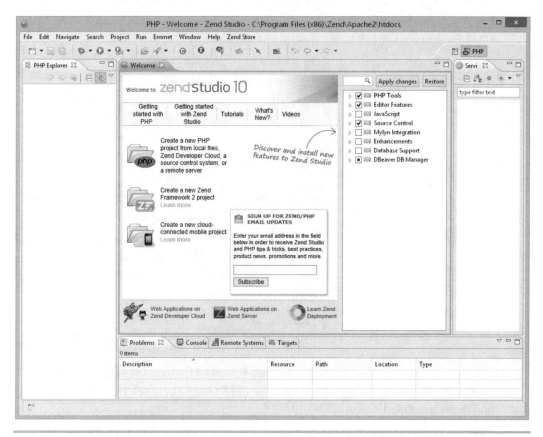

Figure 5-3 Zend Studio provides an environment and support tailored to PHP.

2. I recommend that you enter your email address and click Subscribe to receive the Zend Studio PHP Tips and Tricks newsletter.

3. Review once again the Zend Studio plugins and decide if you want to change the selections that you made during installation. We don't discuss any of the plugins in this book,

but you might want to explore some on your own. If you make any changes, click Apply Changes, and click the X in the Welcome tab to close it.

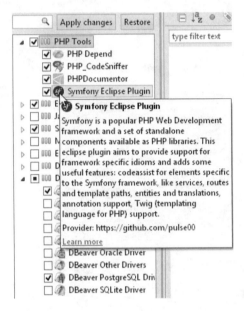

4. Check for and install an upgrade by clicking Window | Preferences | Install/Update | Available Software Sites, select the Zend Studio Update Site, click Edit on the right, and then click OK.

5. Create a PHP project in which to store the files you create in this chapter by clicking File | New | Local PHP Project. Enter a project name, such as **Project05**; if the location isn't already c:\program files (x86)\zend\apache2\htdocs, make it so, and click Finish.

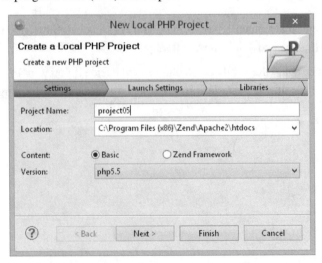

6. If you want to bring in the listings from this book, you can import them into your project. Click File | Import | General | File System | Next. For the From Directory, browse to the folder into which you place this book's files (c:\program files (x86)\zend\apache2\htdocs\ chapter05 suggested earlier), select the individual files you want, browse to the Into Folder, select the folder (Project) you just created, click OK, and click Finish.

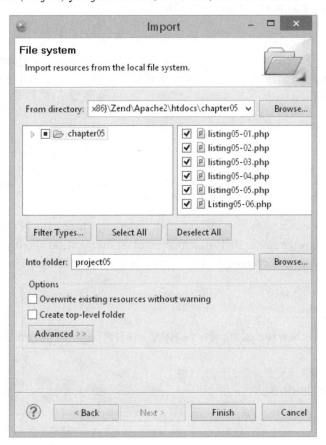

PHP Introduction

PHP is a way within a web page of telling the server that you want something done. It may be to open another web page, write in a file, or extract information from a database. Whatever it is, in an HTML page, the developer has decided that he or she needs something from the server. This is the job of PHP. Note that it started from an HTML page, so the first question is how to put PHP on an HTML page. The second question is what can be done with it once it is there.

Integrating PHP with HTML

Putting PHP in an HTML file is very simple:

- You change the file extension to .php.
- You surround the PHP code with `<?php ... ?>`.

The .php extension tells the server that the file needs to go through the PHP interpreter. The `<?php ... ?>` tells the PHP interpreter that it needs to process whatever is in the middle and to replace the PHP lines of script with HTML code sent to the browser so it can interact with the server.

NOTE

In some situations, you can use `<? ... ?>` without the `php`, but unless you are developing for a very controlled environment like an intranet, we strongly suggest that you include the `php` to make sure your script works in all environments and to simply alert or remind whoever is looking at the script that they are looking at PHP.

Given those two rules, you can put PHP script anywhere in an HTML file. For example, Listing 5-1 shows a single PHP statement to open information about your PHP server in the body of an HTML page that is saved with a .php extension. The result is shown in Figure 5-4.

NOTE

Figure 5-4 shows how Firefox displays the HTML and PHP page using Zend Server with a test PHP server.

Listing 5-1   PHP Example

```
<!DOCTYPE html>
<html>
    <head>
        <meta charset="utf-8">
        <title>Listing 5-1</title>
    </head>
    <body>
        <h1>This is an Example of PHP Embedded in HTML</h1>
        <p>The PHP code displays information about the PHP server.</p>
        <?php
            phpinfo();
        ?>
    </body>
</html>
```

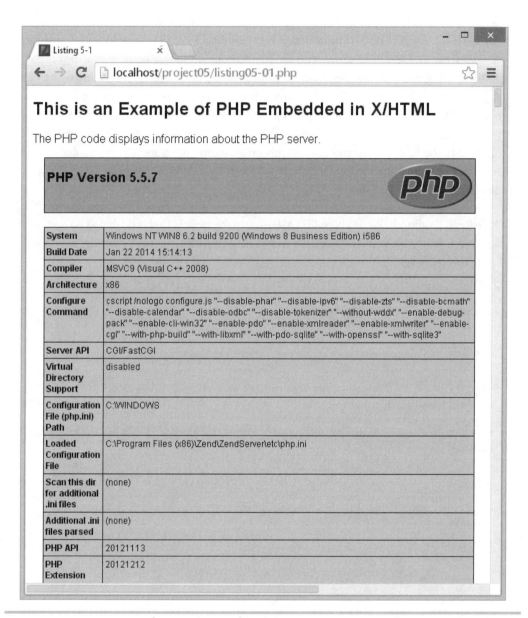

Figure 5-4 PHP operates from any part of an HTML page.

NOTE

The remaining listings in this chapter will not include the `<!DOCTYPE>` and `<meta>` statements to make the listings more compact.

Writing and Testing PHP

As you write and test PHP script with the tools discussed in this book, you will want to do the writing and some testing with Zend Studio, and to do additional testing using the Apache and PHP servers in Zend Server with several browsers. To do that, you need to open a PHP project where Zend Server can see it and create and store your PHP files in the project. That is what was done in "Preparing a PHP Workstation" earlier in this chapter. If you have the listings used in this book, ignore them for a moment, and create a file that has PHP embedded within it. Then look at the result of this code, first within Zend Studio and then in browsers.

1. In Zend Studio, click File | New | HTML File. In the New HTML File dialog box, select the project, project05, you created earlier in this chapter. Enter a name; I'm using "Example" for this purpose.

2. Click Next, select the New HTML File (5) template for HTML5, and click Finish.

3. Between the `<body>` tags, enter:

   ```
   <?php
   phpinfo();
   ?>
   ```

4. Click File | Save As, change the extension to .php, and click OK. Your Zend Studio should look like this:

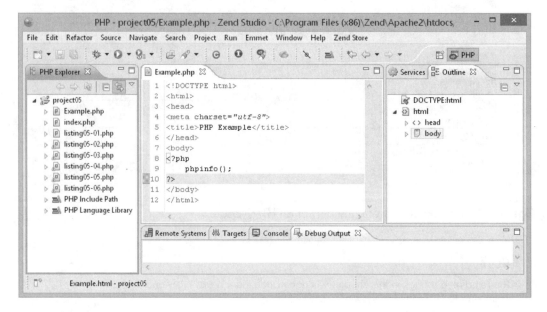

5. To display the results of the code within Zend Studio, click the Run icon | PHP Web Application | OK, confirm the web server URL, and click OK. Here's the result:

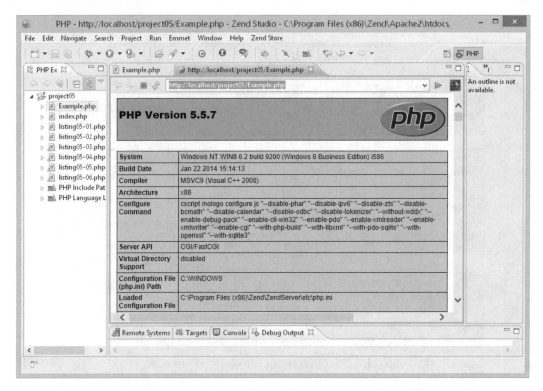

6. You can get the same result outside of Zend Studio by opening a browser and entering the same URL (you can copy it from the display in Zend Studio): localhost/project05/ Example.php. Here it is in Chrome:

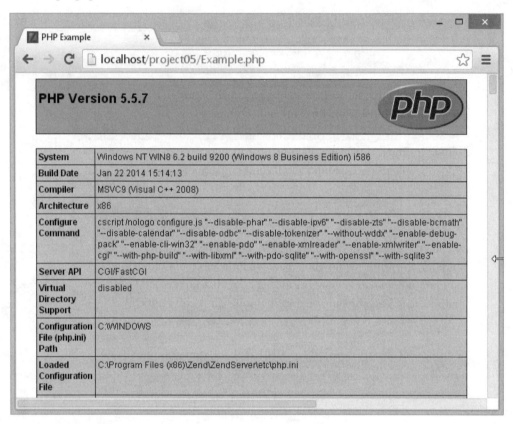

If you do not see the correct results in steps 5 and 6, then most likely, the file location is not where the Apache web server thinks it ought to be. As mentioned earlier, the default location is c:\program files (x86)\zend\apache2\htdocs. Use Windows Explorer to see if the file is there.

If it works in Zend Studio and not in your browser, then make sure the Apache server is running as you tested earlier in "Setting Up Zend Server." If so, look at what is in the browser's address bar. It should be localhost/project05/Example.php.

It is very important, before you go further in this chapter, that you make sure that Zend Studio and Zend Server, along with your browsers, are all working properly. You need to be able to test your work as you go along.

Zend Studio, Apache Friends, and PHP all have forums and user groups that you can contact with questions on how to resolve problems.

PHP Basics

PHP has several basic facilities that both give it power and make it easier to use. These include the ability to display information at any point in your script, adding comments in several ways, and a set of useful coding conventions.

Display Information

In debugging script, it is often helpful to display a comment or a variable while the script is running. PHP gives you two ways to do this with the echo() and print() functions, which are very similar, and for many purposes, they are the same. Listing 5-2 shows both functions, which produce this image with the Run command in Zend Studio:

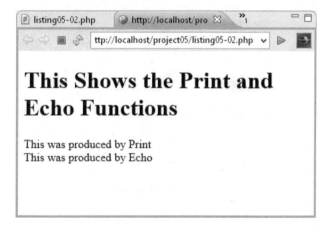

Listing 5-2   print/echo Example

```
<html>
   <head>
      <title>Listing 5-2</title>
   </head>
   <body>
      <h1>This Shows the Print and Echo Functions</h1>
      <?php
         print "This was produced by Print <br />";
         echo "This was produced by Echo";
      ?>
   </body>
</html>
```

Both `print` and `echo`, while called "functions" and included in function lists, are unlike most functions in that their arguments are not required to be in parentheses, although you can use parentheses if you want. The quote marks are required unless the argument is a number, although you can use either single or double quote marks.

Since the information within the quotes is sent to the browser for processing, you can include HTML tags and have them treated as if they are in a line of HTML. The `<br />` in Listing 5-2 shows this. This also means that you can place text on multiple lines within a single set of quotes.

There are only two significant differences between `print` and `echo`. `print` returns a value (1) when it is processed, so you can test to see if that happened (explained later in the chapter). `echo` does not do that, but `echo` can take multiple arguments, separated by commas, while `print` can take only one.

Examples of the various ways that `print` and `echo` can be used are shown in Listing 5-3, with the results shown next:

Listing 5-3   More print and echo Examples

```
<body>    <h1>More Examples of Print and Echo</h1>
   <?php
      print "This is Print with double quotes <br />";
      echo "This is Echo with double quotes <br />";
      print "This is Print with single quotes <br />";
      echo "This is Echo with single quotes <br />";
      print ("This is Print with parens <br />");
      echo ("This is Echo with parens <br />");
      print "Print argument 1<br />"; #Second causes error
      echo "Echo argument 1  ", "Echo argument 2<br />";
      print 1234567890;  //Without quotes
      echo "<br />" , 987654321 , "<br />";
      print "This is on line one,<br />
         while this is on line two, <br />
         and this is on line three.";
      /* echo and print are essentially
         the same with one argument. */
   ?>
</body>
```

NOTE

In Listing 5-3, the echo of a number without quotes cannot start with a zero because PHP interprets that as an octal (base 8) number, which cannot contain a "9," so the whole number would be evaluated as "0."

Commenting Script

PHP allows you to add comments to your script in three ways, one of which was shown in Listing 5-3:

- On a single line starting with #

  ```
  #This is a comment
  ```

- On a single line starting with //

  ```
  //This is also a comment
  ```

- On multiple lines enclosed with /* */

  ```
  /* This is a comment that can
  be on several lines. */
  ```

TIP

It is strongly recommended that you comment your script profusely to make it easier to work with in the future.

Coding Conventions

PHP is fairly easygoing as far as conventions are concerned. In the first three listings, though, you have probably noticed several conventions that should be added to your PHP rules:

● Each PHP statement should end with a semicolon (;). The only exception is the last statement before the closing ?>, which can have a semicolon, but it is not required.

● Text, any combination of letters and numbers, also called a *string,* in an argument needs to be enclosed in quotation marks, either single (' ') or double (" "). (Some differences are explained in a Note later in this section.) Quotation marks must be in like pairs.

● Legitimate numbers, which can have a decimal point, do not have to be in quotation marks.

● Multiple arguments are separated by commas (,).

● Most functions require that their arguments be enclosed in parentheses.

TIP

When you are debugging script and you get the message "Syntax Error," check to see if a semicolon is missing at the end of the previous line or if you have an unclosed/ unmatched quote mark. Often, one of those is the problem.

You may have wondered since quotation marks are used to identify a string, how you display a quotation mark that is part of the string to be printed or echoed. For this purpose, PHP uses the backslash (\) in what is called an *escape sequence,* like this:

```
print "My name is \"Marty\"";
```

Most of the characters that PHP assigns a special use for can be used as a literal character by preceding it with a backslash. In addition, PHP has defined several escape sequences. Here are some of the more common escape sequences:

● \" produces a double quotation mark.

● \' produces a single quotation mark.

● \\ produces a backslash.

● \$ produces a dollar sign.

● \r produces a carriage return.

- \n produces a linefeed.

- \t produces a tab.

NOTE

While either single or double quotation marks can be used to enclose a string, in some circumstances, one or the other is preferable. With single quotation marks enclosing the string, you can use literal double quotation marks without the backslash in the string, as shown next. With single quotation marks, though, escape sequences other than \' or \\ will display the backslash and not perform their function. With double quotation marks, all escape sequences work. For example: `print 'My name is "Marty"';`

Parts of PHP

PHP, while a relatively simple language compared with C or Java, is still very complex, as you would expect of any comprehensive language such as PHP. In this section, we'll take PHP apart and explore PHP information types, statements, variables, operators, and functions. In the following section, we explore control structures, classes, and objects.

NOTE

As with any language, a large number of elements are in each part of the language, far more than can be covered here. To look at the complete list, go to php.net/manual/en/langref.php. Also, w3schools.com/php/ provides a good reference as well as a good tutorial.

Types of Information

PHP is not as sensitive as other languages to the type of information you are working with, and you normally do not have to specify a data type, such as integer or string. PHP will determine it for itself based on the context in which you are using it. It is still a good idea for you to keep in mind the type you are working with. The possible data types are shown in Table 5-1. There is further discussion of these in the next chapter, including how the type is set, unset, and used with variables and arrays.

All of the examples in Table 5-1, except for NULL, are also arrays. Other notes on data types include the following:

- The Boolean FALSE is equivalent to the integer 0, the floating point number 0.0, an empty string or a string of "0", an array of zero elements, or NULL. Everything else is TRUE.

- Integers are, by default, decimal (base 10) numbers. To make a number octal (base 8), precede it with 0 (zero), for example, 02 or 06. To make a number hexadecimal (base 16), precede it with 0x, for example, 0x4 or 0x8.

- Very large integers (larger than 2,147,483,647) are considered floating point numbers.

Data Type	Name	Description	Examples
Arrays	`array`	A set of two or more pieces of data that can be any of these data types in a comma-separated list	[98101, 'WA', 'Seattle', '123 E 3rd']
Booleans	`bool`	Either TRUE or FALSE; not case sensitive, but commonly uppercase	TRUE, FALSE
Floating point numbers	`float`	A fractional number with a decimal; may be negative, and may use scientific notation	7.34, –21.89, 2.31e3
Integers	`int`	A whole number without a decimal; may be negative	43, 928, –4
Null	`null`	The absence of any value	NULL
Strings	`string`	A series of characters (one of 256 letters, numbers, and special characters) enclosed in either single or double quotation marks	"Mike", 'Seattle', "1495 W. 18th St"
Objects	`object`	Data and information to process it, often a piece of script	
Resources	`resource`	A reference to an external element; commonly used with MySQL	

Table 5-1   PHP Data Types

- If you divide two integers, you get a floating point number, unless the numbers are evenly divisible.

- Floating point numbers are not accurate to the last digit because of the infinite progression of fractions like one-third. Therefore, you should not compare two floating point numbers for equality.

- A string containing a number (either integer or floating point) immediately following the left quote can be used as a number. For example, `"18.2"` and `"4 cars"` can both be used as numbers, while `"his 4 cars"` cannot.

- A specific value in an array is identified with a *key*, which can be an integer, a string that evaluates as an integer, the truncated integer portion of a floating point number, the Boolean `TRUE`, which evaluates to the integer `1`, or `FALSE`, which evaluates to the integer `0`.

NOTE

In this book, as in the PHP Manual, two additional pseudo-types are used for discussion purposes only: "mixed" is used for a combination of any of the first six types, and the "numbers" type is used for a combination of integers and floating point.

Variables and Constants

As you write PHP script, you need to name items that you are working with so you can repeatedly refer to them. There are two common types of items you can name:

- **Variables**, which are items that can contain different values at different times during script execution, start with a dollar sign ($) followed by a name that you give them.

- **Constants**, which will contain the same value throughout the execution of your script, are by convention, all uppercase names that you give them. For example, NULL is a constant.

The name that you give to either variables or constants (or any other label in PHP) is case sensitive; can begin with either the letters *a–z* or *A–Z,* or an underscore (_); can be of any length; and can contain letters, numbers, underscores, and the characters in Western European alphabets. While you may find that some special characters will be allowed, the best practice is to not use them.

PHP keywords with specific meanings that you should not use for naming variables, constants, or other labels in PHP are shown in Table 5-2.

A large number of predefined constants in PHP are used for a variety of purposes, like true constants (M_PI = 3.1415926535898 and M_E = 2.718281828459), constants used with particular functions (SORT_NUMERIC and SORT_STRING used with sort functions), constants used to define something (CAL_GREGORIAN and CAL_JULIAN used with calendars), and constants used for formatting (DATE_ATOM and DATE_RFC822 used with the date functions).

abstract	and	array	as	bool	break
callable	case	catch	class	clone	const
continue	declare	default	die	do	echo
else	elseif	empty	enddeclare	endfor	endforeach
endif	endswitch	endwhile	eval	exit	extends
false	final	finally	float	for	foreach
function	global	goto	if	implements	int
include	include_once	instanceof	insteadof	interface	isset
list	namespace	new	null	object	or
print	private	protected	public	require	require_once
return	static	string	switch	throw	trait
true	try	unset	use	var	while
xor.	yield				

Table 5-2   PHP Reserved Keywords

You can find a list of predefined constants within each major section of predefined functions in the PHP Manual – Function Reference at php.net/manual/en/funcref.php.

A good practice is to make variable and constant names more self-descriptive and in the process, stay away from any possibility of conflict with a predefined name. For example, if you are collecting a buyer's name and address, you might be tempted to use $name, $street, and $city. While nothing is wrong with those names, it is a better practice to get in the habit of using compound names that are both more descriptive and stay away from common names, for example, $buyer_name, $buyer_street, and $buyer_city. It may take a couple of seconds more to type these names, but they are not going to be confused with similar names. Also, most programmers get really good at cutting and pasting to reduce typing.

TIP

If you are having trouble finding a bug in a program, look at the names you have assigned variables and constants, and try changing any that could possibly have a conflict with other names, such as changing $name to $buyer_name.

Operators

Having created a variable or a constant, you are going to want to assign it a value. PHP has defined a number of operators of various types to do this, as shown in Table 5-3.

NOTE

Another set of comparison operators, called "ternary operators," will be discussed in the next chapter.

If you combine several operators in a single expression, the order of precedence is as follows, beginning with the highest or first executed: ++, --, !, ~, @, *, /, %, +, -, ., <<, >>, <, <=, >, >=, <>, ==, !=, ===, !==, &, ^, |, &&, ||, =, +=, -=, .=, and, xor, or. You can use parentheses to get around the order of precedence. Other notes about the PHP operators include the following:

- The modulus (%) does not give the percent the first number is of the second; rather, it gives the remainder, that part that is left after whole division.

- The equal sign (=) does not mean "equal"; it means "assign" or "replace." For comparisons, such as "is a equal to b," use the double equal sign (==).

- If $a = 2$ and $b = 2.0$, they are not identical because one is an integer and the other is a floating point number, but they are numerically equal.

Type of Operator	Name	Example	Explanation
Arithmetic			Performs arithmetic
+	Add	`$a + $b`	Sum
−	Subtract	`$a - $b`	Difference
*	Multiply	`$a * $b`	Product
/	Divide	`$a / $b`	Quotient
%	Modulus	`$a % $b`	Remainder
Assignment			Replaces a value with another
=	Assign	`$a = 7;`	Sets `$a` to 7

+=	Increment	`$a = 7;`
		`$a += 2;`
		`returns 9`
			Increments `$a` by 2

.=	Concatenate	`$a = "Joe ";`
		`$a .= "Blow";`
		`returns "Joe Blow"`
			Adds a string to an existing string

[]=	Append	`$array []=` `$something`	Appends `$something` to the end of the array
Bitwise			Turns specific bits in an integer on or off
&	And	`$a & $b`	Sets bits in both `$a` and `$b`
|	Or	`$a | $b`	Sets bits in either `$a` or `$b`
^	Xor	`$a ^ $b`	Sets bits in `$a` or `$b`, but not both
~	Not	`~$a`	Does not sets bits in `$a`
<<	Shift left	`$a << $b`	Shifts bits `$a` by `$b` steps to the left (each step is multiplying by 2)
>>	Shift right	`$a >> $b`	Shifts bits in `$a` by `$b` steps to the right (each step is dividing by 2)
Comparison			Compares two values
==	Equal	`$a == $b`	Returns TRUE if `$a` equals `$b`
===	Identical	`$a === $b`	Returns TRUE if `$a` is identical to `$b`
!= or <>	Not equal	`$a != $b or` `$a <> $b`	Returns TRUE if `$a` is not equal to `$b`
!==	Not Identical	`$a !== $b`	Returns TRUE if `$a` is not identical to `$b`
<	Less than	`$a < $b`	Returns TRUE if `$a` is less than `$b`
>	Greater than	`$a > $b`	Returns TRUE if `$a` greater than `$b`

Table 5-3 PHP Operators *(continued)*

Type of Operator	Name	Example	Explanation
<=	Less than or equal to	$a <= $b	Returns TRUE if $a is less than or equal to $b
>=	Greater than or equal to	$a >= $b	Returns TRUE if $a is greater than or equal to $b
Increment			Changes the value by one
++	Increment	++$a $a++	Adds one to $a and returns $a Returns $a, then adds one to it
--	Decrement	--$a $a--	Subtracts one from $a and returns $a Returns $a, then subtracts one from it
Logical			Logical consequence
and &&	And	$a and $b	Returns TRUE if both $a and $b are TRUE
or ||	Or	$a or $b	Returns TRUE if either $a or $b is TRUE
xor	Xor	$a xor $b	Returns TRUE if either $a or $b is TRUE, but not both
!	Not	!$a	Returns TRUE if $a is not TRUE
Other			
@	Error off	@my_function()	Disables display of errors in expression
` `	Execute	` date `	Executes what is within the back ticks (these are not single quotes), like DOS commands

Table 5-3 PHP Operators

Listing 5-4 shows examples of the use of PHP variables and operators. The results this script returns are shown on the following page.

NOTE

The variable names in the following script, for example, $a or $b, will be replaced with the value contained in the variable when they are displayed with echo or print, unless you *escape* them (treat them as literal characters) by putting a backslash (\) in front of the variable. This is true *both* inside double quotes as well as outside of any quotation marks, and is called *interpolation*. If you use single quotes to enclose a variable name, the name, not the contents, will be displayed.

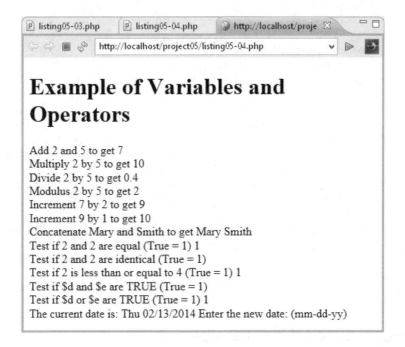

Listing 5-4   Examples of Variables and Operators

```html
<html>
   <head>
      <title>Listing 5-4</title>
   </head>
   <body>
      <h1>Example of Variables and Operators</h1>
      <?php
         //Math
         $a = 2; $b = 5;
         echo "Add $a and $b to get  ", $a + $b, "<br />";
         echo "Multiply $a by $b to get  ", $a * $b, "<br />";
         echo "Divide  $a by $b to get  ", $a / $b, "<br />";
         echo "Modulus  $a by $b to get  ", $a % $b, "<br />";
         //Increment and Concatenate
         $a = 7;
         echo "Increment $a by 2 to get ", $a += 2, "<br />";
         echo "Increment $a by 1 to get ", ++$a, "<br />";
            $first_name = "Mary "; $last_name = "Smith";
         echo "Concatenate $first_name and $last_name to get  ",
            $first_name . $last_name, "<br />";
```

```php
        //Comparison
        $a = "2"; $b = 2.0; $c = 4; $d = $a == $b; $e = $a === $b;
        echo "Test if $a and $b are equal (True = 1)  ", $a == $b,
            "<br />";
        echo "Test if $a and $b are identical (True = 1)  ",
            $a === $b, "<br />";
        echo "Test if $a is less than or equal to $c (True = 1)  ",
            $a <= $c, "<br />";
        //Logical
        echo "Test if \$d and \$e are TRUE (True = 1)  ", $d and $e,
            "<br />";
        echo "Test if \$d or \$e are TRUE (True = 1)  ", $d or $e,
            "<br />";
        //Execute
        echo ` date ` ; /* Executes the date DOS command as you would
                        in Windows' Command Prompt window. */
    ?>
  </body>
</html>
```

Statements and Expressions

PHP scripts contain either comments or statements. A *statement* is anything that is in between semicolons or the opening and closing PHP tags. Often, a statement is a single line of code ending in a semicolon, but you can have several statements on a single line, and you can have statements that take several lines. Most statements contain one or more expressions, but a few are only a single keyword, such as **break** or **else**.

Expressions are anything that has a value or evaluates to a value. *Values* are anything that can be assigned to a variable, so values can be any of the data types: integer, floating point, string, Boolean, array, or object. While the NULL data type is the absence of a value, it is still considered a value for this discussion.

Expressions can contain expressions, or said another way, expressions are building blocks that can be used to build other expressions. For example, $a = 2 is three expressions, 2, $a, and $a = 2.

Functions

A *function* is a piece of script that does something and can be repeatedly called within a larger script. Some internal functions already exist, and some user-defined functions you write. Some functions require *arguments,* which are values that you pass to the function, which uses them to compute a return value. Other functions simply return a value when they are called.

Internal Functions

You can use an internal or predefined PHP function to do many different tasks. To explore the full set of PHP functions, see the online PHP Manual - Function Reference at php.net/manual/en/funcref.php.

The following sections describe a *few* of the more heavily used internal functions as examples in the given category. Again, these are only a small sample of the available functions.

Array Functions   Array functions provide the means to work with arrays in a number of ways. Several of these are shown in Table 5-4 and are demonstrated in Listing 5-5.

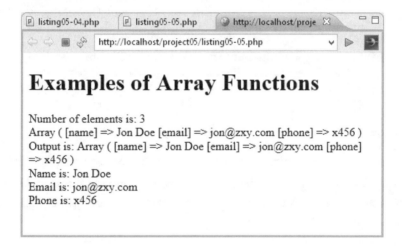

Function	Description	Explanation
array()	Builds an array of arguments	Arguments are a series of key => value statements separated by commas. Keys can be integers or strings. Values can be any type.
count()	Counts elements in an array	Argument is an array name; the elements are the number of key/value pairs.
print_r()	Prints a variable, including an array, in readable form	Argument is a variable (or array) name. With an optional second argument = TRUE, the contents of the variable or array are returned for use by another variable instead of being printed.

Table 5-4   Several Array Functions

Listing 5-5 Examples of Array Functions

```html
<html>
   <head>
      <title>Listing 5-5</title>
   </head>
   <body>
      <h1>Examples of Array Functions</h1>
      <?php
         $nameEntry = array(
            "name" => "Jon Doe", "email" => "jon@zxy.com",
            "phone" => "x456" );
         echo "Number of elements is: ", count($nameEntry), "<br />";
         print_r($nameEntry);
         $output = print_r($nameEntry, true);
         echo "<br /> Output is: ", $output, "<br />";
         echo "Name is: ", $nameEntry["name"], "<br />";
         echo "Email is: ", $nameEntry["email"], "<br />";
         echo "Phone is: ", $nameEntry["phone"], "<br />";
      ?>
   </body>
</html>
```

Date/Time Functions   The date and time functions provide access to and work with the current date and time at the server running the script. A few of these are shown in Table 5-5 and demonstrated in Listing 5-6, shown next.

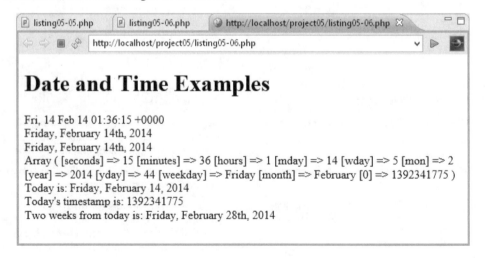

Function	Description	Explanation
date()	Formats a date and time as a string	Requires a format string and optionally a timestamp if the local time is not desired
getdate()	An array of the date and time components	Takes an optional timestamp if the local time is not desired
time()	Current "Unix" timestamp	Returns the number of seconds since 1-1-1970, 00:00:00 GMT to the current moment at your server

Table 5-5 Some Date and Time Functions

Listing 5-6 Examples of Date and Time Functions

```
<html>
    <head>
    <title>Listing 5-6</title>
    </head>
    <body>
        <h1>Date and Time Examples</h1>
        <?php
            echo date(DATE_RFC822), "<br />";
            $date_format = "l, F jS, Y";
            echo date($date_format), "<br />";
            echo date("l, F jS, Y"), "<br />";
            print_r(getdate());
            $date_array = getdate();
            echo "<br />Today is: ", $date_array["weekday"],
                ", ", $date_array["month"], " ", $date_array["mday"],
                ", ", $date_array["year"], "<br />";
            echo "Today's timestamp is: ", time(), "<br />";
                //Seconds since 1-1-1970
            $twoweeks = (14 * 24 * 60 * 60);
                //seconds in 2 weeks
            $twoweeksFrNow = Time() + $twoweeks;
            echo "Two weeks from today is: ",
                date("l, F jS, Y", $twoweeksFrNow), "<br />";
        ?>
    </body>
</html>
```

NOTE

In the results of Listing 5-6, you see that **echo date**(DATE_RFC822), "**
**"; ends with +0000. This says that there is no offset (0000) from GMT (Greenwich Mean Time), which happens because I have not changed the default in Zend Apache server. PHP version 5.1.0 and later checks to see if a valid time zone has been set and will issue a warning if it hasn't. Most Internet hosting services set this, so if you want to use your user's time zone, you're okay. To be sure, though, it is a good idea to set your own time zone in each script (once per script is adequate) using the `date_default_ timezone_set ()` function with a local time zone constant (for example, mine is "America/Los_Angeles" for the Pacific time zone). You can find a list of supported time zone constants at php.net/manual/en/timezones.php (not every major city is included; you must look for cities in your time zone).

When working with dates, there are a large number of constants, formats, and functions within PHP that you can work with. Listing 5-6 demonstrates a couple of these:

- The date() function requires, at a minimum, a format string. The format string can be a predefined date/time constant, such as DATE_RFC822; a literal string, such as "l, F jS, Y" that uses format codes for the various parts of a date and time; or a variable with the format codes.

- Eleven date/time constants provide predefined formatting for the date and time. Four of the more common ones are shown next. You can see all 11 at php.net/manual/en/ class.datetime.php.

Date and Time Constants

```
Atom: 2014-02-16T18:35:23+00:00
RFC822: Sun, 16 Feb 14 18:35:23 +0000
RFC850: Sunday, 16-Feb-14 18:35:23 UTC
RSS: Sun, 16 Feb 2014 18:35:23 +0000
```

- Thirty-five formatting codes can be used to format a date and time in PHP. The codes are case sensitive—a "d" and a "D" mean different formats. Here are four commonly used sets of formatting codes, which are explained in Table 5-6. You can see all of the PHP formatting codes at php.net/manual/en/function.date.php.

Date and Time Formatting Codes

```
l, F jS, Y : Sunday, February 16th, 2014
D, M d, y : Sun, Feb 16, 14
n/j/y g:i:s a : 2/16/14 6:35:23 pm
Y-m-d G:i:s : 2014-02-16 18:35:23
```

- Within the literal format string (within the quote marks), you can include separator characters such as **,** **-** **/** **.** and **:**, as you can see in the previous illustration.

Code	Explanation
D	Three-character day of the week (Mon – Sun)
d	Two-character day of the month with a leading zero (01 – 31)
j	One- or two-character day of the month (1 – 31)
l	Full text day of the week (Sunday – Saturday)
S	Suffix for day of the month, used with code j (st, nd, rd, th)
F	Full text month (January – December)
M	Three-character month (Jan – Dec)
m	Two-character numeric month with a leading zero (01 – 12)
n	One- or two-character numeric month (1 – 12)
Y	Four-digit year (for example, 1986 or 2014)
y	Two-digit year (for example, 86 or 14)
a	am or pm
A	AM or PM
g	One- or two-digit hours in 12-hour format (1 – 12)
G	One- or two-digit hours in 24-hour format (0 – 23
h	Two-digit hours in 12-hour format with leading zeros (01 – 12)
H	Two-digit hours in 24-hour format with leading zeros (00 – 23)
i	Two-digit minutes with leading zeros (00 – 59)
s	Two-digit seconds with leading zeros (00 – 59)

Table 5-6 Explanation of Some of the Date/Time Formatting Codes

Math Functions Math functions allow you to perform mathematical routines. Some of these are shown in Table 5-7 and are demonstrated in Listing 5-7.

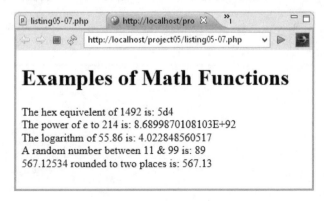

Function	Description	Explanation
`dechex()`	Converts a decimal integer to a hexadecimal number	Returns a string representing the hexadecimal number.
`exp()`	Calculates powers of e	Returns a floating point number of e to the power of the floating point argument.
`log()`	Calculates the natural logarithm	Returns a floating point number of the logarithm of the floating point argument. An optional argument can specify a different base other than the default of e.
`rand()`	Generates a random number	Without an argument, this generates an integer between 0 and 32,768. Optionally, minimum and maximum integers may be specified, separated by a comma.
`round()`	Rounds a number to number of decimal digits	Returns a floating point number after arithmetically rounding a floating point number. Optionally, the precision or number of decimal digits may be specified.

Table 5-7   A Few Math Functions

Listing 5-7   Examples of Math Functions

```html
<html>
  <head>
    <title>Listing 5-7</title>
  </head>
  <body>
    <h1>Examples of Math Functions</h1>
    <?php
      echo "The hex equivalent of 1492 is: ", dechex(1492), "<br />";
      echo "The power of e to 214 is: ", exp(214), "<br />";
      echo "The logarithm of 55.86 is: ", log(55.86), "<br />";
      echo "A random number between 11 & 99 is: ", rand(11,99),
        "<br />";
      echo "567.12534 rounded to two places is: ", round(567.12534, 2),
        "<br />";
    ?>
  </body>
</html>
```

String Functions   String functions allow you to work with strings. You have already seen two string functions, echo() and print(). Several others are shown in Table 5-8, demonstrated in Listing 5-8, and shown next.

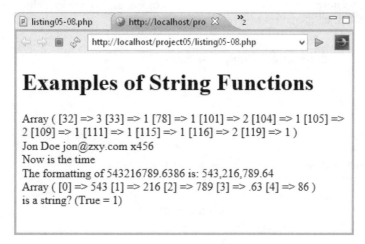

Function	Description	Explanation
count_chars()	Counts occurrence of characters in a string	Arguments are the string and optionally a mode, which determines if the return is an array or a string and what is to be counted. See Note following the illustration.
implode() or join()	Joins array elements to form a string	Arguments are the array and optionally the character, which defaults to a space, to be placed between elements.
is_string()	Determines if a value is a string	Argument is a variable, which is evaluated and returns TRUE if it is a string.
ltrim()	String formed by removing white space and specified characters on left	Arguments are the string and optionally a list of characters to remove. Without a list, spaces, tabs, carriage returns, newlines, and vertical tabs are removed.
number_format()	String formed by formatting a number with a decimal point and thousands separator	A floating point number is formatted with an optional integer number of decimal digits (1, 2, or 4, not 3). Optionally, the decimal point and thousands separator characters can be specified.
str_split()	Splits a string into array elements	Arguments are the string and optionally the number of characters in each element, with a default of 1.
strval()	Converts a numeric variable to a string	Argument must be an integer or floating point number.

Table 5-8   Examples of String Functions

NOTE

The `count_chars()` function has five modes (0 through 4). Modes 0 through 2 are arrays that return the count of 0, all 255 characters; 1, all characters present; and 2, all characters not present. Modes 3 and 4 are strings that list 3, all unique characters present; and 4, all characters not present.

Listing 5-8   Examples of String Functions

```html
<html>
   <head>
      <title>Listing 5-8</title>
   </head>
   <body>
      <h1>Examples of String Functions</h1>
      <?php
         $textString = "Now is the time!";
         $textArray = count_chars($textString, 1);
         print_r($textArray);
         $nameEntry = array(
            "name" => "Jon Doe", "email" => "jon@zxy.com",
            "phone" => "x456"
            );
         echo "<br />", implode("   ",$nameEntry), "<br />";
         $aLongString = "            Now is the time";
         echo ltrim($aLongString), "<br />";
         echo "The formatting of 543216789.6386 is: ",
            number_format(543216789.6386, 2), "<br />";
         print_r(str_split(543216789.6386, 3)) ;
         echo "<br />", $newString, "  is a string? (True = 1) ",
            is_string($newString) , "<br />";
      ?>
   </body>
</html>
```

NOTE

In the next chapter, you'll see a much better display of `count_chars()`.

User-Defined Functions

As you write PHP scripts, you'll often find that you want to repeatedly use the same code. You could simply copy the code to all the places you want to use it, but if you want to change that code, you would have to change it everywhere it was copied. The solution for this is to create a function containing the code you want to repeat and simply call that function everywhere you want to use it. Functions also let you segment or compartmentalize your code, making it easier to debug and maintain.

There is an even bigger reason for using functions. Up to now, all the PHP code in this chapter is meant to run, or execute, as the page is loaded, but *after* the page is displayed, in contrast to some JavaScript that executes *before* the page is displayed. If you don't want the PHP script executed as the page is loaded, you can create a function, place it above the `<!DOCTYPE html>` start of the HTML, and it won't be run until it is called.

Like predefined or internal functions, user-defined (just "user" from here on) functions may optionally have arguments that are passed to them, and may return a value after they are executed. Once a user function has been defined, it is *called,* or used, just like an internal function. The function itself can do anything you can do with PHP, using all of the features of PHP, including calling other functions, or even calling itself to create a recursive function. (You need to limit recursive functions to make sure they can't endlessly act recursively, or an error will result. A good rule of thumb is to limit recursion to no more than 100 times.)

User functions are defined with the **function** and **return** keywords by using this form:

```
function name($argument1, $argument2,...)
{
    [any PHP statements];
    return $returnValue;
}
```

The name that you give to a function uses the same naming rules as variables, constants, and other labels. It is case sensitive; can begin with either the letters *a–z* or *A–Z,* or an underscore (_); can be of any length; and can contain letters, numbers, underscores, and the characters in Western European alphabets.

Listing 5-9 shows an example of a user function with the result shown next. Many other examples are shown in the following chapters.

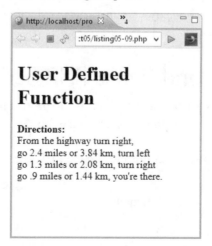

Listing 5-9 User-Defined Function

```html
<html>
   <head>
      <title>Listing 5-9</title>
   </head>
   <body>
      <h1>User-Defined Function</h1>
      <?php
         function tokm($miles)
         {
            $km = $miles * 1.6;
            return $km ;
         }

         echo "<b>Directions:</b>", "<br />", "From the highway
            turn right,", "<br />",
            "go 2.4 miles or ", tokm(2.4), " km, turn left", "<br />",
            "go 1.3 miles or ", tokm(1.3), " km, turn right", "<br />",
            "go .9 miles or ", tokm(.9), " km, you're there.", "<br />";
      ?>
   </body>
</html>
```

In the following chapters, you'll see how to take the pieces of PHP and weave them into a script that actually does something useful like passing data between web pages or between sessions, or reading and writing files on the server to create a guest book, or authenticating a user.

In addition to the online PHP Manual, there are two excellent books on PHP: *PHP: The Complete Reference* by Steven Holzner (McGraw-Hill Education, 2008) and *PHP: A Beginner's Guide* by Vikram Vaswani (McGraw-Hill Education, 2009).

Try This 5-1 Build and Run a PHP Script

Build a PHP script in your IDE that contains the items that follow. When you are done, run the script and correct any problems that you observe.

- Start by creating an HTML5 file and add the PHP section or "envelope." Save it as a PHP file.

- Add `print()` and `echo()` functions.

- Add a comment.

- Add an escape sequence.

- Define two variables and add `echo()` statements that increment one of the variables, and then compare the two variables, displaying the variables as literals.

- Create an array that stores a name and email address, add the content, and then display the information.

- Add a statement that displays today's date in any format and then displays the date one week from today.

- Display a random number between 10 and 99.

- Display the formatting of a string number.

- Create your own function and call it at least twice.

Chapter 5 Self-Test

The following questions are intended to help reinforce your comprehension of the concepts covered in this chapter. The answers can be found in the accompanying online Appendix A, "Answers to the Self-Tests."

1. PHP operates in a browser, true or false?

2. PHP is an interpreted language, true or false?

3. What are three tools that are needed for writing and testing PHP scripts?

4. What are two of the three things that you must do to an HTML file to convert it to a PHP file?

5. PHP code must be in the `<head>` section of an HTML file, true or false?

6. What are two functions to display content in PHP?

7. What set of characters are used to enclose content to be displayed, except for numbers?

8. What are two of the three ways of adding comments to a PHP script?

9. What are three of the four conventions that should—often must—be followed with PHP coding?

10. What is the initial character used in escape sequences, and how are these used?

11. What are four of the eight data types, and what do they represent?

12. How do you differentiate between constants and variables?

13. What are the naming conventions for labels in PHP?

14. What is the difference between =, ==, and ===?

15. What does ++ mean, and what is the difference between ++$a and $a++?

16. What does "order of precedence" mean, and how is it used?

17. What do the terms "statement," "expression," and "value" mean, and how do they relate?

18. What are functions, and what are some examples of internal or premade types of functions?

19. With the date format "l, F jS, Y" what would the date look like?

20. Where do you place a user-defined function you don't want to run until it is called in the body of a script?

Chapter 6

PHP Control and File Handling

Key Skills & Concepts

- `if/else` Statements

- `while` and `do-while` Statements

- `for` and `foreach` Statements

- `switch` Statements

- Basic File Functions

- Additional File Functions

- Session Variables

- Cookies

- Server Variables

PHP is often thought of as simply the mechanism for working with a MySQL database. It is, though, a full-featured programming language with all the features you saw in Chapter 5, as well as a full set of control structures and powerful file-handling tools, browser information features, and techniques for creating and using cookies and session variables. This chapter explores these powerful capabilities of PHP and in the process describes how to use `if-else` and `switch` statements and the conditions that control them, along with `for`, `while`, and `do` loops. The chapter also looks at PHP file management features and functions, the ability to determine the type of browser being used, and how to establish session variables that can protect access to a website. Finally, passing data among web pages using session variables and cookies is discussed.

TIP

It is useful to have the PHP Manual and the PHP Function Reference bookmarked or set up as favorites in your browser, if you don't already, so you can quickly refer to them. The manual is at php.net/manual/en/, and the function reference is at php.net/manual/en/funcref.php.

Control Structures

The scripts so far in this section have been executed from the first statement to the last statement without interruption or change of direction, with the exception of repeated function calls. Often, you will want to ask if the script should go one way or another, or go back and re-execute a particular piece of code. That is the purpose of control structures, which include if/else statements; `while`, `do-while`, `for` statements; and `switch` statements.

`if/else` Statements

if/else statements are the primary decision-making construct in PHP. They allow you to specify that `if` some expression is TRUE, then a group of statements will be executed, `else` a different group of statements will be executed. It takes this form:

```
if (conditional expression) {
   statements executed if TRUE;
   }
else   {
   statements executed if FALSE;
   }
```

The `else` group of statements is optional and is needed only if you want to do something other than continue with the script if the conditional expression is FALSE. Also, you can nest if/else statements using `elseif`, like this:

```
if (conditional expression) {
   statements executed if TRUE;
   }
elseif (second conditional expression) {
   statements executed if second conditional is TRUE;
   }
else {
   statements executed if second conditional is FALSE;
   }
```

In all cases, the conditional expression must result in a Boolean TRUE or FALSE (1 or 0). If a variable simply exists, that is, it has been defined as containing something other than NULL, FALSE, or 0, then it is TRUE.

Many conditional expressions are comparisons that test if two elements are equal, greater than, or less than. Remember that when you test for equality in PHP, you must use a double equal sign (==), not a single one, which means assignment.

Listing 6-1 shows several examples of if/else statements, the results of which are shown next. A number of examples will be shown in the following chapters.

Listing 6-1	if/else Statements

```html
<html>
   <head>
      <title>Listing 6-1</title>
   </head>
   <body>
      <h1>If/Else Examples</h1>
      <?php
         if ($a){  //Tests if $a has been defined
             and is not FALSE or 0
             echo "True", "<br />";
         }
```

```
        else {
            echo "False", "<br />";
        }
        $a = "Something";
        if ($a) {
            echo "True", "<br />";
        }
        else {
            echo "False", "<br />";
        }
        $state = "CA";
        if ($state == "WA" ) {
            echo "Pacific Northwest", "<br />";
        }
        elseif ($state == "OR") {
            echo "Pacific Northwest", "<br />";
        }
        else {
            echo "Somewhere Else", "<br />";
        }
    echo $b ? "True" : "False";
    ?>
  </body>
</html>
```

Ternary Operator

A shorthand method of doing if/else decision making in PHP scripts uses the ternary operator (? :), where ? replaces the if test and follows the conditional expression, and the : replaces else. The following statement produces the same results as the if statement that follows it:

```
echo $a ? "True" : "False", "<br />";
if ($a) {
    echo "True", "<br />";
    }
else {
    echo "False", "<br />";
    }
```

Joining several if statements, as you would with elseif, is not recommended with the ternary operator since PHP's behavior is not defined.

TIP

Use parentheses if you want to use multiple ternary operators.

`while` and `do-while` Statements

The `while` and `do-while` statements are looping constructs that allow you to repeatedly execute a piece of code until a conditional expression is no longer TRUE. The `while` statement is the foundation of this set of statements and takes one of the following forms:

```
while (conditional expression) {
    statements executed while TRUE;
    }

while (conditional expression) :
    statements executed while TRUE;
    endwhile;
```

The `do-while` statement is similar to the `while` statement, except that the conditional expression is at the end of the statement instead of the beginning. The `do-while` statement takes this form:

```
do {
    statements executed while TRUE;
    }
while (conditional expression);
```

The most common conditional expression is to compare a counter with some end value. In other words, to initialize a counter and then to loop though some statements, incrementing the counter with each loop, until the counter exceeds the end value. Listing 6-2 shows examples of this for both `while` and `do-while` using the array function `chr()`, which returns a character based on its number in the standard set of characters, with the results shown next. You can see that in this case there is no difference between `while` and `do-while`.

NOTE

Code in `do-while` is guaranteed to execute at least once, since the condition isn't checked until after the first execution. A `while` statement may not ever execute if the condition immediately evaluates to false.

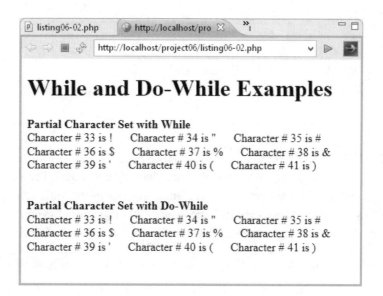

Listing 6-2   `while` and `do-while` Examples

```
<html>
   <head>
      <title>Listing 6-2</title>
   </head>
   <body>
      <h1>While and Do-While Examples</h1>
      <?php
         echo "<b>Partial Character Set with While</b><br />";
         $i = 33;
         while ($i <= 41) {
            echo "Character # ", $i , " is ", chr($i);
            echo "      Character # ", $i + 1 ,
               " is ", chr($i + 1);
            echo "      Character # ", $i + 2 ,
               " is ", chr($i + 2), "<br />";
            $i = $i + 3;
         }
         echo "<br /> <br /> <b>Partial Character Set with
            Do-While</b><br />";
         $i = 33;
         do {
            echo "Character # ", $i , " is ", chr($i);
            echo "      Character # ", $i + 1 ,
               " is ", chr($i + 1);
            echo "      Character # ", $i + 2 ,
```

```
                    " is ", chr($i + 2), "<br />";
              $i = $i + 3;
          }
          while ($i <= 41);
      ?>
   </body>
</html>
```

`for` and `foreach` Statements

The `for` and `foreach` statements are additional looping constructs. The `for` statement, which is similar to its counterpart in other languages, places the initialization of the counter, its conditional limit, and its incrementing all in a series of expressions immediately following the `for`. The `for` statement can take one of the following forms:

```
for (initializing expression; conditional expression; incrementing expression)
    {
    statements executed while TRUE;
    }
for (initializing expression; conditional expression; incrementing expression):
    statements executed while TRUE;
endfor;
```

In its basic form, the `for` expression might be `for ($i = 1; $i <= 5; $i++)`, where `$i++` increments `$i` after it is used. If any of these expressions are handled elsewhere in the script, they can be left blank in the `for` expression, which at its minimum is `for ( ; ; )`.

CAUTION
If the conditional expression never evaluates to true, the loop will never end.

The `foreach` statement is used to iterate through arrays and objects and cannot be used on any other type of variable. It can display the value of each element in an array, or alternatively, it can display the key and the value of each element in an array. Therefore, it has one of the two following forms:

```
foreach ($array as $value) {
    statements executed for each element;
    }

foreach ($array as $key => $value) {
    statements executed for each element;
    }
```

When you first begin to execute a `foreach` statement, the array pointer is automatically reset to the first element in the array. When you end the execution of a `foreach` statement, the array pointer remains at the last element, whose value remains contained by `$value`. You can use `unset($value)` to remove it, and use `reset($array)` to reset the array pointer.

Listing 6-3 shows examples of both `for` and `foreach` statements, with the results shown next. The `for` statement can be used in a manner very similar to `while`. The `foreach` statement makes the display of the `count_chars` array function much easier to read (compare with Listing 5-8).

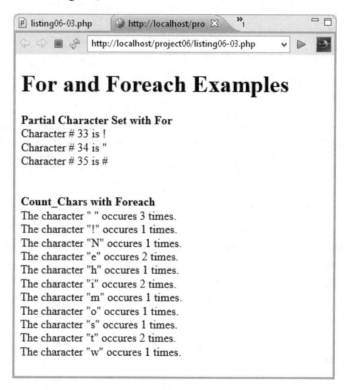

Listing 6-3   `for` and `foreach` Examples

```html
<html>
    <head>
        <title>Listing 6-3</title>
    </head>
    <body>
        <h1>For and Foreach Examples</h1>
        <?php
            echo "<b>Partial Character Set with For</b><br />";
            for ($i = 33; $i <= 35; $i++) {
```

```
        echo "Character # ", $i , " is ", chr($i), "<br />";
    }
    echo "<br /> <br /> <b>Count_Chars with Foreach</b><br />";
    $textString = "Now is the time!";
    $textArray = count_chars($textString, 1);
    foreach ($textArray as $key => $val) {
        echo "The character \"", chr($key) , "\" occurs ",
            $val, " times. <br />";
    }
    ?>
    </body>
</html>
```

TIP

You can exit `for` and `while` loops in two special ways. The first is to exit the current iteration without completing it and continue looping with the next iteration using the keyword `continue`. The second is to stop all looping and go on to the statement after the loop using the keyword `break`.

switch Statements

The `switch` statement is similar to a series of `if/elseif` statements. The `switch` statement is used where you want to compare a single variable to a number of different values and do something different depending on the value. Three additional keywords are used with `switch: case, break,` and `default`, taking this form:

```
switch ($avariable) {
    case 1:
        statements executed when TRUE;
        break;
    case 2:
        statements executed when TRUE;
        break;
    case 3:
        statements executed when TRUE;
        break;
    default:
        statements executed when all are FALSE;
}
```

Each `case` expression in the `switch` statement compares the `switch` variable with the `case` value, which can be a string; if it is equal, the statements following the `case` expression are executed, and then the `break` expression sends the script's flow to the first statement after the `switch`'s closing curly brace. If none of the `case` expressions is successful, the statements following the `default` expression are executed, and the script's flow exits the `switch` statement. Listing 6-4 demonstrates how this works using the random number generator function `rand()`, which provides these results:

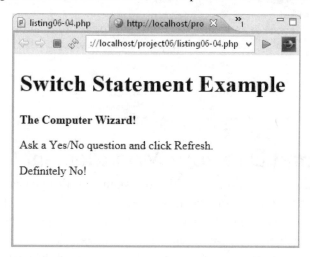

Listing 6-4   `switch` Statement Example

```
<html>
   <head>
      <title>Listing 6-4</title>
   </head>
   <body>
      <h1>Switch Statement Example</h1>
      <p><b>The Computer Wizard!</b></p>
      <p>Ask a Yes/No question and click Refresh.</p>
      <?php
         $randNum = rand(1,5);
         switch ($randNum) {
         case 1:
            echo "Definitely Yes!";
            break;
         case 2:
            echo "Probably Yes!";
            break;
         case 3:
            echo "Definitely Maybe!";
            break;
         case 4:
            echo "Probably No!";
```

```
        break;
    case 5:
        echo "Definitely No!";
        break;
    default:
        echo $randNum, "<br />"; //Display the number
        echo "Computer Malfunction, Try Again";
    }
?>
</body>
</html>
```

PHP File and Directory Management

One of the major benefits of server-side programming is that you can read and write information on the server's storage devices. PHP has an extensive set of functions that let you not only read and write files, but also change file attributes; copy, move, and delete files; work with directories; and much more. In this section we'll discuss and briefly demonstrate some of the more important file functions. In the next chapter, I'll show how to create a user authentication system using the file commands.

Basic File Functions

The basic PHP file process has the following elements:

- Establish a file connection, or *file pointer* (also called a "handle"), between PHP and a file using the fopen() function.

- Write a data string to an opened file by using the fwrite() function.

- Read a certain number of bytes into a string from an opened file by using the fread() function.

- Terminate a file pointer with the fclose() function.

Table 6-1 provides more information about these basic file functions, and Listing 6-5 provides a brief demonstration of how these functions are used.

Function	Description	Explanation
`fclose()`	Terminates a file pointer	The only argument is the file pointer created with `fopen()`. Returns TRUE for a successful close and FALSE otherwise.
`fopen()`	Connects to a file and creates a file pointer	The required arguments are a string with the path and filename, and a string with the mode (see Table 6-2 for the list of modes). Returns a file pointer that can be used with other file functions or FALSE.
`fread()`	Reads a certain number of bytes into a string	The required arguments are the file pointer created with `fopen()` and the number of bytes to be read. Returns a string with data read or FALSE.
`fwrite()`	Writes a string to a file	The required arguments are the file pointer created with `fopen()` and the string to be written. Optionally, the number of bytes to be written can be added. Returns the number of bytes written or FALSE.
`rewind()`	Resets the file pointer to the beginning of the file	The only argument is the file pointer created with `fopen()`. Returns TRUE if successful, and FALSE otherwise.

Table 6-1   Basic File Functions

TIP
The standard name often used for the file pointer variable is `$fp`.

Mode	Explanation
a	Write only, starting at the end of the file or creating a new file, appending new information to what previously existed in the file.
a+	Write and read, starting at the end of the file or creating a new file, appending new information to what previously existed in the file.
r	Read only, from the beginning of the file.
r+	Read and write, from the beginning of the file.
w	Write only, after deleting any file contents or creating a new file.
w+	Write and read, after deleting any file contents or creating a new file.
x	Create a new file and write only, from the beginning of the file. Returns FALSE if the file exists.
x+	Create a new file and write and read, from the beginning of the file. Returns FALSE if the file exists.

Table 6-2   `fopen()` Modes

Figure 6-1 proves that the script in Listing 6-5 does work, providing this response online:

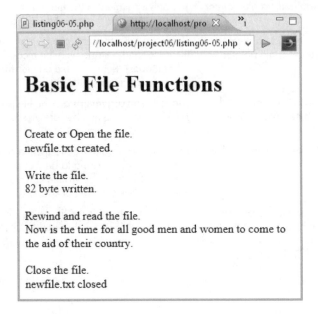

NOTE
You see the multiple lines in the file shown in Figure 6-1 only if you run the script multiple times. The a+ parameter of fopen allows this to happen.

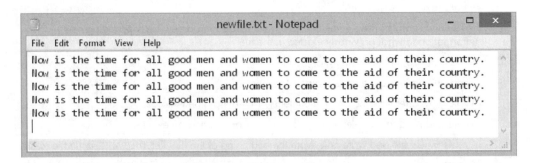

Figure 6-1 Placing \r\n (carriage return, linefeed) at the end of each line causes the file to display as separate lines instead of one continuous string of text. It also can be used to read a line at a time.

Listing 6-5   Basic File Functions

```html
<html>
    <head>
        <title>Listing 6-5</title>
    </head>
    <body>
        <h1>Basic File Functions</h1>
        <?php
            echo "<br />", "Create or Open the file.", "<br />";
                $fp = fopen("newfile.txt", "a+");
                if ($fp){
                    echo "newfile.txt created.", "<br />";
                }
                else {
                    echo "newfile.txt cannot be opened.", "<br />";
                }
            echo "<br />", "Write the file.", "<br />";
                $bytes = fwrite ($fp, "Now is the time for all good men
                and women to come to the aid of their country. \r\n");
                if ($bytes){
                    echo $bytes, " byte written.", "<br />";
                }
                else {
                    echo "File not written.", "<br />";
                }
            echo "<br />", "Rewind and read the file.", "<br />";
                rewind($fp);
                $data = fread ($fp, $bytes);
                if ($data){
                    echo $data, "<br />";
                }
                else {
                    echo "File not read.", "<br />";
                }
            echo "<br />", "Close the file.", "<br />";
                if (fclose ($fp)) {
                    echo "newfile.txt closed", "<br />";
                }
                else {
                    echo "newfile.txt not closed.", "<br />";
                }
        ?>
    </body>
</html>
```

TIP

As your scripts get longer, it becomes very tempting to close up your code, such as putting if statements on one line and not indenting. The problem with that is the code becomes harder to visually check and therefore is prone to problems.

Additional File Functions

Although fread() and fwrite() are very functional, as you've seen, PHP provides a number of other ways to read and write data on a server's storage devices. Both fread() and fwrite() are aimed at reading or writing parts of a file to or from strings. PHP can also read to an array, read a character at a time, read a line at a time, and move around within a file using the functions described in Table 6-3, which are demonstrated in Listing 6-6, the results of which are shown in Figure 6-2.

Function	Description	Explanation
feof()	Determines if the pointer is at end of file (EOF)	The only argument is the file pointer created with fopen(). Returns TRUE if the EOF is reached and FALSE otherwise.
fgetc()	Reads a single character from an open file	The only argument is the file pointer created with fopen(). Returns a string with the character read or FALSE if the EOF is reached.
fgets()	Reads a line designated by \n from an open file	The required argument is the file pointer created with fopen() and, optionally, the number of bytes to be read. Returns a string with data read or FALSE.
file()	Reads an entire file into an array, where each element is a line designated by \n	The required argument is a string with the path and filename. The default is to read as binary data, but you can change that with the FILE_TEXT constant as the second argument.
filesize()	Determines the size of a file	The only argument is a string with the path and filename. Returns the file size in bytes or FALSE.
fseek()	Moves the file pointer of an open file	The required arguments are the file pointer created with fopen() and the number of bytes to move the pointer. The default is to move from the beginning of the file, but adding the SEEK_CUR constant as the third argument adds the number of bytes to the current position, while using the SEEK_END constant as the third argument *adds* the bytes to the EOF. Returns a 0 for success; otherwise, a −1.
ftell()	Provides the current position of the file pointer of an open file	The only argument is the file pointer created with fopen(). Returns the number of bytes from the beginning of the file as an integer, or FALSE.

Table 6-3 Additional File Functions

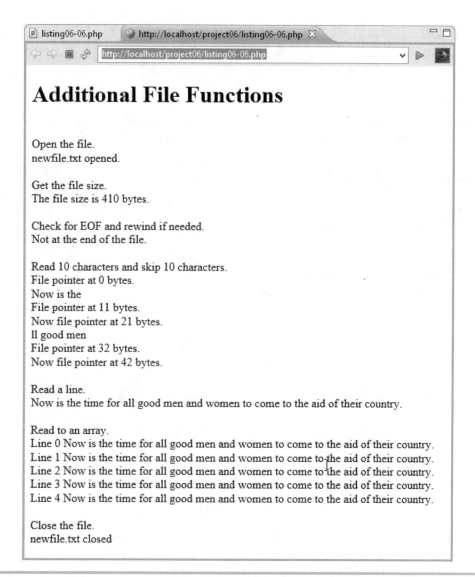

Figure 6-2 PHP gives you a number of ways to read and roam about a file.

TIP

You can read an entire file using the `filesize()` function, as you can see in the following code snippet:

```
$filename = "newfile.txt";
$fp = fopen($filename, "r");
$wholefile = fread($fp, filesize($filename));
```

CAUTION

`fseek()` can move the file pointer beyond the end of a file, so you may want to test for that and use a negative number of bytes with the SEEK_END constant.

NOTE

Listing 6-6 uses the newfile.txt file created with Listing 6-5 after that script has been run five times, creating five lines, each 82 characters or bytes long, for a total of 410 bytes.

Listing 6-6   Additional File Functions

```php
<html>
   <head>
      <title>Listing 6-6</title>
   </head>
   <body>
      <h1>Additional File Functions</h1>
      <?php
        $file = "newfile.txt";           echo "<br />", "Open the file.",
           "<br />";
           $fp = fopen($file, "r");
           if ($fp){
               echo "newfile.txt opened.", "<br />";
           }
           else {
               echo "newfile.txt cannot be opened.", "<br />";
           }
        echo "<br />", "Get the file size.", "<br />";
           $bytes = filesize ($file);
           if ($bytes){
               echo "The file size is ", $bytes, " bytes.", "<br />";
           }
           else {
               echo "File size not available.", "<br />";
           }
        echo "<br />", "Check for EOF and rewind if needed.", "<br />";
           if (feof($fp)){
               rewind($fp);
               echo "Returned to the beginning of the file.", "<br />";
           }
           else {
               echo "Not at the end of the file.", "<br />";
           }
        echo "<br />", "Read 10 characters and skip 10 characters.",
           "<br />";
           echo "File pointer at  ", ftell($fp), " bytes.", "<br />";
```

```php
        while (ftell($fp) < 42) {
            while ($i < 11) {
                $char = fgetc ($fp);
                echo $char ;
                $i++ ;
            }
            $i = 0;
            echo "<br />";
            echo  "File pointer at  ", ftell($fp), " bytes.", "<br />";
            fseek($fp, 10, SEEK_CUR);
            echo "Now file pointer at ", ftell($fp), " bytes.", "<br />";
        }
    echo "<br />", "Read a line.", "<br />";
        rewind($fp);
        $data = fgets ($fp);
        if ($data){
            echo $data, "<br />";
        }
        else {
            echo "File not read.", "<br />";
        }
    echo "<br />", "Read to an array.", "<br />";
        $textArray = file($file);
        foreach ($textArray as $line => $text) {
            echo "Line ", $line, " ", $text, "<br />";
        }
    echo "<br />", "Close the file.", "<br />";
        if (fclose ($fp)) {
            echo "newfile.txt closed", "<br />";
        }
        else {
            echo "newfile.txt not closed.", "<br />";
        }
    ?>
  </body>
</html>
```

TIP

As Listing 6-6 shows, while you are debugging a script, it is very helpful to put in a number of echoes to display what is happening and to comment out specific sections until you isolate a problem. In the final version of the script, the echoes can become comments.

PHP file functions, which number many more than mentioned in this and the previous section, provide a comprehensive ability to work with files. To see the full set of file functions, see php.net/manual/en/ref.filesystem.php.

Cookies and Session and Server Variables

Web pages use variables to temporarily store information while that page is being used. It is likely, though, that you will want to collect and store information from the user, from the script being run, and from the server and to use that information on other pages during the current session, or across multiple sessions. In this section, we'll discuss creating and using session variables, cookies, and server variables to perform that function of collecting and storing. Start by comparing the three objects in Table 6-4.

Session variables, cookies, and server variables are all PHP predefined, or built-in, variables called *superglobals* because they are available throughout a website on as many pages as are contained in the domain. The superglobals used here are $_SESSION, $_COOKIE, and $_SERVER. Their use will be explained in the following sections. All the superglobals discussed in this book have the $_ leading characters and here, as well as in many other reference sources, are displayed in all capital letters, although that is not a requirement. You'll see other superglobals later in this book.

Superglobals are *associative arrays,* arrays whose key, or array index, is a string instead of an integer. Generally, the *key* is an element name, while the *value* is the element value. For example: $_SESSION["name"] = $name; where ["name"] is the *key* for the array element and the contents of $name is its *value*. Some superglobal arrays, such as $_SESSION and $_COOKIE, allow you to define the keys, while others, such as $_SERVER, have predefined keys. You will see examples of these in the sections that follow.

TIP

When you are entering the string for an associative array's key, you can do it without the quotes. However, this is a bad practice because PHP considers the string with quotes to be a different entity than the string without quotes, so it is very easy to confuse the two, creating an error in the script that is hard to find.

Object	Created With	Accessed With	Stored On	Duration
Session variable	$_SESSION	$_SESSION	Server	Session or less
Cookie	setcookie()	$_COOKIE	Client	Until expires
Server variable	Automatically	$_SERVER	Server	Unlimited

Table 6-4 Comparison of External Variables

Session Variables

Session variables allow you to collect and use information across multiple pages in a website during a single *session,* or encounter between a user and a website. To define a session, you must start it with the `session_start()` function, which must precede all other code sent to the client, including <html> and <head>. You can then store information in the `$_SESSION` array. If you go to another page and again start it with the `session_start()` function, you can retrieve the information in the `$_SESSION` array. Listing 6-7a and Listing 6-7b demonstrate this with the results shown here:

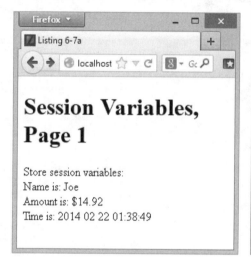
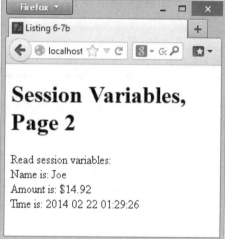

TIP

Testing session variables as described in "Session Variables" should be done with an independent browser and not the browser within Zend Studio. Also, using *http://localhost/* with some Apache servers may not work, although it does with the latest Zend Server. If you have a problem, use http://127.0.0.1/, and it should be fine.

Listing 6-7a   Creating a Session Variable

```php
<?php
   session_start()
?>
<!DOCTYPE html>
<html>
   <head>
      <title>Listing 6-7a</title>
   </head>
```

```
<body>
    <h1>Session Variables, Page 1</h1>
    <?php
        $name = "Joe";
        $amount = "$14.92";
        echo "Store session variables:", "<br />";
            $_SESSION["name"]   = $name;
            $_SESSION["amount"] = $amount;
            $_SESSION["time"]   = time();
        echo "Name is: ", $_SESSION["name"], "<br />";
        echo "Amount is: ", $_SESSION["amount"], "<br />";
        echo "Time is: ", date('Y m d H:i:s', $_SESSION["time"]),
"<br />";
        ?>
    </body>
</html>
```

Listing 6-7b   Using a Session Variable

```
<?php
    session_start()
?>
<!DOCTYPE html>
<html>
    <head>
        <title>Listing 6-7b</title>
    </head>
    <body>
        <h1>Session Variables, Page 2</h1>
        <?php
            echo "Read session variables:", "<br />";
            echo "Name is: ", $_SESSION["name"], "<br />";
            echo "Amount is: ", $_SESSION["amount"], "<br />";
            echo "Time is: ", date('Y m d H:i:s', $_SESSION["time"]),
"<br />";
        ?>
    </body>
</html>
```

NOTE

Session variables have a limited life, which is set by the `session.cache_expire` value in the pnp.ini file on the server. Depending on the use, this can be set from a few minutes to a number of hours in increments of a minute. The default is 180 minutes, or three hours.

Cookies

Cookies store information on client computers. Once a cookie has been stored, or *set*, the same site (really *domain*) that created it will automatically receive that information the next time it is connected to the client. This allows the site to recognize a returning client. Cookies are created with the setcookie() function and accessed with the $_COOKIE superglobal array.

NOTE
Some people do not allow cookies to be stored on their computer due to security concerns.

Using setcookie()

You create and store a cookie using the setcookie() function, which must be placed before any other output in your script, including the <html> and <head> tags. It has the following form:

```
setcookie(name [,value [,expire [,path [,domain [,secure
    [,httponly]]]]]])
```

The name argument is the only one required. The rest are optional and may be left blank if none to the right are present. If you wish to skip an argument and enter one to the right, fill in with the empty string (""), except for $expire, which requires (0). The meaning of the arguments is as follows:

- **name** is the name of the cookie and can be any label using upper- and lowercase letters, numbers, and the underscore.

- **value** is the information you want stored with the cookie, as a string.

- **expire** is the time in seconds since 1/1/1970 that you want the cookie to expire. You can create this with the time() function, which will give you the number of seconds since 1/1/1970 to the current moment, and then add the number of seconds you want the cookie active. For example, time()+(60*60*24*10) would let the cookie be active for ten days from the current time. The default is 0, which means that the cookie will expire at the end of the session.

- **path** is the path on the server where the cookie will be available. If the path is set to "/", the entire domain will have access to the cookie.

- **domain** is the domain where the cookie will be available. If you want the cookie available to all subdomains, precede the domain with a period. For example, .*somedomain*.com.

- **secure**, if set to TRUE, says that the cookie should be sent only over a secure connection such as HTTPS. The default is FALSE.

- **httponly**, if set to TRUE, says the cookie should only be accessible with the HTTP protocol and not on the client via JavaScript. The default is FALSE.

The value argument can be anything that you can put in a string, such as a name or an amount. If you want to store several separate pieces of information in a cookie, you need to use several cookies to do that. From the standpoint of PHP and the server, though, you can think of a set of cookies sent from one site to one client as an array. On the client, they are stored as separate pieces of information, but in PHP, you can address them as elements of a single array. Listing 6-8, later in this chapter, will provide an example of this.

CAUTION
Cookies are viewable by spyware applications, so do not use cookies to store sensitive information like usernames, passwords, and account numbers.

Using $_COOKIE
After a cookie has been set, the next time the domain that set it reconnects with the client, the client will automatically return the cookie information to the server, and it will be stored in the $_COOKIE superglobal array. You must close the connection with the client in which you set the cookie and reopen the connection before $_COOKIE will contain the information.

Listing 6-8a demonstrates a website named "MatTech" storing a customer's first name, the date of her or his last order, and the type of merchandise purchased using cookies that don't expire for 90 days and that are available throughout the domain that set the cookies. Listing 6-8b demonstrates receiving and displaying the information, like this:

Listing 6-8a   Setting a Cookie

```php
<?php
    //Set cookies for name, date, and type of purchase
    $name = "Joe" ;
    $date = time() ;
    $type = "iPods" ;
    $expire = time()+(60*60*24*90);
    setcookie("MatTech[name]", $name, $expire, "/");
    setcookie("MatTech[date]", $date, $expire, "/");
    setcookie("MatTech[type]", $type, $expire, "/");
?>
<!DOCTYPE html>
<html>
    <head>
        <title>Listing 6-8a</title>
    </head>
    <body>
        <h1>Setting Cookies, Page 1</h1>
        <?php
            echo "Cookies set for:", "<br />";
            echo "Name: ", $name, "<br />";
            echo "Date: ", date('m d Y', $date), "<br />";
            echo "Type: ", $type, "<br />";
        ?>
    </body>
</html>
```

Listing 6-8b   Displaying a Cookie

```php
<html>
    <head>
        <title>Listing 6-8b</title>
    </head>
    <body>
        <h1>Displaying Cookies, Page 2</h1>
        <?php
            if (isset ($_COOKIE["MatTech"])) {  //Check if there
                echo "Hello ", $_COOKIE["MatTech"][name], "! <br />";
                echo "Thanks for your order on ", date('M d Y',
                    $_COOKIE["MatTech"][date]), ". <br />";
                echo "Check out our ", $_COOKIE["MatTech"][type], ". <br />";
            }
        ?>
    </body>
</html>
```

TIP

To delete, or unset, a cookie, set a new one with the same name, a value of `""`, and a date prior to the current date, such as `time()-3600`. If you set an array of cookies, you must delete them all. For the cookies set in Listings 6-8a and b, Listing 6-8c shows what is needed to delete them:

Listing 6-8c   Deleting a Cookie

```php
<?php
    //Delete cookies for name, date, and type of purchase
    $expire = time()-(60*60);
    setcookie("MatTech[name]", "", $expire, "/");
    setcookie("MatTech[date]", "", $expire, "/");
    setcookie("MatTech[type]", "", $expire, "/");
?>
```

Server Variables

Server variables provide information about the server, the software that is running on it, the current script that produced the request, and the client and its software. The server in communication with the client produces this information and stores it in the superglobal array $_SERVER. Each web server produces a slightly different set of elements in the array, which are defined by their associative keys. Listing 6-9 is a short script for displaying the $_SERVER array elements on your server. Figure 6-3 shows the server variables generated with the Apache server in Zend Server on my computer.

Listing 6-9   Server Variables Generator

```html
<html>
    <head>
        <title>Listing 6-9</title>
    </head>
    <body>
        <h1>Exploring Server Variables</h1>
        <?php
         foreach ($_SERVER as $key => $value) {
            echo "<b> $key   :   </b> $value ", "<br />";
         }
        ?>
    </body>
</html>
```

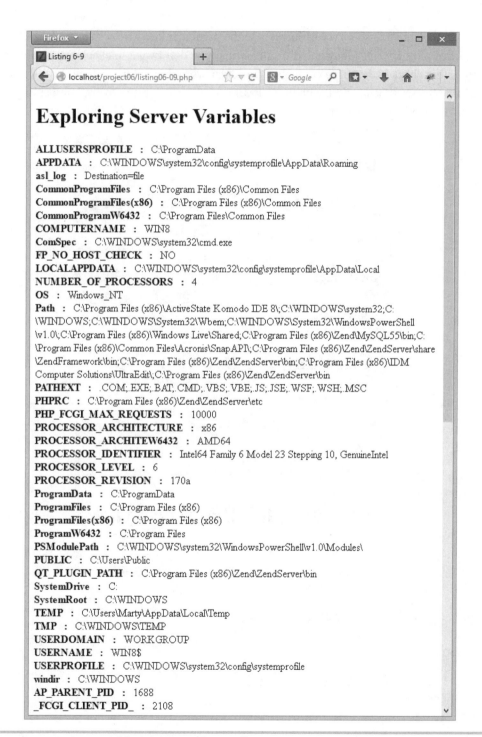

Figure 6-3 Server variables generated by Zend Server.

To look at and use server variables, use the particular key with $\$\_SERVER$. Since the value of most keys is a long and differing string, you don't want to check for equality, but rather check if the string contains a particular word. Listing 6-10 shows how to check which browser is being used, with the following results using, respectively, Internet Explorer, Firefox, and Google Chrome:

Listing 6-10   Checking for Browser Type

```html
<html>
   <head>
      <title>Listing 6-10</title>
   </head>
```

```
<body>
    <h1>Checking for Browser Type</h1>
    <?php
     if(strpos($_SERVER[HTTP_USER_AGENT], "MSIE")) {
         echo "The browser is Internet Explorer. <br />";
     }
     elseif(strpos($_SERVER[HTTP_USER_AGENT], "Trident")) {
         echo "The browser is Internet Explorer. <br />";
     }
     elseif(strpos($_SERVER[HTTP_USER_AGENT], "Firefox")) {
         echo "The browser is Firefox. <br />";
     }
     elseif(strpos($_SERVER[HTTP_USER_AGENT], "Chrome")) {
         echo "The browser is Chrome. <br />";
     }
     else {
         echo "A different browser is being used. <br />";
     }
    ?>
  </body>
</html>
```

NOTE

With Internet Explorer version 9 and before, you could successfully test for "MSIE," but with version 10 and on, that has disappeared and has been replaced with "Trident," so here, that is what I'm testing for.

The `strpos()` function used in Listing 6-10 is both powerful and interesting. Its stated purpose is to find the position of the first occurrence of one string in another string. It is most frequently used, though, to simply find if one string exists in another, as is done in Listing 6-10. The PHP Manual talks of this as finding a "needle in the haystack." There is one catch to using the `strpos()` function if what you are checking for is at the very beginning of the string. For example, if you use `if strpos("Christie is my name", "Christie")` it would return 0, or FALSE, since the position is 0. To correct for this, you would need to use

`if (strpos("Christie is my name", "Christie") === FALSE).`

TIP

To find the complete set of server variables and their meaning, go to php.net/manual/en/reserved.variables.server.php.

Try This 6-1 Create a PHP Script that Writes a File

Create a PHP script that creates and writes a file every four seconds for ten seconds (ten seconds does not sound like very long, but for a computer cycling in thousandths of a second, it is a long time—also for you while you are waiting for it) using `while` or `for` and `if/else` statements to control the timing. Use a `switch` statement to write different information each time the file is written. Create and store a cookie with the filename. Create a second script that reads and displays the cookie and then uses the filename in the cookie to read and display the contents of the file you wrote.

Chapter 6 Self-Test

The following questions are intended to help reinforce your comprehension of the concepts covered in this chapter. The answers can be found in the accompanying online Appendix A, "Answers to the Self-Tests."

1. What is the purpose of control structures in a script?

2. What do `if/else` statements do?

3. `else` statements are optional, true or false?

4. To test if a statement is TRUE or FALSE, you must test for the words "TRUE" or "FALSE," true or false?

5. What is the ternary operator and how is it used?

6. How do `while` and `do-while` differ?

7. What is `for` used for and what is the basic form of its expression?

8. How is `foreach` used?

9. How is the `switch` statement used?

10. PHP's file functions allow you to read and write files on the client, true or false?

11. What does `fopen()` do?

12. How is the mode string used in `fopen()`?

13. What are cookies and how are they used?

14. What are session variables and how are they used?

15. What are server variables and how are they used?

16. What does the `strpos()` function do?

Chapter 7

PHP Arrays and Forms

Key Skills & Concepts

- Creating Arrays

- Working with Arrays

- Looping Through Arrays

- Sorting Arrays

- Navigating in Arrays

- Converting Arrays To and From Strings

- Joining and Splitting Arrays

- Comparing Arrays

- Handling Multidimensional Arrays

- Create a Form in HTML

- Add JavaScript to a Form

- Accepting and Filing Form Data in PHP

This chapter displays the power of PHP as a full-fledged programming language. In Chapters 5 and 6, I briefly introduced and discussed arrays, but these powerful elements are the backbone of PHP, and there is a lot more we need to discuss about them. To these, we'll add a discussion of forms and form handling.

Using Arrays

Arrays are a means of grouping and handling several values with a single entity. Arrays are common in programming languages, but PHP provides an uncommon number of tools to make extensive use of arrays. The values in arrays are generally variables, either strings or numbers, but they can also be constants. Arrays have a single name that stores multiple values using an index, or *key,* to identify individual values. The key can be either an integer or a unique string.

Creating Arrays

Arrays can be created either through assignment, as you do a variable, or through the `array()` function, as you saw in Chapter 5. For example, here are four methods of creating a four-element array of cars:

- Method 1: individual integer assignment

```
$cars[0] = "Ford";
$cars[1] = "Chevy";
$cars[2] = "Honda";
$cars[3] = "BMW";
```

- Method 2: `array()` function integer assignment

```
$cars = array(0 => "Ford", 1 => "Chevy", 2 => "Honda", 3 => "BMW");
```

- Method 3: `array()` function-implied integer assignment

```
$cars = array ("Ford", "Chevy", "Honda", "BMW");
```

- Method 4: `array()` function-associative assignment

```
$cars = array ("Ed" => "Ford", "Sue" => "Chevy", "Kate" => "Honda", "Bob" => "BMW");
```

The first three methods produce the exact same arrays. In the third method, the numeric key is implied with the default start at 0. You can start at 1 or any other number by using the array operator =>. For example, Listing 7-1 produces the array shown next. The fourth method associates a string key with a value, which works just as well as an integer, and may be more meaningful.

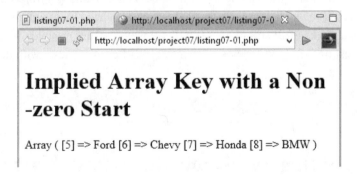

Listing 7-1   Implied Array Key with a Non-zero Start

```
<html>
    <head>
        <title>Listing 7-1</title>
    </head>
    <body>
        <h1>Implied Array Key with a Non-zero Start</h1>
        <?php
            $cars = array(
                5 => "Ford", "Chevy", "Honda", "BMW"
                );
            print_r($cars);
        ?>
    </body>
</html>
```

Working with Arrays

Once you have arrays, PHP provides a number of ways to change and work with them, including adding and removing values, using loops, sorting, navigating in them, converting to and from strings, comparing, and using array operators. There are also many more array functions than discussed in Chapter 5, and you can have multidimensional arrays.

PHP allows you to add, replace, and delete values within an array. You can add a value to an existing array either with a specific key or let PHP use the next implied numeric key. You replace a value by assigning the new value to an existing key, replacing the current value assigned to that key. An existing value can be deleted by assigning nothing ("") to the key, but the key will still exist. We will see ways to fully remove the item later in this chapter. Listing 7-2 shows one or more instances of each of these, with the results shown next.

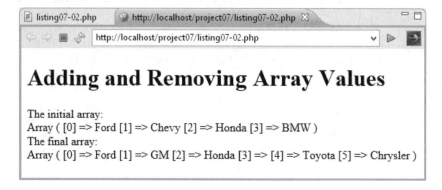

Listing 7-2	Adding and Removing Array Values

```html
<html>
    <head>
        <title>Listing 7-2</title>
    </head>
    <body>
        <h1>Adding and Removing Array Values</h1>
        <?php
            $cars = array(
                "Ford", "Chevy", "Honda", "BMW"
                );o
            echo "The initial array: <br />" ;
            print_r($cars);
            //Add a fifth value
            $cars[4] = "Toyota" ;
            //Add a sixth value with an implied key
            $cars[] ="Chrysler" ;
            //Replace the second value
            $cars[1] = "GM" ;
            //Delete the fourth value
            $cars[3] = "" ;
            echo "<br /> The final array: <br />" ;
            print_r($cars);
            ?>
    </body>
</html>
```

Looping Through Arrays

As you have seen, the `print_r()` function automatically loops through an array and displays the key=>value pairs in an array. You can also do this using **for**, **while**, and **foreach** loops.

Using **foreach**

foreach is structured for use with arrays and uses the simple form foreach ($arrayname **as** $valuename) ; to successively place each of the values in $arrayname into $valuename, as shown in Listing 7-3 with an HTML ordered (numbered) list and displayed next (notice that even though the default numeric keys in an array start with 0, HTML ordered list starts at 1).

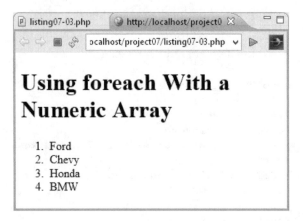

Listing 7-3   Using **foreach** with a Numeric Array

```
<!DOCTYPE html>
<html>
    <head>
        <title>Listing 7-3</title>
    </head>
    <body>
        <h1>Using foreach With a Numeric Array</h1>
        <ol>
        <?php
            $cars = array (
                "Ford", "Chevy", "Honda", "BMW"
                );
                foreach ($cars as $item) {
                    echo "<li>$item" ;
                }
        ?>
        </ol>
    </body>
</html>
```

You can also use `foreach` with an associative array using the form `foreach ($arrayname as $keyname => $valuename) ;` as shown in Listing 7-4 with an HTML unordered (bulleted) list and displayed next.

Listing 7-4   Using `foreach` with an Associative Array

```
<!DOCTYPE html>
<html>
    <head>
        <title>Listing 7-4</title>
    </head>
    <body>
        <h1>Using foreach With an Associative Array</h1>
        <ul>
        <?php
            $cars = array (
                "Ed" => "Ford", "Sue" => "Chevy",
                    "Kate" => "Honda", "Bob" => "BMW"
                );
                foreach ($cars as $key => $item) {
                    echo "<li>$key has a $item" ;
                }
        ?>
        </ul>
    </body>
</html>
```

NOTE

In Listings 7-3 and 7-4, the HTML ordered and unordered lists are for illustrative purposes and are not required.

Using `for`

Using a `for` loop with an array can use the `count()` function or its alias `sizeof()`, which does exactly the same thing: returns the number of elements in an array, with `count()` preferred since it is the original PHP function. Listing 7-5 shows how a `for` loop is used with an array and an HTML ordered list to produce these results:

NOTE

The technique demonstrated in Listing 7-5 with the `for` loop and the `count()` function will not work with associative arrays or with numeric arrays that begin with a number other than 0.

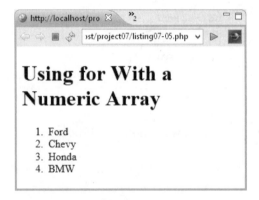

Listing 7-5   Using `for` with a Numeric Array

```php
<!DOCTYPE html>
<html>
    <head>
        <title>Listing 7-5</title>
    </head>
    <body>
        <h1>Using for With a Numeric Array</h1>
        <ol>
        <?php
            $cars = array (
                "Ford", "Chevy", "Honda", "BMW"
                );
                for ($i = 0; $i < count($cars); $i++) {
                    echo "<li>$cars[$i]" ;
                }
        ?>
        </ol>
    </body>
</html>
```

Using `while`

A `while` loop can use a construct very similar to a `for` loop, with the initialization of the index variable just before the `while` and its incrementing within the loop. You can simplify this using the `list()` function, which assigns variables as they are in an array, and the `each()` function, which returns the current `key => value` pair and advances the array pointer, as you see in Listing 7-6 with the results displayed next.

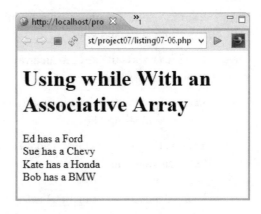

Listing 7-6   Using `while` with an Associative Array

```
<!DOCTYPE html>
<html>
    <head>
        <title>Listing 7-6</title>
    </head>
    <body>
        <h1>Using while With an Associative Array</h1>
        <?php
            $cars = array (
                "Ed" => "Ford", "Sue" => "Chevy",
                    "Kate" => "Honda", "Bob" => "BMW"
                );
                while (list($key, $item) = each($cars)) {
                    echo "$key has a $item <br />" ;
                }
        ?>
    </body>
</html>
```

Sorting Arrays

PHP provides a number of array sorting functions, including

- **sort()** sorts the values in an array in ascending order and reassigns the keys as the default integers 0–9.

- **rsort()** sorts the values in an array in reverse order and reassigns the keys as the default integers 0–9.

- **ksort()** sorts the keys in an array in ascending order and maintains the association between values and keys.

- **krsort()** sorts the keys in an array in reverse order and maintains the association between values and keys.

- **asort()** sorts the values in an array in ascending order and maintains the association between values and keys.

- **arsort()** sorts the values in an array in reverse order and maintains the association between values and keys.

Using the array sort functions is a straightforward process, as you can see in Listing 7-7 with the results shown next:

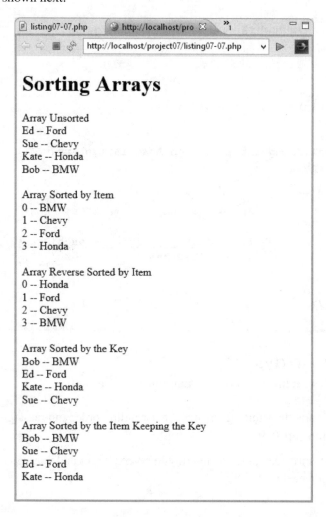

Listing 7-7   Sorting Arrays

```php
<!DOCTYPE html>
<html>
    <head>
        <title>Listing 7-7</title>
    </head>
    <body>
        <h1>Sorting Arrays</h1>
        <?php
            $cars = array (
                "Ed" => "Ford", "Sue" => "Chevy",
                    "Kate" => "Honda", "Bob" => "BMW"
                );
            echo "Array Unsorted <br />" ;
            foreach ($cars as $key => $item) {
                echo "$key -- $item <br />" ;
            }
        sort($cars);
            echo "<br /> Array Sorted by Item <br />" ;
            foreach ($cars as $key => $item) {
                echo "$key -- $item <br />" ;
            }
        rsort($cars);
            echo "<br /> Array Reverse Sorted by Item <br />" ;
            foreach ($cars as $key => $item) {
                echo "$key -- $item <br />" ;
            }
        $cars = array (
            "Ed" => "Ford", "Sue" => "Chevy",
                "Kate" => "Honda", "Bob" => "BMW"
                );
        ksort($cars);
            echo "<br /> Array Sorted by the Key <br />" ;
            foreach ($cars as $key => $item) {
                echo "$key -- $item <br />" ;
            }
        asort($cars);
            echo "<br /> Array Sorted by the Item Keeping
                the Key <br />" ;
            foreach ($cars as $key => $item) {
                echo "$key -- $item <br />" ;
            }
            ?>
    </body>
</html>
```

Navigating in Arrays

In addition to looping, PHP provides several functions to allow you to move one element at a time through an array. These make use of an internal pointer that is initially set at the start of the session at the first element in the array. You can move this pointer within the array and reset it to the first element with these functions:

- `current()` returns the value currently at the pointer in an array and does not move the pointer.

- `key()` returns the key currently at the pointer in an array and does not move the pointer.

- `next()` moves the pointer one element forward in an array and returns the value.

- `prev()` moves the pointer one element back in an array and returns the value.

- `end()` moves the pointer to the last element in an array and returns the value.

- `reset()` moves the pointer to the first element in an array and returns the value.

Listing 7-8 demonstrates moving within an array with the results shown next.

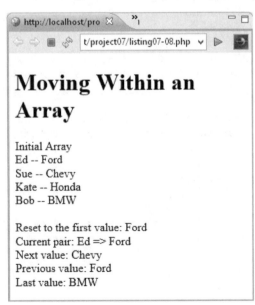

Listing 7-8   Moving Within an Array

```
<!DOCTYPE html>
<html>
    <head>
        <title>Listing 7-8</title>
    </head>
    <body>
        <h1>Moving Within an Array</h1>
        <?php
            $cars = array (
                "Ed" => "Ford", "Sue" => "Chevy",
                    "Kate" => "Honda", "Bob" => "BMW"
                );
                echo "Initial Array <br />" ;
                foreach ($cars as $key => $item) {
                    echo "$key -- $item <br />" ;
                }
                // Because foreach has moved the pointer
                  to the end, we must start with reset().
                echo "<br />Reset to the first value: ",
                    reset($cars), "<br />" ;
                echo "Current pair: ", key($cars), " => ",
                    current($cars), "<br />" ;
                echo "Next value: ", next($cars), "<br />" ;
                echo "Previous value: ", prev($cars), "<br />" ;
                echo "Last value: ", end($cars), "<br />" ;
        ?>
    </body>
</html>
```

TIP

If you try to move beyond the last element in an array, the function will return `false`.

Converting Arrays To and From Strings

PHP provides two functions, `implode()` and `explode()`, to convert an array to a string and a string to an array, as shown in Listing 7-9 with the results shown next. Both `implode()` and `explode()` can have at least two parameters, a delimiter and either an array to be broken into a string in the case of `implode()`, or a string to be converted into an array in the case of `explode()`. The delimiter is a string that separates the elements of either the input or output string. For example, the delimiter used in Listing 7-9 with both `implode()` and `explode()` is ", ", a comma followed by a space. These are placed between the elements of the array.

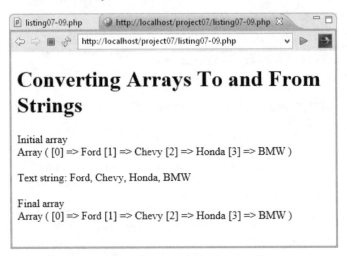

Listing 7-9   Converting Arrays To and From Strings

```
<!DOCTYPE html>
<html>
    <head>
        <title>Listing 7-9</title>
    </head>
    <body>
        <h1>Converting Arrays To and From Strings</h1>
        <?php
            $cars[0] = "Ford";
            $cars[1] = "Chevy";
            $cars[2] = "Honda";
            $cars[3] = "BMW";
            echo "Initial array <br />";
            print_r($cars);
            //Convert to a string
            $carlist = implode(", ", $cars) ;
            echo "<br /><br /> Text string:  ", $carlist ;
            //Convert back to an array
            $cars = explode(", ", $carlist) ;
            echo "<br /><br /> Final array <br />";
            print_r($cars);
            ?>
    </body>
</html>
```

Joining and Splitting Arrays

As you work with arrays, you will want to put arrays together and take them apart. PHP has a number of ways to do both of these.

Joining Arrays

PHP provides several functions and an array operator to join two or more arrays, as shown in Listing 7-10 with the results shown next.

- **Union**, `$a + $b`, joins two arrays based on their unique keys, keeping the original keys.

- **Merge**, `array_merge()`, joins two arrays of values and renumbers their keys if they are numeric.

- **Combine**, `array_combine()`, joins an array of keys with an array of values, which must be of the same length as the keys.

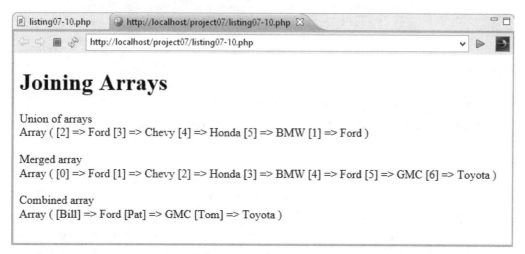

Listing 7-10   Joining Arrays

```
<!DOCTYPE html>
<html>
    <head>
        <title>Listing 7-10</title>
    </head>
    <body>
        <h1>Joining Arrays</h1>
```

```php
<?php
    $cars[2]  = "Ford";
    $cars[3]  = "Chevy";
    $cars[4]  = "Honda";
    $cars[5]  = "BMW";
    $trucks[1] = "Ford";
    $trucks[3] = "GMC";
    $trucks[4] = "Toyota";
    $owners [1] = "Bill";
    $owners [2] = "Pat";
    $owners [3] = "Tom";
    $vehicles = $cars + $trucks;
    echo "Union of arrays <br />";
    print_r($vehicles);
    $vehicles = array_merge($cars, $trucks);
    echo "<br /><br />Merged array <br />";
    print_r($vehicles);
    $vehicles = array_combine($owners, $trucks);
    echo "<br /><br />Combined array <br />";
    print_r($vehicles);
    ?>
    </body>
</html>
```

Splitting and Rearranging Arrays

PHP also gives you several functions to break up and rearrange arrays, as you can see in Listing 7-11 with the results shown next.

- **Slice, `array_slice()`**, removes a sequence of elements from an array based on an offset and optionally a length. If the offset is positive, the starting element is that number of elements from the beginning of the array. If the offset is negative, the starting element is that number of elements in from the end of the array. If the length is positive and less than the total number of elements in the array, then the slice will include the length number of elements. If the length is positive and greater than the number in the array, the slice will include the remaining elements in the array. If the length is negative, then the slice will stop that number of elements from the end of the array. By default, a new set of numeric keys will be created for the resulting array, but you can include the $preserve_keys variable set to TRUE to change that behavior. Said another way, you can pass an optional fourth parameter set to TRUE to change that behavior.

- **Chunk**, `array_chunk()`, divides an array into chunks of equal size based on a size parameter, except that the last chunk may be less and produces a multidimensional array with the results. By default, a new set of numeric keys will be created for the resulting arrays, but you can include the $preserve_keys variable set to TRUE to change that behavior.

- **Splice**, `array_splice()`, removes a sequence of elements based on offset and length parameters as in `array_slice()`, and provides for the insertion of an optional replacement array where the sequence was removed. Keys are replaced by a new set.

- **Flip**, `array_flip()`, exchanges keys and values in an array. If there are multiple occurrences of a value in the original array, only the last one will be used and the others will be lost.

Breaking Up Arrays

The initial array:
Array ([0] => Ford [1] => Chevy [2] => Honda [3] => BMW [4] => Toyota)

Slice out the middle three:
Array ([0] => Chevy [1] => Honda [2] => BMW)

Slice out the last two:
Array ([0] => BMW [1] => Toyota)

Divide into two car chunks:
Array ([0] => Array ([0] => Ford [1] => Chevy)
     [1] => Array ([0] => Honda [1] => BMW)
     [2] => Array ([0] => Toyota))

Splice in this array after removing the last two cars:
Array ([0] => Fiat [1] => Mazda)
Giving this result:
Array ([0] => Ford [1] => Chevy [2] => Honda [3] => Fiat [4] => Mazda)

Given this initial array:
Array ([Ed] => Ford [Sue] => Chevy [Kate] => Ford [Bob] => BMW)
Flipping it produces this result:
Array ([Ford] => Kate [Chevy] => Sue [BMW] => Bob)

Listing 7-11   Breaking Up Arrays

```php
<!DOCTYPE html>
<html>
    <head>
        <title>Listing 7-11</title>
    </head>
    <body>
        <h1>Breaking Up Arrays</h1>
        <?php
            $cars = array(
                "Ford", "Chevy", "Honda", "BMW", "Toyota"
                ) ;
            echo "The initial array: <br />" ;
            print_r($cars);
            echo "<br /><br />Slice out the middle three:<br />";
            $mid_cars = array_slice($cars, 1 , 3) ;
            print_r($mid_cars);
            echo "<br /><br />Slice out the last two:<br />";
            $last_cars = array_slice($cars, -2 , 2) ;
            print_r($last_cars);
            echo "<br /><br />Divide into two car chunks:<br />";
            $car_chunks = array_chunk($cars, 2) ;
            print_r($car_chunks);
            echo "<br /><br />Splice in this array after removing
                the last two cars:<br />";
            $cars2 = array(
                "Fiat", "Mazda"
                ) ;
            print_r($cars2);
            echo "<br />Giving this result:<br />";
            array_splice($cars, -2 , 2, $cars2) ;
            print_r($cars);
            $cars = array (
                "Ed" => "Ford", "Sue" => "Chevy", "Kate" => "Ford",
                    "Bob" => "BMW"
                ) ;
            echo "<br /><br />Given this initial array:<br />";
            print_r($cars);
            echo "<br />Flipping it produces this result:<br />";
            $cars = array_flip($cars) ;
            print_r($cars);
        ?>
    </body>
</html>
```

Comparing Arrays

You can compare arrays in PHP with both array operators and functions. If you have two arrays, `$cars1` and `$cars2`, you can compare them with these operators:

- **Equality**, `$cars1 == $cars2`, is TRUE if `$cars1` and `$cars2` have the same key => value pairs.

- **Identity**, `$cars1 === $cars2`, is TRUE if `$cars1` and `$cars2` have the same key => value pairs, in the same order, and of the same type.

- **Inequality**, `$cars1 != $cars2` or `$cars1 <> $cars2`, is TRUE if `$cars1` and `$cars2` are not equal.

- **Non-identity**, `$cars1 !== $cars2`, is TRUE if `$cars1` and `$cars2` are not identical.

You can also compare arrays with these functions:

- `array_diff()` compares two arrays and creates a new array with the values in the first array that are not in the second.

- `array_diff_assoc()` compares two arrays and creates a new array with the key => value pairs in the first array that are not in the second.

- `array_intersect()` compares two arrays and creates a new array with the values in the first array that are also in the second.

- `array_intersect_assoc()` compares two arrays and creates a new array with the key => value pairs in the first array that are also in the second.

Listing 7-12 shows how the array operators and the array comparison functions can work, with the results shown next.

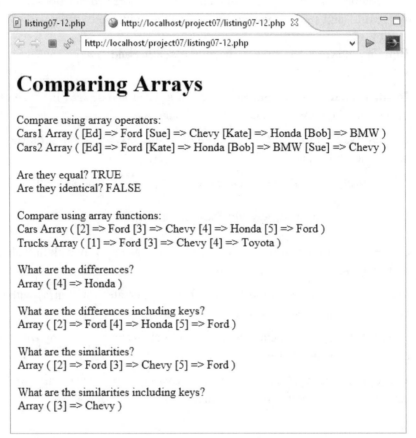

Listing 7-12   Comparing Arrays

```
<!DOCTYPE html>
<html>
    <head>
        <title>Listing 7-12</title>
    </head>
    <body>
        <h1>Comparing Arrays</h1>
        <?php
            echo "Compare using array operators:<br />";
            $cars1 = array (
```

```php
        "Ed" => "Ford", "Sue" => "Chevy", "Kate" =>
            "Honda", "Bob" => "BMW"
        );
echo "Cars1 ";
print_r($cars1);
$cars2 = array (
    "Ed" => "Ford", "Kate" => "Honda", "Bob" =>
        "BMW", "Sue" => "Chevy"
        );
echo "<br />Cars2 ";
print_r($cars2);
echo "<br /><br />Are they equal? ";
if( ($cars1 == $cars2) == TRUE) {
    echo "TRUE"; } else {echo "FALSE"; }
echo "<br />Are they identical? ";
if( ($cars1 === $cars2) == TRUE) {
    echo "TRUE"; } else {echo "FALSE"; }
echo "<br /><br /> Compare using array functions:<br />";
$cars[2] = "Ford";
$cars[3] = "Chevy";
$cars[4] = "Honda";
$cars[5] = "Ford";
echo "Cars ";
print_r($cars);
$trucks[1] = "Ford";
$trucks[3] = "Chevy";
$trucks[4] = "Toyota";
echo "<br />Trucks ";
print_r($trucks);
echo "<br /><br />What are the differences? <br />";
$vehicles = array_diff($cars, $trucks);
print_r($vehicles);
echo "<br /><br />What are the differences including
    keys? <br />";
$vehicles = array_diff_assoc($cars, $trucks);
print_r($vehicles);
echo "<br /><br />What are the similarities? <br />";
$vehicles = array_intersect($cars, $trucks);
print_r($vehicles);
echo "<br /><br />What are the similarities including
    keys? <br />";
$vehicles = array_intersect_assoc($cars, $trucks);
print_r($vehicles);
?>
    </body>
</html>
```

Handling Multidimensional Arrays

PHP allows you to have arrays within arrays, or multidimensional arrays. For example, if you have an array of a person's contact information, like this:

```
$Sue = array ("email" => "sue@anisp.com", "phone" => "555-1234");
```

and then you have an array of contacts, like this:

```
$contacts = array ("Sue", "Tom", "Bob");
```

you can put them in a multidimensional array, like this:

```
$contacts=array(
  "Sue" => array( "email" => "sue@anisp.com", "phone" => "555-1234"),
  "Tom" => array( "email" => "tom@anisp.com", "phone" => "555-5678"),
  "Bob" => array( "email" => "bob@anisp.com", "phone" => "555-4321"));
```

You can refer to a value in a multidimensional array by using both keys, like this:

```
echo "Tom's email is: ", $contacts["Tom"] ["email"], "<br />";
```

You can also use looping functions to work with multidimensional arrays. Basically, you need a loop for each dimension of the array. Listing 7-13 shows using two **foreach()** functions to loop through the contacts array to display the contact information it contains, as shown next.

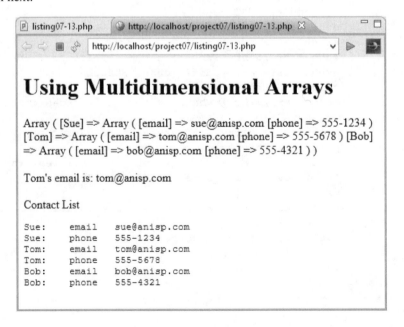

Listing 7-13	Using Multidimensional Arrays

```
<!DOCTYPE html>
<html>
    <head>
        <title>Listing 7-13</title>
    </head>
    <body>
        <h1>Using Multidimensional Arrays</h1>
        <?php
            $contacts=array(
                "Sue"=>array("email"=>"sue@anisp.com",
                    "phone"=>"555-1234"),
                "Tom"=>array("email"=>"tom@anisp.com",
                    "phone"=>"555-5678"),
                "Bob"=>array("email"=>"bob@anisp.com",
                    "phone"=>"555-4321"));
            print_r($contacts);
            echo "<br /><br />Tom's email is: ", $contacts
                ["Tom"] ["email"], "<br />";
            echo "<br />Contact List<pre>";
            foreach ($contacts as $person => $means)
                foreach ($means as $key => $value )
                    echo "$person:\t$key\t$value<br />";
            echo "</pre>";
        ?>
    </body>
</html>
```

NOTE

To use the tab escape character (`\t`) in the `echo` statement that displays the contact list, we must first turn on preformatted text with the HTML `<pre></pre>` tags to display text in a fixed-width font and preserve spaces, line breaks, and tabs.

Building and Handling Forms

The principle way to communicate with a user of a website is through forms. This process requires the combination of HTML, JavaScript, PHP, and eventually MySQL. In Chapters 2 and 4, you were introduced to the basic form creation and validating features of HTML and JavaScript. Here, we'll expand on those and add the form and file capabilities of PHP. In future chapters, you'll see how MySQL adds its functions to working with forms.

Create a Form in HTML

Creating a form in HTML is entering a pair of `<form>` `</form>` tags and then within those tags, entering the fields that you want with the `<input />` tag and `type` attribute. Listing 7-14 shows a simple form that is displayed next:

Listing 7-14   Simple Form

```
<!DOCTYPE html>
<html>
    <head>
        <title>Simple Form</title>
    </head>
    <body>
        <h1>Simple Form</h1>
        <form>
            Name:<input type="text" /><br />
        </form>
    </body>
</html>
```

There are, of course, many other `<input />` types and other form-related tags and attributes, as described in Chapter 2 and Table 2-8 and further enlarged upon in Chapter 4. For the sake of working with a form in PHP, enlarge the HTML form so you have more to work with by adding a second text box with an email address, a pair of radio buttons, a couple of check boxes, and a drop-down list. Also, name all of the fields so we can refer to them later, enclose the fields in a fieldset with a legend, and add submit and reset buttons, as was done in Chapter 4. The resulting form is shown in Listing 7-15 and displayed next.

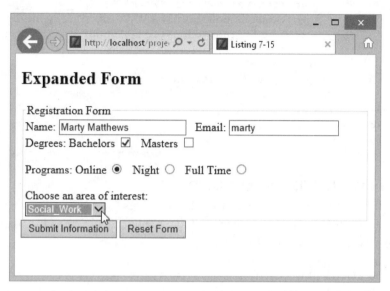

Listing 7-15   Expanded Form

```
<!DOCTYPE html>
<html>
    <head>
        <title>Listing 7-15</title>
    </head>
    <body>
        <h2>Expanded Form</h2>
        <form name="regform">
            <fieldset>
                <legend>Registration Form</legend>
                Name: <input type="text" name="fullname" size =
                    "24"/>  
                Email: <input type="text" name="email" /><br />
                Degrees: Bachelors <input type="checkbox"
                    name="bachelors"/>   Masters <input
                    type="checkbox" name="masters"/><p></p>
                Programs: Online <input type="radio" name="online"/>
                      Night <input type="radio" name="night"/>
                      Full Time <input type="radio" name=
                    "fulltime"/><p></p>
                Choose areas of interest:<br />
```

```
            <select name="Interests" >
            <option selected value="">Interests</option>
            <option value="socialwork">Social_Work</option>
            <option value="clinical">Clinical_Psych</option>
            <option value="education">Education</option>
            </select>
        </fieldset>
        <input type="submit" value="Submit Information">
        <input type="reset" value="Reset Form">
    </form>
    </body>
</html>
```

Add JavaScript to a Form

There are a number of elements that JavaScript brings to forms, as described in Chapter 4. These elements include placing the initial focus and recognizing and validating user input. We add those features to the form next.

Placing Focus in a Form

When a form is first displayed to a user, there is nothing inherent in the display that places the focus or insertion point (the cursor) into the form field to be first filled in. For example, in Listing 7-15 in the last section, the user must click in the Name text box to enter their name. Placing the focus in the text box can be done with JavaScript. You must identify that you will be using JavaScript in the `<head>` section and place an `onload` event handler in the `<body>` tag, as you see in Listing 7-16 (except for the changes in the `<head>` section and in the `<body>` tag, it is the same as Listing 7-15, so I only show the first few lines) as displayed next.

Listing 7-16   Place Focus

```
<!DOCTYPE html>
<html>
    <head>
        <title>Listing 7-16</title>
        <script type= "text/javascript"></script>
    </head>
    <body onload = "document.regform.fullname.focus();">
        <h2>Place Focus</h2>
        <form name="regform">
            <fieldset>
                <legend>Registration Form</legend>
                Name: <input type="text" name="fullname"
                    size="24" />  
                Email: <input type="text" name="email" /><br />
```

Recognizing and Validating User Input

Since JavaScript is running in the client, it can immediately recognize user input and validate that input. For example, in the form shown in Listings 7-15 and 7-16, we want to make sure that the name and email fields are not blank and that the email address has an @ symbol. To do this, we need to add a JavaScript validation function in the **<head>** **<script>** section and an onsubmit event in the **<form>** tag to recognize when the user is trying to leave the form and call the validation function. onsubmit is triggered by the HTML Submit button at the end of the form, which in turn can be triggered by pressing ENTER any place in the form.

There needs to be three conditional (if) statements in the JavaScript validation function, two to test if anything has been entered into the name and email fields, and one to test if the email entry has a @ in it. The @ test uses the JavaScript indexOf() method to look through a string for the existence of another string, the single letter "@" in our case, and returns the position where the second string starts. If the second string does not exist in the first string, indexOf() returns a "-1," so a test for <0 will tell if the "@" is missing. Listing 7-17 shows the changes that have been made to the code shown in Listings 7-15 and 7-16. The alert message that is displayed when an email address does not have an "@" is shown next.

CAUTION

The JavaScript `indexOf()` method is case sensitive. You must capitalize the "O" or it will not work.

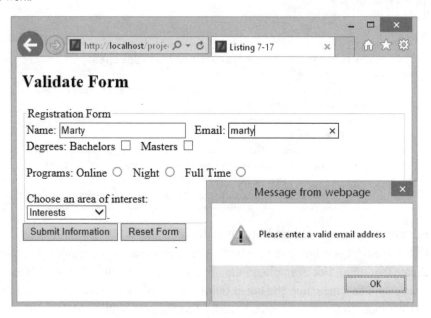

Listing 7-17   Validate Form

```
<!DOCTYPE html>
<html>
    <head>
        <title>Listing 7-17</title>
        <script type= "text/javascript">
        function validateform(){
            if (document.regform.fullname.value==""){
                window.alert("Please provide your full name");
                document.regform.fullname.focus();
                 return false;
            }
            if (document.regform.email.value==""){
                window.alert("Please enter your email address");
                document.regform.email.focus();
                return false;
            }
            if (document.regform.email.value.indexOf("@") < 0){
                window.alert("Please enter a valid email address");
```

```
                document.regform.email.focus();
                return false;
            }
            else {
                window.alert("Thank you for your registration");
                return true;
            }
        }
    </script>
</head>
<body onload = "document.regform.fullname.focus();">
    <h2>Validate Form</h2>
    <form name="regform" onsubmit="return validateform();" >
        <fieldset>
            <legend>Registration Form</legend>
            Name: <input type="text" name="fullname" size =
                "24"/>  
            Email: <input type="text" name="email" /><br />
            Degrees: Bachelors <input type="checkbox"
                name="bachelors"/>   Masters <input
                type="checkbox" name="masters"/><p></p>
            Programs: Online <input type="radio" name="online"/>
                  Night <input type="radio" name="night"/>
                  Full Time <input type="radio" name=
                "fulltime"/><p></p>
            Choose areas of interest:<br />
            <select name="Interests" >
            <option selected value="">Interests</option>
            <option value="socialwork">Social_Work</option>
            <option value="clinical">Clinical_Psych</option>
            <option value="education">Education</option>
            </select>
        </fieldset>
        <input type="submit" value="Submit Registration" />
        <input type="reset" value="Reset Form" />
    </form>
</body>
</html>
```

Accepting and Filing Form Data in PHP

The big difference between PHP and JavaScript is that JavaScript operates in the client and PHP operates in the server and allows you to accept data entered by the user and save it on the server. In this section, we'll use PHP to take the data a user enters into an HTML form, put it into an array, and then write it onto a disk. To do this, the form must have names in all **<input>** fields and must have a Submit button. The form shown in Listing 7-17 meets both of these requirements, and it has been shown that data can be entered into this form and validated, making it a good candidate to demonstrate the collection and filing of form data with PHP.

Collecting Data in a Form

To collect the data that is entered into the form requires that Listing 7-17 be modified to identify the method to be used to transfer the data to PHP, and that optionally you identify where to send the data so PHP can use it.

The HTML **<form>** tag is used to specify both the method of transferring the data collected in the form and where to transfer it. The primary methods used to transfer form data are get and post. These are added to the **<form>** tag using one of the method attributes: method= *"post"* or method= *"get"*. The major difference between the two is how the data is transferred. get transfers data by attaching it to the URL that opens the web page, like this:

```
http://localhost/project07/listing07-18.php?fullname=Marty+Matthews&
email=marty@anisp.com&bachelors=on&online=on&Interests=socialwork
```

The data is added after the actual URL with a ? separating the two. Spaces are marked by a + and successive fields are separated by &.

The post method transfers data in the HTTP header that is sent to the server with a web page request URL, but not in it. This provides a bit of security, since the data being transferred is not quite so obvious.

Identifying where to transfer data is done in the **<form>** tag with the action attribute. If there is no action attribute, then it is expected that the current web page will use the form data (see the next section); otherwise, an action attribute is added to the **<form>** tag with a web page name (such as *awebpage.php*), either by itself if it is in the same directory or folder as the current page, or with a path in front of the page name (for example, */parentfolder/folder/awebpage.php*). Here is an example of the **<form>** tag with both the method and action attributes:

```
<form name= "regform" method= "get" action= "awebpage.php">
```

Extracting Form Data from an Array

PHP provides a set of "superglobal" arrays ($_GET, $_POST, and $_REQUEST) that allow you to utilize form data that is transferred with the get and post **<form>** methods once the form has been transmitted with a Submit button. The $_GET array automatically collects form data from named fields that has been transmitted with the get method, the $_POST array does the same thing with the post method, and $_REQUEST array will collect data from either the `get` method or the `post` method, as well `cookie` (see Chapter 6). `$_GET`, `$_POST`, and `$_REQUEST` are associative arrays built into and immediately usable anywhere in PHP. There is no need to otherwise define them. The indexes or keys for the arrays are the field names defined in the form. For example, in Listing 7-17, if we:

- Add `method="get"` to the **`<form>`** tag so it looks like this:

```
<form name="regform" onsubmit="return validateform();" method="get">
```

- Add the PHP code with either `$_GET` or `$_REQUEST` above `<!DOCTYPE html>`, like this:

```
<?php
print_r($_GET);
?>
<!DOCTYPE html>
<html>
```

- Rename the script with .php.

Then, when the form is filled in and the Submit button is clicked, the array is displayed above the form, as you can see in Figure 7-1 where the keys are field names and the values are what was entered into the fields (the form is also normally reset—blanked out—but I filled it in again so you could see where the values in the array came from).

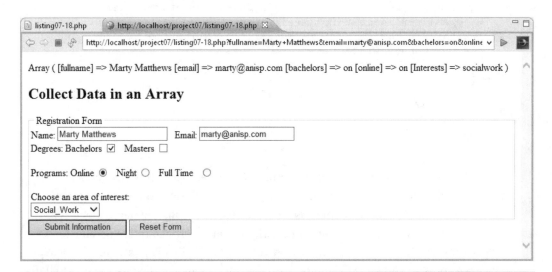

Figure 7-1 PHP's ability to immediately have available information entered into a form is one of its greatest strengths.

TIP

A common question is whether to use $_REQUEST in place of either $_GET or $_POST. There is no inherent difference. They work the same way and give you the same information. The principal reason to use $_GET or $_POST is that it clearly communicates to the script reader how the array got its information, and the reader can then look for the get or post that generated the data.

Writing Data to a File

While it is neat to display information entered into a form, you most likely want to save it in a file. This is done by:

● Converting the $_GET array into a string

● Appending the /r/n carriage return and linefeed escape characters to the end of the new string

● Opening the file so you can write at its end

● Writing an entry or record onto the file and testing to see that was done

This is done by adding to the PHP script at the top of Listing 7-17 as shown here:

```php
<?php
print_r($_GET);
$regrec = implode(", ", $_GET); //turn array into a string
$finalrec = $regrec . "\r\n" ; //add carriage return linefeed
$fp = fopen("regfile.txt", "a"); //open file to write at end
if (fwrite ($fp, $finalrec) == FALSE) {  //write the record
       echo "Cannot write fle.", "<br />";
       }
else {
       echo "File written.", "<br />";
       }
?>
<!DOCTYPE html>
<html>
```

See the discussion of the **implode()** array function earlier in this chapter, and review the file handling discussion in Chapter 6. There are several ways to join or concatenate two strings, but probably the simplest is the concatenation string operator, which is a simple period that is used in the preceding script to join a carriage return and linefeed to one person's registration record. The reason you want to do that is to provide delineation between records so you know where one record ends and another begins. Several PHP file functions depend on the linefeed character (\n) to identify the end of the record, while working with text files uses the carriage return for the same purpose.

You can see the result of writing a file in two ways. The simplest and least elegant is to locate and double-click the file. The result is shown next. The second is to write a small PHP script, shown in Listing 7-18a, that uses the `file()` function to read the named file into an array and then displays the array, shown following the listing.

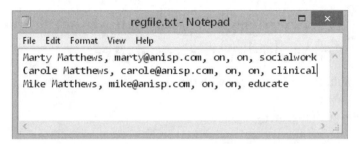

Listing 7-18a   Read Registration File

```html
<!DOCTYPE html>
<html>
    <head>
        <title>Listing 7-18a</title>
    </head>
    <body>
        <h1>Read Registration File</h1>
        <?php
            $regarray = file("regfile.txt");
            print_r($regarray);
        ?>
    </body>
</html>
```

Chapter 8 will demonstrate additional PHP capabilities and how they can be used to create a user authentication system. Also, the work with MySQL in later chapters of this book will demonstrate a much more elegant file-handling capability.

Try This 7-1 Create and Work with a Multidimensional Array

Create a multidimensional array with the `array()` function and then:

- Display it all together
- Extract one item from the array
- Use a loop to display individual `key=>value` pairs
- Sort the array on the values, keeping the association with the keys
- Create a form to enter information into the array
- Use JavaScript to validate some of the information being collected in the form
- Write the array onto a disk file and prove it has been written there

Chapter 7 Self-Test

The following questions are intended to help reinforce your comprehension of the concepts covered in this chapter. The answers can be found in the accompanying online Appendix A, "Answers to the Self-Tests."

1. What are arrays?
2. What are the two principal parts of an array?
3. All arrays have only numeric keys. True or false?
4. Once an array has been created, it can't be changed. True or false?
5. What does the `print_r()` function do?
6. What does the `foreach()` function do?
7. What are three of the six ways that arrays can be sorted?

8. What is the principal construct used to navigate in arrays, and what are some of the ways it is used?

9. What are three ways that array functions allow you to transform arrays?

10. What are three ways that arrays can be compared?

11. What is a multidimensional array?

12. What are the two primary HTML tags used with forms?

13. What are two ways that JavaScript can be used with forms?

14. What are the two ways that information entered into a form can be transferred to a PHP script?

15. What are the PHP superglobal arrays used to collect form information?

Chapter 8

Putting PHP to Use

Key Skills & Concepts

- Create an Index Script

- Add Registration Scripts

- Insert Sign-In Scripts

- Attach a Site Page

In this chapter we'll look at an example of how PHP can be put to use by itself in a user authentication system where we will set up a user login form and then validate the login information. This is not meant to be a system that you might use, but rather an example of how PHP can be used.

User Authentication

User authentication allows you to limit who has access to a website. It requires that all users register for the site, providing a name, a unique ID (usually an email address), and a password. This information is stored in a disk file with the ID and password encrypted so they cannot be misused. The fact that a person has registered (not their ID and password) is placed in a cookie on the user's computer, so he or she will not be asked to register again. A user wishing to enter a site is asked to enter his or her ID and password, which are encrypted and compared against the encrypted value in the file of registered users. If the ID and password correctly match a file entry, the user is admitted to the site. The fact that a user has been admitted to the site (not his or her ID and password) is stored in a session variable so the user can freely move from one site page to another without having to reenter the information.

Figure 8-1 shows a flowchart of a system to perform the user authentication function. It includes six scripts in four areas:

- **The initial entry** in index.php script, which checks if the user has a cookie

- **The registration area** with two scripts, one for the user to enter her or his information, and the other to encrypt the user information, write it to disk, and create and set a cookie

- **The sign-in area** with two scripts, one for the user to enter his or her information, and the other to encrypt the user information, compare it with the disk information, and create and set a session variable
- **A regular site page**, which checks for the presence of the session variable

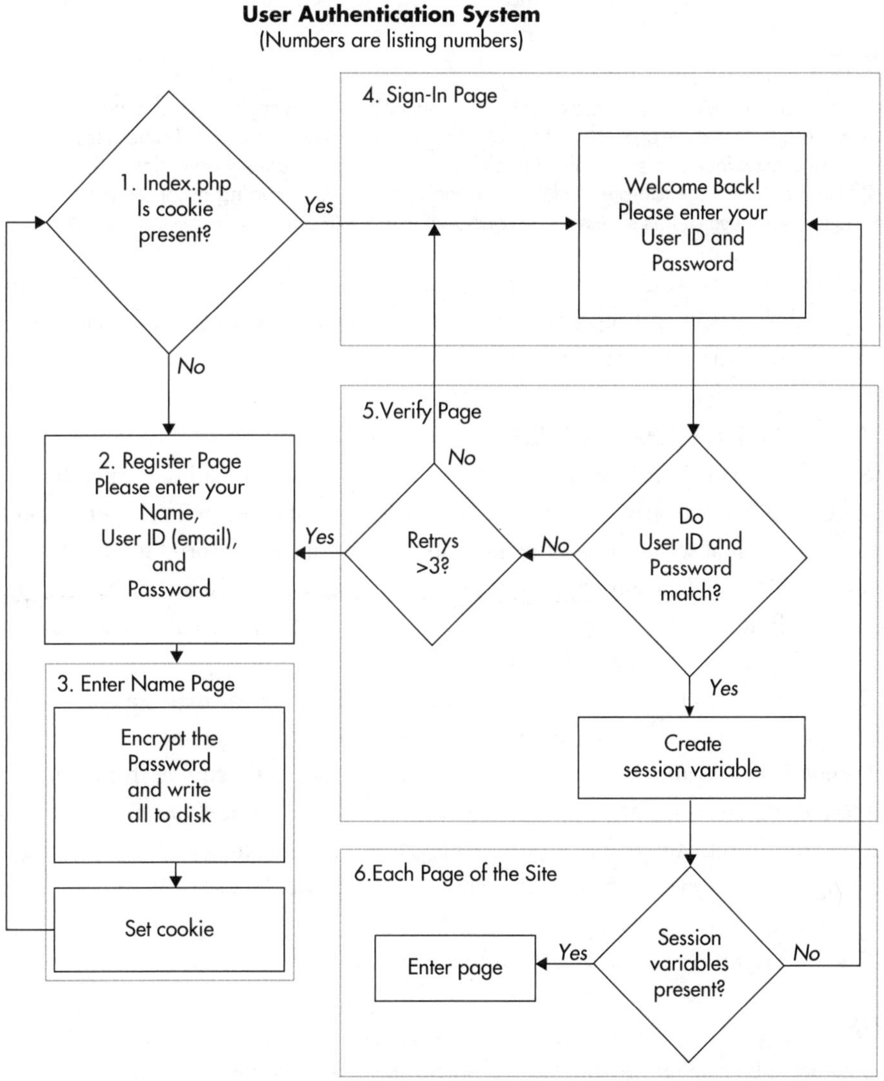

User Authentication System
(Numbers are listing numbers)

Figure 8-1 User authentication system flowchart

Each of these will be discussed in the following sections. I have tried to make these scripts as simple as possible to make the PHP process described here clear. In doing so, I have not included a CSS script to improve the formatting and make the web pages more attractive. As a result, I have used several deprecated HTML formatting attributes such as `width`, `cellpadding`, and `cellspacing` that HTML5 considers obsolete and should be replaced with CSS. I fully agree that CSS is the best way to do the formatting, but my objective here is to focus on PHP and how it can be used by itself.

CAUTION

This user authentication system is meant for demonstration purposes *only* and is *not* intended as a fully secure procedure to protect access to a site. It also is not meant for very many users, since the entire disk file of users is read into memory each time it is used. Use it only as an example of PHP code and possibly as a starting point for your own system. *Any use of this system is at your own risk.*

In later chapters, you'll see how using a database for the files would greatly help a user authentication system and support a large number of users. Also, you will see how a CSS can be applied to a system such as this.

Create an Index Script

When a site is loaded, the script that automatically opens without being specifically requested is the index script, in this case, index.php. For that reason, the user authentication system will use that script to start the authentication. If any other script in the site is opened, the script will check to see if the user has signed in and, if not, will direct the user to sign in. The user will not be able to enter any page on the site if the page has the protection code on it.

The index.php script (see Listing 8-1) has a simple series of PHP statements that asks if the user has a cookie for the site. (The example scripts use a site name of Matthews Technology and the abbreviation "MatTech.") If the user has a cookie from a previous visit to the site and registered there in the last 180 days, a session variable is created with their name, current date, and a retry variable used in signing in. The user is then directed to the signin.php script. If the user does not have a cookie, he or she is sent to the register .php script.

The index.php script has several unique elements:

NOTE

It should again be emphasized that this is a simple example. In normal websites, the index.php should contain the home page information, not only for the reader, but for bookmarking and search engine purposes.

- The script is pure PHP code, has no HTML code, and nothing is displayed to the user from that script. You'll see we do that several times in this system.

- The script uses the isset() function to determine if the cookie exists. Remember that if a domain has set a cookie on a user's computer, it will be automatically returned to the domain's server the next time the user connects to the server as long as the user does not clear their cookies.

- The header("Location:... ") function is used to transfer execution to another web script by using the HTML header to inform the server to send another script. This function *must* be executed before any other output sent to the user, such as an echo statement or the <html> or <head> elements.

TIP

Start out with a lot of echo statements to assist in the debugging, and use HTML <a href=...> (anchor) elements in place of the PHP header statements, since header cannot be used after any output, for example, the echo statements.

Listing 8-1   index.php

```php
<?php
    session_start();
    //Check if user has a cookie.
    if (isset ($_COOKIE["MatTech"])) {
        //If so, set session and go to sign in.
        $_SESSION["name"] = $_COOKIE["MatTech"][name];
        $_SESSION["retry"] = 0;
        $_SESSION["time"] = time();
        header( "Location: signin.php");
    }
    else {
        //If not, go to registration.
        header( "Location: register.php");
    }
?>
```

Add Registration Scripts

As mentioned, there are two registration scripts: register.php, which handles the user input, and enterName.php, which does the processing. It is possible to do all this in one script, as you will see in some of the PHP/MySQL examples later in this book, but the two-script solution provides a clean introduction to this process.

Figure 8-2 The registration form could use a CSS to spruce it up a bit.

Input Form

The register.php script, which you can see in Listing 8-2, is a table containing a form with three fields, Name, User ID, and Password, as shown in Figure 8-2. When the user completes filling out the form and clicks Register, the form action transfers execution to the enterName.php script and populates the $_POST superglobal array with the contents of the form.

TIP

JavaScript can be used with document.body.onload event to automatically go to the first form field, but it is not included here to focus on PHP.

Listing 8-2   register.php

```html
<!--User enters name, ID, and password.-->
<html>
   <head>
      <title>Listing 8-2 Registration Page</title>
   </head>
   <body>
      <div id="form">
         <!-- Go to enterName.php after clicking Register -->
         <form action="enterName.php" method="post" id="registerForm">
         <table width="150" border="1" cellspacing="3" cellpadding="5" >
            <tr height= 50>
               <th colspan= "2" valign="middle" >
                  <p id="head">Welcome to Matthews Technology!</p>
                  <p id="body">Please enter your Name,<br />User ID, and
                     Password</p>
               </th>
            </tr>
            <tr>
               <td width="40">
                  <p class="label">Name:</p>
               </td>
               <td width="100">
                  <input type="text" name="name" value="" size="60" />
               </td>
            </tr>
            <tr>
               <td>
                  <p class="label">User ID:</p>
               </td>
               <td>
                  <input type="text" name="userid" value="" size="60" />
               </td>
            </tr>
            <tr>
               <td>
                  <p class="label">Password:</p>
               </td>
               <td>
                  <input type="password" name="passwd" value="" size="20" />
               </td>
            </tr>
         </table>
            <input type="submit" name="submit" value="Register" />
         </form>
      </div>
   </body>
</html>
```

Encryption and Save to Disk

The enterName.php script, shown in Listing 8-3, is the second pure PHP script. It picks up the name entered at registration and passed to this script through the $_POST superglobal array. This is combined with the current time and the expiration time to create and set a cookie on the user's computer. The user ID and password, entered at registration, are combined and then encrypted with SHA1 (Secure Hash Algorithm 1) for 160-bit encryption. Next, the current time, the user's name, and the encrypted ID and password are placed into an array, and the array is written to disk with the file_put_contents() function because it allows an array to be appended to an existing disk file. System execution is then transferred back to index.php.

Listing 8-3   enterName.php

```php
<?php
/* Cookie is written. Then the user id
 *   and password are encrypted and that and
 *   the name are written to disk. */

        //Information for cookie, expires in 6 months.
        $name = $_POST['name'];
        $date = time();
        $expire = time()+(60*60*24*180);

        //Set cookie.
        setcookie("MatTech[name]", $name, $expire, "/");
        setcookie("MatTech[date]", $date, $expire, "/");

        //Combine userid and password and encrypt it.
        $userPasswd = $_POST['userid'] .= $_POST['passwd'];
        $encryptid_pw = sha1($userPasswd);

        //Build an array of data and write it to disk.
        $entry = array( 'index' => time(),
                    'name' => $name,
                    'encrypt' => $encryptid_pw
                );
        if (!$byteswrite = file_put_contents('namelist.txt',
           $entry, FILE_APPEND)) {
            echo "<br />File not written.<br />";
            }

        //Return to Index.php.
        header( "Location: index.php");
?>
```

Insert Sign-In Scripts

Once again, the two sign-in scripts, signin.php and verify.php, could be in one script, but are split for the clarity of this exercise.

Signing In

Once the user has a cookie on her or his computer, the user goes immediately to signin.php. This is again a form within a table, shown in Figure 8-3 and Listing 8-4. When the user clicks Sign In, the form `action` transfers the execution to verify.php and the `$_POST` superglobal will be populated with the user ID and password that the user entered.

NOTE

You should not get to signin.php without being registered, but the "Not registered? Click here!" is added so you can get back to register.php without having to delete the cookie.

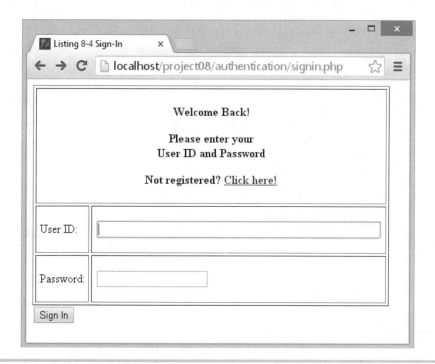

Figure 8-3 The fact that the user ID and password are transmitted over the Internet unencrypted is a major security flaw. Using HTTPS to do this would help.

Listing 8-4	signin.php

```html
<!-- User enters id and password. -->
<html>
   <head>
      <title>Listing 8-4 Sign-In</title>
   </head>
   <body>
      <div id="form">
         <!-- Display the sign-in form. After filling in, go to
            verify script. -->
         <form action="verify.php" method="post" id="signinForm">
         <table width="100" border="1" cellspacing="3" cellpadding="5" >
            <tr height="50">
               <th colspan="2" valign="middle" >
                  <p id="head">Welcome Back!</p>
                  <p id="body">Please enter your<br />User ID
                     and Password</p>
                  <p id="body">Not registered? <a href="register.php">Click
                     here!</a></p>
               </th>
            </tr>
            <tr>
               <td width="50">
                  <p class="label">User ID:</p>
               </td>
               <td width="120">
                  <input type="text" name="userid" value="" size="60" />
               </td>
            </tr>
            <tr>
               <td>
                  <p class="label">Password:</p>
               </td>
               <td>
                  <input type="password" name="passwd" value="" size="20" />
               </td>
            </tr>
         </table>
            <input type="submit" name="submit" value="Sign In" />
         </form>
      </div>
   </body>
</html>
```

Verifying the Input

The verify.php script, which you can see in Listing 8-5, reads the entire namelist.txt file into the $namelist string using the `file_get_contents()` function. It then combines the user ID and password that were entered at sign-in and encrypts that combination. The strpos() function is then used to see if the encrypted combination is contained in $namelist. If the encryption is there, the session variable is updated, and execution is transferred to the original site scripts. If the encryption is not found on the disk file, the $retry variable is incremented and checked to see if it is greater than 3. If so, execution is transferred to register.php; otherwise, the $retry variable execution is stored in the $_SESSION variable, and execution is transferred to signin.php.

Listing 8-5   verify.php

```php
<?php
   session_start();

//   Verify user's id and password, and create session.

        //Read the name list file.
        if(!$namelist = file_get_contents('namelist.txt')) {
           echo "<br />File not read.<br />";
        }

        //Combine the user ID and password and encrypt it.
        $userPasswd = $_POST['userid'] .= $_POST['passwd'];
        $testentry = sha1($userPasswd);

        //Determine if the encrypted user ID and password are in file.
        if(strpos($namelist, $testentry) >= 0){

           //If there, reset the session and enter site.
           $_SESSION["retry"] = "admit";
           $_SESSION["time"] = time();
           header( "Location: enterSite.php");
        }
        else {
           //If not, add to Session Retry and test > 3
           $retry = $_SESSION["retry"];
           $retry++;
           if ($retry > 3) {
              //If greater than 3 go to register.
              header( "Location: register.php");
           }
           else {
              //If less than 3, reset Session Retry and go to Sign in
              $_SESSION["retry"] = $retry;
              header( "Location: signin.php");
           }
        }
?>
```

Attach a Site Page

The code snippet that goes on each regular site page (see Listing 8-6) checks to see if $_SESSION["retry"] is present and equal to "admit." If so, the user is greeted, and execution flows into the regular page, as shown next. Otherwise, execution is returned to index.php, where the user has to prove she has a cookie, or she will have to register, and in either case, she will have to sign in.

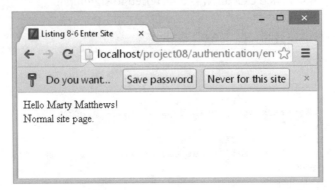

TIP

Instead of including the snippet of PHP code in Listing 8-6 on each regular site page, save just the PHP snippet as its own file; then as the first line of every site page, insert `<?php require_once(enterSite.php); ?>`. One feature of the `require` and `require_once` functions is that the balance of the script on the page will not execute until the code referenced by the function successfully executes. It halts execution with a fatal error. This contrasts with the `include` and `include_once` functions, which do not halt execution of the remaining script. The `_once` prevents the snippet from being loaded more than once.

Listing 8-6   enterSite.php

```php
<?php
   session_start();
//Having successfully signed in...
   //Check to see if the session variable is present and is "admit"
   if (isset($_SESSION["retry"]) && $_SESSION["retry"] == "admit") {
      //If so, continue.
      echo "Hello ", $_SESSION["name"], "!<br />";
   }
   else {
      //If not, return to the site Index page.
      header( "Location: index.php");
   }
?>
```

Many things can be done to enhance this system. The first is probably to make the pieces that collect the user ID and password use HTTPS and thus secure that transfer. The second is to use a CSS to make the data collection forms look better and not use deprecated code. Two other areas that we'll address later in this book are better handling of error messages, such as those returned from disk read and write errors, and handling the user trying to enter unusual characters and other content (like pasting an image) into the form.

Try This 8-1   Create a PHP System of Scripts

Using the example in this chapter, create your own system of scripts that:

- Create and reference a cookie to carry information from session to session and web page to web page within one session.
- Create a form in which a user can enter information.
- Encrypt some of the user information and save it and other user information to disk.
- In a separate session, verify the user information before letting them enter the site.
- In this system, pass user-entered information from a form to the script and from one script to another.

Chapter 8 Self-Test

The following questions are intended to help reinforce your comprehension of the concepts covered in this chapter. The answers can be found in the accompanying online Appendix A, "Answers to the Self-Tests."

1. What function is used to test if something exists?

2. What function is used to transfer to another script and what are its constraints?

3. What is used to transfer data entered into a form to the script itself and what is it called?

4. What should I have used in place of `width`, `cellspacing`, and `cellpadding` attributes?

5. How does one encrypt a password?

6. What is the technique and function used in this example to test if a password is valid?

7. How do you refer to an external piece of PHP code and what are some of its options?

Part III

Creating and Using Relational Databases with MySQL

n Chapters 7 and 8, you saw how with PHP you can read and write a disk file. While that worked, it was limited in that you had to read the entire file into memory and search it there to do what was needed. In Part III, you'll see how MySQL, a full-fledged relational database management system (RDBMS), greatly enhances the process of reading, writing, maintaining, changing, searching, and rearranging information stored in computer files. It is the third major tool used to make websites dynamic, and while a website requires HTML and PHP in addition to MySQL, MySQL does the heavy lifting when it comes to the handling of data.

Chapter 9 introduces databases and describes what makes them relational; how tables, records, fields, keys, and relationships are used; and how to select the data types for different fields. In addition, the chapter shows how to create, initialize, and maintain a MySQL database using phpMyAdmin.

Chapter 10 explores SQL (Structured Query Language), the foundation of MySQL, discussing the basic characteristics of the language. We then introduce MySQL and describe how SQL has been implemented in MySQL. The basic command set for MySQL is described, as is making a database secure.

Chapter 11 describes using the command line to create and use a database and its tables. This will include building, inserting, locating, and deleting records and tables.

Chapter 12 demonstrates how to query, retrieve, and use data from single and multiple tables, including ordering and grouping information and keeping track of where in the table it is being read from or written to.

Chapter 9

Introduction to Relational Databases

Key Skills & Concepts

- Understanding Databases

- Understanding a Relational Database

- Get and Install phpMyAdmin

- Opening and Exploring phpMyAdmin

- Create and Use a Database in phpMyAdmin

With PHP alone, you saw how to use arrays to collect, store, and retrieve small amounts of information and save that information on disk. While the PHP tools work, you can readily see that they would not work well with large volumes of information. For that task, you need a more robust tool, a "database" able to securely handle such volume and provide the means to quickly search for and retrieve information in a number of different ways. In this chapter, we'll look at what a database is, the different kinds of databases, the parts of a database, how a database is used, and how to use phpMyAdmin to set up and maintain a database for use on the Web.

Databases and Relational Databases

A *database* is an organized way of storing information. The key is the word "organized." The primary purpose of a database is to store information in such a way that it can be easily and quickly found and retrieved. A database must facilitate the easy and quick retrieval and use of the data it has collected.

Understanding Databases

In its simplest form, a database is a *table* of information, as shown in the Excel list of books in Figure 9-1. Each book entry is a *row* in the table and is called a *record*. Each piece of information in a book entry, such as the title or author, is a *column* in the table, and is called a *field*.

The table in Figure 9-1 is called a *flatfile,* where all the information in the database is in a single table. Notice that there are several books that have the same author, the same publisher, or the same category. If these fields were made into their own tables

Columns or fields

Table

BkID	Book Title	Author	Publisher	Price	Category
1	Nightfall	Asimov	Bantam	5.99	Sci. Fic.
2	Patriot Games	Clancy	Berkley	4.95	Thriller
3	2010	Clarke	Ballantine	3.95	Sci. Fic.
4	Lie Down with Lions	Follett	Signet	4.95	Mystery
5	A Thief of Time	Hillerman	Harper	4.95	Mystery
6	The Fly on the Wall	Hillerman	Harper	4.95	Mystery
7	Hornet Flight	Follett	Signet	7.99	Thriller
8	The Innocent Man	Grisham	Dell	7.99	Thriller
9	Mission of Honor	Clancy	Berkley	7.99	Thriller

Rows or records

An individual field

Figure 9-1 A database is a table with records and fields.

that can contain additional information, it would simplify the Books table, provide more information, save storage space, and make it easier to change, as you would only have to update in one place. (Savings are very small in this database, but if you have a large database, they would be significant.) The resultant four tables, which are shown in Figure 9-2, form a *relational database*.

BkID	Book Title	Aid	Pid	Price	Cid
3	2010	3	1	3.95	2
5	A Thief of Time	6	5	4.95	1
7	Hornet Flight	4	6	7.99	3
4	Lie Down with Lions	4	6	4.95	1
9	Mission of Honor	2	3	7.99	3
1	Nightfall	1	1	5.99	2
2	Patriot Games	2	3	4.95	3
6	The Fly on the Wall	6	5	4.95	1
8	The Innocent Man	5	4	7.99	3

Aid	Last Name	First Name
1	Asimov	Isaac
2	Clancy	Tom
3	Clarke	Arthur
4	Follett	Ken
5	Grisham	John
6	Hillerman	Tony

Pid	Publisher	Address	City
1	Ballantine	201 E 50th	New York
2	Bantam	666 5th Ave	New York
3	Berkley	200 Madison A	New York
4	Dell	666 5th Ave	New York
5	Harper	10 E 53rd	New York
6	Signet	375 Hudson	New York

Cid	Category	Section
1	Mystry	E-9
2	Sci. Fic.	F-14
3	Thriller	G-10

Figure 9-2 A relational database places repetitive information into separate tables.

Understanding a Relational Database

In a relational database, repeated pieces of information are stored in separate tables and related to one another through their *key,* or index, a unique value assigned to each record in the table. In the table that it indexes, the key is called the *primary key*. When that key is used in another table, it is called a *foreign key*. For example, in the Authors table, the Aid (author ID) is the primary key, but in the Books table, the Aid is a foreign key relating the Authors table to the Books table. The full set of relationships in the Books database is shown next.

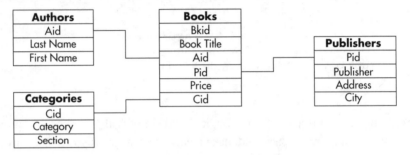

The process of taking a field with repeated values and placing the field in its own table is called *normalization.* It not only reduces the space taken up by a database, but it also significantly enhances the maintainability of a database. Without normalization, if you wanted to change a value in a field, you would have to change all occurrences of the value everywhere in the database. With normalization, you only have to change a single occurrence.

Using phpMyAdmin

phpMyAdmin is an online graphical user interface for working with a MySQL database and is written in PHP. It is an app that can be added into Zend Server. The principal use of phpMyAdmin is to initially create databases and their tables that will be exercised programmatically with PHP and to do occasional maintenance on these databases.

In this section, we'll look at how to get and install phpMyAdmin, explore its interface, review its security and how to change it, create a database with a table, and look at the details of a database specification, including the various data types.

Get and Install phpMyAdmin

With the Zend Server, you will need to separately download and then install phpMyAdmin. Zend provides both instructions and links to do that here:

http://files.zend.com/help/Zend-Server-6/content/installing_phpmyadmin.htm

Open this website, shown in Figure 9-3, and use it and the following steps to install phpMyAdmin on your computer:

1. In the Zend Server phpMyAdmin help page, click the link ("here") in the first step to begin the download process.

2. Click Save As to choose where to save phpMyAdmin. I suggest you save the app in the recommended default, the user's Download folder. Click Save.

3. Double-click the Zend Server icon on your desktop, if you placed one there, or locate the app on the Start menu in Windows 7 and earlier versions or in the Apps screen of Windows 8.

4. Enter your Zend username (usually "admin") and password and click Login. This opens the user interface (UI) discussed in the phpMyAdmin Help page.

5. Click Applications | Apps in the toolbars at the top of the window, and then click Deploy Application.

6. Click Browse (or Choose Files), select the folder where you placed the file, and then select the file and click Open.

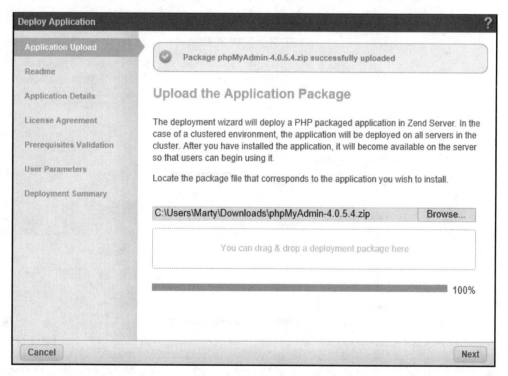

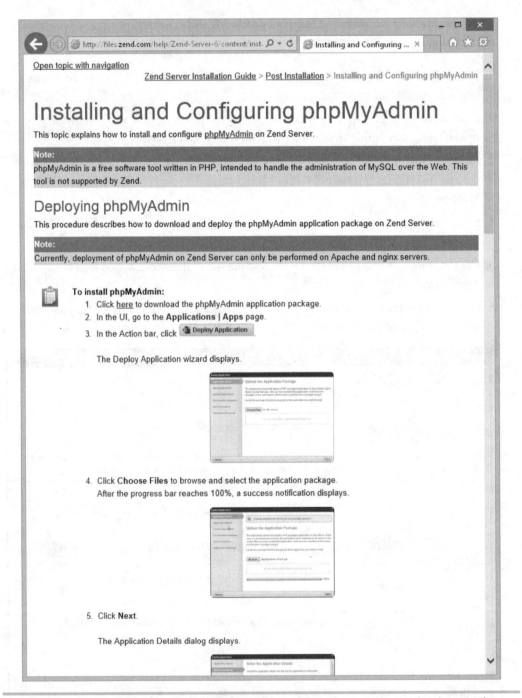

Figure 9-3 phpMyAdmin is a useful tool to take a quick look at a MySQL database without having to write a program to do it.

7. When you are told it has been successfully uploaded, click Next. Review the Readme page and again click Next.

8. Keep the suggested Default Name and Virtual Host (the default server will normally be "localhost"). For the Path, I would enter **phpmyadmin**, but it can be any folder you want. Click Next.

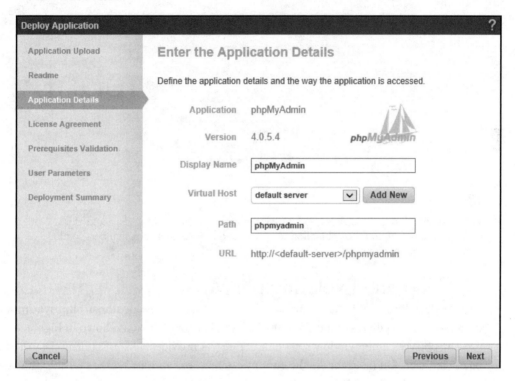

9. Review the License Agreement, click I Have Read, and click Next. You should see the validation that MySQL has been loaded. Click Next.

10. Under most circumstances, keep the default User Parameters and fill in the password you want to use. (If you don't enter a password, especially for the "root" user, you will get an error message when you open phpMyAdmin later in this chapter.) Click Next.

11. Review the Deployment Summary, use Previous to make any corrections you want, and then click Deploy to do that.

12. When the process is complete, click phpMyAdmin to display its details.

TIP

When creating a password, it is good practice to create strong passwords: six to eight characters in length and a combination of upper- and lowercase letters, numbers, and at least one special character.

Opening and Exploring phpMyAdmin

Open and explore phpMyAdmin by opening a browser, typing **localhost/phpmyadmin** in the address bar, and pressing ENTER. phpMyAdmin should open as shown in Figure 9-4.

The phpMyAdmin window shown in Figure 9-4 provides a list of built-in databases on the left side. On the right are the current versions and various settings for the database server (MySQL), the web server (Apache), and phpMyAdmin, as well as documentation for phpMyAdmin. In the middle are general and appearance settings. Across the top are ten tabs that provide a lot of additional information about the resident MySQL databases and the ability to change settings and, in the SQL tab, to do everything you can do in the MySQL command-line client.

If you didn't enter a password, you'll see a warning at the bottom of the window that phpMyAdmin's default settings do not include a password for the default username "root." This means that anybody who knows the username "root," and many people do, can access your database and do what they wish with it. While you are working on your own computer

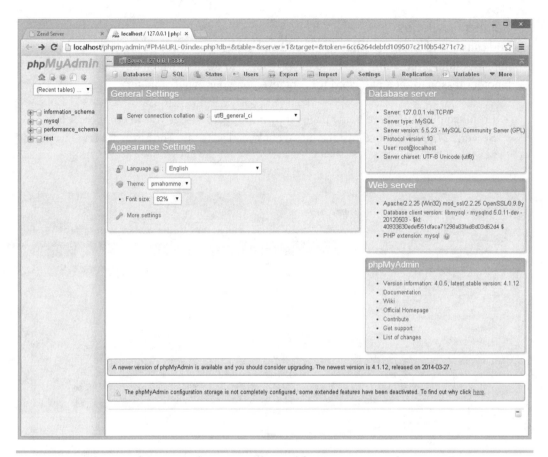

Figure 9-4 phpMyAdmin provides a control panel for setting up and maintaining MySQL.

using localhost (or 127.0.0.1), your risk is not great, but when you upload your site to a commercial host, it becomes critical that you set the username to something other than "root" and use a strong password.

NOTE

If you did not set a password for the "root" user while installing phpMyAdmin, you can use the Update feature in the Zend Server Application Apps window, opposite phpMyAdmin, to do that.

Setting Privileges

You can set and change privileges and add and delete users through the Users tab of phpMyAdmin—providing you have the privileges to do that, which the root user does (another reason to set a password for root, even on your own computer).

1. From the phpMyAdmin home page (shown in Figure 9-4; if you're not there, click Server:127.0.0.1:3306 above the tabs), click the Users tab. The Users Overview opens, as shown in Figure 9-5.

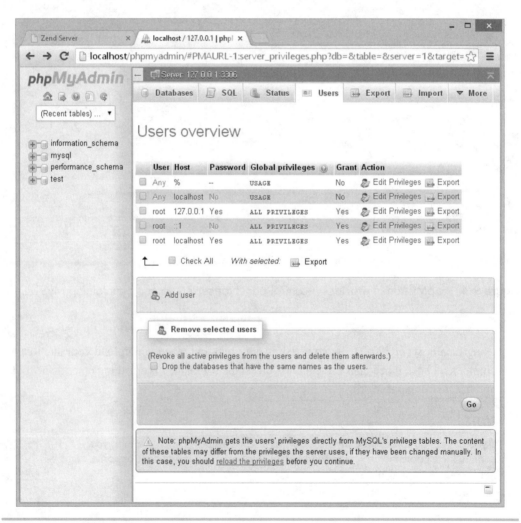

Figure 9-5 MySQL has a comprehensive security system built into it.

You can see that root user is set up (at least in my case) for both localhost and 127.0.0.1, has a password set in both cases, and has all privileges, including the ability to grant privileges to others.

2. Click Edit Privileges on the right end of the first root user listed. The top of the detail privileges page opens. Here you can see the full list of privileges that can be set.

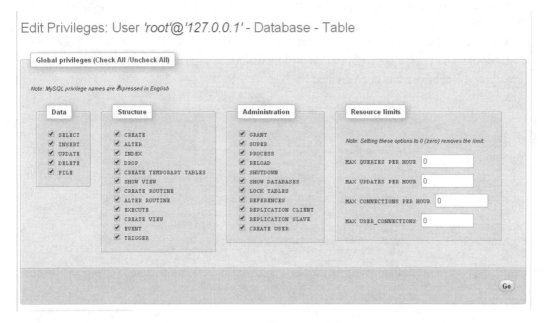

3. Scroll down until you see Change Password, where you can do that if you wish. You can even generate one by clicking Generate to get a 16-character, very strong password created for you. If you do that, be sure to copy the password (select it and press CTRL-C) to a document (open the document and press CTRL-V) that you keep in a secure place. Also, you need to go back to the Zend Server phpMyAdmin entry and use Update to revise your passwords there, or you won't be able to get back into phpMyAdmin.

Create and Use a Database in phpMyAdmin

To fully exercise the features of phpMyAdmin, you need to create a database, add a table to it, and add some data to the table. You can then do queries and manipulate the data.

Create a Database and Its Table

Use the following steps to build the full Books database shown earlier in Figure 9-1.

1. In the phpMyAdmin, click the Databases tab and in the Create Database text box, type **Books** and click Create (Collation will be discussed later). A message appears telling you the database has been created.

Databases

Create database

| Books | | Collation | ▼ | Create |

Database ▲	Action
☐ Books	▣ Check Privileges
information_schema	▣ Check Privileges
☐ mysql	▣ Check Privileges
performance_schema	▣ Check Privileges
☐ test	▣ Check Privileges
Total: 5	

2. Click Books in the left-hand column to open the new database. Under Create Table in the middle, click in the Name text box, type **Books**, press TAB, and type **6** for the Number Of Columns in the Books table (there is nothing that requires the database and table names to be the same). Click Go. The column entry window opens, as shown in Figure 9-6.

3. In the first field, type **Bkid**, leave INT (integer) for the Type, TAB over to Index, select Primary, and click A_I for Auto Increment. Leave the remaining fields blank.

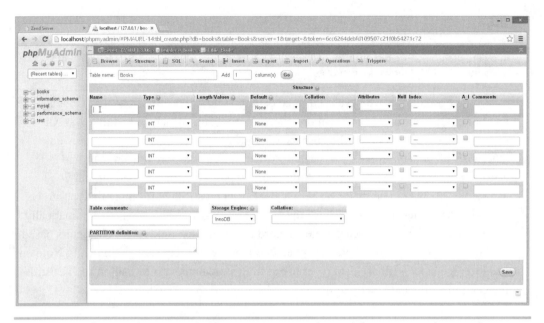

Figure 9-6 phpMyAdmin provides for an extensive column definition (not often used).

4. Fill in the remaining fields as shown next. For the Type, press v to get VARCHAR.

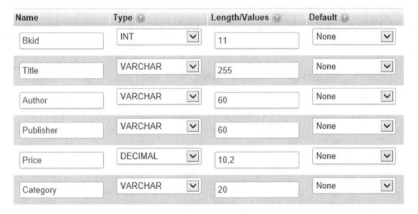

5. When you have completed entering the fields, click Save in the lower-right corner. You will get a message that table Books has been created, as shown in Figure 9-7.

NOTE
Unless you specify otherwise, a NULL or blank field is not allowed and must be filled in by the user. Since we did not specify (check) NULL as we were building the table, all fields have Null No, shown in Figure 9-7.

In the Books table, we have used three data types (INT, VARCHAR, DECIMAL), but a number of types are available, the more common of which are shown in Table 9-1. All data types have a NULL value (the absence of any value) by default if NULL is allowed; otherwise, all data types have a "" (blank) value, which is different from NULL and causes an error with numeric types. All numeric types are signed by default, but you can set the attribute to be UNSIGNED. You can also set an attribute for numeric types to be ZEROFILL, and integer types can have the AUTO_INCREMENT attribute, which automatically increments the field by one each time a record is added. Text fields store characters based on the specified or default character set and collation sequence (see the following Note on collation sequence). Binary data types are used to store nontext information such as still images and audio and video segments.

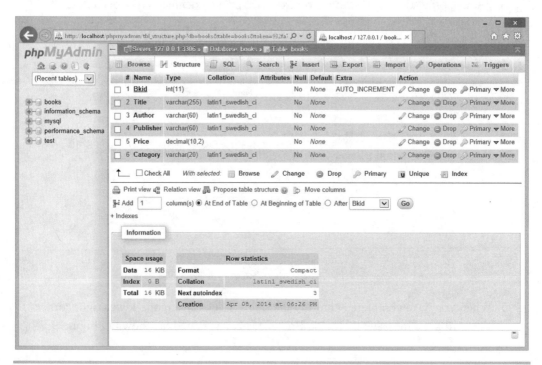

Figure 9-7 The Structure tab provides ways to manage a table's structure.

Type	Name	Length	Contents
Numeric	TINYINT	1 byte	−128 to +127, or 0–255 unsigned.
Numeric	SMALLINT	2 bytes	−32,768 to +32,767 or 0 to 65,535 unsigned.
Numeric	MEDIUMINT	3 bytes	−8,388,608 to +8,388,607 or 0 to 16,777,215 unsigned.
Numeric	INT	4 bytes	−2,147,483,648 to +2,147,483,647 or 0 to 4,294,967,295 unsigned.
Numeric	BIGINT	8 bytes	−9,223,372,036,854,775,808 to +9,223,372,036,854,775,807 or 0 to 18,446,744,073,709,551,615 unsigned.
Numeric	FLOAT(t,d)	4 bytes	Single-precision floating point number of t total digits, of which d are to the right of the decimal place. Good for smaller numbers with up to seven decimal places.
Numeric	DOUBLE(t,d)	8 bytes	Double-precision floating point number of t total digits, of which d are to the right of the decimal place. Good for larger numbers with up to 15 decimal places.
Numeric	DECIMAL(t,d)	Varies	Decimal number of t total digits, of which d are to the right of the decimal place, stored in binary format, packing nine decimal digits into four bytes. Will expand for large numbers.
Text	CHAR(t)	0 to 255	Fixed maximum number of characters (t) padded with blanks on the right, but removed when retrieved. Length is the number of t characters in bytes.
Text	VARCHAR(t)	0 to 65,535	Variable number of characters up to a maximum of (t), not padded. Length is the actual number of characters in bytes plus 1 byte up to 255 characters or plus 2 bytes above 255.
Text	TINYTEXT	0 to 255	Variable number of characters up to a maximum of 255, not padded. Length is the actual number of characters in bytes plus 1 byte.
Text	TEXT	0 to 65,535	Variable number of characters up to a maximum of 65,535, not padded. Length is the actual number of characters in bytes plus 2 bytes.
Text	MEDIUMTEXT	0 to 16,777,215	Variable number of characters up to a maximum of 16,777,215, not padded. Length is the actual number of characters in bytes plus 3 bytes.

Table 9-1 MySQL Data Types *(continued)*

Type	Name	Length	Contents
Text	`LONGTEXT`	0 to 4,294,967,295	Variable number of characters up to a maximum of 4,294,967,295, not padded. Length is the actual number of characters in bytes plus 4 bytes.
Binary	`TINYBLOB`	0 to 255	Variable number of bytes up to a maximum of 255, not padded. Length is the actual number of bytes plus 1 byte.
Binary	`BLOB`	0 to 65,535	Variable number of bytes up to a maximum of 65,535, not padded. Length is the actual number of bytes plus 2 bytes.
Binary	`MEDIUMBLOB`	0 to 16,777,215	Variable number of bytes up to a maximum of 16,777,215, not padded. Length is the actual number of bytes plus 3 bytes.
Binary	`LONGBLOB`	0 to 4,294,967,295	Variable number of bytes up to a maximum of 4,294,967,295, not padded. Length is the actual number of bytes plus 4 bytes.
Date/Time	`DATE`	3 bytes	Stored as YYYY-MM-DD and can range from 1000-01-01 to 9999-12-31.
Date/Time	`TIME`	3 bytes	Stored as HHH:MM:SS, can range from −838:59:59 to 838:59:59, and can be displayed as D HH:MM:SS, where D is the number of days up to a maximum of 34.
Date/Time	`DATETIME`	8 bytes	Stored as YYYY-MM-DD HH:MM:SS and can range from 1000-01-01 00:00:00 to 9999-12-31 23:59:59.
Date/Time	`TIMESTAMP`	4 bytes	Stored as the number of seconds from 1970-01-01 00:00:01 and can go to 2038-01-09 03:13:07. Normally displayed as YYYY-MM-DD HH:MM:SS.
Date/Time	`YEAR(t)`	1 byte	A two-digit or four-digit (YEAR(2) or YEAR(4)) year from 1901 to 2155. Two-digit years 00 to 69 are assumed to be 2000 to 2069, and years 70 to 99 are assumed to be 1970 to 1999.
Set	`ENUM(v1,v2,v3)`	1 or 2 bytes	Stores exactly 1 of up to 65,535 specified string values in a list. Length is dependent on the number of values.
Set	`SET(v1,v2,v3)`	1 to 8 bytes	Stores zero or more of up to 64 specified string values in a list. Length is dependent on the number of values chosen.

Table 9-1 MySQL Data Types

NOTE

As you create a table in phpMyAdmin, you'll notice that the default collation sequence is `latin1_swedish_ci`. This results from its ancestry and is not really a problem, but if you would like to better reflect U.S. English, use `latin1_general_ci`. (This handles most Western European languages. You can select either `ci`, meaning case insensitive, or `cs`, meaning case sensitive.) You can set this on a field-by-field basis or for an entire table by clicking the Operations tab while viewing a table and, under Table Options, selecting `latin1_general_ci` for the collation, as shown next, and clicking Go. You can also set it at the database level through the Operations tab.

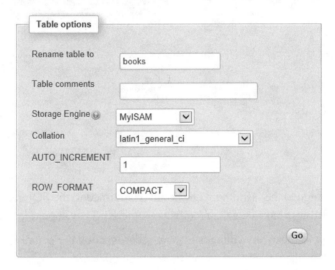

TIP

If a field's data type is `TIMESTAMP`, that field will automatically be filled with the current date and time when the record is created. You want to forbid a manual entry to be made in this field. If you want a field to both have an automatic date and time and allow a manual entry, make its data type `DATETIME` and enter `NOW()` as the default, which provides the current date and time.

Add Records to Your Table

Now that you have a table in phpMyAdmin, add some records to it, and then you can query it.

1. If you closed phpMyAdmin at the end of the last set of steps, restart phpMyAdmin and reopen the Books database and the Books table by clicking the plus sign opposite Books in the left column and clicking the Books table. Finally, click the Structure tab so your window looks like Figure 9-7.

2. Click the Insert tab in the center of the tab row. Enter the information in Table 9-2. In all cases, leave the Bkid field blank. It will be filled in automatically. Uncheck Ignore at the top left of the second record. In the remaining five fields, enter under Value the following nine records, using TAB to go from field to field. After every other record, click Go, Insert, and uncheck Ignore (don't click Ignore in the last record).

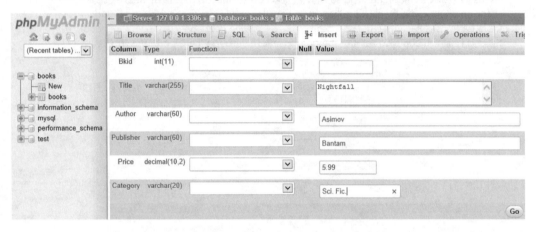

3. After clicking Go the last time, you should be returned to the SQL tab of the Books table. Click the Browse tab to see the records you entered. They should look like Figure 9-8.

4. If you want to make any changes in your records, click the pencil icon on the left of the record. Make the needed changes, and then click Go.

Title	Author	Publisher	Price	Category
Nightfall	Asimov	Bantam	5.99	Sci. Fic.
Patriot Games	Clancy	Berkley	4.95	Thriller
2010	Clarke	Ballantine	3.95	Sci. Fic.
Lie Down With Lions	Follett	Signet	4.95	Mystery
A Thief of Time	Hillerman	Harper	4.95	Mystery
The Fly on the Wall	Hillerman	Harper	4.95	Mystery
Hornet Flight	Follett	Signet	7.99	Thriller
The Innocent Man	Grisham	Dell	7.99	Thriller
Mission of Honor	Clancy	Berkley	7.99	Thriller

Table 9-2 Information for the Books Database

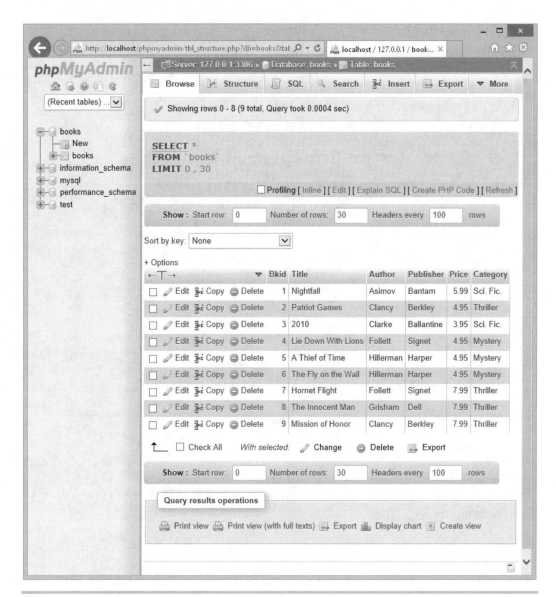

Figure 9-8 Browsing a table in phpMyAdmin lets you sort and review the records that have been entered.

CAUTION

The red "don't enter" icon deletes a record. Although you are given a warning, it is easy to click this icon by mistake, go whipping through the warning, and not realize what you have done until it is too late (there is no undelete). (Can you tell I've done that a couple of times?)

Query Your Table

Queries in phpMyAdmin are very easy to do because phpMyAdmin helps you write the script. Try that next.

1. From the Browse tab (Figure 9-8) in phpMyAdmin, click the SQL tab. The Run SQL Query window will open with the query started, like this:

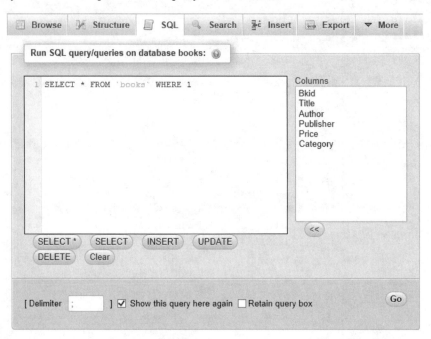

2. Drag over the "1" on the right end of the query, and double-click Price in the Columns list.

3. Click at the right end of the query, type **>5.00;** and click Go. The results are shown next:

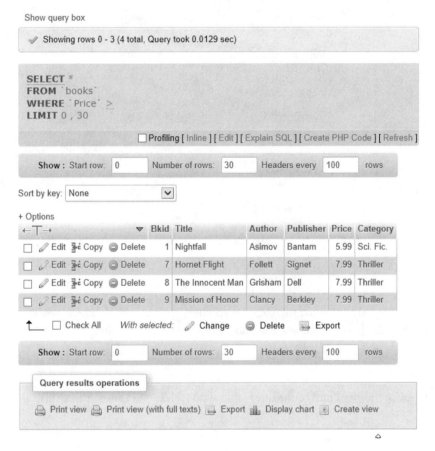

4. Click the SQL tab and do a query of only the Title and Author fields.

5. Drag over the asterisk (which means "all fields") on the left of the beginning query, double-click Title in the Columns list, type a **,** (comma), and double-click Author in the Columns list.

6. Drag over the "1" on the right end of the query, and double-click Category in the Columns list.

7. Click at the right end of the query and type **= "Thriller";** (note the double quotes), like this:

```
SELECT `Title`, `Author` FROM `books` WHERE
`Category` = "Thriller";
```

8. Click Go, with these results:

9. Click the SQL tab once more, and do a query to find a book where you know only part of the title. In this case, use the book with "Lions" in the title.

10. Drag over the "1" on the right end of the query, and double-click Title in the Columns list.

11. Click at the right end of the query and type **LIKE "%Lions";** like this:

```
SELECT * FROM `books` WHERE
`Title` LIKE "%Lions";
```

12. Click Go to get this book:

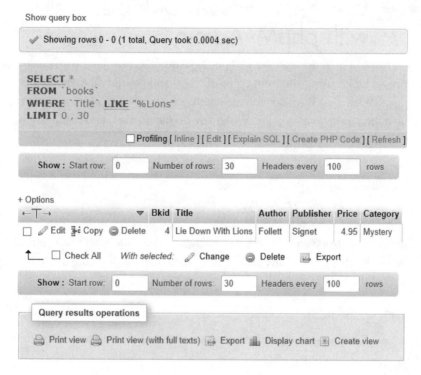

13. phpMyAdmin and your browser can be closed at this point.

As you can see in the previous steps, phpMyAdmin not only aids in creating and maintaining a database, it also allows you to test the MySQL scripts you write to see if they are doing what you want them to do.

Like you saw with PHP in earlier chapters, there is a comprehensive online manual available for MySQL at dev.mysql.com/doc/refman/5.5/en/. Also, an excellent book on MySQL is *MySQL: The Complete Reference,* by Vikram Vaswani (McGraw-Hill/ Professional, 2004).

Try This 9-1 ## Create Your Own Database with phpMyAdmin

Using the example in this chapter and phpMyAdmin, create your own database with one or more tables using different types of fields and possibly a default value such as a timestamp. When you have created the database and table(s), place a few records in the table, and then do several queries. When you do the queries, notice the MySQL script that produces the query results.

Chapter 9 Self-Test

The following questions are intended to help reinforce your comprehension of the concepts covered in this chapter. The answers can be found in the accompanying online Appendix A, "Answers to the Self-Tests."

1. What is a database?

2. What are the three principle parts of a database and their alternative names?

3. What is a relational database?

4. How are the various tables in a relational database related to each other, and what is the element that does this called in two related tables?

5. What is phpMyAdmin?

6. phpMyAdmin is meant to be used as a primary tool on a day-to-day basis, true or false?

7. How do you start or open phpMyAdmin?

8. In a database created with phpMyAdmin, by default, fields must be filled in by the user, true or false?

9. How do you automatically generate an index or key for a database table created with phpMyAdmin?

10. The collation sequence `latin1_swedish_ci` means that text must be in Swedish, true or false?

Chapter 10

Fundamentals of MySQL and SQL

Key Skills & Concepts

- Installing and Using the MySQL Workbench

- Understanding SQL

- Using MySQL

- Reviewing MySQL Word Usage

- Using MySQL Operators

- Exploring MySQL Functions

MySQL is a relational database management system that uses the Structured Query Language (SQL) to store, work with, and retrieve information over the Internet. MySQL is called "the world's most popular open-source database," with many millions of websites using it as a web resource that runs on a web server, as does PHP. That is the way we'll discuss it here, but MySQL can also run on a stand-alone server not connected to the Web. MySQL is built to handle large-volume, multiuser database access. mysql.com says "many of the world's largest and fastest-growing organizations including Facebook, Google, Alcatel Lucent, and Zappos rely on MySQL." MySQL's low or no cost, ease of use, speed, reliability, and usability for small to large sites make it easy to see why it has widespread use.

NOTE

The GNU General Public License discussed here is a model license for free software that was developed for the Swedish GNU operating system. "GNU" is not an acronym, but the name of an antelope-like animal.

About MySQL

MySQL was developed and first released in 1995 by MySQL AB, a Swedish company that is now a part of Oracle. Oracle makes the program available at a number of levels, including under a free-to-the-user GNU General Public License (GPL) in addition to proprietary licenses. GPL stipulates that any system that uses MySQL must be distributed under a similar license. It is this arrangement that makes MySQL available free of charge with the free Zend Server, as well as with WAMP (Windows servers for Apache, MySQL, and PHP) and XAMPP (cross platform servers for Apache, MySQL, PHP, and Perl). As this is written (summer 2014), Zend Server includes MySQL 5.5.23. Oracle offers the MySQL Community Server with MySQL for Windows, Linux, and other operating systems, which can be freely downloaded, but does require some effort to download, set up, integrate, and manage. It also offers MySQL Enterprise, which comes with many tools and technical support to make the job much easier, but for a hefty price. Zend Server, WAMP, and XAMPP make using MySQL relatively easy, free, and a good way to start a project. MySQL is a mature, full-featured, professional relational database management system (RDBMS), as you can see from its website, mysql.com. Many professional web developers believe that PHP and MySQL are the best way to add a database to a website of any size.

TIP
This and the following chapters will require Zend Server to be running and at least one browser to be opened to localhost. With the standard setup you were guided through in earlier chapters, Zend Server with MySQL should automatically start when you start your computer. As described in the last chapter, load a browser and, in the address bar, type **localhost/phpmyadmin**, where you see on the right that MySQL is installed as the database server (see Figure 10-1). On the left, you see that MySQL has its own database with a number of tables that support its use.

TIP
If you have problems seeing your website on http://localhost/, try http://127.0.0.1/.

MySQL gives a website the ability to store, retrieve, and manipulate large amounts of information quickly and efficiently. This allows a website to present a large catalog of items for sale, to provide access to and searchability of a large archive of information, or to register and service a large group of individuals, such as members of an organization.

This chapter will look at the MySQL Workbench as an alternative to phpMyAdmin, SQL as the foundation of MySQL, the structure and use of the MySQL command language, and the basics of working with MySQL directly with a command-line interface and phpMyAdmin.

Installing and Using MySQL Workbench
The MySQL Workbench is a recent graphic interface distributed and maintained by Oracle that allows users to create, manage, and administer MySQL databases. There are two versions of the Workbench: the free Community Edition that can be downloaded from mysql.com, and the extended Standard Edition that can be purchased.

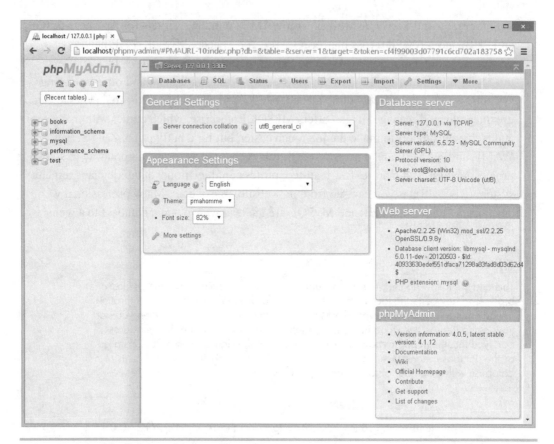

Figure 10-1 "localhost" is the Apache web server running on your computer and provides access to MySQL.

NOTE

phpMyAdmin is an early graphic user interface for MySQL that has been significantly upgraded over time, so today, it is a comprehensive and reliable tool. Because it has been free and open source for some time and included in WAMP, XAMPP, and LAMP (Linux servers for Apache, MySQL, and PHP) server packages, many people (including myself) became familiar with it and continue to use it as the MySQL interface of choice. MySQL Workbench is relatively recent and comes from Oracle. MySQL Workbench is a fully capable interface that many people like. It and phpMyAdmin are much like Ford and Chevy—it depends on your preferences. Try them both and see for yourself (and there are at least half a dozen other MySQL front ends if you want to search them out).

Download and Install MySQL Workbench

Download and install the MySQL Workbench Community Edition with the following steps.

1. Open a browser to mysql.com and click the Downloads tab. Scroll down to MySQL Community Edition and click Download From MySQL Developer Zone.

2. Scroll down to MySQL Workbench and click Download. Scroll down until you see Generally Available (GA) Releases and click Download opposite MSI Installer (assuming you are getting the Windows version).

3. Enter your Oracle user ID and password or sign up for a new one, go through Oracle's questions (part of the reason people stay with phpMyAdmin), and click Download for the third time. Click Run.

4. Click Next three times and then click Install. Click Yes to allow the installation, and when it is done, click Finish. MySQL Workbench will appear as you can see in Figure 10-2.

Figure 10-2   MySQL Workbench is desktop app, whereas phpMyAdmin is a web app.

Create a Database Model

One of the strengths of MySQL Workbench is the ability to create a visual model of a database you want to build, look at it graphically, and then convert to an operating database. To compare to what we did with phpMyAdmin, create a model of a relational database with four relational tables.

1. Within MySQL Workbench, click the Local Instance of MySQL on the Zend Server, enter your password (if you wish, click Save Password), and click OK.

2. Click the File menu and click New Model. A new database model will appear as shown in Figure 10-3.

3. Right-click mydb and click Edit Schema. (A database schema is the detail structure of a database with its tables, columns, and relationships among tables. In MySQL Workbench, the word "schema" is used synonymously with "database.") Type the name you want to use, like **MyBooks** and then click the X in the tab to close the schema.

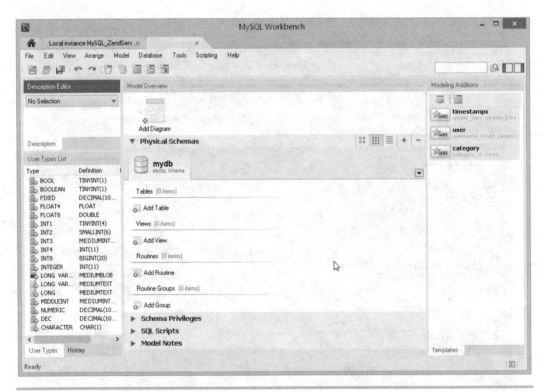

Figure 10-3 Words such as "schema," "triggers," "routines," and "views" pose a bit of a hurdle with MySQL Workbench.

4. Double-click Add Table. Click in the Table Name text box and type **Books**.

5. Click in the Column Name, type **Bkid**, leave INT as the data type, and click in the PK (Primary Key), UQ (Unique Index), and AI (Auto Increment) check boxes by scrolling right. NN (Not Null) will be automatically checked. Repeat this for the following columns:

- Title, VARCHAR(255)
- Aid, INT
- Pid, INT
- Price, DEC
- Cid, INT

6. Then click the X in the tab to close the table and add the following three tables with their columns:

- Authors with Aid, INT, PK, AI; LastName, VARCHAR(30); FirstName, VARCHAR(30)
- Categories with Cid, INT, PK, AI; Category, VARCHAR(20); Section, VARCHAR(20)
- Publishers with PID, INT, PK, AI; Publisher, VARCHAR(50); Address, VARCHAR(60); City, VARCHAR(60)

7. Click Add Diagram. From the catalog tree on the left, drag each of the tables to the grid in the middle so they look like the arrangement in Figure 10-4.

8. At the bottom of the list of icons on the left of the Diagram section, click the last icon to place a connector between existing columns, and then click one of the foreign keys (Aid, Pid, and Cid) in the Books table and the related primary key in its table. A line will appear connecting the two tables, as you see in Figure 10-4.

9. Click the File menu, click Save Model As, locate the folder you want to use, give the model a name, and click Save.

The diagramming part of MySQL Workbench is one of its best features.

Understanding SQL

SQL, or the Structured Query Language, is an efficient means of working with data using statements similar to spoken English. SQL was originally developed at IBM and has since become an international standard that is used by a number of RDBMSs. SQL was designed as a structured, declarative query language for relational databases. SQL statements generally begin with a declarative command, such as CREATE, DELETE,

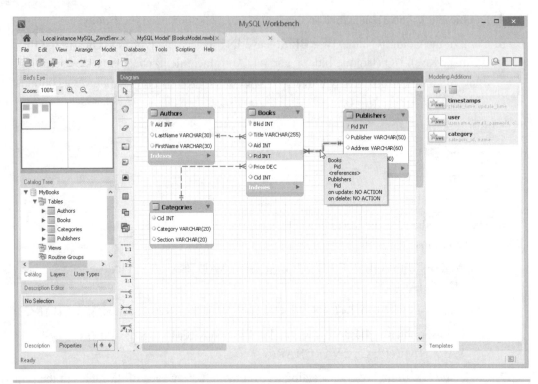

Figure 10-4 The MySQL Workbench diagramming gives you an excellent illustration of your database.

INSERT, OPEN, SELECT, and UPDATE. This is then followed by one or more clauses beginning with one or more of these keywords: FROM, GROUP BY, HAVING, JOIN, ORDER BY, and WHERE. For example, using the Books database and table defined in Chapter 9, a query might be:

```
SELECT * FROM books WHERE price > 5.00 ORDER BY title;
```

This will select all fields (the asterisk) in records from the Books table where the Price is greater than $5.00, and order the resulting list by Title. Listing 10-1 shows additional examples of SQL statements that build the Books table used with phpMyAdmin in Chapter 8 with five fields, three of which are variable-character strings of either 255 or 60 maximum characters. The Bkid field is an integer that must have a value (NOT NULL) and is the primary key for the table. The data for six books is then inserted into the table. In the first five of them, every field has a value, so the fields are not specified. For the sixth book, two of the fields are missing, so the ones that are present must be specified. Then the table is updated to change the price for book 3 and to change the title for book 5 to correct a misspelling. Finally, book 6 is removed from the table.

NOTE

There are two SQL and MySQL coding practices that are followed in this book and that are important to understand:

- Here, and in most other publications, you'll see SQL and MySQL commands and keywords in all uppercase. This is not necessary for the commands and keywords to operate correctly—they are not case sensitive—but it helps to identify those words from other text, and so is recommended.

- Because MySQL and some other implementations of SQL allow multiple statements in the same call to the server, each statement must end with a semicolon (;). I believe that all MySQL statements should end with a semicolon to be consistent with PHP and have followed that practice throughout the remaining chapters of this book.

TIP

In this book I have followed the practice of making object names, such as databases, tables, and columns, all lowercase for human readability. On Windows computers, such names are not case sensitive, so they may be any mixture of cases without affecting machine readability. On Apple Mac and Linux computers, these names *are case sensitive*, and MySQL code will not operate properly if you mix cases. For that reason, as well as human readability, it is a good idea to make all names all lowercase and all commands and keywords all uppercase.

Listing 10-1   Examples of SQL Statements

```
CREATE TABLE books (
     bkid int NOT NULL PRIMARY KEY,
     title varchar(255),
     author varchar(60),
     publisher varchar(60),
     price decimal(10,2));
INSERT INTO books VALUES
     (1, 'Nightfall', 'Asimov', 'Bantam', 5.99);
INSERT INTO books VALUES
     (2, 'Patriot Games', 'Clancy', 'Berkley', 4.95);
INSERT INTO books VALUES
     (3, '2010', 'Clarke', 'Ballantine', 3.95);
INSERT INTO books VALUES
     (4, 'Lie Down with Lions', 'Follett', 'Signet', 4.95);
INSERT INTO books VALUES
     (5, 'A Theif of Time', 'Hillerman', 'Harper', 4.95);
```

```
INSERT INTO books (bkid,title,price) VALUES
    (6, 'The Innocent Man',7.99);
UPDATE books SET price=5.99 WHERE bkid = 3;
UPDATE books SET title='A Thief of Time' WHERE bkid = 5;
DELETE FROM books WHERE bkid = 6;
```

There are, of course, many other SQL commands, keywords, and clauses, as well as a variety of data types and functions. The purpose of the book, though, is to explore how to use MySQL with PHP. While MySQL is closely tied to SQL, there are some differences, so we'll leave SQL with this brief introduction.

Using MySQL

The MySQL server can be used in a variety of ways. In this and the next chapter, we'll look at two of them: directly through the MySQL command-line client and online through the phpMyAdmin user interface. In Chapter 12 and on, we'll look at accessing MySQL programmatically through PHP. In this section, we will briefly look at the command-line client, and in the next major section, we'll explore MySQL with phpMyAdmin.

TIP

The authoritative MySQL manual from Oracle is available for download for free at http://downloads.mysql.com/docs/refman-5.5-en.a4.pdf. I recommend that you add it to your library. The same manual is also available online at http://dev.mysql.com/doc/refman/5.5/en/create-database.html.

The MySQL command-line client is mainly for determining if MySQL is installed and running on a computer, and for doing some quick maintenance on a database. Major setup and maintenance of a database is better done with phpMyAdmin or the MySQL Workbench, while recurring use of a database is done programmatically, which in this book means PHP.

Starting the MySQL Command-Line Client

The MySQL command-line client was placed on your computer when Zend Server was installed and is in the c:/Program Files (86)/zend/mysql55/bin folder.

1. Open Windows Explorer by clicking its icon on the taskbar.

2. Navigate to the c:/Program Files (86)/zend/mysql55/bin folder.

3. Open the MySQL command-line window by double-clicking mysql.exe, as shown in Figure 10-5.

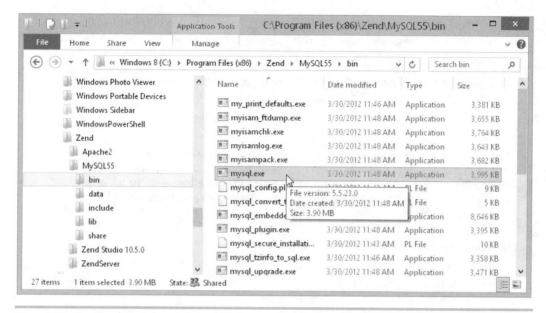

Figure 10-5 Zend Server provides a full suite of web development software, including a full version of MySQL.

4. At the `mysql>` prompt, type

```
select version(), current_date;
```

and press ENTER. Your command window should look like this:

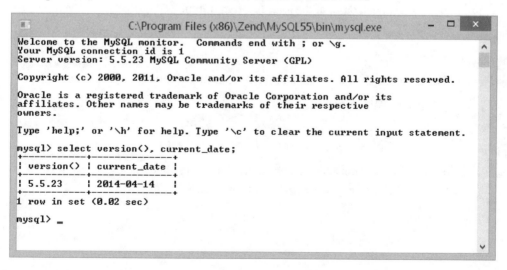

5. If you have been able to do these instructions and get the results shown, then MySQL is properly installed and running. If not, you need to go back over your installation and possibly these instructions to see where the error is.

6. If you are immediately going on to the next section, do so directly. Otherwise, type **exit**, and press ENTER to close the command-line window.

NOTE

Your command-line window starts out with white text on a black background. You can reverse that to what is shown here by clicking the System menu in the upper-left corner, clicking Properties | Colors | Screen Text and clicking the black square on the left of the color bar. Then click Screen Background and click the white square on the right of the color bar. Finally, click OK.

Build a Table on the Command Line

Build a bit of the Books table, do a query on it, and then delete it with these instructions (see Figure 10-6 for the results).

1. If you exited the command-line window, use as much of the immediately preceding instructions as needed to reopen it.

2. To attach the Books table to an existing database, see what databases are available by typing the following at the mysql> prompt:

```
SHOW DATABASES;
```

and pressing ENTER.

3. To use the Test database, at the mysql> prompt, type

```
USE test;
```

and press ENTER.

4. To begin creating the new table, at the mysql> prompt, type

```
CREATE TABLE books (
        bkid int NOT NULL PRIMARY KEY,
        title varchar(255),
        author varchar(60));
```

and press ENTER. This code can be entered all on a single line or, by using SHIFT-ENTER (newline), it can be on several lines as shown here.

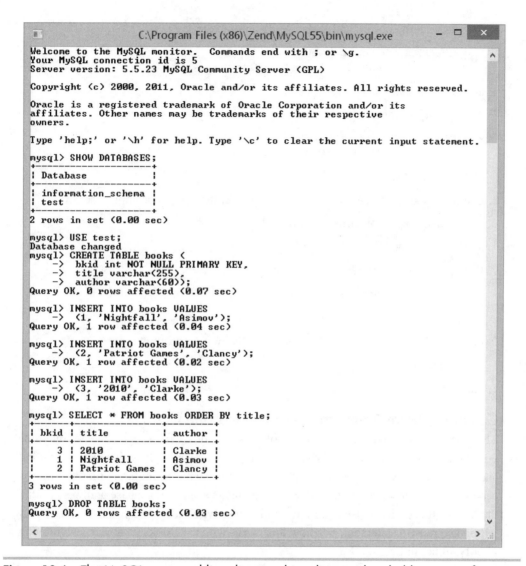

```
C:\Program Files (x86)\Zend\MySQL55\bin\mysql.exe                    _  □  ×
Welcome to the MySQL monitor.  Commands end with ; or \g.
Your MySQL connection id is 5
Server version: 5.5.23 MySQL Community Server (GPL)

Copyright (c) 2000, 2011, Oracle and/or its affiliates. All rights reserved.

Oracle is a registered trademark of Oracle Corporation and/or its
affiliates. Other names may be trademarks of their respective
owners.

Type 'help;' or '\h' for help. Type '\c' to clear the current input statement.

mysql> SHOW DATABASES;
+--------------------+
| Database           |
+--------------------+
| information_schema |
| test               |
+--------------------+
2 rows in set (0.00 sec)

mysql> USE test;
Database changed
mysql> CREATE TABLE books (
    ->   bkid int NOT NULL PRIMARY KEY,
    ->   title varchar(255),
    ->   author varchar(60));
Query OK, 0 rows affected (0.07 sec)

mysql> INSERT INTO books VALUES
    ->   (1, 'Nightfall', 'Asimov');
Query OK, 1 row affected (0.04 sec)

mysql> INSERT INTO books VALUES
    ->   (2, 'Patriot Games', 'Clancy');
Query OK, 1 row affected (0.02 sec)

mysql> INSERT INTO books VALUES
    ->   (3, '2010', 'Clarke');
Query OK, 1 row affected (0.03 sec)

mysql> SELECT * FROM books ORDER BY title;
+-------+---------------+--------+
| bkid  | title         | author |
+-------+---------------+--------+
|    3  | 2010          | Clarke |
|    1  | Nightfall     | Asimov |
|    2  | Patriot Games | Clancy |
+-------+---------------+--------+
3 rows in set (0.00 sec)

mysql> DROP TABLE books;
Query OK, 0 rows affected (0.03 sec)
```

Figure 10-6   The MySQL command-line client is a bit tedious and probably not your first choice for working with MySQL.

5. Add books to the database at the `mysql>` prompt by typing

```
INSERT INTO books VALUES
        (1, 'Nightfall', 'Asimov');
```

and press ENTER. Again, this can be on one or two lines.

6. Continue adding books, and at the `mysql>` prompt, type

```
INSERT INTO books VALUES
        (2, 'Patriot Games', 'Clancy');
```

and press ENTER.

7. At the `mysql>` prompt, type

```
INSERT INTO books VALUES
        (3, '2010', 'Clarke');
```

and press ENTER.

8. List the books in the database, sorted by title. At the `mysql>` prompt, type

```
SELECT * FROM books ORDER BY title;
```

and press ENTER.

9. Delete the table. At the `mysql>` prompt, type

```
DROP TABLE books;
```

and press ENTER.

10. Close the MySQL command-line client. At the `mysql>` prompt, type

```
exit;
```

and press ENTER.

Compare phpMyAdmin to the Command-Line Client

The MySQL command-line client is a tool for small, quick fixes to a database; one-time queries; and for testing how a MySQL command will respond. It is also tedious to use and unforgiving if you make a typo. phpMyAdmin also has a similar, but more powerful, capability that allows you to test MySQL statements against a database and work with the results. It is easier to use and more forgiving of typos, allowing you to correct errors within and reuse a statement. See how this works with the Books database we built with phpMyAdmin in Chapter 9.

1. Open a browser, type **localhost\phpmyadmin** in the address bar, and press **ENTER**.

2. Open the Books database on the left and click the Books table to do a search of that table.

3. Click the SQL tab. You will see the beginning of a SELECT statement.

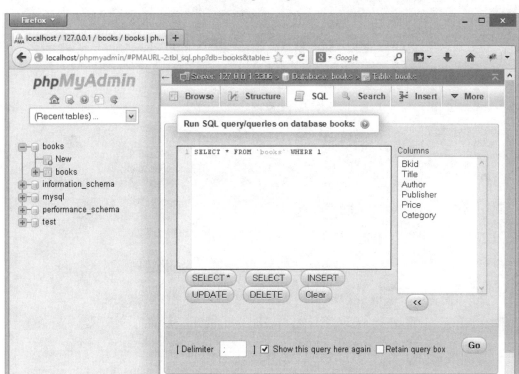

4. Select the 1 at the end of the statement and double-click Author in the Columns list on the right. `'Author'` (the Author column) will replace the 1.

5. Click immediately after `'Author'`, type a space, and then type **= 'Clancy';**. We now have a statement for a MySQL query of the Books table that says "Select all fields in the records in the Books table where the author is Clancy."

```
1 SELECT * FROM `books` WHERE `Author` =
  'Clancy'|
```

6. Click Go. The result is shown in Figure 10-7. It not only answers the query, but also allows you to edit, copy, and delete what was selected.

7. Click Show Query Box at the top to go back and change the query—for example, changing `'Clancy'` to `'Clarke'`. Clicking Go again displays results that reflect the query change.

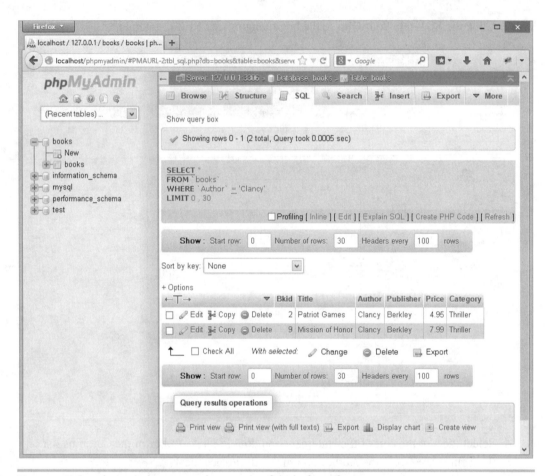

Figure 10-7 phpMyAdmin provides a powerful platform for testing MySQL statements.

Exploring the MySQL Language

MySQL has a number of commands and keywords, a complete set of math and comparison operators, and a number of functions that can be used to build its statements. In the following sections, we'll look at the most important of the operators and functions and demonstrate how they are used. In Chapter 11, we'll explore MySQL commands and other keywords and how all the MySQL elements are put together in statements. It needs to be emphasized that this is not a complete list of every aspect of the language. That is left for the MySQL manual and its over 3,000 pages. We'll begin, though, by looking at MySQL's word usage.

Reviewing MySQL Word Usage

MySQL's language is meant to be human readable and reasonably easy to understand. To do that, MySQL defines various types of words and sets out the rules for their use:

● **Commands** are declarative words that have a specific meaning within MySQL, such as **CREATE**, **SELECT**, and **UPDATE**. They are, by custom, in all capital letters for human readability, but that is not necessary for their proper operation.

● **Keywords** are supporting words for the commands to which MySQL has given a specific meaning. They include **FROM**, **GROUP BY**, **ORDER BY**, and **WHERE**. Once again, they are, by custom, presented in all capital letters, but that is not necessary.

● **Names or identifiers** are words used for specific elements such as databases, tables, and columns. They can contain the letters of the alphabet in either upper or lowercase, the numbers 0 through 9, the dollar sign ($), and the underscore (_). They cannot be over 64 characters in length. They can be within single (') or double quotes ("). Multipart or qualified names are separated by a period (.)—for example, `database_name.table_name.column_name` or `books.books.authors`.

● **Literals** are sets of alphabetic and numeric characters used as values in a statement. There are several types:

   ● **String values** are any combination of alphabetic and numeric characters enclosed in either single (') or double (") quotes. Escape sequences can be embedded in a string.

   ● **Numeric values** are sets of numeric characters that form an integer, decimal, or floating point number. The number may be preceded by either a plus (+) or minus (-) sign. Floating point numbers can be in scientific notation (`4.6E2`).

   ● **Date and time values** are either strings or numbers in a context where a date is expected. Allowable formatting includes the following:

      ● Date strings with delimiters in one of two forms: `'YYYY-MM-DD'` or `'YY-MM-DD'` with most punctuation marks allowable as delimiters, such as `'2016/04/19'` or `'16*04*19'`.

      ● Date strings without delimiters in one of two forms: `'YYYYMMDD'` or `'YYMMDD'`, such as `'20160419'` or `'160419'`.

- Date numbers in either of two forms: YYYYMMDD or YYMMDD, such as 20160419 or 160419.

- Two-digit years 70 to 99 are interpreted as 1970 to 1999, while years 00 to 69 are interpreted as 2000 to 2069.

- Date and time strings with delimiters in one of two forms: 'YYYY-MM-DD HH:MM:SS' or 'YY-MM-DD HH:MM:SS' with most punctuation marks allowable as delimiters, such as '2016/04/19 11:24:30' or '16*04*19 11:24:30'. The separator between date and time can be either a space or the capital letter "T."

- Date and time strings without delimiters in one of two forms: 'YYYYMMDDHHMMSS' or 'YYMMDDHHMMSS', such as '20160419112430' or '160419112430'.

- Date and time numbers in one of two forms: YYYYMMDDHHMMSS or YYMMDDHHMMSS, such as 20160419112430 or 160419112430.

- **Boolean values** are constants expressed by the words TRUE, true, FALSE, or false.

- **User-defined variables**, or just "user variables," are names that can be assigned values within a MySQL statement and then used in other statements. User variables begin with an @ (at sign) followed by a name you give it. The name can contain any alphanumeric characters plus . (period), _ (underscore), and $ (dollar sign), and are not case sensitive. User variables are assigned a value with the assignment character := (semicolon equal sign) or, in the SET clause with just an = (equal sign). Examples of user-defined variables are

  - @book := 'Nightfall'

  - SET @price = 7.99

- **Expressions** are a word or phrase, which can include names, literals, user variables, operators, and functions that provides a value in a MySQL statement.

- **Reserved words** are those for which MySQL has a special usage. There are a large number of reserved words, too many to list here. For that reason, it is a good practice to enclose names, such as database, table, and column names, in either single or double quotes whenever it is possible that a name could be misinterpreted. Also, if you are getting errors for which you cannot find another reason, try putting names in quotes.

- **Comments** are in one of three forms:
  - Begin with a -- (double-dash) to comment to the end of the line.
  - Begin with a # (hash mark) to comment to the end of the line.
  - Begin with /* (slash asterisk) to comment until the following */. Since this is consistent with PHP, it is often used.
- **Escape sequences** are almost the same as those for PHP, as you can see in Table 10-1. All escape sequences begin with a backslash (\) or escape character.

Using MySQL Operators

Within MySQL statements, you can use expressions that include arithmetic, comparison, and assignment operators. For example, in the statement **SELECT * FROM** books **WHERE** price > 5.00, the expression price > 5.00 uses the greater-than comparison operator. As you'll see in later sections of this chapter, there a number of situations where expressions and operators can be used. The operators that MySQL has available are very similar to PHP and include

- Arithmetic operators
- Comparison operators
- Logical operators
- Assignment operators

Escape Sequence	Used to Generate the Following Character
\0	Null
\'	Single quote (')
\"	Double quote (")
\b	Backspace
\n	Newline
\r	Carriage return
\t	Tab
\z	End of file on Windows
\\	Backslash
\%	% in a pattern-matching context
_	_ in a pattern-matching context

Table 10-1   Escape Sequences That Can Be Used in MySQL

Arithmetic Operators

Arithmetic operators, shown in Table 10-2, allow you to perform arithmetic operations within a MySQL statement.

If both values are integers, the calculation will be done with 64-bit precision. If one of the values is unsigned (without a plus or minus), the result will be unsigned. If you are doing arithmetic with very large or very small numbers and the precision of the results is important, read the applicable sections of the manual (12.6.1) carefully. Arithmetic operators apply only to numbers. For dates, you must use the date functions.

Comparison Operators

Comparison operators, shown in Table 10-3, allow you to do comparisons within a MySQL statement.

The result of comparison operations is TRUE (1), FALSE (0), or NULL, where NULL is the absence of a value or is unknown.

TIP
If you want to assign NULL to a value (a variable or an expression), use "IS NULL" and not "=NULL." The reason is that "=NULL" assigns the literal characters "N U L L" to the values, while "IS NULL" assigns '0' to the value, which is, and can be tested for, "FALSE."

Logical Operators

Table 10-4 lists MySQL logical operators that allow you to include logical expressions within statements.

Operator	Description
+	Addition, the sum of two values
−	Subtraction, the difference between two values
*	Multiplication, the product of two values
/	Division, the quotient of two values
% or MOD	Modulus division, the remainder after dividing two values
DIV	Integer division, the integer quotient of two values, which do not have to be integers

Table 10-2 MySQL Arithmetic Operators

Operator	Description (Is a Value...)
=	Equal to another value
>=	Greater than or equal to another value
>	Greater than another value
<=	Less than or equal to another value
<	Less than another value
!= or <>	Not equal to another value
IS NULL	Absent
IS NOT NULL	Not absent
BETWEEN ... AND ...	Between two other values
NOT BETWEEN ... AND ...	Not between two other values

Table 10-3   MySQL Comparison Operators

The result of a logical expression is TRUE (1), FALSE (0), or NULL, where NULL is the absence of a value or is unknown. Examples of logical expressions where x is TRUE and y is FALSE are

- x AND y is FALSE, but if y is TRUE, x AND y is TRUE.
- x OR y is TRUE, but if y is TRUE, x OR y is still TRUE.
- x XOR y is TRUE, but if y is TRUE, x XOR y is FALSE.
- x AND NOT y is TRUE, but if y is TRUE, x AND NOT y is FALSE.

Operator	Description
AND or &&	Logical AND. Both values must be TRUE for the result to be TRUE.
NOT or !	Negates value. NOT TRUE is FALSE.
OR or ||	Logical OR. Either or both values may be TRUE for the result to be TRUE.
XOR	Logical exclusive OR. Either *but not both* values may be TRUE for the result to be TRUE.

Table 10-4   MySQL Logical Operators

Assignment Operators

Assignment operators allow you to assign a value to a user variable. `:=` is the primary assignment operator, but in the `SET` clause, you can use `=`. In all cases other than in the `SET` clause, the `=` is considered a comparison operator. Examples of assignment operators are

- `@name := 'Michael'`
- `SET @date = 160419`

Exploring MySQL Functions

MySQL has a large number of functions that you can use within MySQL statements. The following sections group the more common functions into:

- Arithmetic functions
- Comparison functions
- Control flow functions
- Date and time functions
- Encryption and compression functions
- String functions
- System and information functions

Many of MySQL functions are similar to PHP functions. The benefit of the MySQL functions within a MySQL statement is that they are immediately evaluated by the MySQL server without having to go out to the PHP server.

Function names are immediately followed by a set of parentheses that contains the function's arguments. There can be no space between the function name and the parentheses following it. Functions may have zero or more arguments.

Arithmetic Functions

Arithmetic functions are used in expressions within MySQL statements to perform arithmetic operations. They include the functions shown in Table 10-5.

Examples of arithmetic functions are (use the Books table that was built in Chapter 9):

- `ABS(-64)` returns 64
- `SELECT AVG(Price) FROM books;` returns 5.96778

Function	The Result Is:
ABS()	The absolute value of the argument—the removal of any sign.
AVG()	The average value of the values in a column of a selected table. If DISTINCT is added to the arguments, repeated values in the column are ignored.
CEILING() or CEIL()	The smallest integer greater than the argument.
COUNT()	The number of rows in a selected table that contain the argument. If the argument is * then it is a simple count of rows. If DISTINCT is added to the arguments, rows with repeated argument values are ignored.
FLOOR()	The largest integer less than the argument.
MAX()	The maximum value of the values in a column of a selected table. If DISTINCT is added to the arguments, repeated values in the column are ignored, but the result is the same.
MIN()	The minimum value of the values in a column of a selected table. If DISTINCT is added to the arguments, repeated values in the column are ignored, but the result is the same.
RAND()	A floating point random number between 0 and 1. If an integer constant is added as an argument, it acts as a seed to produce a repeatable set of random numbers.
ROUND(a,b)	Rounds argument a to b number of decimal places. If b is missing, it is assumed to be 0.
SUM()	The sum of the values in a column of a selected table. If DISTINCT is added to the arguments, repeated values in the column are ignored.
TRUNCATE(a,b)	Truncates argument a to b number of decimal places. If b is missing, it is assumed to be 0.

Table 10-5   MySQL Arithmetic Functions

- SELECT CEILING(4.56); returns 5
- SELECT COUNT(*) FROM books; returns 9
- SELECT FLOOR(4.56); returns 4
- SELECT MAX(Price) FROM books; returns 7.99
- SELECT MIN(Price) FROM books; returns 3.95
- SELECT RAND(); returns 0.355812035832379
- SELECT ROUND(7.54); returns 8
- SELECT SUM(Price) FROM books; returns 53.71
- SELECT TRUNCATE(7.54); returns 7

NOTE

You can try out any of these functions using phpMyAdmin, selecting the SQL tab and typing the functions following the SELECT command, and clicking Go as you see in the first and third illustrations next. phpMyAdmin then shows the result as you see in the second and fourth illustrations next.

Comparison Functions

Comparison functions are used in expressions within MySQL statements to compare values. They include the functions shown in Table 10-6.

Examples of comparison functions are

- `COALESCE(NULL, NULL, 1492)` returns 1492

- `GREATEST(4.53, 7.21, 10.83)` returns 10.83

- `5.95 IN(3.99, 4.34, 5.95)` returns 1 or TRUE

- `INTERVAL(10, 4, 8, 12, 15)` returns 2

- `LEAST(4.53, 7.21, 10.83)` returns 4.53

- `'MartyMatthews' LIKE '%Matthews'` returns 1 or TRUE

- `5.95 NOT IN(3.99, 4.34, 5.95)` returns 0 or FALSE

- `STRCMP('Marty', 'MartyMatthews')` returns -1

```
SELECT STRCMP( 'Marty', 'MartyMatthews' )

STRCMP('Marty', 'MartyMatthews')
                              -1
```

Function	The Result Is:
COALESCE()	The first non-NULL argument
GREATEST()	The largest argument
IN()	TRUE if a value is in the set of arguments
INTERVAL()	The index or position of the argument that is not less than the first argument, counting from 0 (if the first argument is less than the second argument, the result is 0)
LEAST()	The smallest argument
LIKE	TRUE if a value matches a specified pattern, which can contain the % wildcard character to replace any number of characters or the _ wildcard character to replace a single character
NOT IN()	TRUE if a value is not in a set of values
NOT LIKE	TRUE if a value does not match a specified pattern
STRCMP()	-1 if the first string is in the second string, 0 if the first string is equal to the second string, and 1 otherwise

Table 10-6   MySQL Comparison Functions

TIP

Do not mix quoted and unquoted arguments. For example, replace (7, 5, 3, 'run') with ('7', '5', '3', 'run').

NOTE

MAX() and GREATEST() and MIN() and LEAST() are easy to confuse. MAX() and MIN() are looking for the maximum or minimum value in a column in a table, while GREATEST() and LEAST() are looking for the largest or smallest value within the function's arguments.

Control Flow Functions

Control flow functions allow you to direct the flow within a MySQL statement based on values and conditions that are present. There are four control flow functions, one of which has two distinct versions, as shown in Table 10-7.

Examples of control flow functions are

- CASE 'Marty' WHEN 'Marty' THEN 'Marty Matthews' WHEN 'Carole' THEN 'Carole Matthews' ELSE 'Michael Matthews' END returns 'Marty Matthews'

- @var:=56, CASE WHEN @var>50 THEN @var ELSE 50 END returns 56

```
SELECT @var :=56,
CASE WHEN @var >50
THEN @var
ELSE 50
END
```

@var:=56	CASE WHEN @var>50 THEN @var ELSE 50 END
56	56

Function	Description
CASE *value* WHEN *comparison1* THEN *result1* WHEN *comparison2* THEN *result2*... ELSE *result3* END	Tests each of the comparisons against the initial value and returns the result when the comparison equals the value. If no comparison equals the value, then the result following ELSE is returned.
CASE WHEN *condition1* THEN *result1* WHEN *condition2* THEN *result2*... ELSE *result3* END	Tests each of the conditions and returns the result of the first condition that is TRUE. If no condition is TRUE, then the result following ELSE is returned.
IF(*condition*, *true_result*, *else_result*)	Tests *condition* and returns the *true_result* if the condition is TRUE; otherwise, the *else_result* is returned.
IFNULL(*value1*, *value2*)	If *value1* is not NULL, *value1* is returned; otherwise, *value2* is returned.
NULLIF(*value1*, *value2*)	Returns NULL if *value1* equals *value2*; otherwise, *value1* is returned.

Table 10-7 MySQL Control Flow Functions

- `@var:=56, IF(@var>50, @var, 50)` returns 56
- `IFNULL(NULL, 450)` returns 450
- `NULLIF(450, 450)` returns NULL

Date and Time Functions

MySQL has a number of date and time functions that can be used in expressions within MySQL statements to work with dates and times. Dates and times in MySQL in their default form look as they did in PHP, with year, month, day, hour, minute, and second divisions in the form YYYY-MM-DD HH:MM:SS. You can see this with the NOW() function to get the full set of values to the current second.

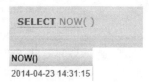

Table 10-8 lists some of the more commonly used date and time functions with some of the synonyms. If you are looking for a function and don't see it here, look at Section 12.13 of the MySQL Manual.

Function	Description
`ADDDATE(date, INTERVAL value unit)` or `DATE_ADD(date, INTERVAL value unit)`	Adds *value* in the units indicated to the *date*. The units can be YEAR, QUARTER, MONTH, WEEK, DAY, HOUR, MINUTE, SECOND, and MICROSECOND and various combinations.
`ADDDATE(date, days)`	Adds *days* to *date*.
`ADDTIME(time1, time2)`	Adds two times.
`CURDATE()` or `CURRENT_DATE()`	Returns the current date as YYYY-MM-DD.
`CURTIME()` or `CURRENT_TIME()`	Returns the current time as HH:MM:SS.
`DATE(datetime)`	Returns the date portion of *datetime* expression.
`DATE_FORMAT(date, format)`	Returns *date* as a string formatted using the codes in Table 10-9.
`DATE_SUB(date, INTERVAL value unit)` or `SUBDATE(date, INTERVAL value unit)`	Subtracts the value in the units indicated to the date. See `ADDDATE()` for *unit*.

Table 10-8 MySQL Date and Time Functions *(continued)*

Function	Description
DATEDIFF(date1, date2)	Returns the number of days after subtracting *date2* from *date1*.
DAYNAME(date) or DAY(date)	Returns the name of the day for *date* (Sunday.. Saturday).
DAYOFMONTH(date)	Returns the day of the month for *date* (1 to 31).
DAYOFWEEK(date)	Returns the day of the week for *date* (1 to 7 with 1 = Sunday..7 = Saturday).
DAYOFYEAR(date)	Returns the day of the month for *date* (1 to 366).
Extract(unit FROM date)	Returns *unit* that is in *date*. See ADDDATE() for *unit*.
HOUR(time)	Returns the hour value that is in *time*.
LAST_DAY(date)	Returns the last day of the month in *date*.
MINUTE(time)	Returns the minute value that is in *time*.
MONTH(date)	Returns the month value (1 to 12) that is in *date*.
MONTHNAME(date)	Returns the month name that is in *date*.
NOW() or CURRENT_TIMESTAMP() or LOCALTIME()	Returns the current date as YYYY-MM-DD HH:MM:SS.
PERIOD_ADD(period, months)	Returns the period in the form YYYMM or YYMM after adding *months* to *period*.
PERIOD-DIFF(period1, period2)	Returns the number of months between *period1* and *period2*, which are in the form YYYMM or YYMM.
QUARTER(date)	Returns the quarter value (1 to 4) that is in *date*.
SECOND(time)	Returns the second value that is in *time*.
TIME_FORMAT(time, format)	Returns *time* as a string formatted using the time codes in Table 10-9.
WEEK(date)	Returns the week value (0 to 53) that is in *date*, assuming Sunday begins the week and week 1 is the first week with a Sunday in the year. You can optionally add a *mode* argument to change the assumptions; see the MySQL Manual.
YEAR(date)	Returns the year value (1000 to 9999) that is in *date*.

Table 10-8 MySQL Date and Time Functions

Examples of date and time functions are

- `ADDDATE(NOW(), 22)` returns 2014-05-15 14:23:47 where `NOW()` is as shown earlier (plus several minutes)

> **SELECT** ADDDATE(NOW( ) , 22)
>
> **ADDDATE(NOW(), 22)**
> 2014-05-15 14:33:37

- `DATEDIFF(CURDATE(),'2014-12-25')` returns –246 since the second date is subtracted from the first
- `DATE_FORMAT(NOW(),'%M %D, %Y %h:%i:%s %P')` returns April 23rd, 2014 02:56:26 P

> **DATE_FORMAT(NOW(), '%M %D, %Y %h:%i:%s %P')**
> April 23rd, 2014 02:55:26 P

- `DAYNAME(CURDATE())` returns Wednesday
- `EXTRACT(MONTH FROM CURDATE())` returns 4
- `LAST_DAY(CURDATE())` returns 2014-04-30

Date and Time Formatting Codes

MySQL provides a number of date and time formatting codes, shown in Table 10-9, that can be used in the `DATE_FORMAT()` function. The codes must each begin with a % and are presented as a string with the appropriate delimiter or space between codes. For example: `'%M %D, %Y'` generates 'April 22nd, 2014'. Zero is an acceptable value for months, days, hours, minutes, seconds, and microseconds because MySQL allows storing incomplete dates. See the example for `DATE-FORMAT()` in the previous section.

Encryption and Compression Functions

You can encrypt, decrypt, compress, and uncompress strings within a MySQL statement using the functions shown in Table 10-10. The string resulting from encryption and compression is best stored using the `VARBINARY` or `BLOB` binary string data types to avoid character set conversion and space removal that can change values with other data types. Several older MySQL encryption functions may have become compromised and are not included in the discussion here.

Function	Description
`%a`	Three-character day of the week name (Sun..Sat)
`%b`	Three-character month name (Jan..Dec)
`%c`	Numeric month (0..12)
`%D`	Day of the month with English suffix (1st, 2nd, 3rd...)
`%d`	Numeric day of the month (00..31)
`%H`	Hour (00..23)
`%h` or `%I`	Hour (01..12)
`%i`	Numeric minutes (00..59)
`%j`	Day of the year (001..366)
`%M`	Month name (January..December)
`%m`	Numeric month (00..12)
`%p`	A or P for AM or PM
`%r`	12-hour time with AM or PM (hh:mm:ss AM/PM)
`%S` or `%s`	Seconds (00..59)
`%T`	24-hour time (hh:mm:ss)
`%U`	Week number (00..53) where Sunday is the first day of the week
`%W`	Full name of the day of the week (Sunday..Saturday)
`%w`	Numeric day of the week (Sunday=0, Saturday=6)
`%Y`	Numeric four-digit year
`%y`	Numeric two-digit year

Table 10-9   MySQL Date and Time Formatting Codes

For examples of encryption and compression functions, a new table was created in the Books database named "users" with three columns: "id," "user," and "pswd."

● `INSERT INTO users (user, pswd) VALUES ('marty', AES_ENCRYPT('passphrase', 'key'));`
`SELECT user, AES_DECRYPT(pswd, 'key') FROM users;` returns "marty passphrase"

```
SELECT user, AES_DECRYPT( pswd, 'key' )
FROM `users`
LIMIT 0 , 30
```

user	AES_DECRYPT(pswd, 'key')
marty	passphrase

Function	Description
AES_DECRYPT(*string*, *key*)	Decrypts *string* that has been encrypted with the Advanced Encryption Standard (AES) using *key*
AES_ENCRYPT(*string*, *key*)	Encrypts *string* using the AES with *key*
COMPRESS(*string*)	Compresses *string* creating a binary string
DECODE(*string*, *key*)	Decodes *string* that has been encoded using *key*
ENCODE(*string*, *key*)	Encodes *string* using *key*
SHA2(*string*)	Returns a checksum for *string* using the Secure Hash Algorithm 2 (SHA2)
UNCOMPRESS(*string*)	Uncompresses *string* from a compressed binary string
UNCOMPRESS_LENGTH(*string*)	Returns the uncompressed length of a compressed *string*

Table 10-10 MySQL Encryption and Compression Functions

- UNCOMPRESS(COMPRESS('amoderatelylargestring')); returns "amoderatelylargestring"

CAUTION
MySQL encryption functions with their keys are sent to the server unencrypted unless a Secure Sockets Layer (SSL) connection is used.

String Functions
The MySQL string functions allow you to manipulate string values within a MySQL statement. Table 10-11 shows the most commonly used string functions.

Examples of string functions are

- CHAR_LENGTH('Seattle') returns 7

- CONCAT('Buggs', 'Bunny') returns "BuggsBunny"

- FORMAT(9876.5432, 2) returns 9,876.54

- INSERT('6718 W 18th Street', 8, 2, '24') returns "6718 W 24th Street"

- LOCATE('car', 'Ft Carson') returns 4

- LTRIM('   something') returns "something"

- RIGHT('something', 5) returns "thing"

- SUBSTR('something', 3, 3) returns "met"

- UPPER('something') returns "SOMETHING"

Function	The Result Is:
CHAR_LENGTH() or CHARACTER_LENGTH()	The number of characters in the argument.
CHAR()	The character represented by each integer in the argument.
CONCAT(*string1, string2,.. stringn*)	The concatenation of several strings.
CONCAT_WS(*separator, string1, string2, ..stringn*)	The concatenation of several strings with *separator* between them.
FIELD()	The position of the first argument in the remaining arguments.
FORMAT(*value, places*)	*Value* formatted with comma separators to the number of *places*.
INSERT(*string1, position, length, string2*)	*Length* characters of *string2* placed at *position* in *string1*.
INSTR(*string1, string2*)	The position of *string2* in *string1*.
LEFT(*string, length*)	The leftmost *length* characters in *string*.
LCASE() or LOWER()	All characters changed to lowercase.
LOCATE(*string1, string2*[, *position*]) or POSITION(*string1* IN *string2*)	The position of *string 1* in *string2*, optionally after *position*.
LTRIM(*string*)	*String* with any leading spaces removed.
QUOTE(*string*)	*String* enclosed in single quote marks; place a backslash before backslashes and single quote marks to escape them.
REPEAT(*string, count*)	*String* repeated *count* times.
REPLACE(*string, find, replace*)	*String* with all occurrences of *find* (which is case sensitive) replaced with *replace*.
REVERSE(*string*)	*String* with the order of the characters reversed.
RIGHT(*string, length*)	The rightmost *length* characters in *string*.
RTRIM(*string*)	*String* with trailing spaces removed.
SPACE(*length*)	A string of *length* spaces.
SUBSTR(*string, position*[, *length*]) or SUBSTRING(*string, position*[, *length*]) or MID(*string, position*[, *length*])	A substring formed from *string* beginning at *position* and optionally of length *length* characters.
TRIM([BOTH | LEADING | TRAILING [*character*] FROM] *string*)	*String* with both leading and trailing spaces removed. Optionally, you can specify *character* to be removed in place of spaces, and you can specify that spaces or *character* are removed from leading, trailing, or both positions. If *character* is specified, then FROM is needed in front of *string*.
UCASE() or UPPER()	All characters changed to uppercase.

Table 10-11 MySQL String Functions

Function	Result Is:
CHARSET()	The character set of the argument
COLLATION()	The collation of the string argument
CURRENT_USER() or USER()	The user name and host name
DATABASE() or SCHEMA()	The name of the current database
DEFAULT()	The default value for a column
FOUND_ROWS()	The number of rows that would be returned if there were no LIMIT clause in a SELECT
LAST_INSERT_ID()	The value of the AUTOINCREMENT column for the last INSERT
ROW_COUNT()	The number of rows updated
VALUES()	The values to be inserted into a table with INSERT
VERSION()	The MySQL version

Table 10-12 MySQL System and Information Functions

System and Information Functions

System and information functions allow you to get information about the MySQL environment and the elements being used. Table 10-12 lists some of the applicable functions.

Examples of system and information functions are

- CHARSET('something') returns "utf8'

- DATABASE() returns "books"

- SELECT SQL_CALC_FOUND_ROWS * FROM books
  WHERE Price > 5.00 LIMIT 2;
  SELECT FOUND_ROWS(); returns 4. SQL_CALC_FOUND_ROWS requests that MySQL keep track of the total number of rows found so that FOUND_ROWS() can report it.

- INSERT INTO books (title, author, publisher, price, category)
  VALUES('The Crystal City', 'Card', 'Thor', '7.99', 'Sci. Fic. ');
  demonstrates the use of the VALUES() function

- LAST_INSERT_id() returns 10 after the INSERT statement earlier

- ROW_COUNT() returns 1 after the INSERT statement earlier

This chapter has introduced MySQL and discussed many of the supporting elements to MySQL statements, including operators and functions. In the next chapter, we'll look in detail at the commands and keywords that are central to MySQL statements. Then we'll look at how to put together and use complete statements. This will then lead to Chapter 12, where we will bring PHP back into the picture to utilize the MySQL statements.

Try This 10-1 Create and Use a MySQL Database

Using either the MySQL command line or phpMyAdmin (phpMyAdmin is probably easier) and the examples in this chapter:

1. Build a small database with one table and four fields, including an index, a name, a dollar amount, and a password. Insert four or five records into your table.

2. Do a query or two, for example: dues < 25, names alphabetical order.

3. In phpMyAdmin, write and execute a statement that generates a random number, multiplies it by 10, and rounds it to produce an integer.

4. Select a name from your database with a name like "Sal" using a wildcard.

5. Generate the current date and time and then format it.

6. Insert a new person in your database that includes an encrypted password. Then retrieve the record and show the password.

Chapter 10 Self-Test

The following questions are intended to help reinforce your comprehension of the concepts covered in this chapter. The answers can be found in the accompanying online Appendix A, "Answers to the Self-Tests."

1. What are three tools that can be used to work directly with MySQL other than programmatically with PHP or other languages?

2. What is SQL and how does it relate to MySQL?

3. How should commands and keywords be presented, and is this mandatory?

4. What are at least four parts of the MySQL language and what do they do?

5. What are the three types of literals?

6. What are at least three ways a date can be represented in a MySQL statement?

7. What are three types of operators with examples of them?

8. What are four types of functions with two examples of each?

9. What is the difference between ROUND and TRUNCATE?

10. What are the two wildcard characters that can be used in MySQL expressions and what do they mean?

11. What formatting characters would I use to get a date that looks like May 15th, 2014?

12. What field types should be used to store passwords and encrypted fields?

Chapter 11

Implementing MySQL Command Statements

Key Skills & Concepts

- Understanding the MySQL Command Structure
- Preparing the MySQL Workbench
- Creating and Using a Database
- Creating a Table and Its Columns
- Reviewing MySQL Data Types
- Working with Data
- Altering Tables and Databases
- Renaming Tables
- Dropping Tables and Databases
- Using Events, Views, and Triggers

In previous chapters you have learned a bit about relational databases, SQL, and MySQL, as well as some of the tools that you can use to work with and create a database with them. Other than in some examples where they were required to demonstrate other elements, MySQL commands and keywords have been ignored. In this chapter, we'll discuss and demonstrate commands and keywords and the statements that marry them together, along with operators and functions, to provide the full power of MySQL. We'll briefly revisit MySQL data types, make extensive use of the MySQL Workbench, and, to a lesser degree, phpMyAdmin and the MySQL command line to demonstrate how MySQL statements, their commands, and keywords operate.

MySQL Commands

MySQL commands are declarative words in MySQL statements that identify an action that is to take place. For example, the words CREATE, INSERT, SELECT, and UPDATE are all MySQL commands that, respectively,

- Create databases and tables and other elements
- Insert information into a table

- Select information from a table
- Update information in a table

MySQL commands can be grouped into the types of statements that use them:

- **Data definition statements** that work with databases, tables, and other elements and include the commands ALTER, CREATE, and DROP
- **Data manipulation statements** that work with the information in tables and include the commands DELETE, INSERT, and SELECT
- **Other statements** that are transactional and administrative in nature and include the commands LOCK TABLES, EXECUTE, and SHOW

In this section we'll review a number of the more frequently used commands, but, as I've said elsewhere in this book, if you don't see a command here that you need, go to the MySQL Manual that was described in Chapter 10.

Understanding the MySQL Command Structure

The MySQL command structure is set up to facilitate the creation and use of a relational database. To do that, it provides for the:

- Creation of a database
- Creation of tables within that database
- Identifying columns and their type, size, and characteristics within a table
- Inserting information into a row of columns
- Indexing the information in a database
- Altering and deleting the columns, tables, and databases
- Replacing and updating information in the table
- Selecting the information in the database and acting on the results
- Joining multiple tables and working with them together

Commands define MySQL statements and are generally the leading word. The remainder of the statement contains keywords, functions, and operators in clauses that modify the command. For example, the statement SELECT NOW(); uses the command SELECT (probably the most commonly used command) and the function NOW() to return the current date and time. You've seen a more complex example in earlier chapters:

```
SELECT * FROM books WHERE price > 5.00;
```

This statement again uses the command SELECT, followed by:

- An asterisk (*) to indicate that all columns or fields ("columns" and "fields" are synonymous) are to be selected
- The keyword FROM
- The table name books
- The keyword WHERE
- The field name price
- The operator >
- The literal 5.00

To repeat what I said in previous chapters, while there are a few exceptions where it isn't needed, most statements need a semicolon (;) at the end. Also, while it isn't needed at all, a good practice for human readability that is generally followed is to put commands and keywords in all capital letters and to put database, table, column, and other object names in lowercase or leading caps. Barring my own fallibility, which is reasonably likely, and that of the amazing technical editor, which is not very likely, all statements in this book will end with a semicolon, all commands and keywords will be in all caps, and all names will be lowercase.

Most keywords are aligned to certain commands and will be discussed with that command. In the next set of sections, we'll discuss the most commonly used commands along with their keywords in the following order, which I believe is how they are most commonly used:

- CREATE databases and tables
- INSERT data into tables
- SELECT data from tables
- REPLACE data in tables
- UPDATE data in tables
- DELETE data in tables
- ALTER tables and databases
- RENAME tables
- DROP tables and databases
- CREATE and use events, views, and triggers

Preparing the MySQL Workbench

In previous chapters we've relied heavily on phpMyAdmin, and to a lesser extent, on the MySQL command line to demonstrate what was being discussed. In this chapter we'll use the MySQL Workbench for that purpose. After downloading and installing MySQL Workbench, as described in Chapter 10, it should have left you with an icon on your desktop, as shown on the right. Use that icon to start MySQL Workbench and the following steps to prepare it to demonstrate the discussions in this chapter.

1. In the MySQL Workbench Home screen, click Database in the toolbar and then click Connect To Database to open a dialog box.

2. Leave Default Schema blank and click OK. (In MySQL Workbench, "schema" is synonymous with "database.")

3. In the Query1 screen that has opened, run your mouse around to the various menus and icons, as shown in Figure 11-1, and read the tooltips to get a feeling for what you can do.

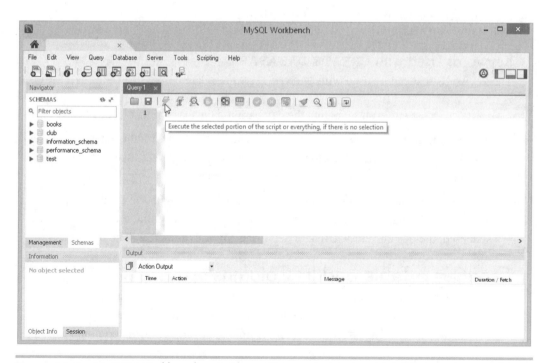

Figure 11-1   MySQL Workbench provides a Query window in which it is easy to try out MySQL statements with existing databases and tables.

In this chapter we'll give the Books database a rest and create a new database named "shop" with initially a single table named "sales." The table will initially have five columns named "id," "ondate," "buyer," "product," and "amount." Later in the chapter we'll add a "tax" column.

Create Databases and Tables

In previous chapters we have created databases and tables using the commands and tools built into phpMyAdmin or MySQL Workbench. Since you only infrequently need to do this, it makes sense to use these tools. MySQL commands, though, can directly create databases and tables, and it is informative to understand how this is done. The MySQL Workbench makes this easy.

Creating and Using a Database

To create a database, you simply enter the command and give the database a name. Then you must tell MySQL to use that database with the statements that follow. The CREATE DATABASE and USE DATABASE commands have the following common formats:

```
CREATE DATABASE database_name;
USE database_name;
```

Keywords Used with **CREATE DATABASE**

The keywords that can be used with CREATE DATABASE are

- IF NOT EXISTS prevents creating the database if a database of that name already exists.

- CHARACTER SET specifies a default character set to be used with the database. See the MySQL Manual for available character sets. If no character set is specified, the one currently active or set as the MySQL default will be used.

- COLLATE specifies a default collation sequence to be used with the database. See the MySQL Manual for available collation sequences. If no collation sequence is specified, the one currently active or set as the MySQL default will be used.

Creating a Table and Its Columns

To create a table, you once again enter the command followed by a name, but in the same statement you must also list the columns in the table along with their data types, size, and special characteristics. The CREATE TABLE command has the following common format:

```
CREATE TABLE table_name (column1_name type(size) characteristics,...
columnn_name type(size) characteristics);
```

Keywords Used with **CREATE TABLE**

There are three common keywords (or phrases) that you can use with CREATE TABLE:

- IF NOT EXISTS prevents creating the table if a table of that name already exists in the database.

- LIKE *old_table_name* creates a new table with the same column names, types, sizes, and characteristics as another table.

- TEMPORARY creates a table that only exists for the current user and is automatically dropped when that user drops their connection.

Keywords Used with Column Characteristics

As you see in the example table discussed here, column characteristics have their own set of keywords. Among the most common are (many keywords can only be used with specific data types):

- AUTO_INCREMENT automatically increments an integer or floating point data type by 1. There can be only one AUTO_INCREMENT column in a table and it cannot have a DEFAULT value.

- CURRENT TIMESTAMP adds the time and date to a TIMESTAMP column.

- DEFAULT provides a default value that immediately follows the keyword. It must be a constant (not an expression or a variable, so you cannot use NOW() or CURRENT_DATE() as a default for a date column, although you can use DEFAULT to add CURRENT_TIMESTAMP to a TIMESTAMP column) and cannot be used with BLOB and TEXT data types.

- FOREIGN KEY specifies the column contains a link to another table's PRIMARY KEY.

- NOT_NULL specifies that the column must contain a value.

- NULL specifies that a column does not need to have a value. If a column does not have NOT_NULL, then MySQL assumes that it is NULL and does not need to have a value.

- ON_UPDATE takes some action, such as inserting the CURRENT_TIMESTAMP, when the record is updated.

- PRIMARY KEY specifies the column is the index for the table and each value is, by definition, both UNIQUE and NOT NULL.

- UNIQUE cannot duplicate any other entry in the column.

Column Name	Data Type	Size	Special Characteristics
id	INTEGER (INT)	11	PRIMARY KEY, AUTO_INCREMENT
ondate	TIMESTAMP		
buyer	VARCHAR	40	
product	VARCHAR	40	
amount	DECIMAL	10,2	

Table 11-1   Columns in the Sales Table

NOTE

The TIMESTAMP data type by itself automatically inserts the current date and time when a new record is created and it automatically updates the field when the record is updated. This is the same as having both DEFAULT CURRENT_TIMESTAMP and ON_UPDATE CURRENT_TIMESTAMP. If you have only DEFAULT CURRENT_TIMESTAMP the current date and time is added when the record is created but is not updated. If you have only ON_UPDATE CURRENT_TIMESTAMP the current date and time is added when the record is updated but is not when it is created.

Create an Example Table

For the example sales table we're building here, the columns, data types, sizes, and characteristics are shown in Table 11-1.

The id is the index for the table, so you tell MySQL it is the PRIMARY KEY. Also, you want MySQL to automatically create the id by incrementing the previous id in the table with AUTO_INCREMENT. The ondate column is really a date and time column of the TIMESTAMP type that is automatically created when the record is added or updated. You could also use DEFAULT CURRENT_TIMESTAMP or ON UPDATE CURRENT_TIMESTAMP if you want the date added only when the record is created or only upon update. The buyer and product columns use the VARCHAR type with a maximum size of 40 characters each. The amount column uses the DECIMAL type 10 characters long with 2 decimal characters.

To create the database and table, perform the following steps in a MySQL Workbench query.

```
Query 1  ×

1 •    CREATE DATABASE shop;
2 •    USE shop;
3 • ⊟  CREATE TABLE sales (
4        id int(11) PRIMARY KEY AUTO_INCREMENT,
5        ondate TIMESTAMP,
6        buyer VARCHAR(40),
7        product VARCHAR(40),
8      ⌐ amount DECIMAL(10,2));
9
```

1. On line 1, type CREATE DATABASE shop;.

2. On line 2, type USE shop;.

3. On line 3, and the needed additional lines, type CREATE TABLE sales (
id INT(11) PRIMARY KEY AUTO_INCREMENT,
ondate TIMESTAMP,
buyer VARCHAR(40),
product VARCHAR(40),
amount DECIMAL(10,2));.

4. Click Execute (the leftmost lightning bolt in the Query1 toolbar).

If there are no errors in typing, all three command statements will execute, as you can see in the Action Output panel at the bottom of the MySQL Workbench (see Figure 11-2). Also, if you click Refresh (two circular arrows) opposite Schemas on the left and then open the database, table, and column elements on the left, you can see the results of your work.

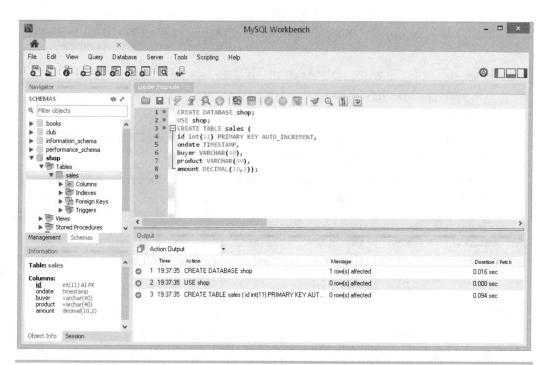

Figure 11-2   The MySQL Workbench provides a very useful set of panes with which to work.

Reviewing MySQL Data Types

Chapter 9 provides a detailed list of common column data types. Here, let's review the most frequently used types for you to keep in mind:

- $INT(n)$, integer number of up to n total digits.

- $DECIMAL(n,d)$, floating point number of up to n total digits, of which d are decimal digits.

- $DOUBLE(n,d)$, double-precision floating point number of n total digits, of which d are decimal digits.

- $CHAR(n)$, string value of a fixed maximum number of n characters padded with blanks on the right, but removed when retrieved.

- $VARCHAR(n)$, string value of a variable number of characters up to a maximum of n, not padded.

- **TEXT**, string value of a variable number of characters up to a maximum of 65,535.

- **BLOB**, binary number of up to a maximum of 65,535 bytes.

- **DATE**, date value stored as YYYY-MM-DD that can range from 1000-01-01 to 9999-12-31.

- **TIME**, time value stored as HHH:MM:SS that can range from –838:59:59 to 838:59:59, and can be displayed as D HH:MM:SS, where D is the number of days up to a maximum of 34.

- **DATETIME**, date and time value stored as YYYY-MM-DD HH:MM:SS that can range from 1000-01-01 00:00:00 to 9999-12-31 23:59:59.

- **TIMESTAMP**, date and time value stored as the number of seconds from 1970-01-01 00:00:01 and can go to 2038-01-09 03:13:07. Normally displayed as YYYY-MM-DD HH:MM:SS.

- $YEAR(n)$, year value of two or four digits ($YEAR(2)$ or $YEAR(4)$) year from 1901 to 2155. Two-digit years 00 to 69 are assumed to be 2000 to 2069, and years 70 to 99 are assumed to be 1970 to 1999.

TIP

If you leave and shut down MySQL Workbench, you can get back to the query screen by opening the program, clicking Database in the menu bar, clicking Connect to Database, clicking Default Schema, typing **shop**, and clicking OK.

Insert Data into Tables

The next step is to load data into a table using the INSERT command, which creates a new row or record ("row" and "record" are synonymous) in the table. INSERT adds a new row at the end of the existing rows in a table. Instead of INSERT, you can use REPLACE, which will overwrite an existing row if it already exists; otherwise, it will perform like a standard INSERT. See "Replacing Data" later in this chapter.

Inserting Data

To insert data, you enter the command followed optionally, but traditionally, by the keyword INTO, then the table name, the list of column names that will receive values, the keyword VALUES or VALUE, and one or more sets of values. The INSERT command can use one of the following three options:

```
INSERT INTO table_name (column1_name,... columnn_name) VALUES (column1_value1,...
column_value1),...(column1_valuen,... columnn_valuen);
```

or

```
INSERT INTO table_name SET column1_name = value1,... columnn_name = valuen;
```

or

```
INSERT INTO table_name (column1_name,... columnn_name) SELECT...;
```

The first format is the most common, although the second is also frequently used. Both of the first two options insert explicit values in specified columns. The third option uses the SELECT command to select values from other table(s). (See "Selecting Data" later in this chapter.) In the first and third option, a value must be provided for each named column. If you do not name the columns, a value must be provided for all columns. If you name the columns and leave one or more columns unnamed, the unnamed columns must have a default value or be automatically set.

Keywords Used with **INSERT**

The common keywords (or phrases) that can be used with INSERT are

- DEFAULT sets a named column to its default value, which is automatically done if you do not name the column. You can also use DEFAULT(*column_name*) with the same result.

- DELAYED puts the inserted values into a buffer and waits until the table is not in use to add the rows.

- `HIGH PRIORITY` overrides a server setting that throttles inserts and updates, and it disables concurrent inserts.

- `IGNORE` ignores any errors that occur while inserting rows into a table. Otherwise, the `INSERT` will abort upon any error and the rows will not be inserted.

- `INTO` is an optional keyword for readability.

- `LOW PRIORITY` waits to insert the rows and prevents the client from doing anything else until no one is reading from the table. This may be a long time. In contrast, `DELAYED` lets the client go on about their work.

- `ON DUPLICATE KEY UPDATE` allows a specified key value to be updated if it is a duplicate.

- `VALUES` or `VALUE`, which are synonymous, provides a list of values for, and in the order of, the columns in the columns list. One `INSERT` statement can have multiple rows of values, each row enclosed in parentheses and separated by commas.

Insert in the Example Table

For the example sales table we're building here, the data to be inserted is shown in Table 11-2. The id and the ondate columns are automatically created when the record is added.

Perform the following steps to insert the data in the sales table of the shop database in a MySQL Workbench query.

```
INSERT INTO sales (buyer, product, amount) VALUES
('Jones', 'Tablet SY8392', 794.23),
('Miller', 'Phone AP5s', 689.99),
('Butler', 'Laptop HP2345', 549.45),
('Staley', 'Phone SG8349', 523.69),
('Connor', 'Tablet AP6', 896.56);
```

Buyer	Product	Amount
Jones	Tablet SY8392	794.23
Miller	Phone AP 5s	689.99
Butler	Laptop HP2345	549.45
Staley	Phone SG8349	523.69
Connor	Tablet AP 6	896.56

Table 11-2 Data to Be Inserted in the Sales Table

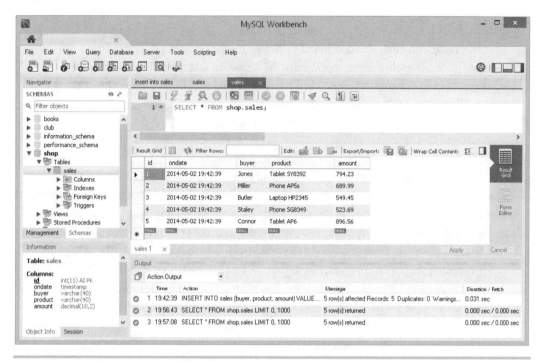

Figure 11-3   The MySQL Workbench can display the inserted rows.

1. On line 1 and the needed additional lines, type:

```
INSERT INTO sales (buyer, product, amount) VALUES
('Jones', 'Tablet SY8392', 794.23),
('Miller', 'Phone AP5s', 689.99),
('Butler', 'Laptop HP2345', 549.45),
('Staley', 'Phone SG8349', 523.69),
('Connor', 'Tablet AP6', 896.56);
```

2. Click Execute.

If there are no errors in typing, the INSERT command statement will execute, as you can see in the Action Output panel at the bottom of the MySQL Workbench. Also, if you right-click the sales table and click Select Rows, you can see the rows you inserted (see Figure 11-3).

Select, Replace, Update, and Delete Data in Tables

Once you have data in a table, you can work with it using the SELECT, REPLACE, UPDATE, and DELETE commands, which retrieve, change, and delete data in a table and allow you to use it in many ways.

Selecting Data

To select data, you enter the command followed by the columns to select from, the keyword FROM, the table name, optionally the keyword WHERE and a conditional expression, and optionally the keyword ORDER BY and a column name. The SELECT command takes the following general form with several of its optional keywords:

```
SELECT column_names FROM table_name WHERE conditional_expression ORDER
BY column_name;
```

In its simplest form, the SELECT command can be used by itself without column names or any keywords to, among other purposes, try out MySQL commands, as you have seen in earlier chapters. The first "column names" represents one or more columns that are to be returned in the selection. You can use an asterisk (*) to represent all columns. The FROM keyword is used to identify the table from which the columns are to be selected, and is required with a column selection, even if you use qualified column names such as table_name.column_name. WHERE precedes a conditional expression that selects the rows to be displayed—for example, amount > 600. ORDER BY precedes a column name on which the selection will be sorted. Here is an example of a full SELECT command with actual column names (see Figure 11-4):

```
SELECT buyer, product, amount FROM sales WHERE amount > 600 ORDER BY buyer;
```

Keywords Used with **SELECT**

The common keywords (or phrases) that can be used with SELECT are

- * indicates that all columns will be included in the selection.

- AS assigns an alias to either a column or table name that precedes it in the form column name AS alias name. The alias name can be used anywhere in the statement, even before the alias assignment. Tables can also be aliased without AS by simply putting the alias name immediately after the table name.

- DISTINCT removes records with duplicate values in the selection columns.

- FROM precedes the table or tables from which the selection will be drawn. Multiple tables are only used when performing a join.

- GROUP BY groups selected rows by one of the columns in a table. This works well with the COUNT() function. See the Tip on COUNT() following this list and the example in "Select from the Example Table."

- HAVING provides a secondary conditional expression after WHERE that allows you to further reduce the selection. This is typically used with GROUP BY to filter after the grouping.

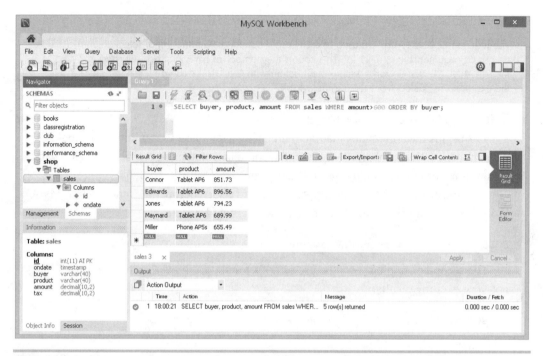

Figure 11-4 The SELECT command's versatility lets it span simple to complex constructs.

- LIMIT limits the number of rows that are returned. A single number following LIMIT returns that number of rows starting with the first row selected. Two numbers following LIMIT, such as LIMIT a, b, returns b rows beginning with the ath row. There is a hitch, though. Row numbers begin at 0, so LIMIT 1, 4 returns four rows beginning with the *second* row.

- ORDER BY precedes the column or columns used in sorting the selected rows. Normal sorting is in ascending order (a to z, 0 to 9). You can sort in reverse order by adding the keyword DESC following the column name in ORDER BY.

- WHERE provides the conditional expression that must be satisfied (be TRUE) for a row to be selected. The expression can contain conditional functions and operators.

NOTE

The order of the keywords in a SELECT statement is important and should normally follow this order: ALL, FROM, WHERE, GROUP BY, HAVING, ORDER BY, LIMIT. An exception is that INTO can also follow the initial set of column names.

TIP

The function COUNT () can be used in a SELECT statement with the initial select column names as arguments in COUNT (). This counts the number of rows that are returned in the SELECT. COUNT () works well in conjunction with GROUP BY as you'll see in one of the examples in "Select from the Example Table."

Select from the Example Table

SELECT begins the commands that facilitate using a database vs. building a database. As a result, there are a number of ways that the command statement can be used. Here we'll look at three of them using the shop database and sales table.

The first example is the standard SELECT you've seen before, here entered into MySQL Workbench. Figure 11-5 shows the result after clicking Execute.

```
SELECT * FROM sales WHERE amount > 600.00 ORDER BY buyer;
```

The second example shows the use of COUNT and GROUP BY. Figure 11-6 shows the not-very-exciting results.

```
SELECT product, COUNT(*) FROM sales GROUP BY product;
```

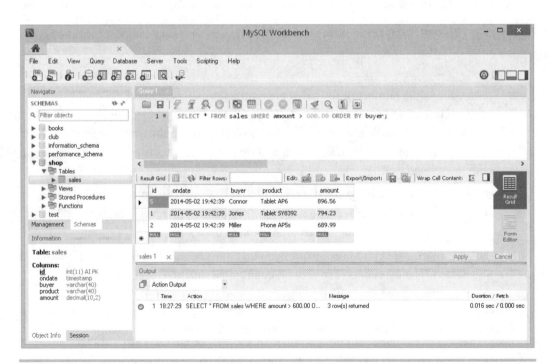

Figure 11-5   The classic SELECT statement

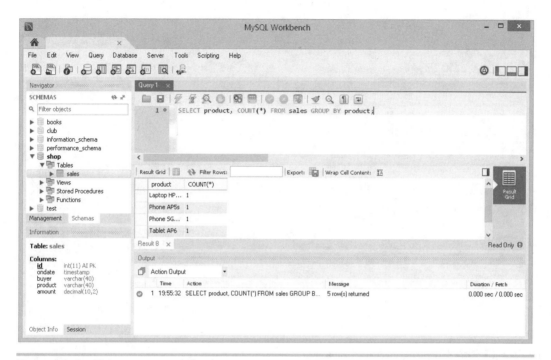

Figure 11-6 Using COUNT and GROUP BY

The third example demonstrates the use of HAVING and LIKE in place of WHERE, although you can use LIKE with WHERE just as well. Figure 11-7 shows the result after clicking Execute.

```
SELECT buyer, product FROM sales HAVING product LIKE 'Tablet%';
```

Replacing Data

The REPLACE command is almost exactly like the INSERT command—you enter the command followed optionally, but traditionally, by the keyword INTO, then the table name, the list of column names that will receive values, the keyword VALUES or VALUE, and one or more sets of values. The REPLACE command can use one of the following three options:

```
REPLACE INTO table_name (column1_name,... columnn_name) VALUES (column1_
value1,... columnn_value1),...(column1_valuen,... column_valuen);
```

or

```
REPLACE INTO table_name SET column1_name = value1,... columnn_name = valuen;
```

or

```
REPLACE INTO table_name (column1_name,... columnn_name) SELECT...;
```

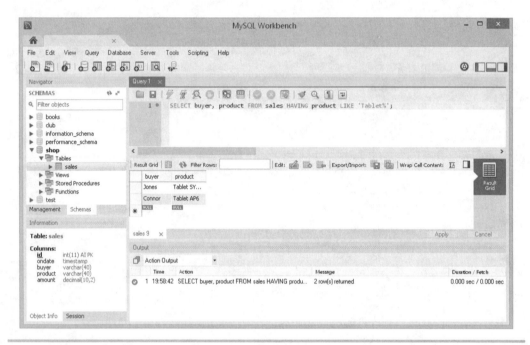

Figure 11-7   Using HAVING and LIKE

The first and second options, which are the most common, insert explicit values in specified columns. The third option uses the SELECT command to select values from other table(s). (See "Selecting Data" earlier in this chapter.) In the first and third options, a value must be provided for each named column. If you do not name the columns, a value must be provided for all columns. If you name the columns and leave one or more columns unnamed, the unnamed columns must have a default value or be automatically set.

With REPLACE you include either the primary key or unique index in the list of column names and in the list of values. If there is no match with an existing primary key or unique index value, then the REPLACE acts exactly like INSERT and a new record is added to the table. If there is a match with an existing primary key or unique index value, then the existing record is deleted and its replacement is added to the table.

One REPLACE statement can have multiple rows of values, each row enclosed in parentheses and separated by commas.

Keywords Used with **REPLACE**

The common keywords (or phrases) that can be used with REPLACE are

- DEFAULT sets a named column to its default value, which is automatically done if you do not name the column. You can also use DEFAULT(*column_name*) with the same result.

- DELAYED puts the replaced values into a buffer and waits until the table is not in use to add the rows.

- INTO is an optional keyword for readability.

- LOW PRIORITY waits to replace the rows and prevents the client from doing anything else until no one is reading from the table. This may be a long time. In contrast, DELAYED lets the client go on about their work.

- VALUES or VALUE, which are synonymous, provides a list of values for, and in the order of, the columns in the columns list.

Replace in the Example Table

For the example sales table, the data to be replaced is shown in Table 11-3.

The id and the ondate columns are automatically created when the record is added.

Perform the following steps to replace the data in the sales table of the shop database in a MySQL Workbench query.

1. On line 1 and the needed additional lines, type:

```
REPLACE INTO sales (id, buyer, product, amount) VALUES
(1, 'Jones', 'Tablet AP6', 794.23),
(6, 'Maynard', ' Tablet AP6', 689.99),
(7, 'Butler', 'Laptop HP2345', 549.45),
(4, 'Staley', 'Phone AP5', 523.69),
(8, 'Edwards', 'Tablet AP6', 896.56);
```

2. Click Execute.

ID	Buyer	Product	Amount
1	Jones	Tablet AP6	794.23
6	Maynard	Tablet AP6	689.99
7	Nelson	Laptop HP2345	549.45
4	Staley	Phone AP5s	523.69
8	Edwards	Tablet AP 6	896.56

Table 11-3 Data to Be Replaced in the Sales Table

The REPLACE command statement will execute, as you can see in the Action Output panel at the bottom of the MySQL Workbench. Also, if you right-click the sales table and click Select Rows you can see the rows you replaced (see Figure 11-8).

Updating Data

To update data, you enter the command followed by the columns to update from, the keyword FROM, the table name, optionally the keyword WHERE and a conditional expression, and optionally the keyword ORDER BY and a column name. The UPDATE command takes the following general form with several of its optional keywords:

```
UPDATE table_name SET column1_name = value1,... columnn_name = valuen
WHERE conditional_expression ORDER BY column_name;
```

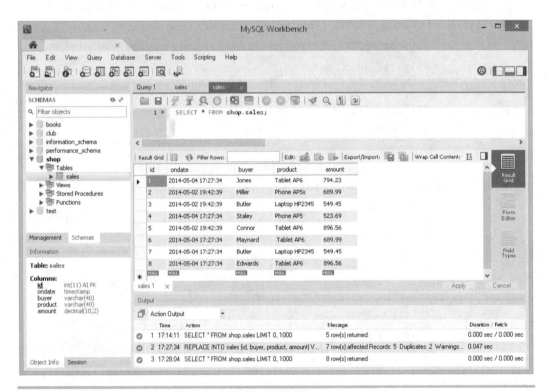

Figure 11-8 Action Output shows the rows replaced.

The first "table name" identifies the table with the columns to be updated. SET identifies one or more columns that are to be updated with the values that follow them. WHERE precedes a conditional expression that selects the rows to be displayed.

Keywords Used with **UPDATE**

The common keywords (or phrases) that can be used with UPDATE are

- DEFAULT sets a named column to its default value, which is automatically done if you do not name the column.

- IGNORE prevents UPDATE from aborting even if there is an error.

- LIMIT limits the number of rows that are returned. A single number following LIMIT returns that number of rows starting with the first row updated. Two numbers following LIMIT, such as LIMIT a, b, returns b rows beginning with the ath row. There is a hitch, though. Row numbers begin at 0, so LIMIT 1, 4 returns four rows beginning with the *second* row.

- LOW PRIORITY waits to update the rows and prevents the client from doing anything else until no one is reading from the table.

- ORDER BY precedes the column or columns used to specify the order in which the rows are updated.

- SET is used to identify the columns and their new values that will update the values in the existing table.

- WHERE provides the conditional expression that must be satisfied (be TRUE) for a row to be updated.

CAUTION

With no WHERE clause, all rows are updated.

Update the Example Table

UPDATE can be used for both surgical one-off corrections and mass corrections of a number of rows. Here we'll look at both of these using the shop database and sales table.

The first UPDATE example gives everybody who purchased on the second of the month a 5 percent discount:

```
UPDATE sales SET amount=amount*.95 WHERE DAYOFMONTH(ondate)=2;
```

When you enter and execute this statement in a newly installed MySQL Workbench, you get an error message that says you are operating in Safe mode and doing an update without referencing the primary key in the WHERE clause, which can have negative consequences, although not in this case. The suggested solution is to change the default with these steps.

1. In MySQL Workbench, click the Edit menu, click Preferences | SQL Queries | "Safe Updates" to clear the default check mark.
2. Click OK and then retry to execute the UPDATE statement.

The UPDATE should now complete, but you now get a warning for each of the dollar amounts that were changed because they are truncated at two decimal digits, as you see in Figure 11-9. You could prevent the warnings by putting SET amount=amount*.95 in the ROUND() function with two decimal digits, like this:

```
ROUND(amount=amount*.95, 2)
```

NOTE
No rows will change if you aren't doing these exercises on the second of the month!

NOTE
You can see the change in Figure 11-9 by comparing it to the dollar amounts in Figure 11-8 for Miller, Butler, and Connor.

The second UPDATE example updates a single field in a single record to correct an error:

```
UPDATE sales SET product='Phone AP5s' WHERE buyer='Staley';
```

	id	ondate	buyer	product	amount
	1	2014-05-...	Jones	Tablet AP6	794.23
	2	2014-05-...	Miller	Phone AP5s	655.49
	3	2014-05-...	Butler	Laptop HP...	521.98
	4	2014-05-...	Staley	Phone AP5s	523.69
	5	2014-05-...	Connor	Tablet AP6	851.73
	6	2014-05-...	Maynard	Tablet AP6	689.99
	7	2014-05-...	Butler	Laptop HP...	549.45
	8	2014-05-...	Edwards	Tablet AP6	896.56
*	NULL	NULL	NULL	NULL	NULL

Deleting Data

The DELETE statement deletes rows using FROM to name the table, optionally using WHERE with a conditional expression to select the rows, and optionally the keyword ORDER BY and

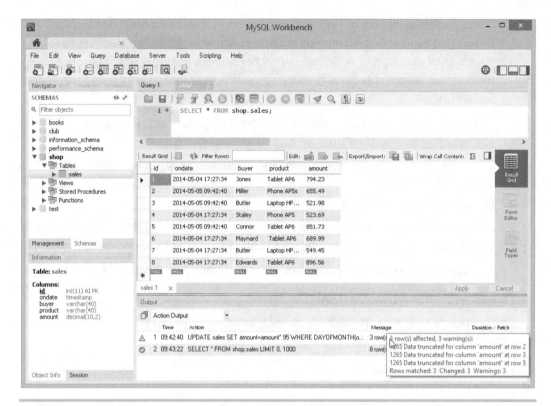

Figure 11-9 Doing an UPDATE and getting a truncation warning

a column name to specify the order in which the deletion occurs. You can also optionally use LIMIT to limit the deletion to a certain number of rows. The DELETE command takes the following general form with several of its optional keywords:

```
DELETE FROM table_name WHERE conditional_expression ORDER BY column_
name LIMIT number_of_ rows;
```

If there is not a WHERE clause, all rows are deleted.

Keywords Used with DELETE

The common keywords (or phrases) that can be used with DELETE are

- FROM precedes the table in which the deletion will occur.

- IGNORE prevents DELETE from aborting even if there is an error.

- LIMIT limits the number of rows that are deleted. A single number following LIMIT deletes that number of rows starting with the first row deleted. Two numbers following LIMIT, such as LIMIT a, b, deletes b rows beginning with the ath row. There is a hitch, though. Row numbers begin at 0, so LIMIT 1, 4 deletes four rows beginning with the *second* row.

- LOW PRIORITY waits to delete the rows and prevents the client from doing anything else until no one is reading from the table.

- ORDER BY precedes the column or columns used in sorting the deleted rows. Normal sorting is in ascending order (a to z, 0 to 9). You can sort in reverse order by adding the keyword DESC following the column name in ORDER BY.

- WHERE provides the conditional expression that must be satisfied (be TRUE) for a row to be deleted. The expression can contain conditional functions and operators.

- QUICK pauses some indexing operations to slightly speed up the deletion.

Delete from the Example Table

DELETE is very similar to the other command statements you saw earlier in this chapter. Here is an example that deletes two rows of the sales table:

```
DELETE FROM sales WHERE amount < 525.00;
```

NOTE

If your dates don't match mine, only one row is going to be deleted with this query because the other one didn't get the 5 percent price reduction.

id	ondate	buyer	product	amount
1	2014-05-...	Jones	Tablet AP6	794.23
2	2014-05-...	Miller	Phone AP5s	655.49
5	2014-05-...	Connor	Tablet AP6	851.73
6	2014-05-...	Maynard	Tablet AP6	689.99
7	2014-05-...	Butler	Laptop HP...	549.45
8	2014-05-...	Edwards	Tablet AP6	896.56
*	NULL	NULL	NULL	NULL	NULL

Alter, Rename, and Drop Tables and Databases

In the previous section we talked about querying, changing, and deleting data within one or more tables. Here we'll talk about changing and deleting tables and databases themselves. While these actions are important and you will most likely need to use them, they are not generally part of your everyday use of MySQL like SELECT, REPLACE, and UPDATE are. As a result, I'll be briefer with these descriptions and you may need to use the MySQL Manual if you need to delve deeply into these commands.

Altering Tables and Databases

Altering tables and databases allows you to change the structure of your database. There is a lot of difference between what you can change in a table and in a database, so they will be discussed separately.

Altering Tables

Altering tables is really altering a table's columns, adding, changing, and dropping (deleting) columns. The general form of an ALTER TABLE statement is

ALTER TABLE *table_name alteration* ;

There are a number of types of alterations; among these are

- ADD COLUMN *column_name column_definition* FIRST or AFTER *column_name*
- ALTER COLUMN *column_name* SET DEFAULT *literal* or DROP DEFAULT
- CHANGE COLUMN *old_column_name new_column_name column_definition* FIRST or AFTER *column_name*
- DROP COLUMN *column_name*
- MODIFY COLUMN *column_name column_definition* FIRST or AFTER *column_name*
- RENAME TO *new_table_name*

NOTE

In the ALTER table alterations, the word "COLUMN" is optional and can be left out. I believe, though, that it helps in human understanding of what is being done, so I recommend that it be included.

The *column_name column_definition* clause is the same as that used in CREATE TABLE described earlier in this chapter. Also, the keyword IGNORE, described earlier, can be used with ALTER TABLE. MODIFY COLUMN is used to change only the *column_definition* including the data type.

The default is that new columns are added at the end after the last existing column. You can change this with the FIRST or AFTER *column_name* clause. FIRST will make the new column the first column; AFTER *column_name* places the new column after the named column. In the CHANGE and MODIFY keywords, this clause will reorder an existing column.

You can use several ADD, ALTER, CHANGE, and DROP alteration clauses in the same ALTER TABLE statement if you separate them with commas.

Here are three examples of ALTER TABLE command statements:

```
ALTER TABLE sales ADD COLUMN tax DECIMAL(10,2);
```

	id	ondate	buyer	product	amount	tax
	1	2014-05-...	Jones	Tablet AP6	794.23	NULL
	2	2014-05-...	Miller	Phone AP5s	655.49	NULL
	5	2014-05-...	Connor	Tablet AP6	851.73	NULL
	6	2014-05-...	Maynard	Tablet AP6	689.99	NULL
	7	2014-05-...	Butler	Laptop HP...	549.45	NULL
	8	2014-05-...	Edwards	Tablet AP6	896.56	NULL
*	NULL	NULL	NULL	NULL	NULL	NULL

```
ALTER TABLE sales ALTER COLUMN amount SET DEFAULT 555.55;
```

```
1 ● ALTER TABLE sales ALTER COLUMN amount SET DEFAULT 555.55;
```

Output

Action Output

Time	Action
⊘ 1 18:52:44	ALTER TABLE sales ALTER COLUMN amount SET DEFAULT 555.55

```
ALTER TABLE sales DROP COLUMN tax;
```

	id	ondate	buyer	product	amount
	1	2014-05-...	Jones	Tablet AP6	794.23
	2	2014-05-...	Miller	Phone AP5s	655.49
	5	2014-05-...	Connor	Tablet AP6	851.73
	6	2014-05-...	Maynard	Tablet AP6	689.99
	7	2014-05-...	Butler	Laptop HP...	549.45
	8	2014-05-...	Edwards	Tablet AP6	896.56
*	NULL	NULL	NULL	NULL	NULL

Altering Databases

ALTER DATABASE allows you to change the default character set and the collation sequence used in the database. The general form of an ALTER DATABASE statement is

ALTER DATABASE *database_name* CHARACTER SET = *character_set_name* or COLLATE = *collation_name*;

The commands SHOW CHARACTER SET; and SHOW COLLATE will provide lists of the character sets and collation sequences that you can use.

Charset	Description	Default collation	Maxlen
big5	Big5 Traditional Chinese	big5_chinese_ci	2
dec8	DEC West European	dec8_swedish_ci	1
cp850	DOS West European	cp850_general_ci	1
hp8	HP West European	hp8_english_ci	1
koi8r	KOI8-R Relcom Russian	koi8r_general_ci	1
latin1	cp1252 West European	latin1_swedish_ci	1
latin2	ISO 8859-2 Central European	latin2_general_ci	1
swe7	7bit Swedish	swe7_swedish_ci	1
ascii	US ASCII	ascii_general_ci	1
ujis	EUC-JP Japanese	ujis_japanese_ci	3

Renaming Tables

Only tables can be renamed—databases cannot. Also, while RENAME TABLE is being executed, no other session can access any of the tables in the RENAME. Finally, temporary tables cannot be renamed with RENAME TABLE, but you can use ALTER TABLE RENAME (see "Altering Tables" earlier in this chapter). The general form of an ALTER DATABASE statement is:

RENAME TABLE *table_name1* TO *new_table_name1*, . . . *table_namen* TO *new_table_namen*;

Dropping Tables and Databases

Dropping tables and databases removes or deletes them. This means that all data contained in the table or tables in the database are lost—they are permanently deleted.

DROP TABLE *table_name1*, . . . *table_namen*;
DROP DATABASE *database_name*;

The keyword (phrase) IF EXISTS can be used to make sure the table or database to be dropped exists. If it doesn't, the statement stops execution and doesn't produce an error message. Also, you can use the TEMPORARY keyword to drop a temporary table. These objects challenge the name "Beginner's Guide," but I think it is important to know that they exist.

Create and Use Events, Views, and Triggers

MySQL supports a number of other objects, including events, views, and triggers that as a group are called "stored programs." Stored programs are MySQL statements and additional keywords that are stored with a database and executed at a later time, either based on a schedule or when they are otherwise called. Events, views, and triggers are examples of stored programs. These objects are relatively new in the MySQL syntax and are on the borderline of being a "Beginner's Guide" subject, I think, though they are important to know about. As a result, we'll briefly look at them here.

Using Events

Events are the scheduled execution of MySQL statements. Events use the MySQL Event Scheduler, which by default is turned off. You can turn it on and prove to yourself that it is on by executing these two command statements:

```
SET GLOBAL event_scheduler = ON;
SHOW PROCESSLIST;
```

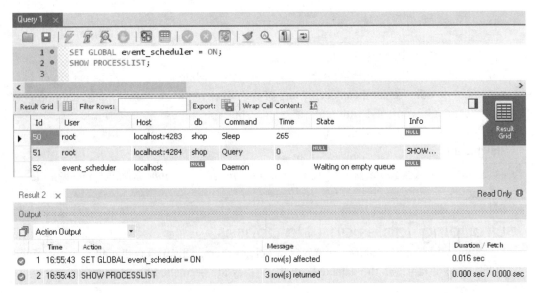

When the Event Scheduler is turned off, it will not show up on the process list. Once turned on, you can turn it off with:

SET GLOBAL event_scheduler = OFF;

Events can be created, altered, and dropped.

Create Events

The general form of a CREATE EVENT statement is

CREATE EVENT *event_name* ON SCHEDULE *schedule* DO *mysql_statement*;

All parts of this CREATE EVENT statement are required. The schedule can be

- At a particular date and time timestamp

  AT CURRENT_TIMESTAMP + INTERVAL 30 MINUTE

- On a periodic interval

  EVERY 10 MINUTE

- On or within a start and/or end date and time

  EVERT 10 MINUTES STARTS CURRENT_TIMESTAMP ENDS CURRENT_TIMESTAMP + INTERVAL 30 MINUTE

NOTE

The time and date values can be in SECOND, MINUTE, HOUR, DAY, WEEK, MONTH, QUARTER, YEAR, and several combinations.

For the mysql_statement, you can use the majority of MySQL statements, but some SELECT and all SHOW statements that simply display information from a table and don't change it have no effect when used in an event, which doesn't display or save information. Additional keywords that you can use with CREATE EVENT include

- IF NOT EXISTS prevents the execution of CREATE EVENT if an event of the same name already exists.

- ON COMPLETION PRESERVE, in the ON SCHEDULE clause, preserves the CREATE EVENT statement after it expires; otherwise, it is automatically and immediately dropped.

- COMMENT allows you to add a comment within quotes in the ON SCHEDULE clause.

An example of using an event is:

CREATE EVENT addtax ON SCHEDULE AT CURRENT_TIMESTAMP + INTERVAL 2 MINUTE
DO UPDATE sales SET tax = ROUND(amount*.092, 2);

This statement allows you to calculate the tax on a group of records on a time-delayed basis, as you can see in Figure 11-10.

Alter and Drop Events

ALTER EVENT allows you to make changes to an existing event. It has the following general form:

ALTER EVENT *event_name* ON SCHEDULE *schedule* DO *mysql_statement*;

This allows you to change any aspect of the event with the contents of the ALTER EVENT statement, including using the keyword RENAME to change the name of the event.

DROP EVENT allows you to delete an existing event. It has this general form:

DROP EVENT *event_name*;

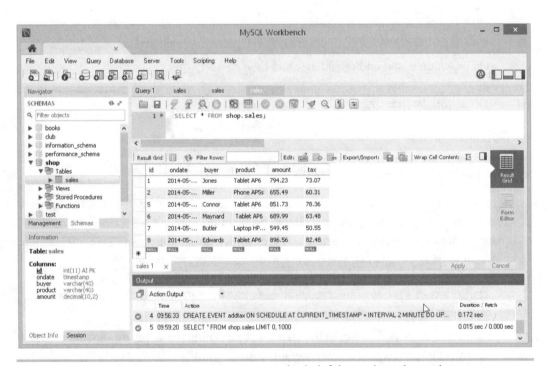

Figure 11-10 Delaying statement execution can be helpful on a heavily used site.

Using Views

Views are, in essence, named SELECT statements that you can repeatedly call using only the name without specifying the full SELECT statement.

Create Views

The general form of a CREATE VIEW statement is

CREATE VIEW *view_name* AS *select_statement*;

An example of creating a VIEW statement and then using it is

```
CREATE VIEW tablets AS SELECT * FROM sales HAVING product LIKE
'Tablet%' ORDER BY buyer;
SELECT * FROM tablets;
```

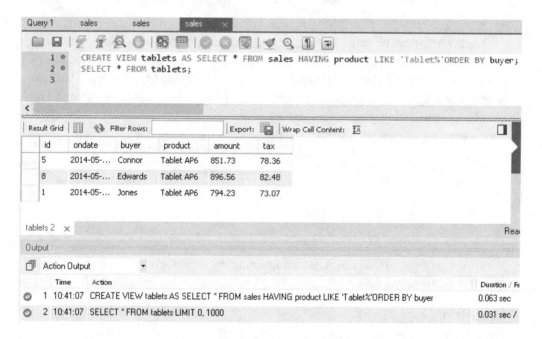

Alter and Drop Views

ALTER VIEW allows you to make changes to an existing view. It has the following general form:

ALTER VIEW *view_name* AS *select_statement*;

This allows you to change any aspect of the view with the contents of the ALTER VIEW statement.

DROP VIEW allows you to delete an existing view. It has this general form:

DROP VIEW *view_name*;

Using Triggers

Triggers are one or more statements that are executed on each row of a particular table when an event occurs within the table.

Create Triggers

The general form of a CREATE TRIGGER statement is

CREATE TRIGGER *trigger_name trigger_time trigger_event* ON *table_name* FOR EACH ROW *trigger_statement(s)*;

Trigger times can be either BEFORE or AFTER the trigger event. Trigger events can be INSERT, UPDATE, or DELETE actions on rows within the named table. FOR EACH ROW executes the following statement(s) on each row affected by the trigger event. There can be only one trigger with a given table with the same trigger time and event. Also, the table must be a permanent (not temporary) table.

An example of creating a TRIGGER statement and then using it is

```
CREATE TRIGGER taxcalc BEFORE INSERT ON sales FOR EACH ROW SET NEW.tax
= ROUND(NEW.amount*.092, 2);
INSERT INTO sales (buyer, product, amount) VALUES
('Linden', 'Tablet AP6', 784.46),
('Meyers', 'Phone AP5c', 469.95),
('Bitts', 'Laptop HP567', 932.75);
```

This allows you to insert the tax after inserting the record, even though you could have done it with the INSERT.

Drop Triggers

DROP TRIGGER allows you to delete an existing trigger. It has this general form:

DROP TRIGGER *trigger_name*;

NOTE
Triggers cannot be altered.

Try This 11-1 Create and Use a Database with MySQL Workbench

Go through this chapter and create and test with MySQL Workbench your own example MySQL statements for each of the following (in MySQL Workbench, try several alternatives to your examples by making simple changes to the statement):

1. Create and use a database.

2. Create a table with various types of columns.

3. Insert data into your table.

4. Select data from your table.

5. Replace data in your table.

6. Update data in your table.

7. Delete data in your table.

8. Alter your table in several ways.

9. Drop a table.

10. Create and use an event.

Chapter 11 Self-Test

The following questions are intended to help reinforce your comprehension of the concepts covered in this chapter. The answers can be found in the accompanying online Appendix A, "Answers to the Self-Tests."

1. What are two types of MySQL statements and what are examples of each?

2. What are the major components of a MySQL statement?

3. What does an asterisk (*) stand for in a MySQL statement?

4. What is a literal?

5. What are the recommended rules to be used in writing MySQL statements?

6. Besides the command CREATE TABLE, what are the other elements in a CREATE TABLE statement?

7. What does AUTO_INCREMENT do and how is it generally used?

8. What is the difference between a primary key and a foreign key?

9. What is the TIMESTAMP data type and how is it used when the record it is in is created and updated?

10. What is the most common data type and size for monetary values and what does the size mean?

11. After creating a database, what else must you do before creating a table?

12. You can only insert one set of values with the INSERT statement, true or false?

13. What primary table-related function is done with a SELECT statement?

14. What are the primary elements of a SELECT statement?

15. How is the COUNT() function used in a SELECT statement?

16. What command and statement are very similar to REPLACE?

17. How does the use of the REPLACE and UPDATE statements differ?

18. DELETE is used to delete a table, true or false?

19. What are several ways the ALTER command and statement can be used?

20. How are stored programs used in MySQL and what are several examples?

21. What must you first do to use events?

22. What is a MySQL event?

23. What are three ways an event can be scheduled?

24. What is a MySQL view?

25. What is a MySQL trigger?

Part IV

Powering Databases with MySQL and PHP

In previous chapters you saw how PHP provides a strong programming language, and then how MySQL provides a full-featured relational database. In Part IV you'll see how PHP and MySQL work together with HTML, CSS, and JavaScript to allow you to build extremely capable and powerful web applications to handle a wide range of needs.

Chapter 12 describes how PHP is used with MySQL to create, access, and query a database. It reviews the types of queries; how information entered into website forms is used to create new records in database tables; and then how information in a database is read, formatted, and displayed on a web page. Finally, the chapter looks at how to detect and handle errors and security issues.

Chapter 13 demonstrates the use of PHP and MySQL to create a web app to register students and the courses they sign up for, including constructing the forms and database tables, validating the data that is entered, querying the database, and presenting the information.

Chapter 14 demonstrates the use of PHP and MySQL to create a web app to handle online purchases. This will include presenting a catalog of items for sale, allowing the selection of items to be purchased, and handling the final checkout. In addition to the database aspects of this, the discussion will include authentication and access control, as well as protecting and encrypting vulnerable information.

Chapter 12

Using a MySQL Database with PHP

Key Skills & Concepts

- Database Manipulation

- Database Information

- Database Administration

- Combining PHP MySQL Functions

- Expanding PHP Form Handling

- Facilitating User Interaction

- Interacting with a Database

- Improving Security

PHP and MySQL are like a teacup and a saucer—you can use either one without the other, but they are meant to be used together. Yes, there are other languages that can be used with MySQL and other databases that can be used with PHP, but I believe that PHP and MySQL is the most frequently used combination. That combination is, of course, the purpose of this book, and bringing the two together is the purpose of this chapter.

Bringing PHP and MySQL Together

Bringing PHP and MySQL together is relatively easy. Almost all web-hosting sites provide both PHP and MySQL, and you have Zend Server or WAMP (Windows servers for Apache, MySQL, and PHP) to test the pair on your computer. Creating web apps with MySQL and PHP is straightforward and not difficult. It is an extension of what you have already learned about PHP and MySQL.

PHP works with MySQL through a set of functions that perform the SQL commands and more. These functions can be split into three categories: database manipulation, database information, and database administration.

Database Manipulation

Manipulating an existing MySQL database with PHP can be broken into these steps:

- Connect to MySQL.
- Perform a query.
- Process the results.
- Release the results from memory.
- Disconnect from MySQL.

The last two steps are optional, but they are a good practice and become mandatory if you are working with multiple databases.

PHP's database manipulation functions for MySQL are the heavy lifters of the group, opening and closing the database, and querying and retrieving database contents, as shown in Table 12-1. There are detailed explanations of these functions in the following sections

Function	Description	Arguments and Comments
`mysqli_close()`	Disconnects from MySQL	Connection ID. Returns TRUE for success or FALSE for failure.
`mysqli_connect()`	Connects to MySQL	Host server name, username, password, database name. Returns the connection ID or FALSE for failure.
`mysqli_create_db()`	Creates a MySQL database	Name of db to be created. Optionally, the connection ID.
`mysqli_fetch_all()`	Gets all result rows as any type of array	Result of a query, type of array: mysqli_assoc, mysqli_num, or mysqli_both (the default).
`mysqli_fetch_array()`	Gets a row as any type of array	Result of a query, type of array: mysqli_assoc, mysqli_num, or mysqli_both (the default).
`mysqli_fetch_assoc()`	Gets a row as an associative array	Result of a query. Field names are the indexes.
`mysqli_fetch_object()`	Gets one or more fields in a row	Result of a query. Optionally, the class name and an array of parameters.
`mysqli_fetch_row()`	Gets a row as an enumerated array	Result of a query. Field numbers are the indexes, beginning with 0.
`mysqli_query()`	Queries a MySQL database	Connection ID. SQL query statement. Returns the result of the query or TRUE if successful, FALSE otherwise.

Table 12-1 Database Manipulation Functions

and many examples of their use in this and the following two chapters. Use Table 12-1 as a reference to come back to after you have seen the function explanations and examples of their use.

NOTE

Throughout this and the remaining chapters' discussion of the PHP MySQL functions, we will precede each function with mysqli, which is the newer "improved (i)" version of the PHP MySQL functions that uses the latest features of MySQL. There is an earlier set of functions preceded with mysql that has been deprecated as of PHP 5.5. There are also two styles of mysqli functions, an object-oriented style ("OOP" for object-oriented programming), and a procedural style. In line with the "Beginner's Guide" nature of this book, we will only discuss the procedural style. For further information about the object-oriented style, see php.net/manual/en/book.mysqli.php. For use in this book and for much of your work, the procedural style functions provide everything that is needed to create full-featured web apps.

NOTE

As with the rest of the book, there are many more PHP MySQL functions than can be discussed here. For the full list, see php.net/mysqli.

Connect to MySQL

Connecting to MySQL is really "logging into" a particular MySQL database server with a username, password, and database name. Like this:

```
mysqli_connect("host_name", "user_name", "password", "database_name");
```

In this book I assume you have installed Zend Server (see Chapter 5) on your computer, used the default username root, and set up password of your choosing. If that is correct, then you could create a variable $conid like this:

```
$conid = mysqli_connect("localhost", "root", "password", "database_name");
```

If mysqli_connect is able to connect, the variable $conid contains the connection identifier that is used in the other PHP MySQL functions. This connection remains open for as long as the script is running. When the script ends, the connection is deleted. As a general rule, you need to specify the connection identifier in other PHP MySQL functions. If a connection is not made, then $conid contains FALSE. Listings 12-1a and 12-1b show how this can be used with the results, first on the left with the words "password" and "database_name" for those values, and then on the right with my password and "books" for the database name.

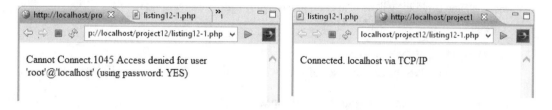

Listing 12-1a   Connect to a Database

```php
<?php
  $conid = mysqli_connect("localhost", "root", "password",
    "database_name");
  if($conid) {
    echo "Connected. " . mysqli_get_host_info($conid);
  }
  else {
    echo "Cannot Connect. " . mysqli_connect_errno() . " " .
      mysqli_connect_error();
  }
  mysqli_close($conid);
?>
```

There are several ways to accomplish the same results. One of the simplest and historically common, and the one that is often used in testing, is shown in Listing 12-1b.

Listing 12-1b   Connect to a Database

```php
<?php
  $conid = mysqli_connect("localhost", "root", "password", "books")
      or die ("Cannot Connect. " . mysqli_connect_errno() . " " .
      mysqli_connect_error());
  echo "Connected. " . mysqli_get_host_info($conid);
  mysqli_close($conid);
?>
```

The or die() clause outputs its message and terminates the script. This is fine for testing, but it should not be used in an active website because it just terminates the current script without giving the user any option but to go to another site.

Perform a Query

The query is a MySQL SELECT statement, which can be assigned to a PHP variable:

```
$query = "SELECT * FROM books WHERE price > 5.00";
```

To perform the query, it needs to be in a query statement:

```
$result = mysqli_query($conid, $query);
if(!$result) {
    echo "Couldn't do query. " . mysqli_error($conid);
}
```

The SELECT statement itself could be in the `mysqli_query()` function in place of the `$query` variable, but having it as a separate statement adds to the human readability and to ease debugging (finding and correcting errors). Also, note the `!` in the `if` statement, meaning "not"—that is, asking "if $result is FALSE," in essence, if the query failed.

Process Results

Once you have done the query, you will want to do something with the data. The variable `$result` contains a resource that allows other PHP MySQL functions to get individual rows and fields in the database. These can be displayed or otherwise processed. There are several functions that can be used to get the information, depending on what you want to do with it. The two most commonly used functions are `mysqli_fetch_assoc($result)`, which gets an associative array with the field names as the indexes, and `mysqli_fetch_row($result)`, which gets an enumerated array with field numbers (beginning at zero) as the indexes.

```
while($row = mysqli_fetch_assoc($result)) {
        echo $row['Bkid']. " - ". $row['Title']. " - ". $row['Author'].
          " - ". $row['Price']. "<br />";
    }
```

```
while($row = mysqli_fetch_row($result)) {
    echo $row[0]. " - ". $row[1]. " - ". $row[2].
        " - ". $row[4]. "<br />";
    }
```

Notice that in the preceding two examples, only some of the fields are displayed (publisher and category have been left out) to simplify the example.

Complete the Query

To complete the query, you simply need to free the memory that is taken up with the result of the query and then close the connection. Neither of these is mandatory; both tasks are also done when the script closes, but they are simple steps that are a good habit to get into so they won't be forgotten when they are needed. The two functions look like this:

```
mysqli_free_result($result);
mysqli_close($conid);-
```

Put It Together

The composite of all of these functions to perform a MySQL database query is shown in Listing 12-2, the result of which looks like this:

Listing 12-2   Query of Books Database

```
<!DOCTYPE html>
<html>
    <head>
        <title>Listing 12-2</title>
    </head>
    <body>
        <h1>Query the Books Database</h1>
```

```
<h3>List books priced above $5.00</h3>
<?php
 //Connect to the database Books
$conid = mysqli_connect("localhost", "root", "password", "books");
if(!$conid) {
   echo "Couldn't connect. " . mysqli_connect_error();
}
//Select books > $5.00
$query = "SELECT * FROM books WHERE price > 5.00";
$result = mysqli_query($conid, $query);
if(!$result) {
   echo "Couldn't do query. " . mysqli_error($conid);
}
//Display the books selected
while($row = mysqli_fetch_row($result)) {
   echo $row[0] . " - ". $row[1] . " - ". $row[2] . " - $".
      $row[4] . "<br />";
}
//Free memory and close the database
mysqli_free_result($result);
mysqli_close($conid);
?>
</body>
</html>
```

Database Information

As you use a MySQL database with PHP, you will need or want information about the database and its tables, rows, and fields. PHP has a number of functions for this purpose, many of which are shown in Table 12-2.

TIP

Database information functions are particularly useful to debug a script; to find out what is happening in your database; to find what table, row, and field you are accessing; or to find what error messages you are receiving.

How you use the database information functions depends on what you want to do. Here are some examples:

● **mysqli_affected_rows()**, which gets the number of rows affected by the last INSERT, UPDATE, REPLACE, or DELETE SQL query, provides this information to use with control functions to iterate through a set of rows. It is for types of queries other than SELECT or SHOW, which get the same information from **mysqli_num_rows()**.

Function	Description	Arguments and Comments
`mysqli_affected_rows()`	Gets number of rows affected by previous operation	Connection ID
`mysqli_character_set_name()`	Gets name of character set	Connection ID
`mysqli_connect_errno()`	Connect error code or number	Returns the error code of the last connection if it fails
`mysqli_connect_error()`	Connect error description	Returns the description of the error from the last connection
`mysqli_errno()`	Returns the error number from the previous operation	Connection ID
`mysqli_error()`	Returns the error message from the previous operation	Connection ID
`mysqli_fetch_fields()`	Returns the column name, table name, length of field, or type of a specified field	Result pointer from a query
`mysqli_get_client_info()` `mysqli_get_host_info()` `mysqli_get_server_info()`	Returns the client version, the type of host connection, or the MySQL server version	Connection ID
`mysqli_info()`	Returns detailed information about the last query	Connection ID
`mysqli_insert_id()`	Gets the ID or key last generated by AUTO_ INCREMENT	Connection ID
`mysqli_num_fields()` `mysqli_num_rows()`	Gets the number of fields or rows in the last query	Result pointer from the last query
`mysqli_stat()`	Gets the current server status	Connection ID

Table 12-2 Database Information Functions

- **mysqli_error()**, which returns the textual error message from the most recent MySQL operation, can be displayed with an or die() function or an echo statement.

- **mysqli_insert_id()**, which returns the ID or key that was automatically created through AUTO_INCREMENT by the last INSERT query, is used to reference the record that was just created.

- **mysqli_num_rows()**, which gets the number of rows affected by the last SELECT or SHOW SQL query, provides this information to use with control functions to iterate through a set of rows. It is for types of queries other than INSERT, UPDATE, REPLACE, or DELETE, which get the same information from **mysqli_affected_rows()**.

Database Administration

The database administration functions perform several maintenance duties on a database. Several of these functions are shown in Table 12-3.

Examples of how several of the database administration functions might be used are

- mysqli_data_seek, which moves the MySQL row pointer to a specific row, can be used with mysqli_fetch_row to get a specific row.

- mysqli_ping, which checks to see if a script is still connected to a MySQL server and reconnects it if it isn't, can be used after a lengthy idle period to possibly reestablish a connection.

- mysqli_real_escape_string, which "escapes" (adds backslashes to) the special characters in a string so they cannot easily include malicious code when included in a SQL statement, should be used with any string that is sent to MySQL that could possibly contain special characters.

NOTE

mysqli_real_escape_string takes into account the particular character set being used and can be specific to a particular connection.

Function	Description	Arguments and Comments
mysqli_data_seek()	Moves the row pointer to specified row	Result pointer from a query and the new row number (beginning at 0).
mysqli_field_seek()	Sets the result pointer to specified field number	Result pointer from the last query and the new field number (beginning at 0).
mysqli_free_result()	Frees the memory used by the last query	Result pointer from a query.
mysqli_ping()	Checks if a MySQL server connection exists, and if not, tries to reconnect	Connection ID. Returns TRUE if connection exists, FALSE otherwise.
mysqli_real_escape_string()	Escapes special characters in a string for use in SQL	Connection ID. String to be escaped.
mysqli_set_charset()	Sets the character set	Connection ID. Character set name.

Table 12-3   Database Administration Functions

Combining PHP MySQL Functions

Listing 12-3 combines a number of the PHP MySQL functions by returning to the Books database used earlier, having the user enter part of a title, and searching for and displaying the full book information. Among the other features are

- Use a form that returns to the PHP in the same script.
- Pause on the form until Submit is clicked.
- Strip the title that is entered of any white space, and make sure it is not blank.
- Escape special characters with `mysqli_real_escape_string`.
- Display the error text on a query error with `mysqli_error`.
- Display the book that is found using an associative array.

Listing 12-3 has several features that need further discussion, which you will see later in this chapter and in future chapters. Both the initial form and the output of this script are displayed in Figure 12-1.

Listing 12-3   Combining PHP MySQL Functions

```
<!DOCTYPE html>
<html>
    <head>
    <meta charset="utf-8">
        <title>Listing 12-3</title>
        </head>
        <body>
            <h1>Query the Books Database</h1>
            <h3>Search for a Title</h3>
            <p>Precede and/or follow the entry with % if not a
                complete title.</p>
            <?php
             tryagain:
            //Wait for submit
                if (!$_POST['submit']) {
            //Enter form information
            ?>
                <form action="<?=$_SERVER['PHP_SELF']?>" method="post">
                    <p>Book Title: <input type="text" name="title" /></p>
                    <p><input type="submit" name="submit" value="Submit" /></p>
                </form>
            <?php
                }
                else {
```

Figure 12-1 The query form disappears when the results are displayed.

```
//Connect to the Book database
   $conid = mysqli_connect("localhost", "root", "password",
      "books");
   if(!$conid) {
      echo "Couldn't connect. " . mysqli_connect_error();
   }
//Remove white space, check for blank, and remove special
   characters
   if (($title = trim($_POST['title'])) == '') {
      echo "Please enter a title.";
      $_POST['submit']=NULL;
      goto tryagain;
   }
   else {
```

```
        //Escape special characters in the title
            $title = mysqli_real_escape_string($conid, $_POST['title']);
        }
    //Select the book based on a partial title
        $query = "SELECT * FROM books WHERE Title LIKE '$title'";
        $result = mysqli_query($conid, $query);
        if(!$result) {
            echo "Couldn't do query. " . mysqli_error($conid);
        }
    //Display book with associative array
        while($row = mysqli_fetch_assoc($result)) {
            echo $row['Title']. " - ". $row['Author']. " - ".
                $row['Publisher']. " - $". $row['Price']. "<br />";
        }
        mysqli_free_result($result);
        mysqli_close($conid);
        }
    ?>
    </body>
</html>
```

NOTE

There is a large body of thought in the programming community that says that using goto is a bad practice because it can lead to disjointed code that goes off in multiple directions that can't be easily followed, and can generally be replaced with a compact loop. I don't disagree with that as a general rule, and, like many general rules, there are exceptions that make sense. Listing 12-3 is an example where using goto simplifies the code and is easy to follow. When tempted to use goto ask yourself if using it would simplify your code, or if a loop would be more understandable.

Working with Forms and Databases

In Chapters 2, 4, and 7 you have been introduced to forms in HTML, JavaScript, and PHP, respectively. In this chapter we'll expand on PHP form handling and then focus on the MySQL aspects of forms. In particular, we'll look at how PHP and MySQL collect and store data in a database table, and then how they retrieve data from a database and display it in a web page.

Expanding PHP Form Handling

PHP acts as both a partner and an intermediary among HTML, JavaScript, and MySQL. Listing 12-3 is a good example of this:

- You start in HTML to set up the web page with its titling.

- Go into PHP to check if the form has been submitted.

- Jump back to HTML to display the form.
- Go back to PHP to:
  - Connect to the MySQL database.
  - Clean up what was entered on the HTML form.
  - Check to make sure something was entered.
  - Query the MySQL database to see if the requested information is there.
  - Fetch the information from the MySQL database.
  - Display the information on the HTML web page.
  - Handle all the possible error conditions.

    You can see that PHP is playing several critical roles, including:

- Facilitating the dynamic user interaction on a static HTML web page.
- Interacting with a MySQL database.
- Providing error handling and security.

Facilitating User Interaction

When working with forms, HTML defines what the user sees—the form itself—and PHP processes the information that is entered into the form. It is a partnership that requires communication between them. Some of the ways this happens is described in the following sections, which uses Listing 12-3 as an example.

HTML `<form method`

On the HTML side, the HTML `<form` tag `method` attribute initializes either the `$_POST` or `$_GET` PHP superglobal array that is used to transfer information entered on the form to PHP using the field names that are defined by HTML in the form. For example, HTML `<form method="post">` and `<input name="title">` allow PHP to use `$_POST['title']` to pick up the value entered into the title field on the form.

HTML `<input type="submit"`

HTML `<input type="submit"` creates a button on the form that the user can click to indicate they have completed entry. The name and value of the button do not have to be "submit" and can be anything the web page creator wants. The type, of course, must be "submit." The name is what is used in the superglobal array, and the value is what is actually displayed on the button. When Submit is selected on the form, the `<form` action takes over and PHP can learn of this using the `$_POST['submit']` superglobal element.

HTML `<form action`

The HTML `<form` tag also uses the `action` attribute or its absence to determine where the focus—in this instance, PHP—should go to continue processing the form after the form has been submitted by the user. If there is no `action` attribute, then the focus is transferred to the first PHP code at the beginning of the script. This can be before or after the start of the HTML. The `action` attribute can also have the URL (web address) of a script to which the focus is transferred. Finally, as is the case in Listing 12-3, the `action` attribute can have a snippet of PHP code to transfer the focus to PHP in the current script. This is exactly the same as *not* having an `action` attribute. The only reason for having `action="<?=$_SERVER['PHP_SELF']?>"` is that it is more obvious to the human reader what is happening.

PHP `$_POST['submit']`

PHP, for its part, watches the superglobal array entry (`$_POST['submit']` in Listing 12-3), which is initially NULL or FALSE, and goes to work when it sees that the `submit` entry has something in it. PHP does this by asking if `$_POST['submit']` is FALSE. In other words, the form has not been submitted. If correct, HTML displays the form, and PHP waits until the form is submitted, when it can then go on and interact with MySQL and the database.

Interacting with a Database

When PHP sees that the form has been submitted, it connects with the database, removes any white space in the entry, and determines if the entry is blank. If so, it asks for a title to be entered, sets the superglobal array entry `$_POST['submit']` to NULL and goes back to watching for the form to be submitted. When that happens, and the title is found to not be blank, PHP looks for and escapes (places backslashes in front of) any special characters. (This may seem like it's not an important step, but just adding this one line of code greatly increases the security of your program.) Finally, the Books table is queried for the title and, if it is found, the row or record in the table with that title is fetched and displayed.

Improving Security

The user can enter anything into a web form that they want to. It can be malicious, silly, or just typing errors. PHP provides several functions and features to improve the safety of handling user input, but no matter how much you do, you need to be aware that *there is nothing you can do to be 100 percent safe*. That said, you should still do what you can in an unobtrusive way to protect your website and its users. Some of what you can do is relatively simple, as you'll see here, but some of it is beyond the scope of this book, and you are encouraged to continue to explore this subject as your knowledge of web programming grows. The PHP Manual has an extensive section on security (php.net/manual/en/security.php) and is worth a review. Here we'll focus on handling user input.

PHP provides functions that work toward cleaning up user input, as shown in Table 12-4.

HTML codes that a user places in his or her form input operate as they are designed in HTML to do. If the user places "Super" in their entry, then the bold tags turn the word "Super" into bold. Obviously, turning a word bold is not a security issue, but there are other sets of tags that might be. `htmlentities()` and `htmlspecialcharacters()` convert HTML tags into their HTML entities, so "Super" becomes <b>Super</b> and is displayed as "Super." `strip_tags()` simply removes the HTML tags altogether, so "Super" becomes "Super."

`htmlentities()` and `htmlspecialcharacters()` are the same except that `htmlspecialcharacters()` limits itself to the five characters: ampersand (&), double quote ("), single quote ('), less than (<), and greater than (>). Both functions will convert these characters into &amp, &quot, &#039 or &apos, &lt, and &gt. By default, both functions will not convert single quotes, although they will convert double quotes. You can use the flag `ENT_QUOTES` to convert both types of quotes. Both functions are dependent on the character set being used. The default is UTF-8, but you can add an optional third argument to specify other character sets.

Function	Description	Arguments and Comments
`htmlentities()`	Converts HTML code into their HTML entities	String to convert. Optionally, flags on quote handling.
`htmlspecial characters()`	Converts specific characters into their HTML entities	String to convert. Converts only &, ", ', <, and >. Optionally, flags for additional handling.
`strip_tags()`	Removes all HTML and PHP tags	String to strip. Optionally, a list of tags to keep.
`trim()`	Removes white space on either end of a string	String to be trimmed. Strips blanks, tabs, newline, carriage return, NULL, vertical tab.
`mysqli_real_ escape_ string()`	Escapes (adds slashes in front of) special characters in a MySQL query	Connection ID. String to be escaped. Must be connected to a MySQL database.
`addslashes()`	Escapes (adds slashes in front of) special characters in a string	String to be escaped.

Table 12-4 Security-Related Functions

Listing 12-4 shows examples of these functions in use, with the results shown next.

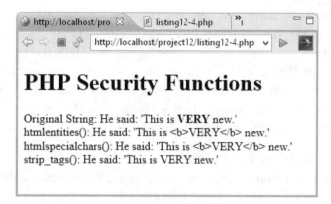

Listing 12-4   Examples of PHP and MySQL Security Functions

```
<!DOCTYPE html>
<html>
    <head>
    <meta charset="utf-8">
    <title>Listing 12-4</title>
    </head>
    <body>
      <h1>PHP Security Functions</h1>
      <?php
            $astr = "He said: 'This is <b>VERY</b> new.'" ;
            $new1 = htmlentities($astr);
            $new2 = htmlspecialchars($astr, ENT_QUOTES);
            $new3 = strip_tags($astr);
            echo "Original String: ", $astr, "<br/>";
            echo "htmlentities(): ", $new1, "<br/>";
            echo "htmlspecialchars(): ", $new2, "<br/>";
            echo "strip_tags(): ", $new3 ;
      ?>
    </body>
</html>
```

NOTE

Don't let what `echo` displays confuse you. `htmlentities()` and `htmlspecialcharacters()` do convert the HTML and quotes as requested, but what you see echoed may not look that way.

Using Magic Quotes

You may have heard about something called "Magic Quotes" as a way to protect yourself from malicious user input. Magic Quotes was a feature of PHP that automatically added a backslash to escape single quotes, double quotes, backslash, and NULL characters. The concept and feature of Magic Quotes have been deprecated and now removed from PHP because it provided a false sense of security, and it is felt that it is better to do this on a case-by-case and database-by-database basis. With MySQL, using `mysqli_real_escape_string()` is much preferable, as is using `htmlentities()` for HTML.

Combining Security Functions

You can combine several security functions in a single user function that you can reuse in multiple scripts. For example, if you want a function that will clean up input that will go into MySQL, you might create and use the following function:

```php
<?php
   function cleanmysql($astr) {
        $astr = trim($astr);
        $astr = mysql_real_escape_string($astr);
        $astr = htmlentities($astr);
        return($astr);
 }
?>
```

You can then add the previous code to your PHP programs and use it with this code:

```php
$newfield = "";
$newfield = cleanmysql($_POST['newfield']);
```

In the following chapters, you'll see examples of additional ways of combining PHP and MySQL with HTML, CSS, and JavaScript to create comprehensive web applications.

Try This 12-1 Create a Script that Uses an Existing Database

Create a script that performs the following tasks, similar to what was shown in Listing 12-3, but with the Shop database and Sales table created in Chapter 11.

1. Use a form that returns to the PHP in the same script.

2. Pause on the form until Submit is clicked.

3. Strip what the user has entered of any white space, and make sure it is not blank.

4. Escape special characters that the user has entered.

5. Connect to the database and table to insert information the user has entered.

6. Query the database and table to retrieve the information that was entered.

7. Display the error text for the connection and query errors.

8. Display the information that was retrieved.

Chapter 12 Self-Test

The following questions are intended to help reinforce your comprehension of the concepts covered in this chapter. The answers can be found in the accompanying online Appendix A, "Answers to the Self-Tests."

1. How does PHP interact with MySQL?

2. You can use either the `mysql` or `mysqli` set of functions, true or false?

3. If you don't connect using the `mysqli_connect` function, what is the value of the function?

4. What is the value of `mysqli_connect` if you do connect?

5. How is the `or die` clause used and when should you use it?

6. What is the code snippet to use in place of the `or die` clause?

7. You must free the query results and close the database at the end of your script, true or false?

8. What is very useful in debugging PHP MySQL interaction?

9. If you use `AUTO_INCREMENT` to automatically generate the key for a database record, how can you get the value of the key?

10. How can you check to see if a script is still connected to a MySQL server?

11. When working with forms, HTML defines what the user sees, and PHP processes the results, true or false?

12. What is the name of and two form-related examples of the entities that collect form input and pass the results to PHP?

13. How does the script know when the user has completed filling in a form?

14. A script must have `action="<?=$_SERVER['PHP_SELF']?>"` if the PHP code is in the same script as the HTML, true or false?

15. What is the best PHP MySQL function to use to clean up user input on a form?

Chapter 13

Registering and Responding to Users

Key Skills & Concepts

- Design a Template

- Create a CSS

- Design a Database

- Create a Script for Authentication

- Authenticate Individual Pages

- Create a Script for Database Entry

- Create a Script for Database Update

- Create a Script for Database Deletion

- Create a Script for Database Selection

- Create a Script for Database Listing

This chapter combines many of the elements described in the first 12 chapters of this book into a single web app to demonstrate how they fit together. HTML will, of course, be the foundation holding all the rest. A CSS style sheet will be used for the common styles used throughout the app. A template will be used to provide a common layout. JavaScript is used for both event handling as well as form validation. PHP will be used both for its own services and to access the MySQL databases, and MySQL will host the database tables.

In this chapter, we'll look at the design of a web app, the creation of a template for the page layout, the building of a CSS file, and the initial construction of the database tables in phpMyAdmin. We'll finally go into depth on the construction of the various JavaScript, PHP, and MySQL elements of the needed scripts.

"Go into depth" is meant very literally. This chapter offers a total of 26 scripts, plus the template and the CSS. In the process, records from several MySQL tables are written, read, selected, updated, and deleted. Multiple tables (three of them) are accessed together to utilize a relational database, and data is passed among scripts in several ways, including sending several pieces at the same time.

In summary, this chapter provides a comprehensive example of how to fully utilize HTML, CSS, JavaScript, PHP, and MySQL to build a significant, data-driven website.

TIP

Remember that all the scripts in this chapter, as in the rest of the book, are available online. See the book's Introduction for details.

Application Design

In this chapter, we'll build an application for students to select and register for classes. It is based on four database tables and five components of the application, as shown schematically in Figure 13-1. The components are

- Administrator Authentication
- Database Entry and Maintenance
- Class List and Selection
- Student Entry and Update
- Registration and Confirmation

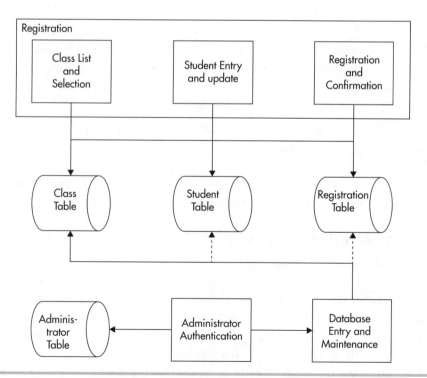

Figure 13-1   The Class Selection and Registration Application uses a relational database with five components.

These components can be grouped into Authentication, Maintenance, and Registration (where Registration contains the last three components: Class List and Selection, Student Entry and Update, and Registration and Confirmation).

Each of the components has one or more scripts and interacts with one or more tables. The Administrator Authentication component is the User Authentication application we built in Chapter 8, updated to use MySQL in place of PHP direct disk access.

TIP

While an application like this may look daunting, it was built with a lot of copying, cutting, and pasting. Many of the scripts are very similar, with only changes in the names. And you have the scripts from this book available to you online as starting points.

The functioning of the application will follow these steps:

- Administrators of this system would sign on and be authenticated. With that, they can then add to, update, and maintain all of the database tables.

- A student would go online, see a list of classes, and then select a class for which they want to register.

- To register for the selected class, the student would first enter their email address. If the script finds the email address in the database, the student's name and address information would be presented for the student to update. If the email address is not found, the student is asked to enter their information.

- With the selected class information and the student's information, a registration record is built and presented to the student to confirm.

A major feature of this application is the passing of multiple pieces of information among the scripts by use of cookies, session variables, and as a part of the URL.

Design Template and CSS

Since you will have a number of separate web pages in this application, you want them to have a consistent look. The best way to do that is to have a template that you use to build every page. This is very easy to do with Zend Studio; for the period while you are building the application, simply replace the standard PHP template with the template for the application. That way, each time you call for a new page, you will get the application template. You will see how to do this in a moment.

You also want a single CSS for use throughout the application. The easiest way to do that is to build the CSS up front and attach it to the template. It will then be called in each page built with the template.

It is not easy to think through an application and decide up front how the template should look and what the styles should be in the CSS. It is easier to just start out writing the scripts and see what develops. The problem is that you will likely not get the consistent look you want, and you will probably end up going back and changing something on earlier pages. It is worth the investment to build and use these tools first and try to stay with them.

Design a Template

To create a template, the first step is to sketch out what various sections of your standard web page will contain, and then how each section is sized and formatted. A common layout for a page, which will be used in this exercise and is shown in Figure 13-2, has

- A heading or banner at the top with the logo and general information
- A horizontal navigation or menu bar beneath the heading for the application-wide options
- A vertical navigation or menu bar down the left side for local options
- One or two columns of page-specific content in the middle-right area
- A footer at the bottom with copyright and contact information and possibly broad navigation options

After deciding what content will go where, the next step is to decide the size of the overall page and the individual sections. Today, most screens are larger than 1280×1024. Therefore, if you use 1024×768, which we will use as the overall page size, you have a safety margin. The size of the individual sections varies depending on their content. For this exercise we'll use

- **Heading**   1000 pixels wide × 100 pixels high
- **Horizontal navigation bar**   1000 pixels wide × 60 pixels high
- **Vertical navigation bar**   150 pixels wide × 500 pixels high
- **Main content**   830 pixels wide × 500 pixels high
- **Footer**   1000 pixels wide × 60 pixels high

You may also need to consider smart phones and tablets and their screen sizes. If that is important to your web app, search for tools that adjust sizes based on the screen type.

The sections will be created using `divs`, floating the left and right columns in the middle to the left and right, and placing the footer at the bottom. The headings and titles

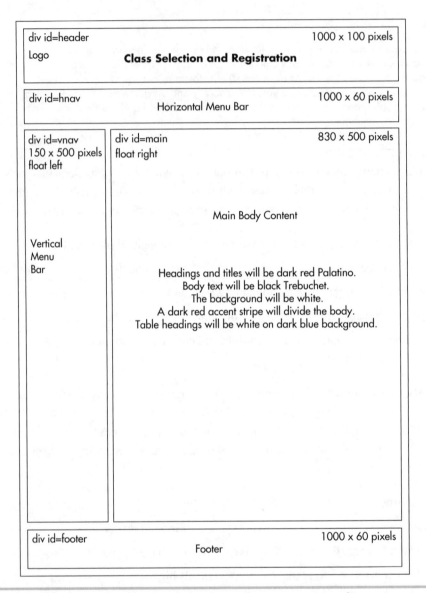

Figure 13-2 The template for the Class Selection and Registration Application

will use the Palatino font, and the body text will use Trebuchet. Both of these translate well to the Mac (Trebuchet is Helvetica on the Mac). We'll use a white background with a dark red accent stripe and dark red headings. The body text will be black, and the headings in the tables will be white on a dark blue background.

Create the Template

The template itself is just a script that is used as the starting point for all other pages. You therefore want the template to have all of the standard features you want on all pages. This starts out with the `<div>` elements that divide the page. In addition to the five `<div>` elements shown in Figure 13-2, we add one called "wrapper" that is an overall `<div>` that contains the others, but is separate from the `<body>`.

TIP

When you initially enter your `<div>` elements, enter a comment with the ID name in the ending element so that you can distinguish it from the others, like this:

```
<body>
    <div id="wrapper">
        <div id="header">

        </div> <!-- id="header" -->
        <div id="hnav">

        </div> <!-- id="hnav" -->
        <div id="vnav">

        </div> <!-- id="vnav" -->
        <div id="main">

        </div> <!-- id="main" -->
        <div id="footer">

        </div> <!-- id="footer" -->
    </div> <!-- id="wrapper" -->
</body>
```

With the `<div>` elements in place, next enter all the common elements that will appear on all pages, such as logos, titling, menus, and common footer information. This example keeps it simple, as shown in Listing 13-1 and Figure 13-3 (without formatting):

- A logo and a title in the heading
- A four-option menu in the horizontal navigation bar
- A heading and a two-option menu in the vertical navigation bar
- A heading, a paragraph, and a footnote in the main content section
- Copyright and contact notices in the footer

Figure 13-3 The unformatted template content

For the most part, everything in the template is relatively straightforward, reflecting work we have done elsewhere in this book. Two minor exceptions are the automatically updating copyright date using the PHP `date()` function and the `mailto` HTML construct.

The PHP `date()` function is discussed in Chapter 5, but the `date_default_timezone_set()` function was only briefly covered. PHP version 5.1.0 and later check to see if a valid time zone has been set and will issue a warning if it hasn't. Most Internet hosting services set this by default, so if you want to use your host's time zone, you're okay. To be sure, though, it is a good idea to set your own time zone in each script (once per script is adequate). You can find a list of supported time zone constants at http://us.php.net/manual/en/timezones.php (not every major city is included; you must look for other cities in your time zone).

The mailto HTML construct combines with an email address to open the default email message client and to create a URL for sending a message to the stated email address, like this:

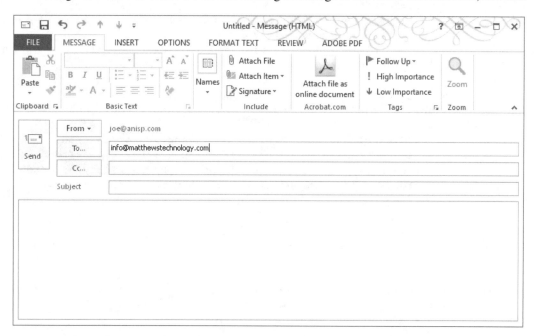

The other item whose absence you might have noticed is that although we said there would be accent stripes on the page, there are no <hr> elements (horizontal rules or lines) in the template. This is because Firefox does not handle the formatting (setting a height and color) of <hr> elements well, and we can accomplish the same thing with single-sided borders in the CSS.

Listing 13-1   Site Template

```php
<?php
   session_start();
?>
<!DOCTYPE html>
<html>
   <head>
    <title>Class Registration Template</title>
    <link rel= "stylesheet" type= "text/css"
       href= "/ClassRegistration/registration.css"/>
    <script language="JavaScript" type="text/javascript"></script>
   </head>
```

```
<body>
 <div id="wrapper">
    <div id="header">
     <img src="/ClassRegistration/MatTechLogo.gif"
     alt="Matthews Technology" />
     <h1 id="title">Class Selection and Registration</h1>
    </div> <!-- id="header" -->

    <div id="hnav">
     <table width="400" border="0" cellspacing="2" cellpadding="2">
      <tr>
         <td><a class="hmenu" href="index.php">Home</a> </td>
         <td><a class="hmenu" href="about.php">About</a> </td>
         <td><a class="hmenu" href="support.php">Support</a> </td>
         <td><a class="hmenu" href="maintain.php">Maintain</a>
         </td>
      </tr>
     </table>
    </div> <!-- id="hnav" -->

    <div id="vnav">
     <table width="120" border="0" cellspacing="2" cellpadding="2">
      <tr>
         <th class="vhead">Go To: </th>
      </tr>
      <tr>
         <td><a class="vmenu" href="classlist.php">Class
         List</a></td>
      </tr>
      <tr>
         <td><a class="vmenu" href="nameentry.php">Student
         Entry</a></td>
      </tr>
     </table>
    </div> <!-- id="vnav" -->

    <div id="main">
     <h1 id="mainhead">Spring Class Schedule</h1>
     <p id="mainpara">Click Register to do so for class.</p>
     <p class="red">*A footnote.</p>
    </div> <!-- id="main" -->

    <div id="footer">
     <p id="copyright">
      Copyright &copy:2008 -
      <?php
         date_default_timezone_set('America/Vancouver');
         echo date('Y');
```

```
  ?>
  Matthews Technology
  </p>
  <p id="contact">
   <a href="mailto:info@matthewstechnology.com">
      Contact us by clicking here.</a>
  </p>
  </div> <!-- id="footer" -->
 </div> <!-- id="wrapper" -->

 </body>
</html>
```

NOTE

While a template is a good idea for preparing a starting place for each page, you can't change the template and have the page it created automatically change. You can do that with the PHP `include()`, `include_once()`, `require()`, and `require_once()` functions as discussed in Chapter 8.

Create a CSS

The CSS for the Class Selection and Registration Application takes up where we left off with CSS in Chapter 3's Listing 3-12, creating the final product shown in Listing 13-2. The effect that this CSS has on the template is pronounced, as you can see in Figure 13-4 (unfortunately, you can't see the color here, but it improves the visual appeal).

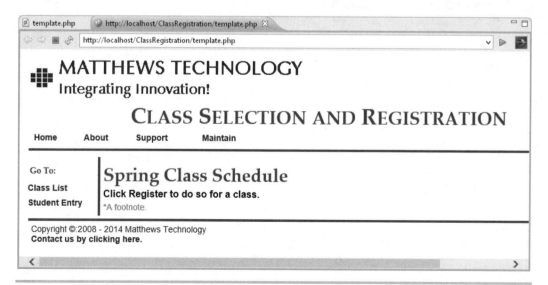

Figure 13-4   The CSS makes major changes in the appearance of the template.

For the most part, the Registration CSS reflects the work that was done in Chapter 3 and shown in Listing 3-12. The major exceptions are the selectors for the `<a>` tag, the links used in the horizontal and vertical navigation bars. The CSS provides formatting for four states of the `<a>` tag with these selectors:

- `a:link` represents the link before it has been clicked, selected, or pointed at.
- `a:visited` represents the link after it has been clicked and the associated code has been executed.
- `a:focus` represents the link as it has been selected but not executed with the keyboard.
- `a:hover` represents the link as it is being pointed at by the mouse.

The `:link`, `:visited`, `:focus`, and `:hover` selectors are called *pseudo-classes,* which allow you to format specific states. Actually, there is another, `:active`, which is the tag as it is being clicked and the associated code executed, something that generally happens rather rapidly. The `:link` pseudo-class is the same as the tag by itself (just a), but just a also covers named anchors to bookmarks or named areas on the current page, so `:link` is preferable.

When using the link pseudo-classes, it is important to put them in the order `:link`, `:visited`, `:focus`, `:hover`, and `:active`; because of the cascading of the style sheet, the last element takes precedence, so if `:link` is last, `:hover` would not appear.

Listing 13-2   Registration CSS

```css
/* registration.css */

body    {
        width : 1000px;
        margin : 0;
        padding : 0;
        }

div, h1, h2, p    {
        margin : 0;
        padding : 0;
        }

h2      {
        color : #8b0000;
        font : 600 24px "Palatino Linotype" ;
        }

P, textarea    { font : 14px "Trebuchet", "Helvetica", sans-serif ; }
```

```
.red    { color : red; }

a:link    {
        color : #00008b;
        font : 600 14px "Trebuchet", "Helvetica", sans-serif;
        text-decoration : none;
        }

a:visited    {
        color : #00ffff;
        font : 600 14px "Trebuchet", "Helvetica", sans-serif;
        text-decoration : none;
        }

a:focus  {
        color : #daa520;
        font : 600 14px "Trebuchet", "Helvetica", sans-serif;
        text-decoration : underline;
        }

a:hover  {
        color : #daa520;
        font : 600 14px "Trebuchet", "Helvetica", sans-serif;
        text-decoration : underline;
        }

th       {
        margin : 5px;
        padding : 5px;
        text-align : right;
        color : #ffffff;
        font : 600 14px "Trebuchet", "Helvetica", sans-serif;
        background : #00008b;
        }

div#header  {
        top : 0px;
        left : 0px;
        height : 100px;
        margin : 5px;
        padding : 5px;
        }

h1#title  {
        color : #8b0000;
        font : small-caps 600 36px /1.0em "Palatino Linotype" ;
        text-align : center;
```

```
            vertical-align : top;
            padding-bottom : 10px;
        }

    div#hnav {
            margin : 5px;
            margin-left : 15px;
            padding : 5px;
            padding-top : 10px;
            border-bottom : 4px solid #8b0000;
        }

    div#vnav {
            float : left;
            width : 100px;
            margin : 5px;
            padding : 5px;
        }

    #vhead   {
            color : #8b0000;
            font : 700 14px "Palatino Linotype" ;
            margin : 5px;
            padding : 5px;
        }

    div#main  {
            float : right;
            width : 850px;
            margin : 5px;
            padding : 5px;
            border-left : 4px solid #8b0000;
        }

    h1#maintitle  {
            color : #8b0000;
            font : 600 30px /1.5em "Palatino Linotype" ;
            text-align : left;
            vertical-align : top;
        }

    div#footer {
            clear: both ;
            margin : 5px;
            margin-left : 15px;
            padding : 5px;
            border-top : 4px solid #8b0000;
        }
```

Database Design

As mentioned earlier and shown in Figure 13-1, four tables are in the Class Registration database:

- **Class**, a list of available classes
- **Student**, a list of students
- **Registration**, a list of students registered for a particular class
- **Administrator**, a list of administrators allowed to edit the database

Three of the tables—Class, Student, and Registration—form a relational database with the Class ID and Student Email being foreign keys used in the Registration table. This allows the storing of only the keys in the Registration table, yet having available all of the information in the Class and Student tables while looking at a registration.

The tables will be built in phpMyAdmin to quickly get them online. Assuming you have Zend Server installed with the Apache2 web server, as discussed in earlier chapters, use these steps to do that:

1. Start a browser and in the address bar, type **localhost/phpmyadmin**, and press ENTER.

2. Click the Databases tab and under Create Database, type **ClassRegistration**, click the down arrow in the Collation drop-down list, click latin1_general_ci, and click Create.

3. Click ClassRegistration in the list below your new database entry, and under Create Table, type **class**, press TAB, type **6** for the number of fields, and click Go on the right.

4. In the form that is presented, type in the information shown in Table 13-1. (*AI* stands for Auto Increment, which is a check box you must tab or scroll to the right to see, and is used when a key is automatically created by MySQL.)

Field	Type	Length	Other
class_id	SMALLINT		AI
class_title	VARCHAR	60	
class_start	DATE		
class_descr	VARCHAR	255	
class_cost	DECIMAL	6,2	
class_instr	VARCHAR	20	

Table 13-1 Class Table

TIP

To quickly fill in the Type field, from the Name field, press TAB and press s for SMALLINT, or v for VARCHAR, or t for TIMESTAMP, or d for DECIMAL. To get DATE you have to press d three times.

5. Click Save. The Class table will be created. Click Structure in the Class row near the top. You'll see how your new table was created, as shown in Figure 13-5. Note that classid was automatically established as the primary key.

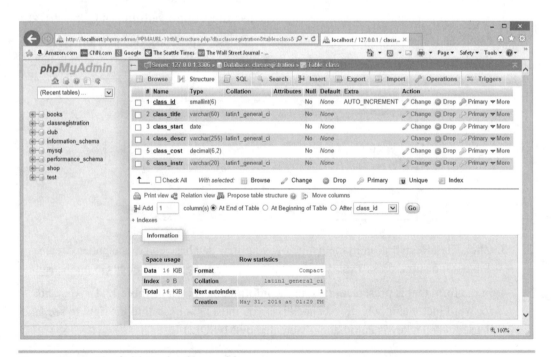

Figure 13-5 The fields in the Class table

Field	Type	Length	Other
student_email	VARCHAR	60	Primary Key
student_name	VARCHAR	60	
student_phone	VARCHAR	30	
student_date	TIMESTAMP		Current Timestamp

Table 13-2   Student Table

6. Click ClassRegistration in the left column. Under Create Table, type **student**, press TAB, type **4** for the number of fields, and click Go.

7. In the form that is presented, type in the information shown in Table 13-2. (The Primary Key is selected in the Index drop-down list. The Current Timestamp is selected in the Default drop-down list. Null is the check box of that name. It means that the field can be left blank. TAB to the right to see all of these.)

8. Click Save and then click Structure. The Student table will be created and then displayed as shown in Figure 13-6.

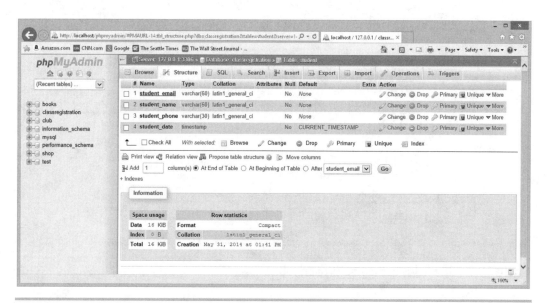

Figure 13-6   The fields in the Student table

Field	Type	Length	Other
reg_id	SMALLINT		AI
class_id	SMALLINT		
student_email	VARCHAR	60	
reg_date	TIMESTAMP		Current Timestamp

Table 13-3 Registration Table

9. Click ClassRegistration in the left column. Under Create Table, type **registration**, press TAB, type **4** for the number of fields, and click Go.

10. In the form that is presented, type in the information shown in Table 13-3.

11. Click Save and then click Structure. The Registration table will be created and then displayed as shown in Figure 13-7.

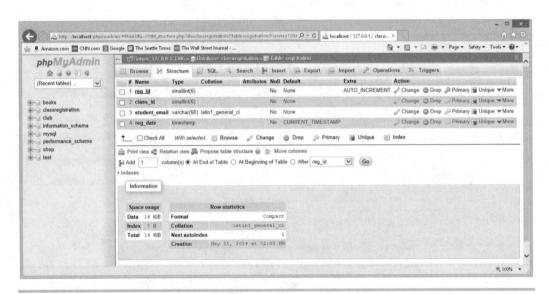

Figure 13-7 The fields in the Registration table

Field	Type	Length	Other
admin_id	VARCHAR	20	Primary Key
admin_password	VARCHAR	100	
admin_name	VARCHAR	60	
admin_date	TIMESTAMP		Current Timestamp

Table 13-4 Administrator Table

12. Click ClassRegistration in the left column. Under Create Table, type **administrator**, press TAB, type **4** for the number of fields, and click Go.

13. In the form that is presented, type in the information shown in Table 13-4.

14. Click **Save**. The Administrator table will be created as shown in Figure 13-8.

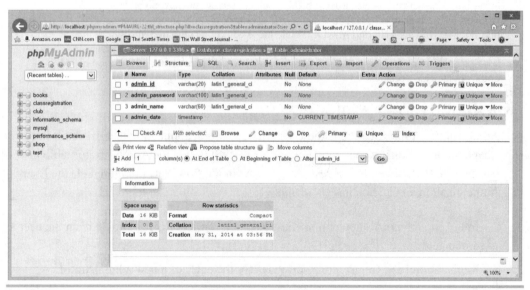

Figure 13-8 The fields in the Administrator table

Creating the Scripts

As you saw in Figure 13-1, the Class Selection and Registration Application has five modules:

- Administrator Authentication
- Database Entry and Maintenance
- Class List and Selection
- Student Entry and Update
- Registration and Confirmation

Each of these modules will have one or more scripts and will interact with one or more of the database tables. We will address them in the order shown in the preceding list, primarily because we need a method to enter classes into the database. (The class entry could be done in phpMyAdmin, but we need an online way to do this for a complete system.)

NOTE

In the following scripts, as was true with User Authentication, often, a given function is handled with a pair of scripts: one with the HTML and possibly a small amount of PHP, and another with just PHP and MySQL. While these could be combined in a single script, we prefer to do it with two scripts because we believe that it's easier to debug, it keeps each script simpler, and it's a more intuitive way of transferring information to and from the PHP portion.

Administrator Authentication

Administrator Authentication is the User Authentication application that was built in Chapter 8, except that we are now going to use MySQL and the Administrator table in place of the PHP direct disk access. As you saw in the flowchart in Figure 8-1, the User Authentication application has six scripts:

- Index.php (adminAuthen.php in Class Registration) checks if a cookie is on the user's computer.
- Registration Page (register.php) provides for the entry of a new administrator.
- Enter Name Page (enterName.php) encrypts the password and writes the record to the table.
- Sign-In Page (signin.php) provides for the entry of a user ID and password.
- Verify Page (verify.php) checks to see if the user ID and password are on the table.
- Each Page (enterSite.php) (the other pages in the application) checks if a session variable is present.

These will mostly be used as they were written in Chapter 8. Begin with these steps to create the necessary project and folder in Zend Studio, and then import the User Authentication scripts into it.

1. In Zend Studio, click File | New| Local PHP Project.

2. Type **ClassRegistration** as the project name, and click Finish.

3. In the Project list on the left, right-click ClassRegistration and click New | Folder. Type **AdministratorAuthentication** as the folder name, and click Finish.

4. Right-click AdministratorAuthentication and click Import. Click File System and click Next.

5. Click Browse | This PC, locate the Authentication folder from Chapter 8 (it should be in C:\Program File (x86)\Zend\Apacke2\hdocs\project08\), click each of the six PHP scripts (leave out namelist.txt), as shown in Figure 13-9, and click Finish.

6. Right-click index.php within the AdministratorAuthentication folder and click Rename. Select just the word "index," type **adminAuthen**, and press ENTER. We'll leave the other script names unchanged.

You can now modify each of the scripts.

Change adminAuthen.php

In adminAuthen.php, we only need to replace the cookie name MatTech with Admin. The resulting script should look like Listing 13-3.

Listing 13-3   adminAuthen.php

```php
<?php
    session_start();
    //Check if user has a cookie.
    if (isset ($_COOKIE["Admin"])) {
    //If so, set session and go to sign in.
    $_SESSION["name"] = $_COOKIE["Admin"][name];
    $_SESSION["retry"] = 0;
    $_SESSION["time"] = time();
    header( "Location: signin.php");
    }
    else {
    //If not, go to registration.
    header( "Location: register.php");
    }
?>
```

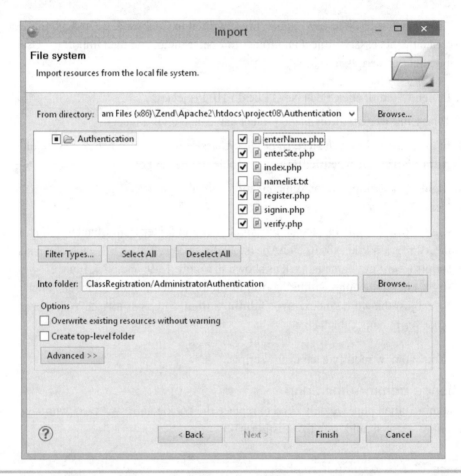

Figure 13-9 The work you did in Chapter 8's User Authentication can be imported into the Class Registration system.

Change register.php

In register.php, we need to embed the User Authentication `<div id="form">` in the `<div id= "main">` of the template. Also, the vertical navigation bar needs to be turned into a placeholder, and a number of other small changes need to be made, as shown in Listing 13-4. Pay particular attention to the `<div id="main">` section, which has the majority of the changes; the balance is very similar to the template, which will not be shown in future listings. Figure 13-10 shows how register.php displays.

NOTE

At the very beginning of the script, there is the `session_start()` statement, which is easily missed. Without it, you can't use the `$_SESSION[]` global variables.

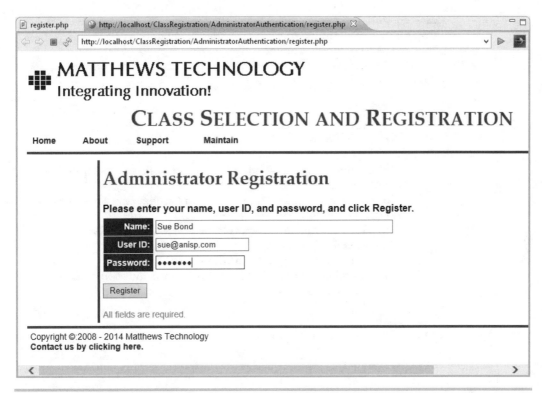

Figure 13-10   Entry of a new administrator

Listing 13-4   register.php

```php
<?php
   session_start();
?>
<!DOCTYPE html>
<html>
   <head>
         <meta charset="utf-8">
      <title>Administrator Registration Page</title>
      <link rel= "stylesheet" type= "text/css" href=
         "/ClassRegistration/registration.css"/>
      <script language="JavaScript" type= "text/javascript"></script>
   </head>
<!-- Put cursor in the first field -->
   <body onload="document.form1.admin_name.focus();">
<!-- From template -->
      <div id="wrapper">
```

```html
<div id="header">
    <img src="/ClassRegistration/MatTechLogo.gif"
        alt="Matthews Technology" />
    <h1 id="title">Class Selection and Registration</h1>
</div> <!-- id="header" -->

<div id="hnav">
    <table width="400" border="0" cellspacing="2"
        cellpadding="2">
    <tr>
      <td><a href="/ClassRegistration/index.php">Home</a>
      </td>
      <td><a href="/ClassRegistration/index.php">About</a>
      </td>
      <td><a href="/ClassRegistration/index.php">Support
      </a> </td>
      <td><a href="/ClassRegistration/
          AdministratorAuthentication/adminAuthen.php">
          Maintain</a> </td>
    </tr>
    </table>
</div> <!-- id="hnav" -->

    <div id="vnav">
<!-- Placeholder only -->
        <table width="120" border="0" cellspacing="2"
          cellpadding="2">
        <tr>
          <td id="vhead"> </td>
        </tr>
        <tr>
          <td> </td>
        </tr>
        <tr>
          <td> </td>
        </tr>
        </table>
    </div> <!-- id="vnav" -->

<!-- END Pure Template -->
    <div id="main">
        <h1 id="maintitle">Administrator Registration</h1>
        <br />
<?php
  if($_SESSION["errmsg"] < 1 ){
?>
```

```
        <p id="mainpara">Please enter your name, user ID, and password,
           and click Register.</p>
<?php
    }
    elseif ($_SESSION["errmsg"] == 1) {
?>
        <p class="red">Your name is required.</p>
        <p class="red">Please RE-enter your name, user ID, and password,
           and click Register.</p>
<?php
    }
    elseif ($_SESSION["errmsg"] == 2) {
?>
        <p class="red">A User ID is required.</p>
        <p class="red">Please RE-enter your name, user ID, and password,
           and click Register.</p>
<?php
    }
    elseif ($_SESSION["errmsg"] == 3) {
?>
        <p class="red">A Password is required.</p>
        <p class="red">Please RE-enter your name, user ID, and password,
           and click Register.</p>
<?php
    }
    else {
?>
        <p class="red">   </p>
        <p class="red">Please RE-enter your name, user ID, and password,
           and click Register.</p>
<?php
    }
?>
<!-- From User Authentication -->
    <div id="form">
<!-- Go to enterName.php after clicking Register -->
    <form action="enterName.php" method="post" name="form1">
        <table width="300" border="0" cellspacing="1" cellpadding="3">
        <tr>
            <th width="30%">Name:</th>
            <td width="50%">
              <input type="text" name="admin_name" value=""
                 size="60" />
            </td>
        </tr>
```

```html
<tr>
    <th>User ID:</th>
    <td>
        <input type="text" name="admin_id" value=""
            size="20" />
    </td>
</tr>
<tr>
    <th>Password:</th>
    <td>
        <input type="password" name="admin_password"
            value="" size="20" />
    </td>
</tr>
</table>
    <br />
    <input type="submit" name="submit" value="Register"
        />
</form>
</div> <!-- id=form -->
<!-- End User Authentication -->
<!-- Begin from template -->
<br />
    <p class="red">All fields are required.</p>
</div> <!-- id="main" -->
<div id="footer">
    <p id="copyright">Copyright &copy;2008 -
        <?php
            date_default_timezone_set('America/Vancouver');
            echo date('Y');
        ?>
        Matthews Technology </p>
    <p id="contact">
        <a href="mailto:info@matthewstechnology.com">Contact us
            by clicking here.</a> </p>
</div> <!-- id="footer" -->
</div> <!-- id="wrapper" -->
</body>
</html>
```

NOTE

The PHP code in this script calls a $_SESSION variable and therefore requires the session_start() function at the very top of the script, which is in the template.

enterName.php

While this script bears some resemblance to the User Authentication script of the same name, a lot has changed so that it could use MySQL in place of PHP direct disk access. The major parts of the script, which is shown in Listing 13-5, are

- Connecting to a MySQL server and selecting the ClassRegistration database.

- Getting the three fields from the registration form (`admin_name`, `admin_id`, and `admin_password`), removing any white space, checking for a blank entry, removing special characters, and then assigning the results to new variables.

- Creating and setting a cookie on the user's computer with the person's name, the current date, and an expiration date 180 days in the future.

- Encrypting the password.

- Checking to see if the combination of the user ID and encrypted password are already on file.

- If the user ID and password are not on the file, add a record to the administrator table so that the contents of `$userid` go into the `admin_id` field, `$encryptpasswd` goes into `admin_password`, and `$name` goes into `admin_name`.

- When the record has been successfully written, the adminAuthen script is reloaded. Since there is now a cookie on the user's computer, she or he is transferred to the signin.php script.

- If the user ID and password are on the file, the user has in essence "signed in," so the script writes a set of `$_SESSION` variables and leaves the authentication area.

- Error messages in this and other scripts in this app that in the past would have used the `or die` construct now use `if`, `echo`, and `exit` to be more informative. Errors that the user can correct, like leaving a blank field, store an error number in a `session` variable and use the `tryagain` label to return to register.php, where an error message is displayed as you see next.

Administrator Sign In

A User ID is required.
Please RE-enter your user ID and password, and click Sign In.

| User ID: | |
| Password: | |

Sign In

All fields are required.

NOTE

Remember that in Chapter 9 we recommended setting a password for the MySQL database. The scripts in this chapter support that and show *"password"* where you need to enter your own password (the word "password" is *not* a good choice for a password).

Listing 13-5   enterName.php

```php
<?php
    session_start();
//Connect to the ClassRegistration database
    $connection = mysqli_connect("localhost", "root", "password",
        "classregistration");
    if (!$connection) {
        echo "Cannot connect to MySQL. " . mysqli_connect_error();
        exit();
    }
//Remove white space, check for blank, and remove special characters
    if (($name = trim($_POST['admin_name'])) == '') {
        $_SESSION["errmsg"] = 1;
        goto tryagain;
    }
    else {$name = mysqli_real_escape_string($connection, $name);
    }
    if (($userid = trim($_POST['admin_id'])) == '') {
        $_SESSION["errmsg"] = 2;
        goto tryagain;
    }
    else {$userid = mysqli_real_escape_string($connection, $userid);
    }
    if (($userPasswd = trim($_POST['admin_password'])) == '') {
        $_SESSION["errmsg"] = 3;
        goto tryagain;
    }
    else {$userPasswd = mysqli_real_escape_string($connection, $userPasswd);
    }
//Set cookie, expires in 180 days.
    $date = time() ;
    $expire = time()+(60*60*24*180);
    setcookie("Admin[name]", $name, $expire, "/");
    setcookie("Admin[date]", $date, $expire, "/");

//Encrypt the password.
    $encryptpasswd = sha1($userPasswd);
```

```
//See if match in the administrator table
    $query = "SELECT admin_id, admin_password, admin_name
        FROM administrator
        WHERE admin_id= '$userid' AND admin_password=
            '$encryptpasswd'";
    $result = mysqli_query($connection, $query);
    if (!$result) {
        echo "Select from administrator failed. " . mysqli_error($connection);
        exit();
    }
//Determine if the user ID and password are on file.
    $row = mysqli_fetch_object($result);
    $db_userid = $row->admin_id;
    $db_password = $row->admin_password;
    $db_name = $row->admin_name;

    if($db_userid != $userid || $db_password != $encryptpasswd){

//Add record to the administrator table
        $query = "INSERT INTO administrator(admin_id, admin_password,
            admin_name) VALUES('$userid', '$encryptpasswd', '$name')";
        $result = mysqli_query($connection, $query);
        if (!$result) {
            echo ("Insert to administrator failed. " .
                mysqli_error($connection));
            exit();
        }
tryagain:
    //Return to adminAuthen.php.
        header( "Location: adminAuthen.php");
    }
    else {

    //If on file, get name, reset the session, and enter site.
        $_SESSION["name"] = $db_name;
        $_SESSION["retry"] = "admit";
        $_SESSION["time"] = time();
        header( "Location:
            /ClassRegistration/Maintenance/systementry.php");
    }
?>
```

CAUTION

SQL requires single quotes around all non-numeric values, both strings *and* variables.

deletecookie.php

As you are building and testing this or any other application that creates cookies, you need to delete the cookie so you can again test the application. As you saw in Chapter 6, you can do this with a very simple script, as shown next:

```php
<?php
//Delete cookie for name and date.
$expire = time()-(60*60);
setcookie("Admin[name]", $name, $expire, "/");
setcookie("Admin[date]", $date, $expire, "/");
?>
```

signin.php

As was done in register.php, for signin.php, we need to embed the User Authentication `<div id= "form">` in the `<div id= "main">` of the template. Again, the vertical navigation bar is simply a placeholder, and other small changes are made. Listing 13-6 shows only the `<div id= "main">` section of the script; the balance is very similar to the template and register.php. Figure 13-11 shows how signin.php displays.

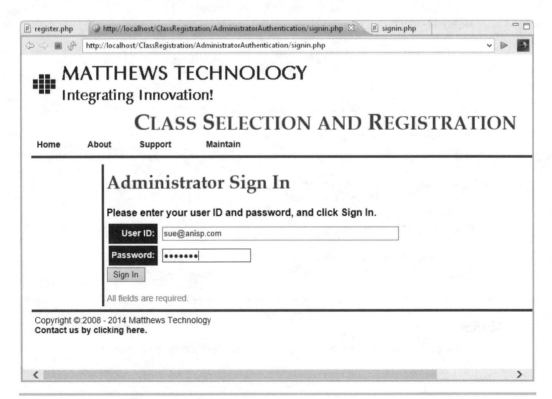

Figure 13-11   Signing in of an administrator

Listing 13-6   signin.php (in part)

```php
    <div id="main">
     <h1 id="maintitle">Administrator Sign In</h1>
     <br />
<?php
    $retry = $_SESSION["retry"];
    if($retry < 1 ){
?>
     <p id="mainpara">Please enter your user ID and password, and
        click Sign In.</p>
<?php
    }
    elseif ($_SESSION["errmsg"] == 1) {
?>
     <p class="red">A User ID is required.</p>
     <p class="red">Please RE-enter your user ID and password, and
        click Sign In.</p>
<?php
    $_SESSION["errmsg"] = NULL;
    }
    elseif ($_SESSION["errmsg"] == 2) {
?>
     <p class="red">A Password is required.</p>
     <p class="red">Please RE-enter your user ID and password, and
        click Sign In.</p>
<?php
    $_SESSION["errmsg"] = NULL;
    }
    else {
?>
     <p class="red">   </p>
     <p class="red">Please RE-enter your user ID and password, and
        click Sign In.</p>
<?php
    }
?>
    <!-- From User Authentication -->
     <div id="form">
    <!-- Display the sign-in form. After filling in, go to verify page. -->
        <form action="verify.php" method="post" id="signinForm">
         <table width="200" border="0" cellspacing="3" cellpadding="5" >
          <tr>
             <th width="60">User ID:</th>
             <td width="120">
              <input type="text" name="userid" value="" size="60" />
             </td>
```

```
        </tr>
        <tr>
          <th>Password:</th>
          <td>
          <input type="password" name="passwd" value="" size="20" />
          </td>
        </tr>
        </table>
        <input type="submit" name="submit" value="Sign In" />
        </form>
  </div>  <!-- id="form" -->
        <!-- End User Authentication -->
        <!-- Begin from template -->
        <br />
        <p class="red">All fields are required.</p>
  </div>  <!-- id="main" -->
```

verify.php

The verify.php script is very similar to enterName.php. userid and passwd, which are brought in from signin.php, are cleaned up, the password is encrypted, and then it and the user ID are compared with what is in the database. If they match, the session variables are updated, and the focus is transferred to the first site page. If there is not a match, the user is given three tries back in signin.php, and after which is sent to register.php to re-register. Listing 13-7 shows this script.

TIP

The result of a SELECT query is not FALSE, and the query does not fail if the sought items are not found. You must separately compare what was found to what you were looking for to determine the outcome. This is demonstrated in verify.php.

Listing 13-7 *verify.php*

```php
<?php
   session_start();
//Connect to the ClassRegistration database
   $connection = mysqli_connect("localhost", "root", "password",
        "classregistration");
   if (!$connection) {
      echo "Cannot connect to MySQL. " . mysqli_connect_error();
      exit();
   }
//Remove white space, check for blank, and remove special characters
   if (($userid = trim($_POST['userid'])) == '') {
```

```php
      $_SESSION["errmsg"] = 1;
      goto tryagain;
   }
   else {$userid = mysqli_real_escape_string($connection, $userid);
   }
   if (($userPasswd = trim($_POST['passwd'])) == '') {
      $_SESSION["errmsg"] = 2;
      goto tryagain;
   }
   else {$userPasswd = mysqli_real_escape_string($connection, $userPasswd);
   }
//Encrypt the password.
   $encryptpasswd = sha1($userPasswd);
//See if match in the administrator table
   $query = "SELECT admin_id, admin_password, admin_name
         FROM administrator
         WHERE admin_id= '$userid' AND admin_password=
            '$encryptpasswd'";
   $result = mysqli_query($connection, $query);
   if (!$result) {
      echo "Select from administrator failed. " . mysqli_error($connection);
      exit();
   }
//Determine if the user ID and password are on file.
   $row = mysqli_fetch_object($result);
   $db_userid = $row->admin_id;
   $db_password = $row->admin_password;
   $db_name = $row->admin_name;
   if($db_userid != $userid || $db_password != $encryptpasswd){
tryagain:
   //If not, add to Session Retry and test > 3
      $retry = $_SESSION["retry"];
      $retry++;
      if ($retry > 3) {
   //If greater than 3 go to register.
      header( "Location: register.php");
      }
      else {
   //If less than 3 reset Session Retry and go to Sign in
         $_SESSION["retry"] = $retry;
         header( "Location: signin.php");
      }
   }
   else {
//If on file, get name, reset the session, and enter site.
   $_SESSION["name"] = $db_name;
   $_SESSION["retry"] = "admit";
```

```php
$_SESSION["time"] = time();
header( "Location: /ClassRegistration/Maintenance/systementry.php");
}
?>
```

enterSite.php

enterSite.php is a snippet of code, shown in Listing 13-8, that can either be placed on each page in the site or be included on each page using the PHP `require_once()` function. We'll demonstrate both in the following scripts. When this is in a separate script in this application, it is called "doorway.php." This snippet checks to see if the `$_SESSION` variable `retry` has been set and contains `admit`. If so, it retrieves the user's name for use in the script (in real use, the `echo` statement would be removed from the snippet and placed elsewhere in the script). If not, the adminAuthen.php script is loaded.

Listing 13-8   enterSite.php

```php
<?php
session_start();
//Check to see if session retry is "admit."
if (isset($_SESSION["retry"]) && $_SESSION["retry"] == "admit") {
    //If so, continue.
    echo "Hello ", $_SESSION["name"], "!<br />";
}
else {
    header( "Location: adminAuthen.php");
}
?>
```

Database Entry and Maintenance

The Database Entry and Maintenance component is used to enter, update, and delete information for the database. It is needed for all four tables, but for this exercise, we'll do it for the Class table so that we can put some classes in it. In the process, it will demonstrate the MySQL INSERT, UPDATE, and DELETE functions. Database Entry and Maintenance has three subcomponents, each with one or more scripts:

- System entry
- New class entry
- Class update and delete

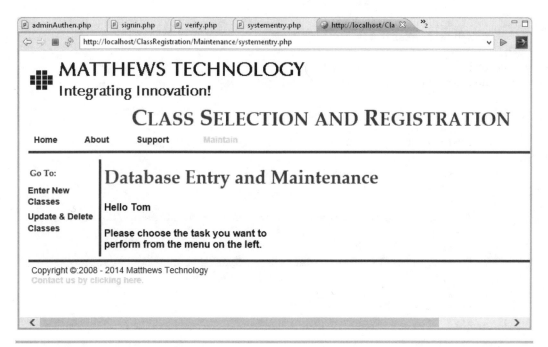

Figure 13-12 systementry.php

System Entry

systementry.php, the starting place for Database Entry and Maintenance, allows you to choose what you want to do and then sends you on your way. It is the script to which Administrator Authorization sends you, and it's the script you return to when you are done with any of the others in this component. It has no database elements and little PHP, as you can see in Figure 13-12.

Begin by creating a new PHP script based on the template we've built here, cut and paste the enterSite.php snippet, and modify the middle section and the vertical menu to what is shown here. Listing 13-9 shows the PHP code at the beginning of the script that comes from the enterSite.php snippet and the vnav and main divisions of the script. The balance of the script is straight out of the template.

Listing 13-9   systementry.php

```php
<?php
   session_start();

//Check to see if session retry is "admit."
if (isset($_SESSION["retry"]) && $_SESSION["retry"] == "admit") {
```

```
        //If so, continue.
        $name = $_SESSION["name"];
    }
    else {
        header( "Location: adminAuthen.php");
    }
    ?>
        <div id="vnav">
          <table width="120" border="0" cellspacing="2" cellpadding="2">
            <tr>
              <td id="vhead">Go To: </td>
            </tr>
            <tr>
              <td><a href="classentry.php">Enter New Classes</a> </td>
            </tr>
            <tr>
              <td><a href="classupdate.php">Update & Delete Classes</a>
              </td>
            </tr>
          </table>
        </div> <!-- id="vnav" -->
        <div id="main">
          <h1 id="maintitle">Database Entry and Maintenance</h1>
          <br />
          <p id="mainpara">Hello
    <?php
        echo $name;
    ?>
          </p>
          <br />
          <p id="mainpara">Please choose the task you want to<br />
            perform from the menu on the left.</p>
          <!-- <p class="red">*A footnote.</p> -->
        </div> <!-- id="main" -->
```

Class Entry

Class Entry starts with classentry.php, which begins with the template, adds a form
for entering new classes, JavaScript for positioning the cursor on the first field, and
finally calls addclass.php to add the class to the database. addclass.php is very similar to
enterName.php described earlier and is simpler because it doesn't need the cookie and
encryption elements. Figure 13-13 shows the screen during class entry, Listing 13-10
shows classentry.php, and Listing 13-11 shows addclass.php. When Class Entry is used,
after entering a class, you are returned to classentry.php to enter another class or either
click System Entry to return to that screen or click Class Update & Delete to go there.

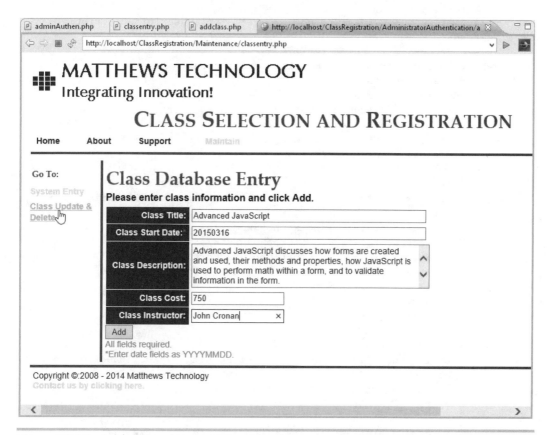

Figure 13-13 With a template, a CSS, and another page from which you can get some of the code, building a new page is relatively simple.

Most of the full classentry.php is shown in Listing 13-10 so you can see the changes in the early part of the script. The footer portion was left out because it is unchanged.

Listing 13-10 classentry.php

```php
<?php
require_once "doorway.php" ;
?>
<!DOCTYPE html PUBLIC >
<html>
    <head>
     <title>Class Database Entry</title>
     <link rel= "stylesheet" type= "text/css" href=
        "/ClassRegistration/registration.css"/>
```

```
            <script language="JavaScript" type= "text/javascript"></script>
        </head>
        <!-- Put cursor in the first field -->
        <body onload="document.form1.class_title.focus();">
         <div id="wrapper">
            <div id="header">
             <img src="/ClassRegistration/MatTechLogo.gif"
               alt="Matthews Technology" />
             <h1 id="title">Class Selection and Registration</h1>
            </div> <!-- id="header" -->

            <div id="hnav">
             <table width="400" border="0" cellspacing="2" cellpadding="2">
              <tr>
                 <td><a href="../index.php">Home</a> </td>
                 <td><a href="../about.php">About</a> </td>
                 <td><a href="../support.php">Support</a> </td>
                 <td><a href="../adminAuthen.php">Maintain</a> </td>
              </tr>
             </table>
            </div> <!-- id="hnav" -->

            <div id="vnav">
             <table width="120" border="0" cellspacing="2" cellpadding="2">
              <tr>
                 <td id="vhead">Go To: </td>
              </tr>
              <tr>
                 <td><a href="systementry.php">System Entry</a> </td>
              </tr>
              <tr>
                 <td><a href="classlist.php">Class Update & Delete</a></td>
              </tr>
             </table>
            </div> <!-- id="vnav" -->

            <div id="main">
             <h1 id="maintitle">Class Database Entry</h1>
<?php
        if($_SESSION["errmsg"] < 1 ){
?>
            <p id="mainpara">Please enter class information and click Add.</p>
<?php
           }
        elseif ($_SESSION["errmsg"] == 1) {
?>
            <p class="red">A Class Title is required.</p>
            <p class="red">Please RE-enter class information and click Add.</p>
```

```php
<?php
      $_SESSION["errmsg"] = NULL;
   }
   elseif ($_SESSION["errmsg"] == 2) {
?>
      <p class="red">A Start Date is required.</p>
      <p class="red">Please RE-enter class information and click Add.</p>
<?php
      $_SESSION["errmsg"] = NULL;
   }
   elseif ($_SESSION["errmsg"] == 3) {
?>
      <p class="red">A Class Description is required.</p>
      <p class="red">Please RE-enter class information and click Add.</p>
<?php
      $_SESSION["errmsg"] = NULL;
   }
   elseif ($_SESSION["errmsg"] == 4) {
?>
      <p class="red">A Class Cost is required.</p>
      <p class="red">Please RE-enter class information and click Add.</p>
<?php
      $_SESSION["errmsg"] = NULL;
   }
   elseif ($_SESSION["errmsg"] == 5) {
?>
      <p class="red">An Instructor is required.</p>
      <p class="red">Please RE-enter class information and click Add.+
<?php
      $_SESSION["errmsg"] = NULL;
   }
   else {
?>
      <p class="red">   </p>
      <p class="red">Please RE-enter your user ID and password, and click
        Sign In.</p>
<?php
   }
?>
        <!-- Class Entry form -->
        <form action="addclass.php" method="post" name="form1">
         <table width="600px" border="0" cellspacing="1" cellpadding="3">
            <tr>
            <th width="18%">Class Title:</th>
            <td width="60%">
               <input type="text" name="class_title" value=""
                 size="60" />
            </td>
```

```
        </tr>
        <tr>
         <th>Class Start Date:<span class="red">*</span></th>
         <td>
            <input type="text" name="class_start" value=""
            size="60" />
         </td>
        </tr>
        <tr>
         <th>Class Description:</th>
         <td>
            <textarea name="class_descr" cols="60"
            rows="4"></textarea>
         </td>
        </tr>
        <tr>
         <th>Class Cost:</th>
         <td>
            <input type="text" name="class_cost" value=""
            size="20" />
         </td>
        </tr>
        <tr>
         <th>Class Instructor:</th>
         <td>
            <input type="text" name="class_instr" value=""
            size="20" />
         </td>
        </tr>
      </table>
      <p><input type="submit" value="Add" /></p>
     </form>

     <p class="red">All fields required.<br />
     *Enter date fields as YYYYMMDD.</p>
    </div> <!-- id="main" -->
```

Listing 13-11   addclass.php

```php
<?php
    session_start();
//Connect to the ClassRegistration database
    $connection = mysqli_connect("localhost", "root", "password",
        "classregistration");
    if (!$connection) {
        echo "Cannot connect to MySQL. " . mysqli_connect_error();
        exit();
    }
```

```php
//Remove white space, check for blank, and remove special characters
    if (($title = trim($_POST['class_title'])) == '') {
        $_SESSION["errmsg"] = 1;
        goto tryagain;
    }
    else {$title = mysqli_real_escape_string($connection,
        $title);
    }
    if (($start = trim($_POST['class_start'])) == '') {
        $_SESSION["errmsg"] = 2;
        goto tryagain;
    }
    else {$start = mysqli_real_escape_string($connection,
        $start);
    }
    if (($descr = trim($_POST['class_descr'])) == '') {
        $_SESSION["errmsg"] = 3;
        goto tryagain;
    }
    else {$descr = mysqli_real_escape_string($connection,
        $descr);
    }
    if (($cost = trim($_POST['class_cost'])) == '') {
        $_SESSION["errmsg"] = 4;
        goto tryagain;
    }
    else {$cost = mysqli_real_escape_string($connection,
        $cost);
    }
    if (($instr = trim($_POST['class_instr'])) == '') {
        $_SESSION["errmsg"] = 5;
        goto tryagain;
    }
    else {$instr = mysqli_real_escape_string($connection,
        $instr);
    }
//Add record to the class table
    $query = "INSERT INTO class(class_title, class_start, class_descr,
        class_cost, class_instr)
        VALUES('$title', '$start', '$descr', '$cost', '$instr')";
    $result = mysqli_query($connection, $query);
    if (!$result) {
        echo "insert into class failed. " . mysqli_error($connection);
        exit();
    }
tryagain:
//Return to classentry.php.
    header( "Location: classentry.php");
?>
```

Class Update and Delete

The Class Update and Delete function has three subelements:

- Displaying the list of classes and letting the user select one to update or delete
- Displaying and updating the class selected
- Displaying and deleting the class selected

These three elements have in total five scripts, as discussed next.

Display the Class List   To update or delete a class, you must first have a list of classes from which to choose the one you want to update or delete. That is the function of classlist.php. This script begins with a PHP/MySQL section using SELECT to get all the records from the class table and ordering them by the class start date. The first record or row in the database table is then picked up and sent to an HTML table, which proceeds to loop through the remaining rows using a PHP do-while loop and displaying each as a row in the HTML table. Finally, each row of the table has two links: one for updating that particular record, and the other for deleting it. Figure 13-14 shows what the class list looks like on the screen, and Listing 13-12 shows the PHP and <div id= "main"> segments of the script to perform this function.

NOTE

The class_id used to get the correct record from the class table is passed to both classupdate.php and classdelete.php scripts in the link URL that loads them.

Listing 13-12   classlist.php

```php
<?php
require_once "doorway.php" ;

//Connect to the ClassRegistration database
    $connection = mysqli_connect("localhost", "root", "password",
"classregistration");
    if (!$connection) {
        echo "Cannot connect to MySQL. " . mysqli_connect_error();
        exit();
    }
//Get records from the class table
    $query = "SELECT * From class ORDER BY class_start";
    $result = mysqli_query($connection, $query);
    if (!$result) {
        echo "Select from class failed. " . mysqli_error();
```

MATTHEWS TECHNOLOGY
Integrating Innovation!

CLASS SELECTION AND REGISTRATION

Home   About   Support   Maintain

Go To:

Add New
Classes

System Entry

Class List

Choose to Update or Delete a class.

Class ID	Class Title	Class Start	Class Description	Class Cost	Class Instructor		
1	Introduction to Websites	02/14/15	This class provides the beginner with the foundation material needed to begin building web sites. It introduces the student to the Web, and then dives into HTML and how to write basic scripts to place text and images in a site.	$250	John Staley	Update	Delete
4	Exercising the Server with PHP	02/18/15	Exercising the Server with PHP introduces PHP with an overview of the language, describing the various elements it makes available, and then how PHP is used to work on and with the server to dynamically handle information.	$450	Alice Bailey	Update	Delete
3	Adding JavaScript Dynamic Elements	03/01/15	Adding JavaScript Dynamic Elements introduces JavaScript by providing an overview of the language, describing its various elements, and how JavaScript is used to create a number of dynamic elements.	$550	Jim Jones	Update	Delete
2	Adding Style to a Web Page	03/16/15	Adding Style to a Web Page covers both the elements of good design, what makes a web page attrative, as well as how to create and use a cascading style sheet (CSS) to add consistent style through out a web site.	$400	Bess Pretty	Update	Delete
6	Advanced JavaScript	03/16/15	Advanced JavaScript discusses how forms are created and used, their methods and properties, how JavaScript is used to perform math within a form, and to validate information in the form.	$750	John Cronan	Update	Delete
5	Building Databses with MySQL	04/24/15	Building Databases with MySQL introduces the SQL (Structured Query Language) as the foundation of MySQL and discusses the basic characteristics of the language and how these have been implemented in MySQL.	$500	Andy Roony	Update	Delete
7	Accessing a MySQL Database with PHP	05/03/15	Accessing a MySQL Database with PHP discusses how PHP is used with MySQL to create and query a database including taking information form an HTML form and storing it in the database, and displaying, updating, and deleting database information.	$750	Marty Matthews	Update	Delete

Figure 13-14   The class list lets you not only see the classes, but also choose to update or delete classes.

```
      exit();
  }
?>

    <div id="main">
     <h1 id="maintitle">Class List</h1>
     <p id="mainpara">Choose to Update or Delete a class.</p>
```

```html
<!-- Class List -->
<table width="850" border="1" frame="void" rules="all"
  cellspacing="1" cellpadding="2">
  <!-- Display the column headings -->
  <tr>
    <th class="list" width="40">Class ID</th>
    <th class="list" width="110">Class Title</th>
    <th class="list" width="60">Class Start</th>
    <th class="list" width="400">Class Description</th>
    <th class="list" width="50">Class Cost</th>
    <th class="list" width="50">Class Instructor</th>
    <th class="list" width="50"> </th>
    <th class="list" width="40"> </th>
  </tr>

  <!-- Loop through and display the classes -->
  <?php while ( $classrow = mysqli_fetch_assoc($result) ) {   ?>

  <tr>
    <td align="center"><?php echo $classrow ['class_id']; ?></td>
    <td><?php echo $classrow ['class_title']; ?></td>
    <td align="center"><?php echo date('m/d/y',
      strtotime($classrow ['class_start'])); ?></td>
    <td><?php echo $classrow ['class_descr']; ?>   </td>
    <td align="right">$<?php echo number_format($classrow
      ['class_cost'],0,'.',','); ?> </td>
    <td><?php echo $classrow ['class_instr']; ?></td>
    <td><a href="classupdate.php?recordID=<?php echo
      $classrow ['class_id']; ?>">Update</a></td>
    <td><a href="classdelete.php?recordID=<?php echo
      $classrow ['class_id']; ?>">Delete</a></td>
  </tr>
  <?php } ?>
</table>

<p class="red"> </p>
</div> <!-- id="main" -->
```

Updating a Class   Updating a class is a combination of entering a new one and displaying an existing one. It uses an input form like entering a new record, but provides the current value for a particular field using a PHP-produced array for the class being updated. That class is found using the class_id passed from the class list and MySQL SELECT. Once the desired changes have been made on the screen, the updateclass.php script is called, and the record is replaced on the database table with MySQL UPDATE.

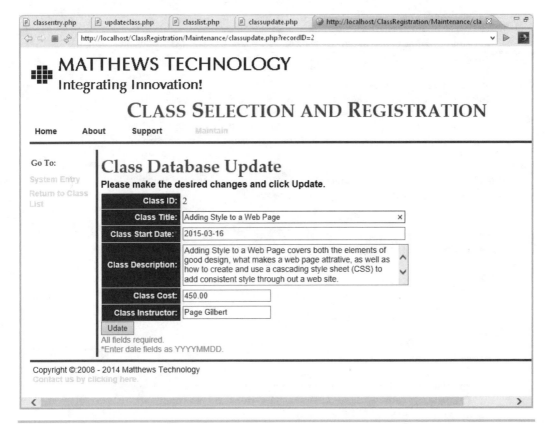

Figure 13-15 The Class List and Class Update screens and scripts are very similar.

The `class_id` is again passed to updateclass.php using the URL, while the other fields are brought over using the form's POST method. Figure 13-15 shows the Class Update screen, while Listings 13-13 and 13-14 show portions of classupdate.php and updateclass.php, respectively.

Listing 13-13   classupdate.php

```php
<?php
   require_once "doorway.php" ;

//Get Class ID from classlist.php
   $classid = ($_GET['recordID']);

//Connect to the ClassRegistration database
   $connection = mysqli_connect("localhost", "root", "password",
```

```php
        "classregistration");
    if (!$connection) {
        echo "Cannot connect to MySQL. ", mysqli_connect_error($connection);
        exit();
    }
//Get records from the class table
    $query = "SELECT * FROM class WHERE class_id = $classid";
    $result = mysqli_query($connection, $query);
    if (!$result) {
        echo "Select from class failed. ", mysqli_error($connection);
        exit();
    }
//Get class (row)from database
    $classrow = mysqli_fetch_assoc($result);

?>
    <div id="main">
     <h1 id="maintitle">Class Database Update</h1>

<?php
        if($_SESSION["errmsg"] < 1 ){
?>
        <p id="mainpara">Please make the desired changes and click Update.</p>
<?php
        }
    elseif ($_SESSION["errmsg"] == 1) {
?>
        <p class="red">A Class Title is required.</p>
        <p class="red">Please RE-make the desired changes and click
           Update.</p>
<?php
        $_SESSION["errmsg"] = NULL;
    }
    elseif ($_SESSION["errmsg"] == 2) {
?>
        <p class="red">A Start Date is required.</p>
        <p class="red">Please RE-make the desired changes and click
           Update.</p>
<?php
        $_SESSION["errmsg"] = NULL;
    }
    elseif ($_SESSION["errmsg"] == 3) {
?>
        <p class="red">A Class Description is required.</p>
        <p class="red">Please RE-make the desired changes and click
           Update.</p>
<?php
        $_SESSION["errmsg"] = NULL;
    }
    elseif ($_SESSION["errmsg"] == 4) {
?>
```

```
        <p class="red">A Class Cost is required.</p>
        <p class="red">Please RE-make the desired changes and click
          Update.</p>
<?php
        $_SESSION["errmsg"] = NULL;
    }
    elseif ($_SESSION["errmsg"] == 5) {
?>
        <p class="red">An Instructor is required.</p>
        <p class="red">Please RE-make the desired changes and click
          Update.</p>
<?php
        $_SESSION["errmsg"] = NULL;
    }
    else {
?>
        <p class="red">   </p>
        <p class="red">Please RE-make the desired changes and click
          Update.</p>
<?php
    }
?>

    <!-- Class Entry form -->
    <form action="updateclass.php?recordID=<?php echo $classrow
        ['class_id'];
      ?>" method="post" name="form1">
      <table width="600px" border="0" cellspacing="1" cellpadding="3">
       <tr>
        <th width="18%">Class ID:</th>
        <td width="60%"><?php echo $classrow ['class_id']; ?></td>
       </tr>
        <tr>
        <th>Class Title:</th>
        <td>
           <input type="text" name="class_title" value="<?php
             echo $classrow ['class_title']; ?>" size="60" />
        </td>
       </tr>
       <tr>
        <th>Class Start Date:<span class="red">*</span></th>
        <td>
           <input type="text" name="class_start" value="<?php
             echo $classrow ['class_start']; ?>" size="60" />
        </td>
       </tr>
       <tr>
        <th>Class Description:</th>
        <td>
           <textarea name="class_descr" cols="60" rows="4"><?php
             echo $classrow ['class_descr']; ?></textarea>
```

```
       </td>
      </tr>
      <tr>
       <th>Class Cost:</th>
       <td>
          <input type="text" name="class_cost" value="<?php echo
           $classrow ['class_cost']; ?> " size="20" />
       </td>
      </tr>
      <tr>
       <th>Class Instructor:</th>
       <td>
           <input type="text" name="class_instr" value="<?php
            echo $classrow ['class_instr']; ?>" size="20" />
       </td>
      </tr>
      </table>
      <p><input type="submit" value="Update" /></p>
    </form>

   <p class="red">All fields required.<br />
       *Enter date fields as YYYYMMDD.</p>

   </div> <!-- id="main" -->
```

NOTE

To keep this code as simple as possible, I have not escaped all user input, such as
$classid in the classupdate.php script in Listing 13-13. In a production environment, all
user-inputted values should be escaped to protect from hackers.

Listing 13-14	updateclass.php

```php
<?php
   session_start();

//Connect to the ClassRegistration database
   $connection = mysqli_connect("localhost", "root", "password",
      "classregistration");
   if (!$connection) {
       echo "Cannot connect to MySQL. ", mysqli_connect_error($connection);
       exit();
   }
//Get Class ID from classupdate.php
   $classid = ($_GET['recordID']);

//Remove white space, check for blank, and remove special characters
```

```php
    if (($title = trim($_POST['class_title'])) == '') {
       $_SESSION["errmsg"] = 1;
       goto tryagain;
    }
    else {$title = mysqli_real_escape_string($connection,
       $title);
    }
    if (($start = trim($_POST['class_start'])) == '') {
       $_SESSION["errmsg"] = 2;
       goto tryagain;
    }
    else {$start = mysqli_real_escape_string($connection,
       $start);
    }
    if (($descr = trim($_POST['class_descr'])) == '') {
       $_SESSION["errmsg"] = 3;
       goto tryagain;
    }
    else {$descr = mysqli_real_escape_string($connection,
       $descr);
    }
    if (($cost = trim($_POST['class_cost'])) == '') {
       $_SESSION["errmsg"] = 4;
       goto tryagain;
    }
    /* adding a zero forces this to be a number not a string. */
    else {$cost = mysqli_real_escape_string($connection,
       $cost + 0);
    }
    if (($instr = trim($_POST['class_instr'])) == '') {
       $_SESSION["errmsg"] = 5;
       goto tryagain;
    }
    else {$instr = mysqli_real_escape_string($connection,
       $instr);
    }

//Update a record on the class table
    $query = "UPDATE class SET class_title='$title', class_start='$start',
       class_descr='$descr', class_cost='$cost', class_instr='$instr' WHERE
       class_id='$classid' ";
    $result = mysqli_query($connection, $query);
    if (!$result) {
       echo "Insert into class failed. ", mysqli_error($connection);
       exit();
    }
```

```
tryagain:
//Return to classlist.php if successful.
   header( "Location: classlist.php");
?>
```

NOTE

In the updateclass.php you'll see that I added a zero to the Class Cost. The reason is that when the user inputs the value, it is a string that causes the MySQL UPDATE to produce an error saying that a string cannot be inserted into a decimal type field. Adding the zero (+ 0) forces PHP to convert the field to a number, which can then be inserted into a decimal field. It is probably more elegant to cast it back to a floating point number using (float) $_POST['class_cost'] instead of adding the 0.

Deleting a Class   classdelete.php has many of the elements of classupdate.php. The PHP at the beginning of the script is exactly the same and won't be repeated in the listing that follows. It simply gets the class or record that will be deleted. This record is presented in a table like classupdate.php, but here the information is just listed and can't be changed. While there are no input fields, the HTML table is in a form that the contents can be passed on to deleteclass.php, which does the actual deletion using MySQL's DELETE. Figure 13-16 shows classdelete.php on the screen, while Listings 13-15 and 13-16 show portions of classdelete.php and deleteclass.php, respectively.

Listing 13-15   classdelete.php

```
<div id="main">
 <h1 id="maintitle">Class Delete</h1>
 <p class="red"><b>If you are sure you want to delete this class,
    click Delete.</b></p>

<!-- Class Entry form -->
<form action="deleteclass.php?recordID=<?php echo $classrow
 ['class_id']; ?>" method="post" name="form1">
 <table width="600px" border="0" cellspacing="1" cellpadding="3">
    <tr>
     <th width="18%">Class ID:</th>
     <td width="60%"><?php echo $classrow ['class_id']; ?></td>
    </tr>
    <tr>
     <th>Class Title:</th>
     <td><?php echo $classrow ['class_title']; ?></td>
    </tr>
```

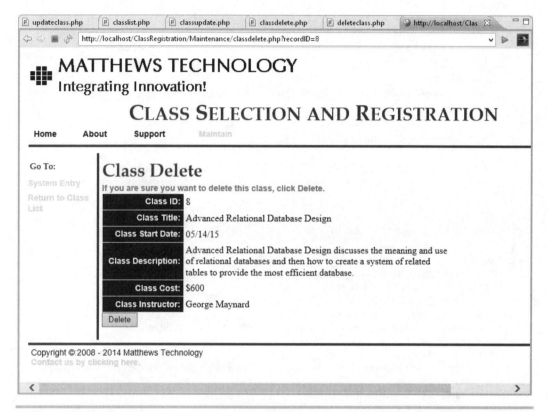

Figure 13-16 classdelete.php is getting a confirmation that the user wants to delete the record.

```
<tr>
 <th>Class Start Date:</th>
 <td><?php echo date('m/d/y',strtotime($classrow
  ['class_start'])); ?></td>
</tr>
<tr>
 <th>Class Description:</th>
 <td><?php echo $classrow ['class_descr']; ?></td>
</tr>
<tr>
 <th>Class Cost:</th>
 <td>$<?php echo number_format($classrow ['class_cost'],
  0,'.',','); ?> </td>
</tr>
```

```
    <tr>
     <th>Class Instructor:</th>
     <td><?php echo $classrow ['class_instr']; ?></td>
    </tr>
  </table>
  <p class="red"><input type="submit" value="Delete" /></p>
 </form>

 <p class="red"> </p>

 </div><!-- id="main" -->
```

Listing 13-16   deleteclass.php

```php
<?php
//Get Class ID from classupdate.php
   $classid = ($_GET['recordID']);

//Connect to the ClassRegistration database
   $connection = mysqli_connect("localhost", "root", "password",
"classregistration");
   if (!$connection) {
      echo "Cannot connect to MySQL. " . mysqli_connect_error($connection);
      exit();
   }
//Delete a record from the class table
   $query = "DELETE FROM class WHERE class_id='$classid' ";
   $result = mysqli_query($connection, $query);
   if (!$result) {
      echo "Insert into class failed. ", mysqli_error($connection);
      exit();
   }
//Return to classlist.php.
   header( "Location: classlist.php");
?>
(2)Class Registration
```

The class registration process is comparatively simple in comparison to, and after having gone through, the authentication and the maintenance processes. There are six steps to registration, as shown in Figure 13-17, each with one or two scripts.

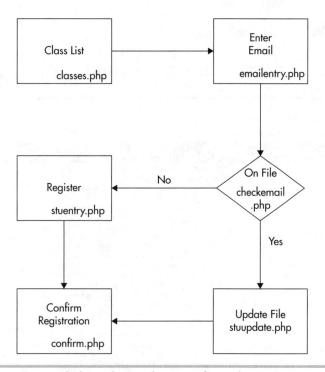

Figure 13-17   The steps needed to select and register for a class

Class List and Selection

The class list script, classes.php, is almost exactly the same as classlist.php used with updating and deleting classes. The major differences are that the Update and Delete links have been replaced by a Register link, a different script is called at the end, and some titling has changed. It is not even worth a new listing; see Listing 13-12. What you see on the screen is also very similar, as shown in Figure 13-18.

Student Email Entry

The student email entry script brings the selected class along with it to ask students to enter their email address to determine if they have previously registered for a course. If so, they are passed on to the stuupdate.php script, where they can update their student

MATTHEWS TECHNOLOGY
Integrating Innovation!

CLASS SELECTION AND REGISTRATION

Home   About   Support   Maintain

Class List

Choose a class and click Register.

Class ID	Class Title	Class Start	Class Description	Class Cost	Class Instructor	
1	Introduction to Websites	02/14/15	This class provides the beginner with the foundation material needed to begin building web sites. It introduces the student to the Web, and then dives into HTML and how to write basic scripts to place text and images in a site.	$250	John Staley	Register
4	Exercising the Server with PHP	02/18/15	Exercising the Server with PHP introduces PHP with an overview of the language, describing the various elements it makes available, and then how PHP is used to work on and with the server to dynamically handle information.	$450	Alice Bailey	Register
3	Adding JavaScript Dynamic Elements	03/01/15	Adding JavaScript Dynamic Elements introduces JavaScript by providing an overview of the language, describing its various elements, and how JavaScript is used to create a number of dynamic elements.	$550	Jim Jones	Register
2	Adding Style to a Web Page	03/16/15	Adding Style to a Web Page covers both the elements of good design, what makes a web page attrative, as well as how to create and use a cascading style sheet (CSS) to add consistent style through out a web site.	$450	Page Gilbert	Register
6	Advanced JavaScript	03/16/15	Advanced JavaScript discusses how forms are created and used, their methods and properties, how JavaScript is used to perform math within a form, and to validate information in the form.	$700	John Cronan	Register
5	Building Databses with MySQL	04/24/15	Building Databases with MySQL introduces the SQL (Structured Query Language) as the foundation of MySQL and discusses the basic characteristics of the language and how these have been implemented in MySQL.	$500	Andy Roony	Register
7	Accessing a MySQL Database with PHP	05/03/15	Accessing a MySQL Database with PHP discusses how PHP is used with MySQL to create and query a database including taking information form an HTML form and storing it in the database, and displaying, updating, and deleting database information.	$750	Marty Matthews	Register
8	Advanced Relational Database Design	05/14/15	Advanced Relational Database Design discusses the meaning and use of relational databases and then how to create a system of related tables to provide the most efficient database.	$600	George Maynard	Register

Figure 13-18 The class list for registration is very similar to the class list for updating and deleting.

record if they wish. Otherwise, they are sent to stuentry.php, where they can fill out the registration. Three scripts are used in this process:

● **emailentry.php,** an entry form for the email address and its confirmation, which displays the class for which the student is registering, is partially shown in Listing 13-17. Figure 13-19 shows what email entry looks like on the screen.

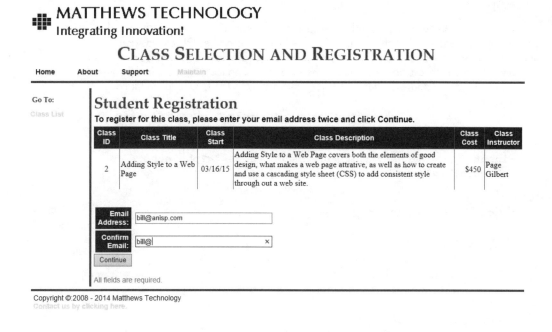

Figure 13-19 The email entry carries the class information with it.

- **emailvalid.js**, a JavaScript form validation script, checks if both an email address and its confirmation have been entered, that they are both valid addresses, and that they are the same. It is shown in Listing 13-18. Here are three of the messages that are produced:

- **checkemail.php** checks if the email address is on file, as shown in Listing 13-19. The student's email address is compared with the email addresses in the student table, and if a match is found, stuupdate.php is loaded; otherwise, stuentry.php is loaded. In both cases, the class ID and student email address are passed on to the next script.

NOTE

The following three lines of code from emailentry.php contain two separate ways of passing the `classid` to checkemail.php. The first way uses the URL, as was done earlier in several maintenance scripts; the second uses a hidden field and `post`. Only one is needed. checkemail.php will use the second, getting the `classid` in the same way as the email address. The `onsubmit` statement calls the JavaScript validation functions.

```
<form action="checkemail.php?recordID=<?php echo $classid ?>"
method="post"
  onsubmit="return validate_form(this);" name="form1">
<input type="hidden" name="classid" value="<?php echo
$classid; ?>"/>
```

Listing 13-17   emailentry.php

```
<div id="main">
<h1 id="maintitle">Student Registration</h1>
<p id="mainpara">To register for this class, please enter your
   email address twice and click Continue.</p>

<!-- From Class List -->
<table width="850" border="1" frame="void" rules="all"
   cellspacing="1" cellpadding="2">
   <!-- Display the column headings -->
   <tr>
      <th class="list" width="40">Class ID</th>
      <th class="list" width="150">Class Title</th>
      <th class="list" width="60">Class Start</th>
      <th class="list" width="450">Class Description</th>
      <th class="list" width="50">Class Cost</th>
      <th class="list" width="50">Class Instructor</th>
   </tr>

   <!-- Display the selected class. -->
   <tr>
      <td align="center"><?php echo $classrow ['class_id']; ?></td>
      <td><?php echo $classrow ['class_title']; ?></td>
      <td align="center"><?php echo date('m/d/y',strtotime($classrow
         ['class_start'])); ?></td>
      <td><?php echo $classrow ['class_descr']; ?>   </td>
      <td align="right">$<?php echo number_format($classrow
         ['class_cost'],0,'.',','); ?> </td>
      <td><?php echo $classrow ['class_instr']; ?></td>
   </tr>
</table>
```

```
<p> </p>
<p> </p>

<div id="form">
<!-- Display the email entry form. After filling in, go
   to check email page. -->
<form action="checkemail.php" method="post"
   onsubmit="return validate_form(this);" name="form1">
   <input type="hidden" name="classid" value="<?php echo
      $classid; ?>"/>
   <table width="200" border="0" cellspacing="3" cellpadding="5">
      <tr>
         <th width="100">Email Address:</th>
         <td width="80">
         <input type="text" name="email" value="" size="40" />
         </td>
      </tr>
      <tr>
         <th width="100">Confirm Email:</th>
         <td width="80">
         <input type="text" name="conemail" value="" size="40" />
         </td>
      </tr>
   </table>
   <input type="submit" name="submit" value="Continue" />
</form>
</div>  <!-- id="form" -->

<!-- Begin from template -->
<br />
<p class="red">All fields are required.</p>
 </div>  <!-- id="main" -->
```

Listing 13-18   emailvalid.js

```
// JavaScript Document
function validate_required(field,alerttxt)
{
   with (field)
   {
     if (value==null||value==""){
        alert(alerttxt);
        return false;
     }
```

```
    else {return true;}
    }
}

function validate_email(field,alerttxt)
{
    with (field)
    {
    apos=value.indexOf("@");
    dotpos=value.lastIndexOf(".");
    if (apos<1||dotpos-apos<2){
     alert(alerttxt);
     return false;
    }
    else {return true;}
    }
}

function validate_equal(field1,field2,alerttxt)
{
    if (field1.value==field2.value)
     {return true;}
    else {
       alert(alerttxt);
       return false;}
}

function validate_form(thisform)
{
    with (thisform)
    {
    if (validate_required(email,"Please enter an email address.")==false)
     {email.focus();return false;}
    if (validate_email(email,"Please enter a valid email address.")==false)
     {email.focus();return false;}
    if (validate_required(conemail,"Please confirm your email address.")==false)
     {conemail.focus();return false;}
    if (validate_email(conemail,"Please enter a valid email address.")==false)
     {conemail.focus();return false;}
    if (validate_equal(email,conemail,"The two email addresses are not the
     same.")==false) {conemail.focus();return false;}
    if (email && conemail)
     form1.submit();
    }
}
```

Listing 13-19   checkemail.php

```php
<?php
   session_start();

//Connect to the ClassRegistration database
   $connection = mysqli_connect("localhost", "root", "password",
      "classregistration");
   if (!$connection) {
      echo "Cannot connect to MySQL. ", mysqli_connect_error($connection);
      exit();
   }
//Remove white space, check for blank, and remove special characters
   if (($classid = trim($_POST['classid'])) == '') {
      echo "A blank class ID was found.";
      exit();
   }
   else {$classid = mysqli_real_escape_string($connection, $classid);
   }
   if (($email = trim($_POST['email'])) == '') {
      echo "A blank email was found.";
      exit();
   }
   else {$email = mysqli_real_escape_string($connection, $email);
   }

//See if match in the administrator table
   $query = "SELECT student_email FROM student
      WHERE student_email= '$email'";
   $result = mysqli_query($connection, $query);
   if (!$result) {
      echo "Select from student failed. ", mysqli_error($connection);
      exit();
   }
//Determine if the student email is on file.
   $row = mysqli_fetch_object($result);
      $db_email = $row->student_email;

   if($db_email != $email ){
//If not, go to new student entry passing both the classid and the email
      header( "Location: stuentry.php?classid=$classid&email=$email");
         }
   else {
```

```
//If on file, go to student update, again with the classid and the email.
    header( "Location: stuupdate.php?classid=$classid&email=$email");
}
?>
```

New Student Entry

The student entry script (stuentry.php, shown in Listing 13-20) receives both the class ID and student email address from checkemail.php. The class ID is used to display the class being registered for. The student is asked to enter his or her name and phone number (probably more fields in real life), as shown in Figure 13-20, and then, on clicking Continue, is taken to enterstu.php with the class ID and email address along with the name and phone number.

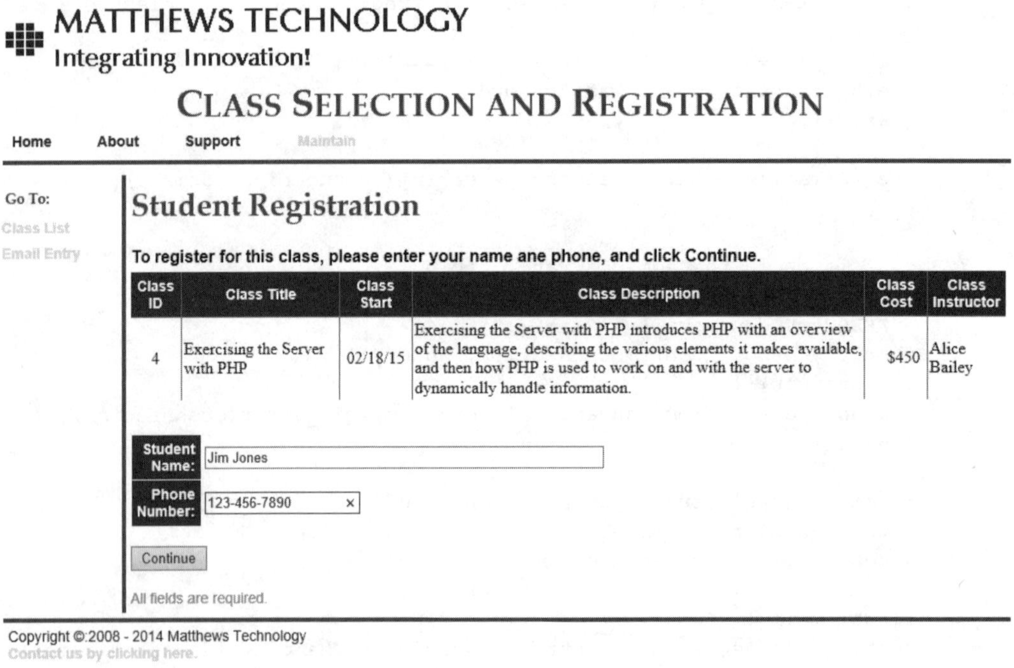

Figure 13-20 Student registration continues to display the class so the student is reminded what he or she is registering for.

Listing 13-20   stuentry.php

```php
<?php
//Get Class ID from checkemail.php
    $classid = ($_GET['classid']);

//Get email address from checkemail.php
    $email = ($_GET['email']);

//Connect to the ClassRegistration database
    $connection = mysqli_connect("localhost", "root", "password",
        "classregistration");
    if (!$connection) {
        echo "Cannot connect to MySQL. ", mysqli_connect_error($connection);
        exit();
    }
//Get records from the class table
    $query = "SELECT * From class WHERE class_id = $classid";
    $result = mysqli_query($connection, $query);
    if (!$result) {
        echo "Select from class failed. ", mysqli_error($connection);
        exit();
    }
//Get class (row) from class table
    $classrow = mysqli_fetch_assoc($result);
?>
    <div id="main">
    <h1 id="maintitle">Student Registration</h1>
    <br />
    <p id="mainpara">To register for this class, please enter
        your name and phone, and click Continue.</p>

    <!-- From Class List -->
    <table width="850" border="1" frame="void" rules="all"
        cellspacing="1" cellpadding="2">
        <!-- Display the column headings -->
        <tr>
            <th class="list" width="40">Class ID</th>
            <th class="list" width="150">Class Title</th>
            <th class="list" width="60">Class Start</th>
            <th class="list" width="450">Class Description</th>
            <th class="list" width="50">Class Cost</th>
            <th class="list" width="50">Class Instructor</th>
        </tr>
```

```
        <!-- Display the selected class. -->
        <tr>
            <td align="center"><?php echo $classrow ['class_id']; ?></td>
            <td><?php echo $classrow ['class_title']; ?></td>
            <td align="center"><?php echo date('m/d/y',strtotime($classrow
                ['class_start'])); ?></td>
            <td><?php echo $classrow ['class_descr']; ?>   </td>
            <td align="right">$<?php echo number_format($classrow
                ['class_cost'],0,'.',','); ?> </td>
            <td><?php echo $classrow ['class_instr']; ?></td>
        </tr>
        </table>
        <p> </p> <!-- Inserts two blank lines -->
        <p> </p>

<div id="form">
<!-- Go to enterstu.php after clicking Continue -->
<form action="enterstu.php?classid=<?php echo $classid
    ?>&email=<?php echo $email ?>" method="post" name="form1">
    <table width="300" border="0" cellspacing="1" cellpadding="3" >
    <tr>
        <th width="30%">Student Name:</th>
        <td width="50%">
            <input type="text" name="stu_name" value=""
                size="60" />
        </td>
    </tr>
    <tr>
        <th>Phone Number:</th>
        <td>
            <input type="text" name="phone" value=""
                size="20" />
        </td>
    </tr>
    </table>
    <br />
        <input type="submit" name="submit" value="Continue" />
</form>
</div> <!-- id=form -->
```

enterstu.php (see Listing 13-21) receives the class ID and the student email address, name, and phone number from stuentry.php. It writes the latter three items to the student table and then loads confirm.php, passing the class ID and email address to it.

Listing 13-21   enterstu.php

```php
<?php
//Connect to the ClassRegistration database
   $connection = mysqli_connect("localhost", "root", "password",
      "classregistration");
   if (!$connection) {
      echo "Cannot connect to MySQL. ", mysqli_connect_error($connection);
      exit();
}
//Get Class ID from checkemail.php
   $classid = ($_GET['classid']);

//Get email address from checkemail.php
   $email = ($_GET['email']);

//Remove white space, check for blank, and remove special characters
   if (($name = trim($_POST['stu_name'])) == '') {
      echo "A blank student name was found.";
      exit();
   }
   else { $name = mysqli_real_escape_string($connection, $name);
   }
   if (($phone = trim($_POST['phone'])) == '') {
      echo "A blank phone was found.";
      exit();
   }
   else { $phone = mysqli_real_escape_string($connection, $phone);
      }
//Add record to the student table
   $query = "INSERT INTO student(student_email, student_name, student_phone)
      VALUES('$email', '$name', '$phone')";
   $result = mysqli_query($connection, $query);
   if (!$result) {
      echo "Insert into student failed. ", mysqli_error($connection);
      exit();
   }

//Go to confirm.php with class id and email.
   header( "Location: confirm.php?classid=$classid&email=$email");
?>
```

Existing Student Update

Student update (stuupdate.php; see Listing 13-22) maintains the class display while displaying the student's database record and allowing the student to change the name and phone number fields, as you see in Figure 13-21. The student cannot change the email

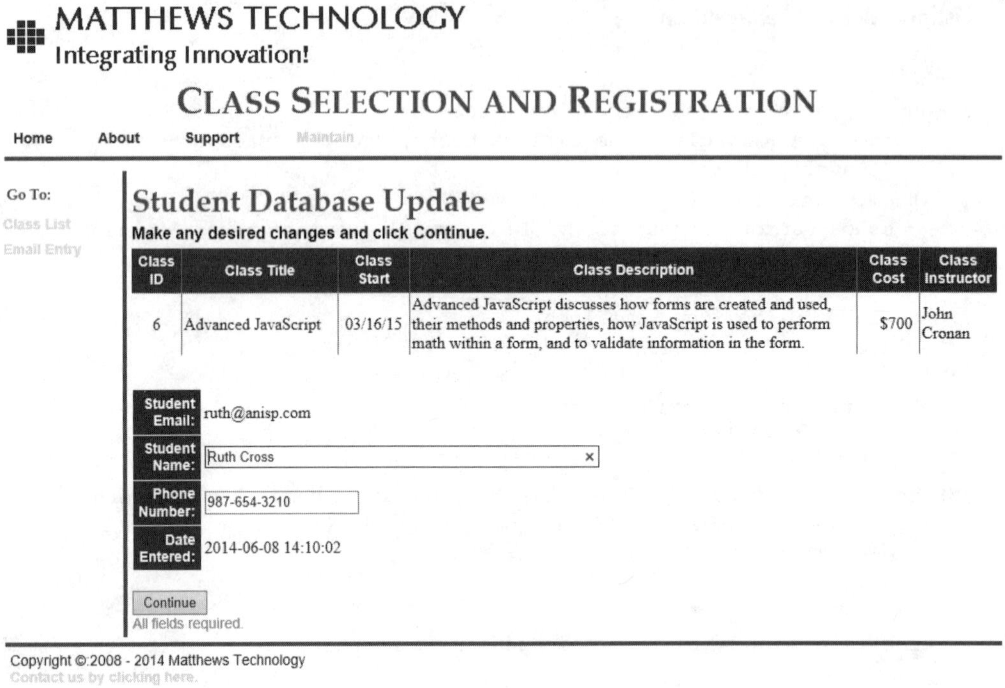

■■ MATTHEWS TECHNOLOGY
■■ Integrating Innovation!

CLASS SELECTION AND REGISTRATION

Home   About   Support   Maintain

Go To:

Class List

Email Entry

Student Database Update
Make any desired changes and click Continue.

Class ID	Class Title	Class Start	Class Description	Class Cost	Class Instructor
6	Advanced JavaScript	03/16/15	Advanced JavaScript discusses how forms are created and used, their methods and properties, how JavaScript is used to perform math within a form, and to validate information in the form.	$700	John Cronan

Student Email:	ruth@anisp.com
Student Name:	Ruth Cross ×
Phone Number:	987-654-3210
Date Entered:	2014-06-08 14:10:02

Continue
All fields required.

Copyright ©:2008 - 2014 Matthews Technology
Contact us by clicking here.

Figure 13-21   Student update allows the changing of fields the student entered.

address because it is the record key (this is possible, but it is a complexification—it becomes the deletion of the original record and the entry of a new record), and the registration date is supplied by the system. When the student is done updating and clicks Continue, he or she is taken to updatestu.php with the information from this page.

Listing 13-22   stuupdate.php

```php
<?php
//Connect to the ClassRegistration database
   $connection = mysqli_connect("localhost", "root", "password",
      "classregistration");
   if (!$connection) {
      echo "Cannot connect to MySQL. ", mysqli_connect_error($connection);
      exit();
   }
//Get Class ID from checkemail.php
   $classid = ($_GET['classid']);
```

```php
//Get email address from checkemail.php
    $email = ($_GET['email']);

///Get record from the class table
    $query = "SELECT * From class WHERE class_id = $classid";
    $result = mysqli_query($connection, $query);
    if (!$result) {
        echo "Select from class failed. ", mysqli_error($connection);
        exit();
    }
//Get class (row) from class table
    $classrow = mysqli_fetch_assoc($result);

//Get record from the student table
     $query = "SELECT * From student WHERE student_email = '$email'";
    $result1 = mysqli_query($connection, $query);
    if (!result1) {
        echo "Select from student failed. ", mysqli_error($connection);
        exit();
    }
//Get student (row) from student table
    $sturow = mysqli_fetch_assoc($result1);
?>

    <div id="main">
     <h1 id="maintitle">Student Database Update</h1>
     <p id="mainpara">Make any desired changes and click Continue.</p>

     <!-- From Class List -->
     <table width="850" border="1" frame="void" rules="all"
        cellspacing="1" cellpadding="2">
        <!-- Display the column headings -->
        <tr>
         <th class="list" width="40">Class ID</th>
         <th class="list" width="150">Class Title</th>
         <th class="list" width="60">Class Start</th>
         <th class="list" width="450">Class Description</th>
         <th class="list" width="50">Class Cost</th>
         <th class="list" width="50">Class Instructor
        </tr>

        <!-- Display the selected class. -->
        <tr>
         <td align="center"><?php echo $classrow ['class_id']; ?></td>
         <td><?php echo $classrow ['class_title']; ?></td>
         <td align="center"><?php echo
          date('m/d/y',strtotime($classrow ['class_start'])); ?></td>
         <td><?php echo $classrow ['class_descr']; ?>   </td>
```

```
    <td align="right">$<?php echo
     number_format($classrow ['class_cost'],0,'.',','); ?> </td>
    <td><?php echo $classrow ['class_instr']; ?></td>
    </tr>
    </table>
    <p> </p> <!-- Inserts two blank lines -->
    <p> </p>
    <!-- Begin Student Update -->
 <div id="form">
    <!-- Go to updatestu.php after clicking Continue -->
    <form action="updatestu.php?classid=<?php echo $classid
     ?>&email=<?php echo $email ?>" method="post" name="form1">
    <table width="300" border="0" cellspacing="1" cellpadding="3" >
     <tr>
        <th width="30%">Student Email:</th>
        <td width="50%"><?php echo $sturow ['student_email']; ?></td>
     <tr>
     <tr>
        <th>Student Name:</th>
        <td>
         <input type="text" name="stu_name" value="<?php echo
           $sturow ['student_name']; ?>" size="60" />
        </td>
     </tr>
     <tr>
        <th>Phone Number:</th>
        <td>
         <input type="text" name="phone" value="<?php echo
           $sturow ['student_phone']; ?>" size="20" />
        </td>
     </tr>
     <tr>
        <th width="30%">Date Entered:</th>
        <td width="50%"><?php echo $sturow ['student_date']; ?></td>
     </tr>
     </table>
     <br />
     <input type="submit" name="submit" value="Continue" />
    </form>
 </div> <!-- id=form -->
 <p class="red">All fields required.</p>
 </div> <!-- id="main" -->
```

updatestu.php (see Listing 13-23) receives the class ID and the student email address, name, and phone number from stuupdate.php. It updates the latter three items to the student table and then loads confirm.php, passing the class ID and email address to it.

Listing 13-23   updatestu.php

```php
<?php
//Connect to the ClassRegistration database
   $connection = mysqli_connect("localhost", "root", "password",
      "classregistration");
   if (!$connection) {
      echo "Cannot connect to MySQL. ", mysqli_connect_error($connection);
      exit();
}
//Get Class ID from stuupdate.php
   $classid = ($_GET['classid']);

//Get email address from stuupdate.php
   $email = ($_GET['email']);

//Remove white space, check for blank, and remove special characters
   if (($name = trim($_POST['stu_name'])) == '') {
      echo "A blank student name was found.";
      exit();
   }
   else { $name = mysqli_real_escape_string($connection,
      $name);
   }
   if (($phone = trim($_POST['phone'])) == '') {
      echo "A blank phone was found.";
      exit();
   }
   else { $phone = mysqli_real_escape_string($connection, $phone);
   }
//Update a record on the student table
   $query = "UPDATE student SET student_name='$name', student_phone='$phone'
      WHERE student_email='$email' ";
   $result = mysqli_query($connection, $query);
   if (!$result) {
      echo "Update of student failed. ", mysqli_error($connection);
      exit();
   }

//Go to confirm.php with class id and email.
   header( "Location: confirm.php?classid=$classid&email=$email");
?>
```

Registration and Confirmation

The final registration confirmation, confirm.php (shown in Listing 13-24), receives the class ID and email address from either enterstu.php or updatestu.php. It uses these to

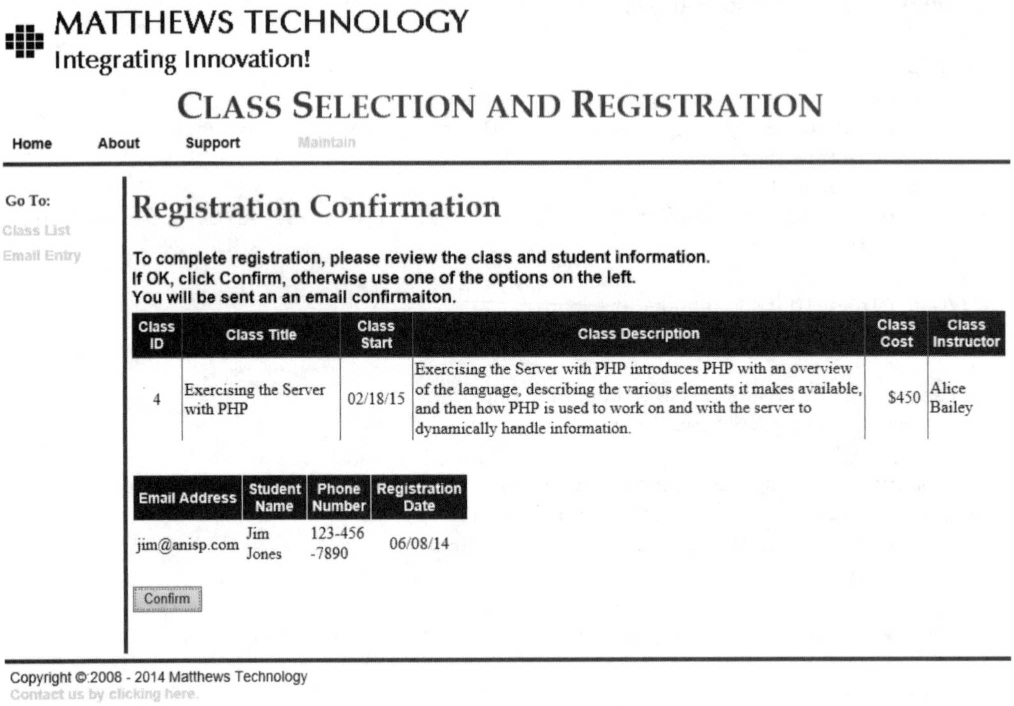

∷: MATTHEWS TECHNOLOGY
Integrating Innovation!

CLASS SELECTION AND REGISTRATION

Home   About   Support   Maintain

Go To:

Class List

Email Entry

Registration Confirmation

To complete registration, please review the class and student information.
If OK, click Confirm, otherwise use one of the options on the left.
You will be sent an an email confirmaiton.

Class ID	Class Title	Class Start	Class Description	Class Cost	Class Instructor
4	Exercising the Server with PHP	02/18/15	Exercising the Server with PHP introduces PHP with an overview of the language, describing the various elements it makes available, and then how PHP is used to work on and with the server to dynamically handle information.	$450	Alice Bailey

Email Address	Student Name	Phone Number	Registration Date
jim@anisp.com	Jim Jones	123-456 -7890	06/08/14

Confirm

Copyright ©2008 - 2014 Matthews Technology
Contact us by clicking here.

Figure 13-22   The student is given one more opportunity to make changes, and then the registration is confirmed.

retrieve and display both the class and student's information from the database. The student is asked to confirm these, as shown in Figure 13-22. When they click Confirm, sendemail.php is loaded with the class ID and email address passed to it.

Listing 13-24   confirm.php

```php
<?php
//Connect to the ClassRegistration database
    $connection = mysqli_connect("localhost", "root", "password",
        "classregistration");
    if (!$connection) {
        echo "Cannot connect to MySQL. ", mysqli_connect_error($connection);
        exit();
    }
//Get Class ID from checkemail.php
    $classid = ($_GET['classid']);
```

```php
//Get email address from checkemail.php
   $email = ($_GET['email']);

///Get record from the class table
   $query = "SELECT * From class WHERE class_id = $classid";
   $result = mysqli_query($connection, $query);
   if (!$result) {
      echo "Select from class failed. ", mysqli_error($connection);
      exit();
   }
//Get class (row) from class table
   $classrow = mysqli_fetch_assoc($result);

//Get record from the student table
   $query = "SELECT * From student WHERE student_email = '$email'";
   $result1 = mysqli_query($connection, $query);
   if (!result1) {
      echo "Select from student failed. ", mysqli_error($connection);
      exit();
   }
//Get student (row) from student table
   $sturow = mysqli_fetch_assoc($result1);
?>
   <div id="main">
    <h1 id="maintitle">Registration Confirmation</h1>
    <br />
    <p id="mainpara">To complete registration, please review
       the class and student information.<br />
       If OK, click Confirm, otherwise use one of the
       options on the left.<br />
       You will be sent an email confirmation.</p>

    <!-- From Class List -->
    <table width="850" border="1" frame="void" rules="all"
       cellspacing="1" cellpadding="2">
       <!-- Display the column headings -->
       <tr>
        <th class="list" width="40">Class ID</th>
        <th class="list" width="150">Class Title</th>
        <th class="list" width="60">Class Start</th>
        <th class="list" width="450">Class Description</th>
        <th class="list" width="50">Class Cost</th>
        <th class="list" width="50">Class Instructor</th>
       </tr>

       <!-- Display the selected class. -->
       <tr>
        <td align="center"><?php echo $classrow ['class_id']; ?></td>
```

```
         <td><?php echo $classrow ['class_title']; ?></td>
         <td align="center"><?php echo
         date('m/d/y',strtotime($classrow ['class_start'])); ?></td>
         <td><?php echo $classrow ['class_descr']; ?>   </td>
         <td align="right">$<?php echo number_format($classrow
         ['class_cost'],0,'.',','); ?> </td>
         <td><?php echo $classrow ['class_instr']; ?></td>
      </tr>
   </table>
   <p> </p> <!-- Inserts two blank lines -->
   <p> </p>

   <div id="form">
      <!-- Go to enterstu.php after clicking Continue -->
      <form action="sendemail.php?classid=<?php echo
      $classid ?>&email=<?php echo $email ?>"
      method="post" name="form1">
      <table width="300" border="0" cellspacing="1" cellpadding="3" >
      <!-- Display the column headings -->
       <tr>
          <th class="list" width="40">Email Address</th>
          <th class="list" width="150">Student Name</th>
          <th class="list" width="60">Phone Number</th>
          <th class="list" width="450">Registration Date</th>
       </tr>

      <!-- Display the selected class. -->
       <tr>
          <td align="center"><?php echo $sturow ['student_email']; ?></td>
          <td><?php echo $sturow ['student_name']; ?></td>
          <td><?php echo $sturow ['student_phone']; ?>   </td>
          <td align="center"><?php echo
          date('m/d/y',strtotime($sturow ['student_date'])); ?></td>
       </tr>
       </table>
       <br />
       <input type="submit" name="confirm" value="Confirm" />
      </form>
   </div> <!-- id=form -->
   <br />
   <p class="red"> </p>
   </div> <!-- id="main" -->
```

Send Email Confirmation

sendemail.php, shown in Listing 13-25, is where we make the relational database do its thing. The class ID and email address are used to build a new record that is written to the register table. Then `mysqli_insert_id` is used to get the registration ID ($regid) that was automatically generated when the new registration record was generated. Next, the class ID, the email address, and the registration ID are used to retrieve records from the class, student, and registration tables, respectively. This information is then used to prepare and send an email confirmation of the registration. The email message uses a long concatenation (the .) of $msg_client to form the message body, which is then sent with the PHP mail function.

Listing 13-25   sendemail.php

```php
<?php
//Connect to the ClassRegistration database
    $connection = mysqli_connect("localhost", "root", "password",
        "classregistration");
    if (!$connection) {
        echo "Cannot connect to MySQL. ", mysqli_connect_error($connection);
        exit();
    }
//Get Class ID from confirm.php
    $classid = ($_GET['classid']);

//Get email address from confirm.php
    $email = ($_GET['email']);

//Add record to the registration table
    $query = "INSERT INTO registration(class_id, student_email)
        VALUES('$classid', '$email')";
    $result = mysqli_query($connection, $query);
    if (!$result) {
        echo "Insert to registration failed. ", mysqli_error($connection);
        exit();
        }
//Get the registration ID generated by insert.
    $regid = mysqli_insert_id($connection);

///Get record from the class table
    $query = "SELECT * From class WHERE class_id = $classid";
    $result = mysqli_query($connection, $query);
    if (!$result) {
        echo "Select from class failed. ", mysqli_error($connection);
        exit();
    }
//Get selected class (row) from class table
    $classrow = mysqli_fetch_assoc($result);

//Get record from the student table
    $query = "SELECT * From student WHERE student_email = '$email'";
    $result1 = mysqli_query($connection, $query);
    if (!result1) {
```

```php
        echo "Select from student failed. ", mysqli_error($connection);
        exit();
    }
//Get selected student (row) from student table
    $sturow = mysqli_fetch_assoc($result1);

//Get record from the registration table
    $query3 = "SELECT * FROM registration WHERE reg_id = '$regid'";
    $result3 = mysql_query($connection, $query3);
    if (!result3) {
        echo "Select from registration failed. ", mysqli_error($connection);
        exit();
    }
//Get registration (row) from registration table
    $regrow = mysqli_fetch_assoc($result3);

//Confirmation Email
$to_client = $sturow['student_name']. ' <'.$sturow['student_email'].'>';
$sub_client = 'Class Registration';
$msg_client = 'Thank you for your class registration. Here is the
        necessary information:'."\n\n";
$msg_client .= 'Registration number: '.$regrow['reg_id']."\n";
$msg_client .= 'Class ID: '. $classid . "\n";
$msg_client .= 'Class Title: '.$sturow['class_title']."\n";
$msg_client .= 'Class Start Date: '.$sturow['class_start']."\n";
$msg_client .= 'Class Cost: '. "$" . $sturow['class_cost']."\n";
$msg_client .= 'Registration date: '.$regrow['reg_date']."\n";
$msg_client .= "\n\n";
$msg_client .= 'Your Email Address: '.$sturow['email_address']."\n";
$msg_client .= 'Your Name: '.$sturow['student_name']. "\n";
$msg_client .= 'Your Phone: '.$sturow['student_phone']."\n\n";
$msg_client .= 'Please contact us to arrange payment at:'."\n";
$msg_client .= 'info@matthewstechnology.com'."\n";
$msg_client .= "\n\n";
$msg_client .= 'Thanks again,'."\n\n";
$msg_client .= 'Matthews Technology'."\n\n";
$addl_headers_client = 'From: Matthews Technology
    <info@matthewstechnology.com>'."\n\n";

mail($to_client,$sub_client,$msg_client,$addl_headers_client);
?>
    <div id="main">
     <h1 id="maintitle">Class Database Update</h1>
     <p id="mainpara">Thank you for completing class registration!<br />
      Please click Complete.</p>
```

```
<div id="form">
  <!-- Go to classes.php after clicking Complete -->
  <form action="classes.php" method="post" name="form1">
  <input type="submit" name="submit" value="Complete" />
  </form>
</div> <!-- id=form -->
<p class="red"> </p>

</div> <!-- id="main" -->
```

An application like Class Selection and Registration can always be expanded and improved. You make decisions as you are building it that, when you are done, you second-guess and think, in most cases for not more than 15 seconds, about going back and doing a major overhaul. Some things that might be changed in this application include

- Putting the database connection code (shown next), which is the same in every script that uses the database, in a separate script that is included in the others by using `require_once`. This also helps security by putting the username and password in only one place instead of in every script. Most Internet hosting services have a way you can hide a script like this.

```
//Connect to the ClassRegistration database
  $connection = mysqli_connect("localhost", "root", "password",
    "classregistration");
  if (!$connection) {
    echo "Cannot connect to MySQL. ", mysqli_connect_error($connection);
    exit();
  }
```

- Expanding the database entry and maintenance component to include the maintenance of the student and registration tables. This would involve simply copying the class table scripts and changing the table names.

- Expanding the student table and the supporting scripts to include additional student fields such as address, city, state, and ZIP code.

- Adding a payment system—using PayPal makes this very easy to do. With PayPal, you can accept credit and debit cards, as well as bank transfers, by using simple HTML links or a shopping cart. Check their website at paypal.com; click Business, and then under Need To Accept Credit Cards? click On Your Website.

I'm sure you can think of many other changes to make to this application. The key is that now you have the tools to make those changes and links to many resources for additional tools. What you can do with these tools is limited only by your imagination.

Try This 13-1 Change This Web App for Your Likes

Take this web app and change it for your tastes and needs. For example:

1. Change the template for a different layout.

2. Redo the CSS for a new look with different colors.

3. Change the user and products from classes and students to objects of your choice, like concerts and attendees, or doctors and patients.

4. Take some of the HTML and PHP script pairs and combine them into one script.

5. Look at the scripts in detail and see if you can come up with more efficient ways of accomplishing the same objective. If you come up with a cool and efficient way of doing something, email it to me (info@matthewstechnology.com) and I'll consider adding it to the next edition of this book.

Chapter 13 Self-Test

The following questions are intended to help reinforce your comprehension of the concepts covered in this chapter. The answers can be found in the accompanying online Appendix A, "Answers to the Self-Tests."

1. What are the series of steps needed to create a functioning web app?

2. What is a method that eases the process of making a web app?

3. What are some of the parts of a web page to consider when building a web app?

4. What is a method of using recurring snippets of code in several scripts?

5. What are two methods demonstrated in this chapter to transfer information from script to script?

6. What are two methods demonstrated in this chapter of combining HTML and PHP?

7. What are two methods demonstrated in this chapter of handling user input errors?

8. What are two uses of JavaScript in this chapter?

9. What statement must be in a script to use SESSION variables?

10. How does SQL identify non-numeric values?

11. You can assume that you have found the values you are looking for if a SELECT query is not FALSE, true or false?

12. What is a simple way to force PHP to turn a string number into a number?

Chapter 14

Handling Online Purchases

Key Skills & Concepts

- Design Template and CSS

- Database Design

- Book List and Selection

- Customer Sign-in and Verification

- Sales and Confirmation

- Building an Invoice

- Deleting Sales

- Writing an Invoice Record

This chapter takes what you did in Chapter 13 a step further by applying much of the Student Registration System to the sales of books to customers. It will have three similar tables, Books, Customer, and Sales, and one unique table, Invoice. It will use scripts similar to Chapter 8's User Authentication System to register and sign in customers and to add to and update the Customer table. The display of books will be a single display page to which you could add further detail pages if you wish. When the customer decides to purchase a product, they are taken through the sign-in and sales process and then to the concluding of the sale. The major new material in this chapter will be the conclusion of the sale in which an invoice is produced and the information emailed to the customer. You could, of course, add options to this for a means of payment, such as PayPal, which provides an easy-to-use process for payment. Figure 14-1 shows a summary flowchart. Individual detail will be presented as we move through the creation process.

NOTE
The Administrator and Maintenance sections of Chapter 13's Class Registration System could be easily plugged into this chapter's Book Sales System to set up and maintain its tables. Here, since you have already done that, we'll leave them out.

Again, this chapter, like Chapter 13, combines many of the elements described in the first 12 chapters of this book into a single web app to demonstrate how they fit together

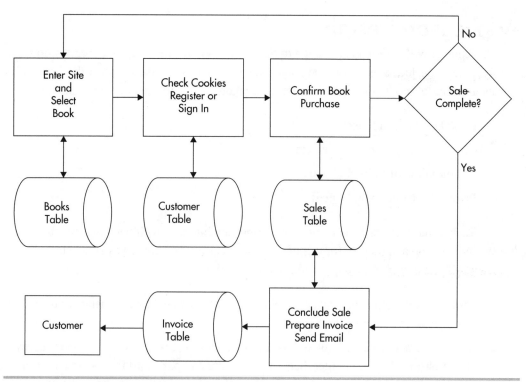

Figure 14-1   Online Sales System summary

using HTML, CSS, a template, JavaScript, PHP, and MySQL. We'll briefly modify the template and CSS from Chapter 13, quickly create the database tables with phpMyAdmin, use similar JavaScript scripts for validating the input, and go through the sign-in and authentication process, because, while it follows what was done in Chapter 13, there are some significant differences. We'll then go into more depth with the invoice processing setup elements and needed scripts, which are all new.

In summary, this chapter shows you how to repurpose existing scripts and then provides a comprehensive example of invoice processing utilizing the HTML, CSS, JavaScript, PHP, and MySQL fundamentals from the earlier chapters to build another significant, data-driven website.

TIP

Once more, all the scripts in this chapter are available online. See the book's Introduction.

Application Design

This chapter will build an application to display books, handle a customer registration and signing in, conclude a purchase, and prepare an invoice. It is based on the four database tables and four sets of scripts shown schematically in Figure 14-1. The major components are

- Book Display and Selection
- Customer Sign-in and Authentication
- Confirmation of Individual Sale
- Invoice Preparation and Email

Each of the sections has one or more scripts and interacts with one or more tables. We will pick up and modify for this purpose scripts from Chapter 13 as applicable. The functioning of the application will follow these steps:

- Customer will come to the site and review a list of books to buy and then possibly select a book that they want to purchase.
- If the customer selects a book to buy, he or she will be asked to either register if they are a first-time buyer, or enter their email address and password if they are a returning buyer. If the script finds the email address and password in the database, the user's name and address information will be presented for them to update. If the email address and password are not found, the customer is given three tries and then asked to register.
- With the selected book information and the user's information, a sales record is built and presented to the user to confirm.
- With a sale confirmation, a sales record will be written and the customer asked if they want to shop for another book.
- When the customer is done shopping, an invoice is created and presented to the customer for approval. When the customer approves, the invoice is written in the Invoice table and an email is sent to the customer to complete the transaction.

Design Template and CSS

As in Chapter 13 and with larger web apps, a template is useful to provide a consistent look over a number of separate web pages. You also want a single CSS for use throughout the application. Here, we'll start off with the CSS and template from Chapter 13 and make only minor modifications to them.

TIP
A major factor to note here is how simply and easily the class registration app is transformed to the book sales app. You can do the same for your own apps by expanding on the work shown here.

Design a Template
The template in this chapter will mirror the template in Chapter 13, except that here, there will not be a vertical navigation bar, we'll change the folder from classregistration to booksales, and reflect the CSS name change. The resulting page will contain these elements:

- A heading or banner at the top with the logo and general information
- A horizontal navigation or menu bar beneath the heading for the application-wide options
- One or two columns of page-specific content in the middle of the page
- A footer at the bottom with copyright and contact information

After deciding what content will go where, the next step is to decide the size of the overall page and the individual sections. Again for simplicity, we'll use almost the same dimensions as those in Chapter 13 without the vertical navigation bar (we make a slight increase in the heading to accommodate the larger logo and title):

- **Heading**   1000 pixels wide × 110 pixels high
- **Horizontal navigation bar**   1000 pixels wide × 60 pixels high
- **Main content**   1000 pixels wide × 500 pixels high
- **Footer**   1000 pixels wide × 60 pixels high

The sections will be created using divs with floating columns, and the fonts will be Palatino and Trebuchet, all as they were in Chapter 13.

Create the Template
The template created for this chapter, Listing 14-1, mirrors what was done in Chapter 13 and reflects work done elsewhere in this book. We will change the name and the logo used to reflect the products to be sold, QuickSteps Books, as you can see in Figure 14-2.

Listing 14-1   Site Template

```php
<?php
    session_start();
?>
<!DOCTYPE html>
```

Figure 14-2 The Sales template has only minor changes from Chapter 13's template.

```html
<html>
  <head>
   <title>Sales Template</title>
   <link rel= "stylesheet" type= "text/css"
      href= "/booksales/booksales.css"/>
   <script language="JavaScript" type="text/javascript'></script>
  </head>

  <body>
   <div id="wrapper">
      <div id="header">
       <h1 id="logo"><img src="/booksales/quicksteps_logo.jpg"/>
          QuickSteps Books</h1>
       <h1 id="title">Book Selection and Purchasing</h1>
      </div> <!-- id="header" -->

      <div id="hnav">
       <table width="400" border="0" cellspacing="2" cellpadding="2">
        <tr>
           <td><a href="/booksales/index.php">Home</a> </td>
           <td><a href="/booksales/index.php">About</a> </td>
           <td><a href="/booksales/index.php">Support</a> </td>
           <td><a href="/booksales/index.php">Maintain</a>
           </td>
        </tr>
       </table>
```

```
  </div> <!-- id="hnav" -->
  <div id="main">
   <h1 id="mainhead">Recent QuickSteps Books</h1>
   <p id="mainpara">Click a Title to Purchase the Book</p>
   <p class="red">*A footnote.</p>
  </div> <!-- id="main" -->

  <div id="footer">
   <p id="copyright">
    Copyright &copy:2008 -
    <?php
       date_default_timezone_set('America/Vancouver');
       echo date('Y');
    ?>
    Matthews Technology
   </p>
   <p id="contact">
    <a href="mailto:info@matthewstechnology.com">
       Contact us by clicking here.</a>
   </p>
  </div> <!-- id="footer" -->
 </div> <!-- id="wrapper" -->
 </html>
```

Create a CSS

The CSS for the Book Selection and Sales app is again very similar to the CSS in Chapter 13 with only minor changes in the logo and titling, as shown in Listing 14-2 and as you saw in Figure 14-2.

Listing 14-2   Booksales CSS

```
/* sales.css */

body    {
        width : 1000px;
        margin : 0;
        padding : 0;
        }

div, h1, h2, p    {
        margin : 0;
        padding : 0;
        }

h2      {
        color : #8b0000;
```

```
        font : 600 24px "Palatino Linotype" ;
     }

P, textarea   { font : 14px "Trebuchet", "Helvetica", sans-serif ; }

.red   { color : red; }

a:link   {
         color : #00008b;
         font : 600 14px "Trebuchet", "Helvetica", sans-serif;
         text-decoration : none;
     }

a:visited   {
         color : #00ffff;
         font : 600 14px "Trebuchet", "Helvetica", sans-serif;
         text-decoration : none;
     }

a:focus   {
         color : #daa520;
         font : 600 14px "Trebuchet", "Helvetica", sans-serif;
         text-decoration : underline;
     }

a:hover   {
         color : #daa520;
         font : 600 14px "Trebuchet", "Helvetica", sans-serif;
         text-decoration : underline;
     }

th       {
         margin : 5px;
         padding : 5px;
         text-align : right;
         color : #ffffff;
         font : 600 14px "Trebuchet", "Helvetica", sans-serif;
         background : #00008b;
     }

th.list     {text-align : center;}

tr.tab      {text-align : left; vertical-align: bottom;}

td.tab      {text-align : left; vertical-align: bottom;}
```

```css
div#header   {
        top : 0px;
        left : 0px;
        height : 110px;
        margin : 5px;
        padding : 5px;
        }


h1#logo     {
        color : #8b0000;
        font : small-caps 700 italic 58px /1.0em "Trebuchet" ;
        text-align : left;
        vertical-align : top;
        padding-bottom : 5px;
        }

h1#title  {
        color : #8b0000;
        font : small-caps 600 36px /1.0em "Palatino Linotype" ;
        text-align : center;
        vertical-align : top;
        padding-bottom : 10px;
        }

div#hnav  {
        margin : 5px;
        margin-left : 15px;
        padding : 5px;
        padding-top : 10px;
        border-bottom : 4px solid #8b0000;
        }

div#vnav  {
        float : left;
        width : 100px;
        margin : 5px;
        padding : 5px;
        }

#vhead    {
        color : #8b0000;
        font : 700 14px "Palatino Linotype" ;
        margin : 5px;
        padding : 5px;
        }
```

```
div#main   {
        float : right;
        width : 850px;
        margin : 5px;
        padding : 5px;
        border-left : 4px solid #8b0000;
      }

h1#maintitle   {
        color : #8b0000;
        font : 600 30px /1.5em "Palatino Linotype" ;
        text-align : left;
        vertical-align : top;
      }

div#footer   {
        clear: both ;
        margin : 5px;
        margin-left : 15px;
        padding : 5px;
        border-top : 4px solid #8b0000;
      }
```

Database Design

As mentioned earlier and shown in Figure 14-1, there are four tables in the Book Sales database:

- **Books**, a list of available books
- **Customer**, a list of customers
- **Sales**, a list of sales of a particular book
- **Invoice**, a list of invoices for a particular customer and date

These tables form a two-way relational database, with the Books ISBN and Customer Email being foreign keys used in the Sales table, and the Sales ID and Customer Email being the foreign keys used in the Invoice table. This allows the storing of only the keys in the Sales and Invoice tables and yet having available all of the information in the detail tables while looking at a transaction.

Field	Type	Length	Other
book_isbn	VARCHAR	20	Primary
book_title	VARCHAR	60	
book_author	VARCHAR	20	
book_image	VARCHAR	40	
book_descr	VARCHAR	255	
book_price	DECIMAL	6,2	

Table 14-1   Books Table

As in the past, the tables will be built and, in the case of the Books table, initially populated in phpMyAdmin to quickly get them online. Use these steps to do that:

1. In phpMyAdmin, click the Databases tab and under Create Database, type **booksales**, click the down arrow in the Collation drop-down list, click latin1_general_ci, and click Create.

2. Click booksales in the list below your new database entry, and under Create Table, type **books**, press TAB, type **6** for the number of fields, and click Go on the right.

3. In the form that is presented, type in the information shown in Table 14-1.

NOTE

The easiest way to handle images in a database is to store the path to an image in the database and have the images in a folder within the folder with the web pages. I'm using a "books" folder within the "booksales" folder that contains the web pages, so my path is /booksales/books/image_name.

4. Click Save. The Books table will be created. Click Insert in the Books row near the top and populate the table. You can see how I did it with Print View in Figure 14-3.

5. Click booksales in the left column. Under Create Table, type **customer**, press TAB, type **8** for the number of fields, and click Go.

6. In the form that is presented, type in the information shown in Table 14-2. Here, unlike the Customer table, we'll make the name list more realistic with both first and last names and full address with a separate ZIP code so the desired sorting can be done.

7. Click Save and then click Structure. The Customer table will be created and then displayed.

8. Click booksales in the left column. Under Create Table, type **sales**, press TAB, type **6** for the number of fields, and click Go.

SQL result

Host: 127.0.0.13306
Database: booksales
Generation Time: Jun 15, 2014 at 07:18 PM
Generated by: phpMyAdmin 4.0.5 / MySQL 5.5.23
SQL query: SELECT * FROM `books` LIMIT 0, 30 ;
Rows: 10

book_isbn	book_title	book_author	book_image	book_descr	book_price
007174035x	Computing for Seniors QuickSteps	Marty Matthews	/booksales/books/compsen.jpg	Follow along and quickly learn how to navigate the Windows operating system; get online; use core programs such as Word, Excel, and Quicken; and secure your computer.	20.00
007176805x	Windows 7 for Seniors QuickSteps	Marty Matthews	/booksales/books/win7sen.jpg	Follow along and quickly learn how to customize your desktop, manage files, connect to the internet, use email, add hardware and software, print documents, and secure your system.	20.00
0071772472	Windows 7 SP1 QuickSteps	Marty Matthews	/booksales/books/win7sp1.jpg	Fully updated to cover Windows 7 SP1, Windows Live Mail 2011, and Internet Explorer 9, this book includes color screenshots and clear explanations that show you how to maximize the powerful features and upgrades available in Windows 7.	20.00
0071772650	Facebook for Seniors QuickSteps	Carole Matthews	/booksales/books/facesen.jpg	In Facebook for Seniors QuickSteps, color photos and screenshots with clear instructions show you how to enjoy the benefits of the world's most popular social networking site.	20.00
0071798463	Windows 8 QuickSteps	Marty Matthews	/booksales/books/win8.jpg	Follow along and learn how to navigate the touch interface, customize your desktop, store data, manage files, connect to the Internet, use email, add hardware and software, download apps, work with photos, and enjoy multimedia.	20.00
0071805877	Microsoft® Office 2013 QuickSteps	Carole Matthews	/booksales/books/office13.jpg	Full-color screenshots on every page with clear instructions make it easy to use the latest release of Microsoft's powerful productivity suite.	30.00
0071805893	Excel® 2013 QuickSteps	John Cronan	/booksales/books/excel13.jpg	Follow along and quickly learn how to create workbooks, enter and edit data, use formulas and functions, create charts and tables, analyze data, extend Excel, and more.	25.00
0071805974	Word 2013 QuickSteps	Carole Matthews	/booksales/books/word13.jpg	Take control and learn how to create and format documents, apply templates and themes, use mail merge, add tables and illustrations, use special features such as forms and translation, save Word documents as web pages, and much more.	25.00
0071821503	iPad for Seniors QuickSteps	Marty Matthews	/booksales/books/ipadsen.jpg	Follow along and quickly learn how to set up your iPad, navigate the touch screen, use apps and email, and browse the Internet.	25.00
0071832580	Windows 8.1 for Seniors QuickSteps	Marty Matthews	/booksales/books/win81sen.jpeg	Full-color screenshots on every page with clear instructions make it easy to use this versatile operating system on any device and navigate the interface with a touchscreen, keyboard, or mouse.	25.00

Print

Figure 14-3 The populated Books table

Field	Type	Length	Other
customer_email	VARCHAR	60	Primary Key
customer_passwd	VARCHAR	255	
customer_fname	VARCHAR	30	
customer_lname	VARCHAR	30	
customer_street	VARCHAR	60	
customer_city_st	VARCHAR	60	
customer_zip	VARCHAR	30	
customer_phone	VARCHAR	30	

Table 14-2 Customer Table

Field	Type	Length	Other
sales_id	INT		AI, PRIMARY KEY
invoice_no	INT		
book_isbn	VARCHAR	20	
customer_email	VARCHAR	60	
sales_amount	DECIMAL	6,2	
sales_date	TIMESTAMP		Current Timestamp

Table 14-3 Sales Table

9. In the form that is presented, type in the information shown in Table 14-3.

10. Click Save and then click Structure. The Sales table will be created and then displayed.

11. Click booksales in the left column. Under Create Table, type **invoice**, press TAB, type **7** for the number of fields, and click Go.

12. In the form that is presented, type in the information shown in Table 14-4.

13. Click Save and then click Structure. The Invoice table will be created and then displayed.

Field	Type	Length	Other
invoice_no	INT		AI, PRIMARY KEY
customer_email	VARCHAR	60	
invoice_amount	DECIMAL	6,2	
invoice_tax	DECIMAL	6,2	
invoice_freight	DECIMAL	6,2	
invoice_total	DECIMAL	6,2	
invoice_date	TIMESTAMP		Current Timestamp

Table 14-4 Sales Table

Creating the Book List and Customer Sales Scripts

We'll break the Book Selection and Sales Application into two parts. The first part, which is discussed in this section, is very similar to what we did in the Student Registration app and will cover the listing of books, the customer selection of one, customer sign-in or registration, and the confirmation of a purchase. The second part, discussed later in the chapter, will cover the creation of an invoice and the sending of an email version. The first part is made up of three modules:

- Book List and Selection
- Customer Sign-in and Verification
- Sale and Confirmation

Each of these modules will have one or more scripts and will interact with one or more of the database tables. There are six steps to a sale, as shown in Figure 14-4, each with one or more scripts. We will address them in the order shown in the preceding list.

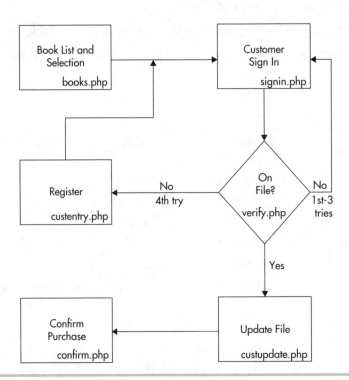

Figure 14-4 The steps needed to select and purchase a book

Book List and Selection

The book list and selection process is very similar to the class list and selection process in Chapter 13, and we can modify the scripts used there to create books.php. The major differences are the handling to display the book covers, the field changes, and some titling has changed. See Listing 14-3. What you see on the screen when the script is run with the QuickSteps database entries is shown in Figure 14-5. If the customer should decide to click Purchase to buy a book, they are transferred to signin.php; otherwise, they leave the site.

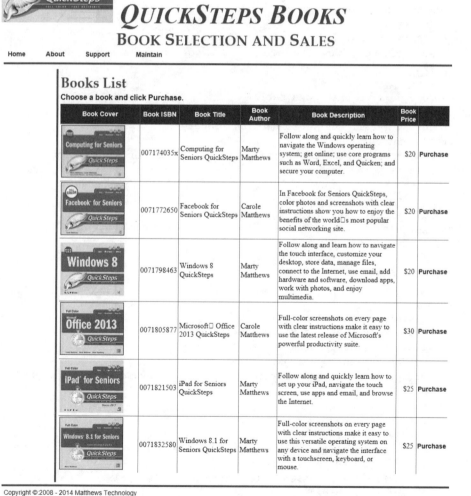

Figure 14-5   The book selection list with the QuickSteps database

NOTE

Listing 14-3 shows the entire script. The remaining HTML scripts in this chapter will not repeat the introductory code down through the end of the horizontal navigation bar (`hnav`) and the closing code beginning with `<div id="footer">`. Both of these sections are common to all HTML scripts and are in the template.

Listing 14-3   books.php

```php
<?php
    session_start();
//Connect to the booksales database
    $connection = mysqli_connect("localhost", "root", "password",
        "booksales");
    if (!$connection) {
        echo "Cannot connect to MySQL. ", mysqli_connect_error($connection);
        exit();
    }
//Get records from the Books table
    $query = "SELECT * From books ORDER BY book_isbn";
    $result = mysqli_query($connection, $query);
    if (!$result) {
        echo "Select from books failed. ", mysqli_error($connection);
        exit();
    }

//Initialize the session variables
    $_SESSION["onfile"] = NULL;
    $_SESSION["shop"] = NULL;
?>
<!DOCTYPE html>
<html>
    <head>
            <meta charset="utf-8">
        <title>Book List and Selection</title>
        <link rel= "stylesheet" type= "text/css" href=
            "/booksales/booksales.css"/>
        <script language="JavaScript" type= "text/javascript"></script>
    </head>
    <body>
        <div id="wrapper">
            <div id="header">
                <h1 id="logo"><img src="/booksales/quicksteps_logo17.jpg"/>
                    QuickSteps Books</h1>
                <h1 id="title">Book Selection and Sales</h1>
            </div> <!-- id="header" -->
            <div id="hnav">
```

```html
    <table width="400" border="0" cellspacing="2" cellpadding="2">
      <tr>
       <td><a href="/booksales/index.php">Home</a> </td>
       <td><a href="/booksales/index.php">About</a> </td>
       <td><a href="/booksales/index.php">Support</a> </td>
       <td><a href="/booksales/index.php">Maintain</a> </td>
       </tr>
     </table>
  </div> <!-- id="hnav" -->

<div id="main">
   <h1 id="maintitle">Books List</h1>
   <p id="mainpara">Choose a book and click Purchase.</p>

   <!-- Book List -->
   <table width="850" border="1" frame="void" rules="all"
      cellspacing="1" cellpadding="2">
      <!-- Display the column headings -->
       <tr>
          <th class="list" width="180">Book Cover</th>
          <th class="list" width="40">Book ISBN</th>
           <th class="list" width="150">Book Title</th>
          <th class="list" width="80">Book Author</th>
            <th class="list" width="340">Book Description</th>
          <th class="list" width="20">Book Price</th>
          <th class="list" width="40"> </th>
       </tr>

       <!-- Loop through and display the books (first Book retrieved
          above). -->
       <?php while ( $bookrow = mysqli_fetch_assoc($result) ) {   ?>

       <tr>
          <td><img src="<?php echo $bookrow ['book_image']; ?>"
             width="140" height="112"></td>
          <td align="center"><?php echo $bookrow ['book_isbn'];
             ?></td>
          <td><?php echo $bookrow ['book_title']; ?></td>
          <td><?php echo $bookrow ['book_author']; ?></td>
          <td><?php echo $bookrow ['book_descr']; ?>   </td>
          <td align="right">$<?php echo number_format($bookrow
             ['book_price'],0,'.',','); ?> </td>
          <td><a href="signin.php?bookisbn=<?php echo $bookrow
             ['book_isbn']; ?>">Purchase</a></td>
       </tr>
          <?php } ?>
     </table>
```

```
            <p class="red"> </p>
        </div> <!-- id="main" -->
        <div id="footer">
            <p id="copyright">
                Copyright &copy:2008 -
                <?php
                    date_default_timezone_set('America/Vancouver');
                    echo date('Y');
                ?>
                Matthews Technology
            </p>
            <p id="contact">
                <a href="mailto:info@matthewstechnology.com">Contact us
                by clicking here.</a>
            </p>
        </div> <!-- id="footer" -->
    </div> <!-- id="wrapper" -->
</body>
</html>
```

Customer Sign-in and Verification

If the customer decides to buy a book, they are sent to signin.php, which brings the selected book along with it, asks returning customers to enter their email address and password and click Continue, or, if not an existing customer, to click Register. If they enter an email address and password, their presence is validated with signinvalid.js and verified to be in the database with verify.php. If the entry was successful, the customer is passed on to custupdate.php where they can update their customer record if they wish, which is written to the database with updatecust.php. Otherwise, they are sent to custentry .php, where they can register. This in turn is validated with regvalid.js and written to the database with entercust.php. Eight scripts in three sets are therefore used in this process:

- **signin.php,** which is validated with signinvalid.js and verified with verify.php

- **custupdate.php,** which is written to the database with updatecust.php

- **custentry.php,** which is validated with regvalid.js and written to the database with entercust.php

NOTE

regvalid.js is a simple validating script similar to those in Chapter 13 and to signinvalid .js, shown later in this chapter, that makes sure the customer information is entered as requested.

signin.php

signin.php is an entry form for customers to enter their email address and password. It displays the book the customer is purchasing. It allows the customer to click Continue if they are an existing customer or to click Register if not. The script is partially shown in Listing 14-4. Figure 14-6 shows what sign-in looks like on the screen.

TIP

In Listing 14-4, note in the $query statement the single quotes around $bookisbn. Without these single quotes, the all-numeric values work fine, but as soon as you have a non-numeric value, the ones with an "x" for a check digit will display an error. When you are referring to a non-numeric value, SQL requires that you put it in single quotes. PHP, though, will interpret the single quote as a literal value and not the value within the variable $bookisbn.

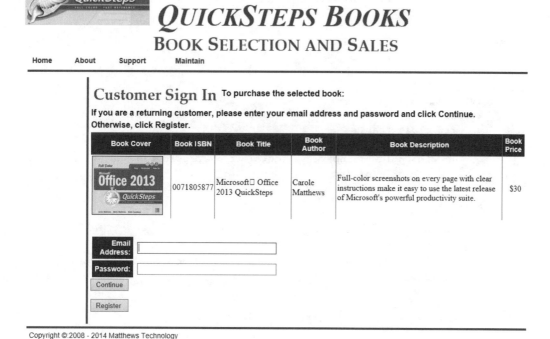

Figure 14-6 The sign-in script carries the book information with it.

Listing 14-4 signin.php

```php
<?php
   session_start();
//Get Book ISBN from books.php
   $bookisbn = ($_GET['bookisbn']);

//Connect to the booksales database
   $connection = mysqli_connect("localhost", "root", "password",
      "booksales");
   if (!$connection) {
      echo "Cannot connect to MySQL. ", mysqli_connect_error($connection);
      exit();
   }
//Get records from the Book table
   $query = "SELECT * FROM books WHERE book_isbn = '$bookisbn'";
   $result = mysqli_query($connection, $query);
   if (!$result) {
      echo "Select from books failed. ", mysqli_error($connection);
      exit();
   }
//Get book (row) from database
   $bookrow = mysqli_fetch_assoc($result);
?>

   <div id="main">
     <table width="500" border="0" cellspacing="2" cellpadding="2">
        <tr class="tab">
           <td><h1 id="maintitle">Customer Sign In</h1></td>
           <td><p id="mainpara" align="left"> To purchase the selected
              book:</p></td>
        </tr>
     </table>
     <?php
        if ($_SESSION["onfile"] == "yes"){
        ?>
           <p class="red">The email address you entered was already on
           file.</p>
        <?php
        }
        elseif ($_SESSION["onfile"] == "no") {
        ?>
           <p class= "red">The email address you entered was not on file.</p>
        <?php
        }
        $_SESSION["onfile"] = NULL;
```

```
    ?>
    <p id="mainpara">If you are a returning customer, please enter
       your email address and password and click Continue.</p>
    <p id="mainpara">Otherwise, click Register.</p>
    <!-- From Book List -->
    <table width="850" border="1" frame="void" rules="all"
       cellspacing="1" cellpadding="2">
       <!-- Display the column headings -->
       <tr>
          <th class="list" width="150">Book Cover</th>
          <th class="list" width="50">Book ISBN</th>
          <th class="list" width="150">Book Title</th>
          <th class="list" width="80">Book Author</th>
          <th class="list" width="360">Book Description</th>
          <th class="list" width="20">Book Price</th>
       </tr>

       <!-- Display the selected book. -->
       <tr>
          <td><img src="<?php echo $bookrow ['book_image']; ?>"
             width="140" height="112"></td>
          <td align="center"><?php echo $bookrow ['book_isbn']; ?></td>
          <td><?php echo $bookrow ['book_title']; ?></td>
          <td><?php echo $bookrow ['book_author']; ?></td>
          <td><?php echo $bookrow ['book_descr']; ?>   </td>
          <td align="right">$<?php echo number_format($bookrow
             ['book_price'],0,'.',','); ?> </td>
       </tr>
    </table>
    <p> </p> <!-- Inserts two blank lines -->
    <p> </p>

<div id="form">
<!-- Display the sign in form. After filling in, go to the verify
   registration script. -->
<!-- The onsubmit statement calls the JavaScript validation functions.
   -->
    <form action="verify.php?bookisbn=<?php echo $bookisbn; ?>"
       method="post"  onsubmit="return validate_form(this);" name="form1">
       <table width="200" border="0" cellspacing="3" cellpadding="5" >
          <tr>
             <th width="100">Email Address:</th>
             <td width="80">
                <input type="text" name="email" value="password"
                   size="40" />
             </td>
          </tr>
```

```
        <tr>
           <th width="100">Password:</th>
           <td width="80">
              <input type="password" name="password" value=""
                 size="41" />
           </td>
        </tr>
     </table>
     <input type="submit" name="submit" value="Continue" />
  </form>
  <p> </p>

  <!-- Alternatively go directly to registration. -->
  <form action="custentry.php?bookisbn=<?php echo $bookisbn; ?>"
     method="post" name="form2">

     <input type="submit" name="submit" value="Register " />
  </form>
</div> <!-- id="form" -->
```

signinvalid.js

signinvalid.js is a JavaScript form validation script that checks if both the email address and password have been entered. signinvalid.js, which is shown in Listing 14-5, is identified at the beginning of signin.php with this script statement:

```
<script language="JavaScript" type= "text/javascript"
src="signinvalid.js"> </script>
```

Listing 14-5   signinvalid.js

```
// JavaScript Document
function validate_required(field,alerttxt)
{
   with (field)
```

```
   {
   if (value==null||value=="")
    {alert(alerttxt);return false;}
   else {return true;}
   }
}

function validate_form(thisform)
{
   with (thisform)
   {
   if (validate_required(email,"Please enter an email
address.")==false)
    {email.focus();return false;}
   if (validate_required(password,"Please enter a password.")==false)
    {password.focus();return false;}
   if (email && password)
    return true;
   }
}
```

verify.php

verify.php checks if the email address and password are on file, as shown in Listing 14-6. The customer's combination of email address and encrypted password is compared with what is in the Customer table, and if a match is found, custupdate.php is loaded. The customer is given three tries to correctly enter an email address and password and is sent back to signin.php each time they make a mistake. After three tries, they are sent to custentry.php to register. For custupdate.php, the book ISBN and customer email address are passed on; for both signin.php and custentry.php, only the book ISBN is passed on.

Listing 14-6 verify.php

```php
<?php
   session_start();
//Get Book ISBN from signin.php
   $bookisbn = ($_GET['bookisbn']);

//Connect to the booksales database
   $connection = mysqli_connect("localhost", "root", "password", "booksales");
      if (!$connection) {
      echo "Cannot connect to MySQL. ", mysqli_connect_error($connection);
      exit();
   }
```

```php
//Remove white space and remove special characters
   $email = mysqli_real_escape_string($connection, trim($_POST['email']));

   $Passwd = mysqli_real_escape_string($connection,
      trim($_POST['password']));

//Encrypt the password.
   $encryptpasswd = sha1($Passwd);

//See if match in the Customer table
   $query = "SELECT customer_email, customer_passwd, customer_fname,
      customer_lname
         FROM customer
         WHERE customer_email= '$email' AND customer_passwd=
            '$encryptpasswd'";
   $result = mysqli_query($connection, $query);
   if (!$result) {
      echo "Select from customer failed. ", mysqli_error($connection);
      exit();
   }

//Determine if the email and password are on file.
   $row = mysqli_fetch_object($result);
   if ($row){
     $db_email = $row->customer_email;
     $db_passwd = $row->customer_passwd;
     $db_fname = $row->customer_fname;
     $db_lname = $row->customer_lname;
   }

   if(!$row || $db_email != $email || $db_passwd != $encryptpasswd){

//If not, add to Session Retry and test > 3
     $retry = $_SESSION["retry"];
     $retry++;
     if ($retry > 3) {
   //If greater than 3 go to customer entry.
         header( "Location: custentry.php?bookisbn=$bookisbn" );
     }
     else {
   //If less than 3 reset Session Retry and go to Sign in
         $_SESSION["retry"] = $retry;
         $_SESSION["onfile"] = "no";
         header( "Location: signin.php?bookisbn=$bookisbn");
     }
   }
   else {
```

```
//If on file, get name, reset the session, and enter site.
    $_SESSION["fname"] = $db_fname;
    $_SESSION["lname"] = $db_lname;
    $_SESSION["retry"] = "admit";
    $_SESSION["time"] = time();
    header( "Location: custupdate.php?bookisbn=$bookisbn&email=$email");
}
?>
```

TIP

As you work through this application, remember that you are working in four environments: HTML, JavaScript, PHP, and MySQL, and you have to use the elements and techniques applicable to that environment. You must not mix them up. In working with a non-numeric variable, say, for email, in PHP, it is $email; in JavaScript, it is email; in MySQL, it is '$email'; and in HTML, it is <?php echo $email; ?>. It is easy to be working along and forget where you are and, for example, use the PHP $email directly in HTML and leave off the <?php echo ?>. (This Tip is the result of my doing just that.)

New Customer Entry

The customer entry or registration script (custentry.php, shown in Listing 14-7) receives the book ISBN from verify.php. The book ISBN is used to display the book being purchased. The customer is asked to enter his or her name, address, phone number, email, and password, as shown in Figure 14-7, and then, on clicking Continue, is taken to entercust.php with the book ISBN and email address to write a new record in the Customer table.

Listing 14-7   custentry.php

```php
<?php
//Connect to the booksales database
    $connection = mysqli_connect("localhost", "root", "password",
        "booksales");
    if (!$connection) {
        echo "Cannot connect to MySQL. ", mysqli_connect_error($connection);
        exit();
    }
//Get Book ISBN from verify.php
    $bookisbn = ($_GET['bookisbn']);

//Get records from the Books table
    $query = "SELECT * From books WHERE book_isbn = '$bookisbn'";
    $result = mysqli_query($connection, $query);
```

QUICKSTEPS BOOKS
BOOK SELECTION AND SALES

Home   About   Support   Maintain

Customer Registration

To purchase this book, please enter the information below, and click Continue.

Book Cover	Book ISBN	Book Title	Book Author	Book Description	Book Price
	0071805877	Microsoft□ Office 2013 QuickSteps	Carole Matthews	Full-color screenshots on every page with clear instructions make it easy to use the latest release of Microsoft's powerful productivity suite.	$30

First Name:

Last Name:

Street:

City & State:

ZIP:

Phone Number:

Email:

Password:

Continue

All fields are required.

Copyright ©:2008 - 2014 Matthews Technology
Contact us by clicking here.

Figure 14-7 Customer sales continue to display the book so the customer is reminded what he or she is purchasing.

```php
    if (!$result) {
        echo "Select from books failed. ", mysqli_error($connection);
        exit();
    }
//Get book (row) from Books table
    $bookrow = mysqli_fetch_assoc($result);
?>
    <div id="main">
        <h1 id="maintitle">Customer Registration</h1>
        <br />
```

```
<p id="mainpara">To purchase this book, please enter the
   information below, and click Continue.</p>

<!-- From BookList -->
<table width="850" border="1" frame="void" rules="all"
   cellspacing="1" cellpadding="2">
   <!-- Display the column headings -->
    <tr>
        <th class="list" width="180">Book Cover</th>
        <th class="list" width="40">Book ISBN</th>
         <th class="list" width="150">Book Title</th>
      <th class="list" width="80">Book Author</th>
        <th class="list" width="340">Book Description</th>
      <th class="list" width="20">Book Price</th>
   </tr>

   <!-- Display the selected book. -->
   <tr>
      <td><img src="<?php echo $bookrow ['book_image']; ?>"
         width="140" height="112"></td>
      <td align="center"><?php echo $bookrow ['book_isbn'];
         ?></td>
      <td><?php echo $bookrow ['book_title']; ?></td>
      <td><?php echo $bookrow ['book_author']; ?></td>
      <td><?php echo $bookrow ['book_descr']; ?>   </td>
      <td align="right">$<?php echo number_format($bookrow
         ['book_price'],0,'.',','); ?> </td>
   </tr>
</table>
<p> </p> <!-- Inserts two blank lines -->
<p> </p>
<!-- Begin customer Entry -->
<div id="form">
   <!-- Go to entercust.php after clicking Continue -->
   <form action="entercust.php?bookisbn=<?php echo $bookisbn
      ?>&email=<?php echo $email  ?>"
      onsubmit="return validate_form(this);" method="post"
         name="form1">
      <table width="200" border="0" cellspacing="1"
         cellpadding="3" >
         <tr>
           <th width="50">First Name:</th>
           <td width="150">
              <input type="text" name="fname" value="" size="60"
                 />
         </tr>
```

```html
        <tr>
          <th width="50">Last Name:</th>
          <td width="150">
            <input type="text" name="lname" value="" size="60"
              />
          </td>
        </tr>
        <tr>
          <th width="50">Street:</th>
          <td width="150">
            <input type="text" name="street" value=""
              size="60" />
          </td>
        </tr>
        <tr>
          <th width="50">City & State:</th>
          <td width="150">
            <input type="text" name="city_st" value=""
              size="60" />
          </td>
        </tr>
        <tr>
          <th width="50">ZIP:</th>
          <td width="150">
            <input type="text" name="zip" value="" size="20"
              />
          </td>
        </tr>
        <tr>
          <th width="50">Phone Number:</th>
          <td width="150">
            <input type="text" name="phone" value="" size="20"
              />
          </td>
        </tr>
        <tr>
          <th width="50">Email:</th>
          <td width="150">
            <input type="text" name="email" value="" size="20"
              />
          </td>
        </tr>
        <tr>
          <th width="50">Password:</th>
          <td width="150">
            <input type="password" name="passwd" value=""
              size="21" />
          </td>
```

```
            </tr>
            </table>
            <br />
            <input type="submit" name="submit" value="Continue" />
        </form>
    </div> <!-- id=form -->
```

entercust.php

entercust.php (see Listing 14-8) receives the book ISBN and the customer name, address, phone, email, and password from custentry.php. It writes these items to the Customer table and then loads confirm.php, passing the book ISBN and email address to it.

Listing 14-8   entercust.php

```php
<?php
    session_start();

//Connect to the booksales database
    $connection = mysqli_connect("localhost", "root", "password",
        "booksales");
    if (!$connection) {
        echo "Cannot connect to MySQL. ", mysqli_connect_error($connection);
        exit();
    }
//Get Book ISBN from custentry.php
    $bookisbn = ($_GET['bookisbn']);

//Remove white space and remove special characters
    $fname = mysqli_real_escape_string($connection, trim($_POST['fname']));
    $lname = mysqli_real_escape_string($connection, trim($_POST['lname']));
    $street = mysqli_real_escape_string($connection, trim($_POST['street']));
    $city_st = mysqli_real_escape_string($connection,
        trim($_POST['city_st']));
    $zip = mysqli_real_escape_string($connection, trim($_POST['zip']));
    $phone = mysqli_real_escape_string($connection, trim($_POST['phone']));
    $email = mysqli_real_escape_string($connection, trim($_POST['email']));
    $passwd = mysqli_real_escape_string($connection, trim($_POST['passwd']));

//Encrypt the password.
    $encryptpasswd = sha1($passwd);

//See if email already in the Customer table
    $query = "SELECT customer_email FROM customer
        WHERE customer_email= '$email'";
    $result = mysqli_query($connection, $query);
```

```php
if (!$result) {
    echo "Select from customer failed. ", mysqli_error($connection);
    exit();
}

//Determine if the email is on file.
$row = mysqli_fetch_object($result);
if ($row) {
    $db_email = $row->customer_email;
}

if(!$row || $db_email != $email){

//If not on file, add record to the Customer table
    $query = "INSERT INTO customer(customer_email, customer_passwd,
        customer_fname, customer_lname, customer_street,
        customer_city_st, customer_zip, customer_phone)
      VALUES('$email', '$encryptpasswd', '$fname', '$lname',
        '$street', '$city_st', '$zip', '$phone')";
    $result = mysqli_query($connection, $query);
    if (!$result) {
    echo "Insert into customer failed.  ", mysqli_error($connection);
    exit();
    }

//Go to confirm.php with book isbn and email.
    header( "Location: confirm.php?bookisbn=$bookisbn&email=$email");

}
else {
    //If email on file, go to Sign in
       $_SESSION["onfile"] = "yes";
       header( "Location: signin.php?bookisbn=$bookisbn");
    }
?>
```

Existing Customer Update

Customer update (custupdate.php; see Listing 14-9) maintains the book display while displaying the customer's database record and allowing the customer to change the name, address, and phone number fields, as you see in Figure 14-8. The customer cannot change the email address because it is the record key (it requires the deletion of the original record and the entry of a new record), and the sales date is supplied by the system. When the customer is done updating and clicks Continue, he or she is taken to updatecust.php with the information from this page.

QUICKSTEPS BOOKS

BOOK SELECTION AND SALES

Home   About   Support   Maintain

Customer Registration

To purchase this book, please enter the information below, and click Continue.

Book Cover	Book ISBN	Book Title	Book Author	Book Description	Book Price
	0071805893	Excel☐ 2013 QuickSteps	John Cronan	Follow along and quickly learn how to create workbooks, enter and edit data, use formulas and functions, create charts and tables, analyze data, extend Excel, and more.	$25

First Name:	Geo
Last Name:	Maynard
Street:	PO 245
City & State:	Geneva, OH
ZIP:	44501
Phone Number:	1234567890

Continue
All fields required.

Copyright ©:2008 - 2014 Matthews Technology
Contact us by clicking here.

Figure 14-8   Customer update allows the changing of fields the customer entered.

Listing 14-9   custupdate.php

```php
<?php
   session_start();
//Connect to the booksales database
   $connection = mysqli_connect("localhost", "root", "password",
      "booksales");
   if (!$connection) {
      echo "Cannot connect to MySQL. ", mysqli_connect_error($connection);
      exit();
   }
//Get Book ISBN from verify.php
   $bookisbn = ($_GET['bookisbn']);
```

```php
//Get email address from verify.php
    $email = ($_GET['email']);

//Get records from the Books table
    $query = "SELECT * From books WHERE book_isbn = '$bookisbn'";
    $result = mysqli_query($connection, $query);
    if (!$result) {
        echo "Select from books failed. ", mysqli_error($connection);
        exit();
    }
//Get book (row) from Books table
    $bookrow = mysqli_fetch_assoc($result);

//Get record from the Customer table
    $query = "SELECT * From customer WHERE customer_email = '$email'";
    $result1 = mysqli_query($connection, $query);
    if (!$result1) {
        echo "Select from customer failed. ", mysqli_error($connection);
        exit();
    }
//Get customer (row) from Customer table
    $custrow = mysqli_fetch_assoc($result1);

?>
    <div id="main">
      <h1 id="maintitle">Customer Registration</h1>
      <br />
      <p id="mainpara">To purchase this book, please enter the
         information below,
         and click Continue.</p>

      <!-- From BookList -->
      <table width="850" border="1" frame="void" rules="all"
         cellspacing="1" cellpadding="2">
         <!-- Display the column headings -->
          <tr>
             <th class="list" width="180">Book Cover</th>
             <th class="list" width="40">Book ISBN</th>
             <th class="list" width="150">Book Title</th>
            <th class="list" width="80">Book Author</th>
             <th class="list" width="340">Book Description</th>
            <th class="list" width="20">Book Price</th>
         </tr>

         <!-- Display the selected book. -->
         <tr>
           <td><img src="<?php echo $bookrow ['book_image']; ?>"
               width="140" height="112"></td>
```

```
      <td align="center"><?php echo $bookrow ['book_isbn'];
         ?></td>
      <td><?php echo $bookrow ['book_title']; ?></td>
      <td><?php echo $bookrow ['book_author']; ?></td>
      <td><?php echo $bookrow ['book_descr']; ?>   </td>
      <td align="right">$<?php echo number_format($bookrow
         ['book_price'],0,'.',','); ?> </td>
   </tr>
</table>
<p> </p> <!-- Inserts two blank lines -->
<p> </p>
<!-- Begin customer Update -->
<div id="form">
      <!-- Go to updatecust.php after clicking Continue -->
      <form action="updatecust.php?bookisbn=<?php echo $bookisbn
         ?>&email=<?php echo $email  ?>"
         onsubmit="return validate_form(this);" method="post"
         name="form1">
      <table width="200" border="0" cellspacing="1"
         cellpadding="3" >
      <tr>
         <th width="50">First Name:</th>
         <td width="150">
            <input type="text" name="fname" value="<?php echo
               $custrow ['customer_fname']; ?>" size="60" />
      </tr>
         <tr>
            <th width="50">Last Name:</th>
            <td width="150">
               <input type="text" name="lname" value="<?php echo
                  $custrow ['customer_lname']; ?>" size="60" />
            </td>
         </tr>
         <tr>
           <th width="50">Street:</th>
           <td width="150">
              <input type="text" name="street" value="<?php echo
                 $custrow ['customer_street']; ?>" size="60" />
           </td>
         </tr>
        <tr>
          <th width="50">City & State:</th>
          <td width="150">
             <input type="text" name="city_st" value="<?php
                echo $custrow ['customer_city_st']; ?>"
                size="60" />
          </td>
        </tr>
```

```
                        <tr>
                           <th width="50">ZIP:</th>
                           <td width="150">
                              <input type="text" name="zip" value="<?php echo
                                 $custrow ['customer_zip']; ?>" size="20" />
                           </td>
                        </tr>
                        <tr>
                           <th width="50">Phone Number:</th>
                           <td width="150">
                              <input type="text" name="phone" value="<?php
                                 echo $custrow ['customer_phone']; ?>" size="20"
                                 />
                           </td>
                        </tr>
                     </table>
                        <br />
                        <input type="submit" name="submit" value="Continue" />
                  </form>
            </div> <!-- id=form -->
```

updatecust.php

updatecust.php (see Listing 14-10) receives the book ISBN and the customer email address, name, address, and phone from custupdate.php. It updates the name, address, and phone in the Customer table and then loads confirm.php, passing the book ISBN and email address to it.

Listing 14-10 updatecust.php

```php
<?php
   session_start();
//Connect to the booksales database
   $connection = mysqli_connect("localhost", "root", "password", "booksales");
   if (!$connection) {
      echo "Cannot connect to MySQL. ", mysqli_connect_error($connection);
      exit();
   }
//Get Book ISBN from custupdatephp
   $bookisbn = ($_GET['bookisbn']);

//Get email address from custupdate.php
   $email = ($_GET['email']);

//Remove white space and remove special characters
   $fname = mysqli_real_escape_string($connection, trim($_POST['fname']));
```

```php
$lname = mysqli_real_escape_string($connection, trim($_POST['lname']));
$street = mysqli_real_escape_string($connection, trim($_POST['street']));
$city_st = mysqli_real_escape_string($connection, trim($_POST['city_st']));
$zip = mysqli_real_escape_string($connection, trim($_POST['zip']));
$phone = mysqli_real_escape_string($connection, trim($_POST['phone']));

//Update a record on the Customer table
    $query = "UPDATE customer SET customer_fname='$fname',
        customer_lname='$lname', customer_street='$street',
        customer_city_st='$city_st', customer_zip='$zip',
        customer_phone='$phone'
        WHERE customer_email='$email' ";
    $result = mysqli_query($connection, $query);
    if (!$result) {
        echo "Update of customer failed. ", mysqli_error($connection);
        exit();
    }
//Go to confirm.php with book isbn and email.
        header( "Location: confirm.php?bookisbn=$bookisbn&email=$email");
?>
```

Sales and Confirmation

The sales confirmation, confirm.php (shown in Listing 14-11), receives the book ISBN and email address from either entercust.php or updatecust.php. It uses these to retrieve and display both the book and customer's information from the database. The customer is asked to confirm these, as shown in Figure 14-9, and given the choice of continuing shopping or going to checkout using either saleconfirmshop.php or saleconfirm.php, both of which are loaded with the book ISBN and email address.

Listing 14-11   confirm.php

```php
<?php
    session_start();
//Connect to the booksales database
    $connection = mysqli_connect("localhost", "root", "password", "booksales");
    if (!$connection) {
        echo "Cannot connect to MySQL. ", mysqli_connect_error($connection);
        exit();
    }
//Get Book ISBN from verify.php
    $bookisbn = ($_GET['bookisbn']);

//Get email address from verify.php
    $email = ($_GET['email']);
```

QUICKSTEPS BOOKS
BOOK SELECTION AND SALES

Home   About   Support   Maintain

Purchase Confirmation

**To complete the purchase, please review the book and customer information.
If OK, click CONFIRM, otherwise use one of the other options at the bottopm.**

Book Cover	Book ISBN	Book Title	Book Author	Book Description	Book Price
Excel 2013 QuickSteps	0071805893	Excel□ 2013 QuickSteps	John Cronan	Follow along and quickly learn how to create workbooks, enter and edit data, use formulas and functions, create charts and tables, analyze data, extend Excel, and more.	$25

First/Last Name:	Geo	Maynard		
Street:	PO 245			
City State:	Geneva, OH	**ZIP:**	44501	
Phone Number:	1234567890			
Email:	geo@anisp.com			

Complete the purchase:
CONFIRM and continue shopping>

CONFIRM and checkout

Click as appropriate:
CANCEL THE SALE

Edit my customer information.

Copyright ©:2008 - 2014 Matthews Technology
Contact us by clicking here.

Figure 14-9 The customer is given one more opportunity to make changes, and then the sale is confirmed.

```
//Get records from the Books table
   $query = "SELECT * From books WHERE book_isbn = '$bookisbn'";
   $result = mysqli_query($connection, $query);
   if (!$result) {
      echo "Select from books failed. ", mysqli_error($connection);
      exit();
   }
//Get book (row) from Books table
   $bookrow = mysqli_fetch_assoc($result);
```

```php
//Get record from the Customer table
    $query = "SELECT * From customer WHERE customer_email = '$email'";
    $result1 = mysqli_query($connection, $query);
    if (!$result1) {
        echo "Select from customer failed. ", mysqli_error($connection);
        exit();
    }
//Get customer (row) from Customer table
    $custrow = mysqli_fetch_assoc($result1);
?>
        <div id="main">
            <h1 id="maintitle">Purchase Confirmation</h1>
            <br />
            <p id="mainpara">To complete the purchase, please review the
                book and customer information.<br />
                If OK, click CONFIRM, otherwise use one of the other options
                at the bottom.</p>

            <!-- From BookList -->
            <table width="850" border="1" frame="void" rules="all"
                cellspacing="1" cellpadding="2">
                <!-- Display the column headings -->
                <tr>
                    <th class="list" width="180">Book Cover</th>
                    <th class="list" width="40">Book ISBN</th>
                    <th class="list" width="150">Book Title</th>
                    <th class="list" width="80">Book Author</th>
                    <th class="list" width="340">Book Description</th>
                    <th class="list" width="20">Book Price</th>
                </tr>

                <!-- Display the selected book. -->
                <tr>
                    <td><img src="<?php echo $bookrow ['book_image']; ?>"
                        width="140" height="112"></td>
                    <td align="center"><?php echo $bookrow ['book_isbn'];
                      ?></td>
                    <td><?php echo $bookrow ['book_title']; ?></td>
                    <td><?php echo $bookrow ['book_author']; ?></td>
                    <td><?php echo $bookrow ['book_descr']; ?>
                          </td>
                    <td align="right">$<?php number_format($bookrow
                        ['book_price'],0,'.',','); ?> </td>
                </tr>
            </table>
                <!-- End book display. -->
            <p> </p> <!-- Inserts two blank lines -->
            <p> </p>
```

```html
<div id="customer">
    <!-- Display customer. -->
<table width="300" border="0" cellspacing="1" cellpadding="3" >
        <tr>
          <th width="20%">First/Last Name:</th>
          <td width="40%"><?php echo $custrow
            ['customer_fname']; ?></td>
          <td width="40%"><?php echo $custrow
            ['customer_lname']; ?></td>
        </tr>
        <tr>
          <th width="20%">Street:</th>
          <td width="80%"><?php echo $custrow
            ['customer_street']; ?></td>
        </tr>
        <tr>
          <th width="20%">City State:</th>
          <td width="40%"><?php echo $custrow
            ['customer_city_st']; ?></td>
          <th width="20%">ZIP:</th>
          <td width="20%"><?php echo $custrow
            ['customer_zip'];
            ?></td>
        </tr>
        <tr>
          <th width="20%">Phone Number:</th>
          <td width="20%"><?php echo $custrow
            ['customer_phone']; ?></td>
        </tr>
        <tr>
          <th width="20%">Email:</th>
          <td width="20%"><?php echo $custrow
            ['customer_email']; ?></td>
        </tr>
    </table>
    </div> <!-- id=customer -->
    <!-- End customer display -->
    <div id="wrapup">
      <h2>Complete the purchase: </h2>
      <p .red><a href="saleconfirmshop.php?bookisbn=<?php
        echo $bookisbn ?>&email=<?php echo $email ?>"CONFIRM
        and continue shopping</a></p>
      <p> </p>
      <p .red><a href="saleconfirm.php?bookisbn=<?php
        echo $bookisbn ?>&email=<?php echo $email ?>">CONFIRM
        and checkout</a></p>
      <p> </p>
        <p> </p>
      <h2>Click as appropriate: </h2>
```

```
        <p><a href="repbooks.php?email=$email">CANCEL THE
            SALE</a></p>
        <p> </p>
        <p><a href="custupdate.php?bookisbn=<?php echo $bookisbn
            ?>&email=<?php echo $email ?>">Edit my customer
            information.</a></p>
    </div> <!-- id=wrapup -->
```

saleconfirm.php

saleconfirm.php, shown in Listing 14-12, completes the sale of an individual book by writing a record in the Sales table with the book ISBN and email address as foreign indexes that have been passed to it. Upon completion, it calls checkout.php.

Listing 14-12   saleconfirm.php

```php
<?php
    session_start();
//Connect to the booksales database
    $connection = mysqli_connect("localhost", "root", "password",
        "booksales");
    if (!$connection) {
        echo "Cannot connect to MySQL. ", mysqli_connect_error($connection);
        exit();
    }
//Get Book ISBN from verify.php
    $bookisbn = ($_GET['bookisbn']);

//Get email address from verify.php
    $email = ($_GET['email']);

//Get records from the Books table
    $query = "SELECT * From books WHERE book_isbn = '$bookisbn'";
    $result = mysqli_query($connection, $query);
    if (!$result) {
        echo "Select from books failed. ", mysqli_error($connection);
        exit();
    }
//Get book (row) from Books table
    $bookrow = mysqli_fetch_assoc($result);

    $price = $bookrow ['book_price'];

//Add record to the Sales table
        $query = "INSERT INTO sales(book_isbn, customer_email, sales_amount)
          VALUES('$bookisbn', '$email', '$price')";
        $result2 = mysqli_query($connection, $query);
```

```
if (!$result2) {
echo "Insert into customer failed.  ", mysqli_error($connection);
exit();
}

//Go to checkout.php with ISBN and email address.
header( "Location: checkout.php?bookisbn=$bookisbn&email=$email");
?>
```

saleconfirmshop.php

The only difference between salesconfirmshop.php and salesconfirm.php is that salesconfirmshop.php allows the customer to return to shopping instead of checking out, and so the last line of code is changed to:

```
header( "Location: repbooks.php?email=$email");
```

NOTE
You could use one file with a different query parameter instead of two separate files, but I wanted to leave it as two to emphasize the difference.

repbooks.php

repbooks.php is the same as the original books list books.php, except that repbooks.php handles an active customer that is already in the process of buying and so doesn't need to enter their email and password upon selecting a book. Their email address is passed to repbooks.php by salesconfirmshop.php and goes directly to confirm.php, passing along the email address with this changed line of code:

```
<td><a href="confirm.php?bookisbn=<?php echo $bookrow ['book_isbn'];
    ?>&email=<?php echo $_GET['email'];   ?>">Purchase</a></td>
```

Invoicing

The invoicing section of the book sales web app has three elements: invoicing, which creates and displays the books being purchased on an invoice; writing a record to the Invoice table and an email invoice to the customer; and deleting a sales record if the customer decides at the last minute they do not want to buy.

Building an Invoice

Building an invoice is done with the checkout.php script, which picks up uninvoiced sales for a particular customer from the Sales table, places them in a list, adds up the total of the sales, and adds tax and freight to produce the total invoice amount.

checkout.php is called by salesconfirm.php, which passes the customer's email address. The email address is used to get the customer's record from the Customer table to provide the name and address information for the invoice.

Next, the last or most recently written record is retrieved from the Invoice table to get the last used invoice number, to which 1 is added for the invoice number of the current invoice being built. This is done by ordering a select of the Invoice table by invoice number in descending (DESC) order, as you see in this statement:

```
$query = "SELECT * From invoice ORDER BY invoice_no DESC";
```

The invoice itself is made up of three sections:

- The name and address section, which also includes the current date and the invoice number.

- The listing of books that have been purchased. These are found by iterating through the Sales table, looking for records belonging to the current customer based on email address that have not been invoiced based on a zero value in the Sales table's invoice number.

  The actual iteration is done with a do/while loop with a MySQL select outside of the loop and a fetch in the loop. Also, within the loop is a select from the Books table to get the book in the current sales record.

- The final section is used to total the sales and add tax and freight.

From the invoice display, the customer can delete any of the book sales by clicking Delete on the right of the book, which calls delsale.php. When the customer is satisfied with the invoice, they can click Complete This Purchase, which calls compinv.php.

Listing 14-13 displays checkout.php without the common template areas. Figure 14-10 shows the resulting invoice.

Listing 14-13   checkout.php

```php
<?php
    session_start();

//Connect to the booksales database
    $connection = mysqli_connect("localhost", "root", "password",
        "booksales");
    if (!$connection) {
        echo "Cannot connect to MySQL. ", mysqli_connect_error($connection);
```

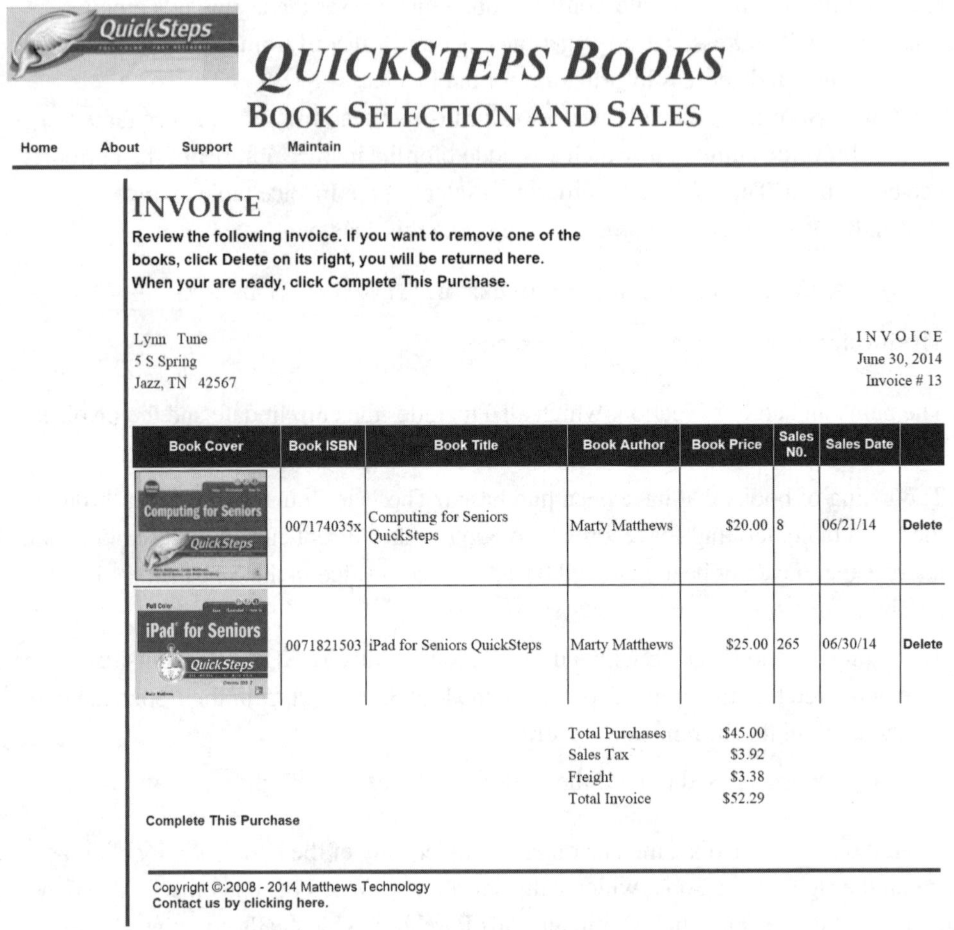

QUICKSTEPS BOOKS
BOOK SELECTION AND SALES

Home   About   Support   Maintain

INVOICE

Review the following invoice. If you want to remove one of the
books, click Delete on its right, you will be returned here.
When your are ready, click Complete This Purchase.

Lynn Tune
5 S Spring
Jazz, TN 42567

INVOICE
June 30, 2014
Invoice # 13

Book Cover	Book ISBN	Book Title	Book Author	Book Price	Sales NO.	Sales Date	
	007174035x	Computing for Seniors QuickSteps	Marty Matthews	$20.00	8	06/21/14	Delete
	0071821503	iPad for Seniors QuickSteps	Marty Matthews	$25.00	265	06/30/14	Delete

Total Purchases $45.00
Sales Tax $3.92
Freight $3.38
Total Invoice $52.29

Complete This Purchase

Copyright ©:2008 - 2014 Matthews Technology
Contact us by clicking here.

Figure 14-10 The invoice totals the books that have been purchased and adds tax and
freight to it.

```php
    exit();
  }

//Get email address from saleconfirm.php
  $email = ($_GET['email']);

//Get record from the Customer table
  $query = "SELECT * FROM customer WHERE customer_email = '$email'";
  $result1 = mysqli_query($connection, $query);
```

```php
    if (!$result1) {
        echo "SELECT from customer failed. ", mysqli_error($connection);
        exit();
    }
//Get customer (row) from Customer table
    $custrow = mysqli_fetch_assoc($result1);

//Get record from the Invoice table
    $query = "SELECT * FROM invoice ORDER BY invoice_no DESC";
    $result4 = mysqli_query($connection, $query);
    if (!$result4) {
        echo "SELECT from invoice failed. ", mysqli_error($connection);
        exit();
    }
//Get first row from Invoice table
    $invoicerow = mysqli_fetch_assoc($result4);
    if ($invoicerow){
        $invoiceNo = $invoicerow['invoice_no'] +1;
    }
    else{
        $invoiceNo = 1;
    }
    date_default_timezone_set('America/Vancouver');
?>
    <div id="main">
        <h1 id="maintitle">INVOICE</h1>
        <p id="mainpara">Review the following invoice. If you want
            to remove one of the </p>
        <p id="mainpara">books, click Delete on its right, you will
            be returned here.</p>
        <p id="mainpara">When you are ready, click Complete This
            Purchase.</p>
        <p > </p>
        <p > </p>

    <div id="cust">
        <!-- Customer -->
        <table width="850" border="0" frame="void" rules="none"
            cellspacing="1" cellpadding="2">
            <tr>
                <td align="left"><?php echo $custrow ['customer_fname'];
                    ?>   <?php echo $custrow ['customer_lname'];
                    ?> </td>
                <td align="right">I N V O I C E</td>
            </tr>
            <tr>
```

```
            <td align="left"><?php echo $custrow ['customer_street'];
                ?> </td>
            <td align="right"><?php echo date('F j, Y');?> </td>
        </tr>
        <tr>
            <td align="left"><?php echo $custrow ['customer_city_st'];
                ?>   <?php echo $custrow ['customer_zip'];
                ?> </td>
            <td align="right">Invoice # <?php echo $invoiceNo;?> </td>
        </tr>
    </table>
    <p> </p> <!-- Inserts two blank lines -->
    <p> </p>
</div> <!-- id="cust" -->
<div id="sales"
    <!-- Sales List -->
    <table width="850" border="1" frame="void" rules="all"
        cellspacing="1" cellpadding="2">
        <!-- Display the column headings -->
        <tr>
            <th class="list" width="150">Book Cover</th>
            <th class="list" width="80">Book ISBN</th>
            <th class="list" width="240">Book Title</th>
            <th class="list" width="120">Book Author</th>
            <th class="list" width="100">Book Price</th>
            <th class="list" width="20">Sales N0.</th>
            <th class="list" width="80">Sales Date</th>
            <th class="list" width="20"> </th>
        </tr>

    <?php
        $purtot = $taxamt = $frtamt = $invtot = 0;

    //Get first record from the Sales table
        $query = "SELECT * FROM sales WHERE customer_email =
            '$email' && invoice_no IS NULL";
        $result5 = mysqli_query($connection, $query);
        if (!$result5) {
            echo "SELECT from books failed. ", mysqli_error($connection);
            exit();
        }
    //Get first row from Sales table
        $salesrow2 = mysqli_fetch_assoc($result5);

    //Loop through and display the books (first Book retrieved above).
```

```php
   do {
      $this_book = $salesrow2 ['book_isbn'];
      $sale_date = $salesrow2 ['sales_date'];

//Get record from the Book table
   $query = "SELECT * FROM books WHERE book_isbn = '$this_book'";
   $result6 = mysqli_query($connection, $query);
   if (!$result6) {
   echo "SELECT from books failed. ", mysqli_error($connection);
   exit();
   }
//Get first book (row)from Books table
   $bookrow2 = mysqli_fetch_assoc($result6);
?>
   <tr>
      <td><img src="<?php echo $bookrow2 ['book_image']; ?>"
         width="140" height="112"></td>
      <td align="center"><?php echo $bookrow2 ['book_isbn']; ?></td>
      <td><?php echo $bookrow2 ['book_title']; ?></td>
      <td><?php echo $bookrow2 ['book_author']; ?></td>
      <td align="right">$<?php echo number_format($bookrow2
         ['book_price'],2,'.',','); ?> </td>
      <td><?php echo $salesrow2 ['sales_id']; ?>   </td>
      <td><?php echo date('m/d/y', strtotime($salesrow2
         ['sales_date'])); ?>   </td>
      <td><a href="delsale.php?deletid=<?php echo $salesrow2
         ['sales_id']; ?>&email=<?php echo $email ?>">Delete</a></td>
      </tr>
<?php
   $purtot = $purtot + $bookrow2 ['book_price'];
   } while ( $salesrow2 = mysqli_fetch_assoc($result5) );

   $taxamt = $purtot * .087; //This should be set to a ZIP Code table
   $frtamt = $purtot * .075; //This should be set to Distance table
   $invtot = $purtot + $taxamt + $frtamt;
?>
</table>
<table width="850" border="0" frame="void" rules="none"
   cellspacing="1" cellpadding="2">

   <tr> </tr>
   <tr> </tr>
   <tr>
      <td class="list" width="480"> </td>
      <td class="list" width="110" align="left">Total Purchases</td>
```

```
         <td class="list" width="100" align="right">$<?php echo
            number_format($purtot,2,'.',','); ?> </td>
         <td class="list" width="190"> </td>
      </tr>
      <tr>
         <td class="list" width="480"> </td>
         <td class="list" width="110" align="left">Sales Tax</td>
         <td class="list" width="100" align="right">$<?php echo
            number_format($taxamt,2,'.',','); ?> </td>
         <td class="list" width="190"> </td>
      </tr>
      <tr>
         <td class="list" width="480"> </td>
         <td class="list" width="110" align="left">Freight</td>
         <td class="list" width="100" align="right">$<?php echo
            number_format($frtamt,2,'.',','); ?> </td>
         <td class="list" width="190"> </td>
      </tr>
      <tr>
         <td class="list" width="480"> </td>
         <td class="list" width="110" align="left">Total Invoice</td>
         <td class="list" width="100" align="right">$<?php echo
            number_format($invtot,2,'.',','); ?> </td>
         <td class="list" width="190"> </td>
      </tr>
   </table>

   <p id="mainpara">  <a href="compinv.php?email=<?php echo
      $email; ?>&purch=<?php echo $purtot; ?>&
      tax=<?php echo $taxamt; ?>&freight=<?php echo $frtamt;
      ?>&invoice=<?php echo $invtot; ?>">
      Complete This Purchase</a></p>
   <p > </p>
   <p > </p>

   </div> <!-- id="main" -->
```

Deleting Sales

Deleting a sale, which is done with delsale.php and shown in Listing 14-14, is called by checkout.php and returns there after completing the deletion. delsale.php gets the customer's email address and the sales ID of the sales record to be deleted from checkout.php. A MySQL delete is then used to do the actual chore.

Listing 14-14 delsale.php

```php
<?php
   session_start();
//Connect to the booksales database
   $connection = mysqli_connect("localhost", "root", "password", "booksales");
   if (!$connection) {
      echo "Cannot connect to MySQL. ", mysqli_connect_error($connection);
      exit();
   }

//Get email address from checkout.php
   $email = ($_GET['email']);

//Get sales ID from checkout.php
   $salesid = ($_GET['deletid']);

//Delete record from the Sales table
   $query = "DELETE FROM sales WHERE sales_id = $salesid";
   $result = mysqli_query($connection, $query);
   if (!$result) {
      echo "SELECT from invoice failed. ", mysqli_error($connection);
      exit();
   }
//Go back to checkuot.php with email address.
   header( "Location: checkout.php?email=$email");
?>
```

Writing an Invoice Record

The final process to complete the invoice is to write an invoice record to the Invoice table and to send the customer an email record of the event. That is the purpose of compinv.php, which is shown in Listing 14-15 and on the screen in Figure 14-11. `mysqli_insert_id` is used to get the invoice ID ($invid) that was automatically generated when the new invoice was generated. Next, the book ISBN, the email address, and the sales ID are used to retrieve records from the book, customer, and Sales tables, respectively. This information is then used in the email message, which uses a long concatenation (the .) of $msg_client to form the message body.

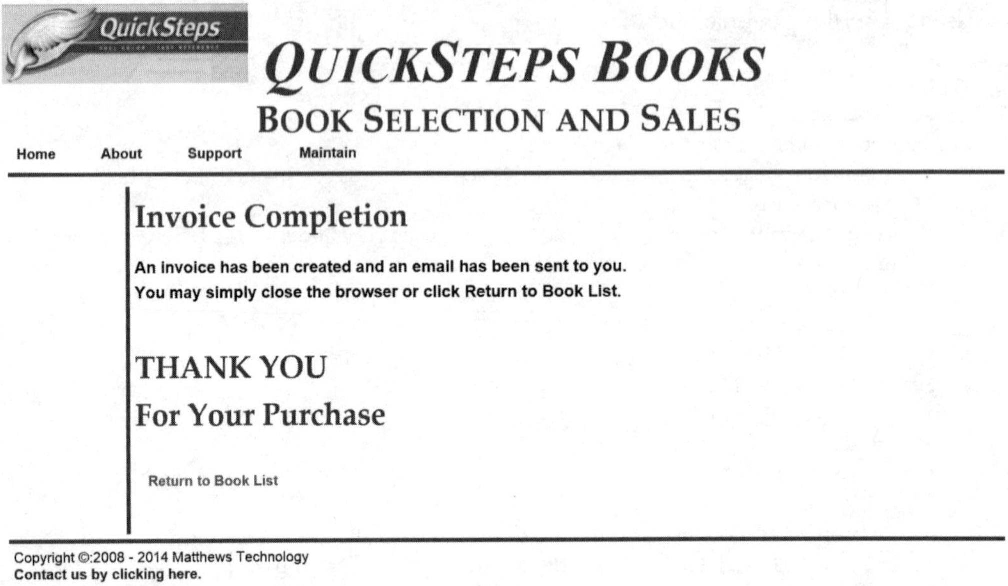

QUICKSTEPS BOOKS

BOOK SELECTION AND SALES

Home   About   Support   Maintain

Invoice Completion

An invoice has been created and an email has been sent to you.
You may simply close the browser or click Return to Book List.

THANK YOU

For Your Purchase

Return to Book List

Copyright ©:2008 - 2014 Matthews Technology
Contact us by clicking here.

Figure 14-11 A Thank You is used as a closing page.

Listing 14-15   compinv.php

```php
<?php
    session_start();
//Connect to the booksales database
    $connection = mysqli_connect("localhost", "root", "password", "booksales");
    if (!$connection) {
        echo "Cannot connect to MySQL. ", mysqli_connect_error($connection);
        exit();
    }

//Get email address from checkout.php
    $email = ($_GET['email']);

//Get record from the Customer table
    $query = "SELECT * FROM customer WHERE customer_email = '$email'";
    $result1 = mysqli_query($connection, $query);
    if (!$result1) {
        echo "SELECT from customer failed. ", mysqli_error($connection);
        exit();
    }
```

```
//Get customer (row) from Customer table
   $custrow = mysqli_fetch_assoc($result1);

//Get purchase total from checkout.php
   $purtot = ($_GET['purch']) + 0;

//Get tax amount from checkout.php
   $taxamt = ($_GET['tax']) + 0;

//Get freight amount from checkout.php
   $frtamt = ($_GET['freight']) + 0;

//Get invoice total from checkout.php
   $invtot = ($_GET['invoice']) + 0;

//Add record to the Invoice table
   $query = "INSERT INTO invoice(customer_email, invoice_amount,
      invoice_tax, invoice_freight, invoice_total )
      VALUES('$email', '$purtot', '$taxamt', '$frtamt', '$invtot' )";
   $result2 = mysqli_query($connection, $query);
   if (!$result2) {
      echo "Insert into invoice failed.  ", mysqli_error($connection);
      exit();
   }

//Get invoice ID generated by insert.
   $invid = mysqli_insert_id($connection);

//Get record from the Invoice table
   $query = "SELECT * FROM invoice WHERE invoice_no = '$invid'";
   $result3 = mysqli_query($connection, $query);
   if (!$result3) {
      echo "SELECT from customer failed. ", mysqli_error($connection);
      exit();
   }
//Get invoice (row) from Invoice table
   $invrow = mysqli_fetch_assoc($result3);

//Get First record from the Sales table
   $query = "SELECT * FROM sales WHERE customer_email = '$email' &&
      invoice_no = 0";
   $result4 = mysqli_query($connection, $query);
   if (!$result4) {
      echo "SELECT from books failed. ", mysqli_error($connection);
      exit();
   }
```

```php
//Get first row from Sales table
    $salesrow = mysqli_fetch_assoc($result4);

//Confirmation Email
$to_client = $custrow['customer_fname'].' '.$custrow['customer_lname'].'
    <'.$custrow['customer_email'].'>';
$sub_client = 'Book Purchase';
$msg_client = 'Thank you for your QuickSteps book purchase.'."\n\n";
$msg_client .= 'Invoice number: '. $invid . "\n";
$msg_client .= 'Invoice date: '. $invrow['invoice_date'] . "\n";
$msg_client .= 'Total Purchases: '. "$" . $purtot . "\n";
$msg_client .= 'Sales Tax: '. "$" . $taxamt . "\n";
$msg_client .= 'Freight: '. "$" . $frtamt . "\n";
$msg_client .= 'Invoice Total: '. "$" . $invtot . "\n";
$msg_client .= "\n\n";
$msg_client .= 'Your Email Address: '.$custrow['customer_email']."\n";
$msg_client .= 'Your Name: '.$custrow['customer_fname'].' '
.$custrow['customer_lname']. "\n";
$msg_client .= 'Your Street: '.$custrow['customer_street']."\n\n";
$msg_client .= 'Your City & ST: '.$custrow['customer_city_st'].'
    '.$custrow['customer_zip']. "\n";
$msg_client .= 'Your Phone: '.$custrow['customer_phone']."\n\n";
$msg_client .= 'Thanks again,'."\n\n";
$msg_client .= 'Matthews Technology'."\n\n";
$addl_headers_client = 'From: Matthews Technology
    <info@matthewstechnology.com>'."\n\n";
mail($to_client,$sub_client,$msg_client,$addl_headers_client);

//Loop through and update the Sales table with the invoice being billed.
    while ( $salesrow = mysqli_fetch_assoc($result4) ) {
        $query = "UPDATE sales SET invoice_no = '$invid' WHERE customer_email
            = '$email' && invoice_no = 0";
        $result5 = mysqli_query($connection, $query);
        if (!$result5) {
            echo "SELECT from books failed. ", mysqli_error($connection);
            exit();
        }
    }
?>
    <div id="main">
        <h1 id="maintitle">Invoice Completion</h1>
        <br />
        <p id="mainpara">An invoice has been created and an email
            has been sent to you. </p>
        <p id="mainpara">You may simply close the browser or click
            Return to Book List. </p>
        <br />
```

```
<p class="red"> </p>
<h1 id="maintitle" align="center">THANK YOU</h1>
<h1 id="maintitle" align="center">For Your Purchase </h1>
<p > </p>
<p > </p>
<p id="mainpara">  <a href="repbooks.php?email=
    <?php echo $email; ?>">
    Return to Book List</a></p>
<p > </p>
<p > </p>
</div> <!-- id="main" -->
```

Try This 14-1 Change This Web App for Your Tastes

Take this web app and change it for your tastes and needs. For example:

- Change the template and CSS for your tastes.

- Change the user and products from books and customers to objects of your choice, like concerts and attendees, or doctors and patients.

- Take some of the HTML and PHP script pairs and combine them into one script.

- Look at the scripts in detail and see if you can come up with more efficient ways of accomplishing the same objective.

Chapter 14 Self-Test

The following questions are intended to help reinforce your comprehension of the concepts covered in this chapter. The answers can be found in the accompanying online Appendix A, "Answers to the Self-Tests."

1. What is a simple and easy way to create web apps?

2. What is a way to include images in a database without taking up a lot of space?

3. How do you need to reference a non-numeric value in an SQL statement?

4. If you use the SQL technique for referencing non-numeric values in PHP, what happens?

5. What are the ways of representing the PHP variable $email in PHP, JavaScript, MySQL, and HTML?

6. How do you reference the most recently written record in a MySQL table with PHP when the table uses an autoincrement index?

7. How do you get an autoincrement index immediately after it is automatically generated?

8. What do you use to concatenate elements in a PHP statement?

Index

Numbers

Symbols

A

N